Nonverbal Behavior in Clinical Settings

Series in Affective Science

Series Editors
Richard J. Davidson
Paul Ekman
Klaus Scherer

The Nature of Emotion: Fundamental Questions
edited by Paul Ekman and Richard J. Davidson

Boo!: Culture, Experiences, and the Startle Reflex
Ronald Simons

Emotions in Psychopathology: Theory and Research
edited by William F. Flack Jr. and James D. Laird

*What the Face Reveals: Basic and Applied Studies of Spontaneous
   Expression Using the Facial Action Coding System (FACS)*
edited by Paul Ekman and Erika Rosenberg

Shame: Interpersonal Behavior, Psychopathology, and Culture
edited by Paul Gilbert and Bernice Andrews

Affective Neuroscience: The Foundations of Human and Animal Emotions
Jaak Panksepp

*Extreme Fear, Shyness, and Social Phobia: Origins, Biological Mechanisms,
   and Clinical Outcomes*
edited by Louis A. Schmidt and Jay Schulkin

Cognitive Neuroscience of Emotion
edited by Richard D. Lane and Lynn Nadel

The Neuropsychology of Emotion
edited by Joan C. Borod

Anxiety, Depression, and Emotion
edited by Richard J. Davidson

Persons, Situations, and Emotions: An Ecological Approach
edited by Hermann Brandstätter and Andrzej Eliasz

Emotion, Social Relationships, and Health
edited by Carol D. Ryff and Burton Singer

Appraisal Processes in Emotion: Theory, Methods, Research
edited by Klaus R. Scherer, Angela Schorr, and Tom Johnstone

Music and Emotion: Theory and Research
edited by Patrik N. Juslin and John A. Sloboda

Handbook of Affective Sciences
edited by Richard J. Davison, Klaus Scherer, and H. Hill Goldsmith

Nonverbal Behavior in Clinical Settings
edited by Pierre Philippot, Robert S. Feldman, and Erik J. Coats

Nonverbal Behavior in Clinical Settings

EDITED BY

Pierre Philippot
Robert S. Feldman
Erik J. Coats

2003

OXFORD

UNIVERSITY PRESS

Oxford   New York
Auckand   Bangkok   Buenos Aires   Cape Town   Chennai
Dar es Salaam   Delhi   Hong Kong   Istanbul   Karachi   Kolkata
Kuala Lumpur   Madrid   Melbourne   Mexico City   Mumbai   Nairobi
Sao Paulo   Shanghai   Taipei   Tokyo   Toronto

Published by Oxford University Press, Inc.
198 Madison Avenue, New York, New York 10016

www.oup.com

Oxford is a registered trademark of Oxford University Press

Library of Congress Cataloging-in-Publication Data
Nonverbal behavior in clinical settings / edited by Pierre Philippot,
   Robert S. Feldman, and Erik J. Coats
      p. cm. — (Series in affective science)
   Includes bibliographical references and index.
   ISBN 0-19-514109-1
   1. Body language   2. Psychotherapy.   I. Philippot, Pierre, 1960–
II. Coats, Erik, J., 1968–   III. Feldman, Robert S. (Robert Stephen), 1947–
IV. Series.
   RC489.N65 N66 2003
   616.89′14—dc21   2002012415

9 8 7 6 5 4 3 2 1

Printed in the United States of America
on acid-free paper

Foreword

KLAUS R. SCHERER

The pioneers in psychiatry and clinical psychology believed that emotion plays a central role in pathology and that emotions are most directly and truthfully expressed through the face, voice, and body. Reflecting this, they recommended that in diagnosis and therapy nonverbal behavior should be treated as a valuable sign of a patient's affective state. Subsequent research on nonverbal communication has shown that these intuitions are correct and that attention to nonverbal cues is extremely important in interacting with emotionally disturbed individuals. Nonetheless, for all practical purposes, therapy in clinical settings has continued to focus on the verbal rather than the nonverbal. There are many reasons for the continued prevalence of the verbal in therapy, including the intellectual influence of psychoanalysis and cognitive therapies, the ease of obtaining verbal reports, the need to classify behaviors and feelings into semantic categories, and the amount of effort and time required to observe and interpret nonverbal behavior. This situation is about to change, as the explosion of research on emotion has finally reached the clinic.

In this volume, leading scholars in the area present research that provides a foundation for understanding and using nonverbal behavior to measure and modify patients' feelings and behavior. Their chapters describe the mechanisms underlying the nonverbal expression of emotion, the role of nonverbal behavior in regulatory and clinical processes, the effects of negative life events and personality dispositions on expressing and inferring, nonverbal behavior patterns in specific clinical disorders, and the interpretation of nonverbal behavior in different clinical populations. These contributions provide pointers for methodologies appropriate in clinical settings and outline the practical significance of placing more emphasis on nonverbal behavior in clinical settings.

Nonverbal Behavior in Clinical Settings represents an important addition to the Oxford Series in Affective Science, demonstrating both the multiple sources of insight from different fields and the potential applications of a multidisciplinary perspective on affect and its disturbances in an important area of professional practice—the clinic.

Acknowledgments

This book is the outcome of a long-standing collaboration among the three coeditors that grew out of an ongoing exchange program between the University of Massachusetts at Amherst and the Catholic University of Louvain at Louvain-la-Neuve, Belgium. Initially funded by the U.S. Information Agency, the exchange program subsequently has been supported for over a decade by the Catholic University of Louvain and the University of Massachusetts. We are particularly grateful to Dean Guillaume Wunsch and to the late Dean Jean Costermans of the Catholic University of Louvain and Dean Glenn Gordon and former Dean Seymour Berger of the University of Massachusetts for their support of this project. In addition, the FRNS (National Sciences Foundation) of Belgium provided indirect support for the book.

Finally, we would like to acknowledge the contributors to this volume. Their first-class chapters represent a state-of-the-art view of the ways in which nonverbal behavior relates to clinical theory and practice; these chapters provide ideas and guidance for both researchers and practitioners.

Contents

Foreword   v

Contributors   xi

1. The Role of Nonverbal Behavior in Clinical Settings: Introduction and Overview   3
   Pierre Philippot, Robert S. Feldman, and Erik J. Coats

Part I. Nonverbal Behavior in Regulatory and Clinical Processes

2. Nonverbal Social Skills and Psychopathology   17
   John E. Perez and Ronald E. Riggio

3. Of Butterflies and Roaring Thunder: Nonverbal Communication in Interaction and Regulation of Emotion   45
   Arvid Kappas and Jean Descôteaux

4. Changes in Nonverbal Behavior During the Development of Therapeutic Relationships   75
   Linda Tickle-Degnen and Elizabeth Gavett

5. What Makes Good Therapists Fail?   111
   Jörg Merten and Rainer Krause

Part II. Nonverbal Behavior in Negative Life Events

6. Selective Processing of Nonverbal Information in Anxiety: Attentional Biases for Threat   127
   Karin Mogg and Brendan P. Bradley

7. The Social and Functional Aspects of Emotional Expression During Bereavement   145
   George A. Bonanno and Anthony Papa

8. Impairments of Facial Nonverbal Communication After
Brain Damage   171
Raymond Bruyer

Part III. Nonverbal Behavior in Specific Clinical Disorders

9. Nonverbal Deficits and Interpersonal Regulation in Alcoholics   209
Pierre Philippot, Charles Kornreich, and Sylvie Blairy

10. Ethology and Depression   233
Antoinette L. Bouhuys

11. Nonverbal Behavior in Schizophrenia   263
Ann M. Kring and Kelly S. Earnst

12. Clinical Implications of Research in Nonverbal Behavior
of Children With Autism   287
Gail McGee and Michael Morrier

Index   319

Contributors

Sylvie Blairy
Free University of Brussels
Department of Psychiatry
Avenue Van Gehuchten, 4
1020 Brussels
Belgium

George A. Bonanno
Department of Counseling and
   Clinical Psychology
525 West 120th Street
Teachers College, Box 218
Columbia University
New York, NY 10027
USA

Antoinette L. Bouhuys
Rijksuniversiteit Groningen
Department of Social Psychiatry
P.O. Box 3001
9700 RB Groningen
The Netherlands

Brendan P. Bradley
Centre for the Study of Emotion
   and Motivation
Department of Psychology
University of Southampton
Highfield
Southampton SO17 1BJ
United Kingdom

Raymond Bruyer
Department of Psychology
University of Louvain
Place du Cardinal Mercier 10
B-1348 Louvain la Neuve
Belgium

Erik J. Coats
Strategic Marketing Corporation
1 Belmont Avenue
Bala Cynwyd, PA 19004
USA

Jean Descôteaux
Université Laval
Ecole de Psychologie
Pavillon Savard
Québec G1K 7P4
Canada

Kelly S. Earnst
University of Alabama at
   Birmingham
Department of Psychology
415 Campbell Hall
Birmingham, AL 35294
USA

Robert S. Feldman
Department of Psychology
University of Massachusetts
Amherst, MA 01003
USA

Elizabeth Gavett
Department of Occupational
   Therapy
Sargent College of Health and
   Rehabilitation Sciences
Boston University
635 Commonwealth Avenue
Boston, MA 02215
USA

Arvid Kappas
International University Bremen
School of Humanities and Social
    Sciences
Res. IV
P.O. Box 750561
D-28725 Bremen
Germany

Charles Kornreich
Free University of Brussels
Department of Psychiatry
Avenue Van Gehuchten, 4
1020 Brussels
Belgium

Rainer Krause
Fachrichtung 6.4 Psychologie
Universtat des Saarlandes
66123 Saarbrucken
Germany

Ann M. Kring
Department of Psychology
3210 Tolman
University of California, Berkeley
Berkeley, CA 94720
USA

Gail McGee
718 Gatewood Road
Emory Autism Resource Center
Emory University School of
    Medicine
718 Gatewood Road
Atlanta, GA 30322
USA

Jörg Merten
Fachrichtung 6.4 Psychologie
Universtat des Saarlandes
66123 Saarbrucken
Germany

Karin Mogg
Centre for the Study of Emotion
    and Motivation
Department of Psychology
University of Southampton
Highfield
Southampton SO17 1BJ
United Kingdom

Michael Morrier
718 Gatewood Road
Emory Autism Resource Center
Emory University School of
    Medicine
718 Gatewood Road
Atlanta, GA 30322
USA

Anthony Papa
Department of Counseling and
    Clinical Psychology
525 West 120th Street
Teachers College, Box 218
Columbia University
New York, NY 10027
USA

John E. Perez
Department of Psychology
Yale University
New Haven, CT 06520
USA

Pierre Philippot
Department of Psychology
University of Louvain
Place du Cardinal Mercier 10
B-1348 Louvain la Neuve
Belgium

Ronald E. Riggio
Department of Psychology
Claremont McKenna College
850 Columbia Avenue
Claremont, CA 91711
USA

Linda Tickle-Degnen
Department of Occupational
    Therapy
Sargent College of Health and
    Rehabilitation Sciences
Boston University
635 Commonwealth Avenue
Boston, MA 02215
USA

Nonverbal Behavior in Clinical Settings

1

The Role of Nonverbal Behavior in Clinical Settings

Introduction and Overview

PIERRE PHILIPPOT, ROBERT S. FELDMAN, AND ERIK J. COATS

> Your face, my thane, is as a book where men
> May read strange matters. To beguile the time,
> Look like the time; bear welcome in your eye,
> Your hand, your tongue: look like the innocent flower,
> But be the serpent under 't.
>
> Shakespeare, *Macbeth*

Nonverbal Behavior: A Historically Neglected Field in Clinical Psychology and Psychotherapy

From the richness and psychological accuracy of his characters, there is no doubt that Shakespeare had quite a "clinical eye." In the quotation above, he stresses the importance of nonverbal behavior, such as facial expression, in deciphering one's inner thoughts and feelings. This quotation also suggests that the meanings of verbal and nonverbal messages do not always parallel each other. Nonverbal messages, under less control than the verbal ones, may often be more indicative of true affect and attitude. From these considerations, it follows that nonverbal behavior should be a major preoccupation in clinical settings. Not only might nonverbal behavior be informative regarding one's spontaneous thoughts and feelings, but also it might be a marker of psychopathological processes or a diagnostic index of psychopathology.

It is thus striking to observe that, until recently, nonverbal behavior has received very little attention from clinical researchers and practitioners. In our opinion, this intriguing state of affairs is just one consequence of the particular conceptions of clinical psychology and psychotherapy that have prevailed. Indeed, with the notable exception of the behavioral approach, the clinical field and most psychotherapeutic approaches have been marked by an overwhelming emphasis and reliance on verbal processes: Often, diagnoses are made solely on the basis of verbal information provided by the client, and therapeutic changes are accomplished by verbal means, such as thought association, interpretation of critical experiences, irrational belief challenge, and other types of change. Until the last decade, there was very little emphasis on the nonverbal processes, especially on nonverbal behavior, as a medium of communication and emotion in clinical settings.

We have commented elsewhere that this state of affairs in clinical psychology and psychotherapy is quite paradoxical (Philippot, 2000). Indeed, on the one hand, psychopathological conditions are marked by emotional and automatic processes: People make judgments about situations, often without a clear idea of why they are doing so; they feel distress, anxiety, guilt, and anger that they cannot control or regulate. Most of these emotional processes are nonverbal and often nonconscious in nature, and it is very difficult to translate them into verbal language (Philippot, Deplus, Baeyens, Schaefer, & Falise, in press; Teasdale, 1999). Yet, on the other hand, these conditions are evaluated via verbal means, and clinical interventions are often verbal.

However, in the last decade, significant changes have appeared in both the clinical and the emotional domains. One change is the recognition that many of the processes active in psychopathology are nonverbal. For instance, preconscious attentive biases for emotional material and automatic emotional information processing have been documented in many disorders (e.g., McNally, 1995; Mogg & Bradley, 1998). A second significant change is that some authors have developed clinical interventions based on, and specifically targeting, emotional processes. For instance, in his now-classic 1988 work, Barlow proposed an etiological model of anxiety based on emotion research and theories. Similarly, Greenberg and Paivio (1997) developed a model of clinical intervention based on emotional information processing that emphasizes the relationships between verbal and nonverbal information processing.

A third significant change is the recent interest of nonverbal behavior researchers in clinical issues (see, e.g., Nowicki & Duke, 1994). As illustrated by this book, the last decade witnessed a dramatic blossoming of research investigating nonverbal encoding and decoding of emotion in virtually all clinical conditions. This research has produced insightful results for understanding and intervention regarding psychopathological disorders.

Finally, the fourth significant change is the growing interest emotion researchers have shown in emotion regulation, such as Gross's work examining the effects of controlling nonverbal expression of emotion (e.g., Gross, 1998).

The results of these changes have today converged to offer new insights regarding the multiple and complex role of nonverbal behavior in clinical settings. Indeed, the start of the new millennium seems a timely moment to gather the rich research findings from these converging areas into an integrated framework—the goal of this book.

To begin the consideration of the applications of nonverbal behavior to clinical and psychotherapeutic areas, this introductory chapter first discusses why the study of nonverbal behavior is particularly relevant to the clinical domain. It then turns to the different dimensions of the large and diverse field of nonverbal behavior in clinical settings. Finally, the chapter presents the organization of the book and the rationale that ties together individual chapters.

The Relevance of Nonverbal Behavior for Clinical Research and Practice

On the one hand, many clinical conditions are related to emotional conditions. As a consequence, the study of emotion regulation and communication has gained considerable prominence in clinical psychology and psychiatry. On the other hand, nonverbal behavior has received considerable attention in emotion research, and its role in emotion communication and regulation is now well established (Matsumoto, 1987).

It also seems reasonable to suspect that nonverbal behavior might play an important role in several clinical conditions. In fact, at least four aspects of nonverbal behavior, as evidenced by fundamental research on emotion and communication, are relevant to clinical issues. First, nonverbal behavior is a constitutive part of the emotional response. Indeed, the first facet of emotion to receive scientific attention was nonverbal behavior. In his seminal work, Darwin (1872/1965) showed the importance of emotional nonverbal behavior as an interaction mean with the environment. Since then, nonverbal behavior has received more attention from researchers than any other aspect of emotion.

Second, nonverbal behavior is a determinant of subjective feeling states. Probably the best-known example of this effect is the facial feedback hypothesis. A wealth of evidence has documented that manipulating facial expression affects feeling states (Laird, 1984; Manstead, 1991; Matsumoto, 1987; McIntosh, 1996). The effect size of facial feedback is generally small (around 13% of explained variance), but is reliably significant. Yet, facial behavior is not the only facet of nonverbal behavior to produce such effects. Stepper and Strack (1993) documented that manipulating posture also has an impact on subjective feeling states and affects later judgment of valenced material, extending previous findings from Duclos et al. (1989), which showed that posture affects mood. Nonverbal behavior thus might be a determinant of the distressing or painful feelings experienced by people affected by psychopathological disorders.

Third, because of its impact on other facets of emotion, nonverbal behavior is involved in the regulation of emotion. The literature on facial feedback mentioned above has shown how facial behavior might modulate feeling states. The effect of facial muscle manipulation has been extended to physiological changes such as heart rate or skin temperature (Hess, Kappas, McHugo, Lanzetta, & Kleck, 1992; Kappas, 1989; Levenson, 1992; Levenson, Carstensen, Friesen, & Ekman, 1991; Levenson, Ekman, & Friesen, 1990). Thus, the voluntary alteration of nonverbal behavior might be used as a strategy to modify painful feelings, although the extent to which this strategy is effective is still controversial (e.g., Gross, 1998; Kappas & Descôteaux, chapter 3 of this volume).

Finally, nonverbal behavior definitely encompasses a larger domain than emotional nonverbal behavior. More generally, nonverbal behavior is an important medium for the communication of inner feelings and intentions (Cacioppo, Petty, Losch, & Kim, 1986; Tcherkassof, 1999). As such, it plays important functions in interaction and social regulation (Patterson, 1991) and in emotion contagion (Hess, Philippot, & Blairy, 1999). From a social interactionist perspective, the mastery of nonverbal behavior is a critical competence for effective and harmonious social functioning (Feldman, Philippot, & Custrini, 1991). On the one hand, this competence includes the sensitivity to and understanding of the nonverbal signals of others. On the other hand, it also addresses the capacity to express nonverbal behaviors that are appropriate to the social and strategic constraints of the situation.

In sum, nonverbal behavior is related to many aspects of affective experience, the elicitation of feelings, and the regulation of emotional experience. Further, nonverbal behavior is a major medium of social communication and interpersonal regulation. It follows that any nonverbal dysfunction might have an effect on the individual's well-being and personal as well as interpersonal functioning. The study of nonverbal behavior thus is necessary to gain full understanding of clinical disorders.

The Dimensions of Nonverbal Behavior in Clinical Settings

In the discussion above, we suggested that nonverbal behavior serves many functions that have direct relevance for the clinical domain. Nonverbal behavior is involved in the generation and modulation of affect, and it plays critical roles in interpersonal communication and regulation. Next, the relevance of nonverbal behavior for clinical settings is examined more directly.

Nonverbal Behavior as a Diagnostic Tool

Nonverbal behavior might help clinicians make clinical diagnoses in several ways. First, nonverbal signs are sometimes the initial and most reliable indicators of disorders, especially those occurring at a young age. For instance, McGee and Morrier show in this volume (chapter 12) how crucial nonverbal symptoms are for the early diagnosis of autism. The ability to determine a diagnosis as early as possible is critically important for many conditions, including autism, as the effectiveness of interventions is generally increased when remediation programs are initiated very soon after the onset of the condition.

Another important way in which nonverbal behavior might help in forming a diagnosis is by providing information about a client's spontaneous affective reactions. Nonverbal behaviors might even provide information of which clients are unaware or that they are unwilling to report. This is particularly important in egodystonic conditions in which the individual does not recognize an important facet of the problem or is negating emotional implications of a situation, attitude, or behavior.

Finally, nonverbal behavior is particularly important for diagnosing the social functioning and social competence of the individual. Nonverbal skills are a constitutive part of more general social competence, and their evaluation can be indicative of how interpersonally adapted an individual is.

Nonverbal Behavior as an Index of Pathological Processes

In other instances, nonverbal behavior is not indicative of a clinical syndrome per se, but it can reveal at a more molecular level that some specific process is at work, a process that exposes possible dysfunctions. For instance, as reported by Greenberg and Paivio (1997), in certain critical situations the message conveyed by nonverbal behavior might differ from the message conveyed verbally. In such instances, nonverbal behavior alerts the clinician that the issue at stake is probably more complex or ambiguous than the client is verbally exposing. It may be that the client's conscious appraisal of the situation does differ from the automatic, unconscious appraisal of it.

Another instance is the case of secondary emotion, which was discussed by Greenberg and Paivio (1997). In this case, the client reports a painful emotion (e.g., anxiety) when confronted by his or her supervisor. However, this anxiety is actually secondary to (i.e., is a consequence of) a primary emotion, for example, anger toward authority figures. Thus, the clinician must identify which emotion is actually the primary one; in this example, it is anger, not anxiety. Determining the "true" target is obviously necessary for therapeutic success. In the case of secondary emotions, nonverbal behavior, concomitant to the secondary emotion but not congruent with it, can alert the clinician of the possibility that another emotion and another target might be of primary importance.

In sum, as a rich medium of communication of inner state and attitude, nonverbal behavior can offer clinicians considerable information that is not conveyed by the verbal channel. As such, it requires special attention in deciphering the pathological processes at work.

Nonverbal Behavior in Emotion and Interaction Regulation

We have reported above several lines of evidence that nonverbal behavior, such as facial expression or posture, may be used to regulate "normal" emotions. This is also the case for "abnormal" or distressing emotions. Although little systematic empirical work has been conducted in this precise domain, some clinical practices have been exclusively based on nonverbal behavior. For instance, dance therapy has been developed on both sides of the Atlantic (e.g., Schmais & Schmais, 1983; Siegel, 1995). It is also a medium of healing in many preliterate cultures.

Another aspect of the use of nonverbal behavior in the therapeutic process is nonverbal training (e.g., Beck & Feldman, 1990; Feldman, McGee, Mann, & Strain, 1993). It consists of teaching a person to encode and decode the nonverbal behaviors that are critical for effective social interactions and interpersonal regulation. Such training may be especially important for conditions marked by a deficit in assertiveness or empathy. Furthermore, certain conditions that are characterized by apparent failures to understand the emotions of others—such as autism—might potentially be remediated by teaching more effective decoding of the emotional displays of others.

Nonverbal Behavior in the Therapeutic Relationship

Last, nonverbal behavior plays many important functions in the creation and maintenance of the therapeutic relationship. At least three aspects of the therapeutic relationship are connected to nonverbal behavior: empathy, evaluation of the therapist by the clients, and feelings of rapport or relatedness.

Some have proposed that nonverbal behavior is the primary medium by which empathy is created and communicated (Hatfield, Cacioppo, & Rapson, 1993; Hoffman, 1984). By unconsciously mimicking a client's nonverbal behavior, a phenomenon of emotional contagion appears in the therapist. This emotional contagion would in turn be communicated nonverbally to the client. Such a phenomenon has already been advocated as a major avenue to psychotherapeutic change by Rogers (1975).

Nonverbal behavior of the therapist has also been reported to influence the client's evaluation of the therapist (e.g., Harper, Wiens, & Matarazzo,

1978). For instance, congruent body movements and mirror-imaged postures have been found to be related positively to perceptions of affiliation and to increased verbal disclosure (Cappella, 1981). Thus, therapists who are nonverbally "in tune" with their clients are perceived more positively by their clients (e.g., as being warmer, more understanding, more involved in the therapeutic process).

Finally, and relatedly, one predictor of positive psychotherapy outcome is the feeling of rapport or relatedness. Some early studies (e.g., Charny, 1966) suggest that mimicry fosters the feeling of rapport. In these studies, clients were reported to be more in tune with the therapist and to feel more understood when the therapist's body posture and movement were similar and attuned to those of the client. More recent evidence has shown this effect in nonclinical settings as well. For instance, in a series of studies, Bernieri and collaborators established this phenomenon in young couples' interactions and in dyads in either a cooperative or an adversarial discussion (Babad, Bernieri, & Rosenthal, 1989; Bernieri, 1988; Bernieri, Gillis, Davis, & Grahe, 1996).

In sum, nonverbal behavior is relevant to many different facets of the clinical setting. Given the ubiquity of nonverbal behavior in human behavior in general, this observation should not be very surprising.

Accordingly, in the last decade a large body of empirical literature has emerged concerning the investigation of nonverbal behavior in the clinical domain. Encompassing a variety of approaches and perspectives, researchers have made important theoretical and empirical strides in elucidating the origins, functions, and consequences of nonverbal behavior. By now, it is clear that nonverbal behavior plays a far greater role than merely reflecting emotional experience: It also plays a central function in psychological adaptation.

The aim of this book is to present contemporary perspectives on the role of nonverbal behavior in psychological regulation, adaptation, and psychopathology. The book includes empirically grounded work and theories that are central to our understanding of the reciprocal influences among nonverbal behavior, psychopathology, and therapeutic processes.

The Current Volume

This book is organized in three sections: "Nonverbal Behavior in Regulatory and Clinical Processes," "Nonverbal Behavior in Negative Life Events," and "Nonverbal Behavior in Specific Clinical Disorders." Following this chapter's general orientation, each section has three or four chapters.

Part I, "Nonverbal Behavior in Regulatory and Clinical Processes," presents the nonverbal processes involved in emotion regulation in everyday life and in therapeutic intervention. It consists of four chapters. Chapter 2, "Nonverbal Social Skills and Psychopathology" by John E. Perez and Ronald E. Riggio, presents a framework for understanding nonverbal social skills in the context of general psychopathology. Nonverbal social skill deficiencies and treatment approaches using social skills training are examined for three clinical categories for which nonverbal social skills are particularly relevant: major depression, social phobia, and schizophrenia. Chapter 3, "Of Butterflies and Roaring Thunder: Nonverbal Communication in Interaction and Regulation of Emotion" by Arvid Kappas and Jean Descôteaux, provides an in-depth and insightful analysis of the function of nonverbal behavior in interpersonal and emotional regulation. It also reviews the current debates regarding the relationship between nonverbal behavior and emotional feeling states.

Also in part I, chapters 4 and 5 address nonverbal behaviors in therapeutic relationships. Chapter 4, by Linda Tickle-Degnen and Elizabeth Gavett, examines changes in nonverbal behavior during the development of therapeutic relationships. Chapter 5, "What Makes Good Therapists Fail?" by Jörg Merten and Rainer Krause, focuses on unconscious emotional processes that occur in the context of the therapeutic relationship and are revealed by nonverbal behaviors.

Part II, "Nonverbal Behavior in Negative Life Events," examines the relationships between nonverbal behavior and challenging negative life conditions. Chapter 6, "Selective Processing of Nonverbal Information in Anxiety: Attentional Biases for Threat" by Karin Mogg and Brendan P. Bradley, addresses a ubiquitous clinical phenomenon: anxiety. These authors specifically investigate how preattentive and attentional biases in the decoding of facial expression of emotion create and maintain social anxiety. Chapter 7, "The Social and Functional Aspects of Emotional Expression During Bereavement" by George A. Bonanno and Anthony Papa, focuses on a specific negative life event: bereavement. The authors review recent empirical findings that correlate long-term recovery from bereavement with three components of emotional reactions during bereavement: facial expressions of emotion, self-reports of emotion, and physiological manifestations of emotion. Chapter 8, "Impairments of Facial Nonverbal Communication After Brain Damage" by Raymond Bruyer, takes a different perspective. Bruyer presents a neurological model of nonverbal behavior and shows how brain damage can alter normal functioning.

Finally, part III, "Nonverbal Behavior in Specific Clinical Disorders," examines nonverbal behavior in specific psychopathological conditions. In chapter 9, Pierre Philippot, Charles Kornreich, and Sylvie Blairy present their research on the nonverbal deficits in alcoholics as well as a model that establishes the importance of deficits in nonverbal skills in the onset and maintenance of alcoholism. In the next two chapters, Antoinette L. Bouhuys ("Ethology and Depression") examines the nonverbal behaviors that are typical of major depression, and Ann M. Kring and Kelly S. Earnst ("Nonverbal Behavior in Schizophrenia") review emotional disturbances in schizophrenia, focusing on the nonverbal emotional displays in this condition. Finally, Gail McGee and Michael Morrier ("Clinical Implications of Research in Nonverbal Behavior of Children With Autism") examine the distinctive nonverbal behavior of autistic children and how the observation of nonverbal behavior is central in the early diagnosis of autism.

A Final Note

The study of nonverbal behavior in clinical settings has come of age. We see this book as a testament to the progress that is being made in applying the basic principles and theories developed by researchers in nonverbal behavior to therapeutic situations. At the same time, the work being done in the clinical domain has important implications for our broader understanding of the role of nonverbal behavior in nonclinical settings. We hope that this book advances our understanding of theoretical and applied issues, both within and outside the clinical domain.

Acknowledgments

The writing of this chapter was facilitated by grants from the Fonds National de la Recherche Scientifique de Belgique (8.4508.95 and 8.4512.98). In addition, support was provided by the University of Louvain (departmental grant) and the College of Behavioral and Social Sciences at the University of Massachusetts at Amherst (Glenn Gordon, Dean).

References

Babad, E., Bernieri, F., & Rosenthal, R. (1989). Nonverbal communication and leakage in the behavior of biased and unbiased teachers. *Journal of Personality and Social Psychology, 56,* 89–94.

Barlow, D. H. (1988). *Anxiety and its disorders: The nature and treatment of anxiety and panic.* New York: Guilford Press.

Beck, L., & Feldman, R. S. (1990). Enhancing children's decoding of facial expression. *Journal of Nonverbal Behavior, 13,* 269–277.

Bernieri, F. (1988). Coordinated movement and rapport in teacher-student interactions. *Journal of Nonverbal Behavior, 12,* 120–138.

Bernieri, F., Gillis, J. S., Davis, J. M., & Grahe, J. E. (1996). Dyad rapport and the accuracy of its judgment across situations: A lens model analysis. *Journal of Personality and Social Psychology, 71,* 110–129.

Cacioppo, J. T., Petty, R. E., Losch, M. E., & Kim, H. S. (1986). Electromyographic activity over facial muscle regions can discriminate the valence and intensity of affective reactions. *Journal of Personality and Social Psychology, 50,* 260–268.

Cappella, J. N. (1981). Mutual influence in expressive behavior: Adult-adult and infant-adult dyadic interaction. *Psychological Bulletin, 89,* 101–132.

Charny, J. E. (1966). Psychosomatic manifestations of rapport in psychotherapy. *Psychosomatic Medicine, 28,* 305–315.

Darwin, C. (1965). *The expression of emotion in man and animals.* Chicago: University of Chicago Press. (Original work published 1872)

Duclos, S. D., Laird, J. D., Schneider, E., Sexter, M., Stern, L., & VanLighten, O. (1989). Emotion-specific effects of facial expressions and postures on emotional experience. *Journal of Personality and Social Psychology, 57,* 100–108.

Feldman, R. S., McGee, G. G., Mann, L., & Strain, P. (1993). Nonverbal affective decoding ability in children with autism and in typical preschoolers. *Journal of Early Intervention, 17,* 1–10.

Feldman, R. S., Philippot, P., & Custrini, R. J. (1991). Nonverbal behavior and social competence. In R. S. Feldman & B. Rimé (Eds.), *Fundamentals of nonverbal behavior* (pp. 329–350). Cambridge, England: Cambridge University Press.

Greenberg, L. S., & Paivio, S. C. (1997). *Working with emotions in psychotherapy.* New York: Guilford Press.

Gross, J. J. (1998). Antecedent- and response-focused emotion regulation: Divergent consequences for experience, expression, and physiology. *Journal of Personality and Social Psychology, 74,* 224–237.

Harper, R., Wiens, A., & Matarazzo, J. (1978). *Nonverbal communication: The state of the art.* New York: Wiley.

Hatfield, E., Cacioppo, J. T., & Rapson, R. L. (1993). *Emotional contagion.* Madison, WI: C. W. Brown.

Hess, U., Kappas, A., McHugo, G. J., Lanzetta, J. T., & Kleck, R. E. (1992). The facilitative effect of facial expression on the self-generation of emotion. *International Journal of Psychophysiology, 12,* 251–265.

Hess, U., Philippot, P., & Blairy, S. (1999). Mimicry: Fact and fiction. In P. Philippot, R. S. Feldman, & E. J. Coats (Eds.), *The social context of nonverbal behavior* (pp. 213–241). New York: Cambridge University Press.

Hoffman, M. L. (1984). Interaction of affect and cognition on empathy. In C. E. Izard, J. Kagan, & R. B. Zajonc (Eds.), *Emotions, cognition, and behavior* (pp. 103–131). Cambridge, England: Cambridge University Press.

Kappas, A. (1989). *Control of emotion.* Unpublished doctoral dissertation, Dartmouth College, Hanover, NH.

Laird, J. (1984). The real role of facial response in the experience of emotion: a reply to Tourangeau and Ellsworth, and others. *Journal of Personality and Social Psychology, 47,* 909–917.

Levenson, R. W. (1992). Autonomic nervous system differences among emotions. *Psychological Science, 3,* 23–27.

Levenson, R. W., Carstensen, L. L., Friesen, W. V., & Ekman, P. (1991). Emotion, physiology, and expression in old age. *Psychology and Aging, 6,* 28–35.

Levenson, R. W., Ekman, P., & Friesen, W. V. (1990). Voluntary facial action generates emotion-specific autonomic nervous system activity. *Psychophysiology, 27,* 363–384.

Manstead, A. S. R. (1991). Expressiveness as an individual difference. In R. S. Feldman & B. Rimé (Eds.), *Fundamentals of nonverbal behavior* (pp. 285–328). Cambridge, England: Cambridge University Press.

Matsumoto, D. (1987). The role of facial responses in the experience of emotion:

More methodological problems and a meta-analysis. *Journal of Personality and Social Psychology, 52,* 769–774.

McIntosh, D. N. (1996). Facial feedback hypotheses: Evidence, implications, and directions. *Motivation and Emotion, 20,* 121–147.

McNally, R. J. (1995). Automaticity and the anxiety disorders. *Behavior Research and Therapy, 33,* 747–754.

Mogg, K., & Bradley, B. P. (1998). A cognitive-motivational analysis of anxiety. *Behavior Research and Therapy, 36,* 809–848.

Nowicki, S., Jr., & Duke, M. P. (1994). Individual differences in the nonverbal communication of affect: The Diagnostic Analysis of Nonverbal Accuracy Scale. *Journal of Nonverbal Behavior, 18,* 9–35.

Patterson, M. L. (1991). A functional approach to nonverbal exchange. In R. S. Feldman & B. Rimé (Eds.), *Fundamentals of nonverbal behavior* (pp. 458–496). Cambridge, England: Cambridge University Press.

Philippot, P. (2000). Une approche cognitive de la pathologie des émotions [A cognitive approach to emotional disorders]. In M. Vanderlinden & J. M. Danion (Eds.), *Neuropsychologie et psychopathologie* (pp. 31–50). Marseille, France: Editions Solal.

Philippot, P., Deplus, S., Baeyens, C., Schaefer, A., & Falise, F. (2001). Le travail émotionnel en psychothérapie: Application du modèle bi-mnésique des émotions au traitement des pathologies des émotions [Emotional work in psychotherapy: Applying the dual memory model of emotion to emotional disorders treatment]. *Revue Francophone de Clinique Comportementale et Cognitive, 6,* 5–8.

Rogers, C. (1975). Empathic: An unappreciated way of being. *The Counseling Psychologist, 5,* 2–9.

Schmais, C., & Schmais, A. (1983). Reflecting emotions: The movement-mirroring test. *Journal of Nonverbal Behavior, 8,* 42–54.

Siegel, E. V. (1995). Psychoanalytic dance therapy: The bridge between psyche and soma. *American Journal of Dance Therapy, 17,* 115–128.

Stepper, S., & Strack, F. (1993). Proprioceptive determinants of affective and nonaffective feelings. *Journal of Personality and Social Psychology, 64,* 211–220.

Tcherkassof, A. (1999). Les indices de préparation à l'action et la reconnaissance des expressions émotionnelles faciales [Action tendencies and emotional facial expression recognition]. *Revue européenne de psychologie appliquée, 49,* 99–105.

Teasdale, J. D. (1999). Multi-level theories of cognition-emotion relations. In T. Dalgleish & M. J. Power (Eds.), *Handbook of cognition and emotion* (pp. 665–682). Chichester, England: Wiley.

PART I

NONVERBAL BEHAVIOR IN REGULATORY AND CLINICAL PROCESSES

2

Nonverbal Social Skills and Psychopathology

JOHN E. PEREZ AND RONALD E. RIGGIO

An important approach to the study of the connections between nonverbal behavior and psychopathology focuses on the notion of skill in nonverbal communication (Riggio, 1992; Rosenthal, 1979). Accordingly, many researchers have considered nonverbal skills as embedded in a broader conceptualization of social skills (Argyle, 1981; Riggio, 1986; Trower, Bryant, & Argyle, 1978). People vary in their abilities to send and receive nonverbal messages, and this skill in nonverbal communication has important implications for social interaction, for the development and maintenance of healthy social relationships, and for psychosocial adjustment in general (Riggio, Watring, & Throckmorton, 1993; Riggio & Zimmerman, 1991).

The importance of nonverbal behavior (e.g., psychomotor activity, speech pauses) in psychopathology was recognized long ago (Griesinger, 1876; Kraepelin, 1913). Moreover, enthusiasm for the study of nonverbal behavior in psychiatric populations blossomed in the 1960s and 1970s. However, this interest waned shortly thereafter, due in part to the emergence of cognitive theories and therapies for psychopathology (e.g., Beck, 1987, 1991).

In the last 15 years, there has been a resurgence of interest in the study of nonverbal behavior and psychopathology. For example, ethological psychiatry—defined as the systematic, quantitative study of the behavior, assessed from an evolutionary frame of reference, of psychiatric patients—has continued to develop and bear fruitful information about the nonverbal behavior of individuals suffering from psychological disorders (see Bouhuys, chapter 10, this volume). Methodological and statistical advances in the field have also allowed detailed behavioral analyses of various mental disorders.

These developments are important because mental status examinations used in the assessment of psychiatric populations rely heavily on the accurate and reliable observation of nonverbal behavior. Information so obtained is used to develop treatment plans and to measure treatment progress. Perhaps most important, nonverbal as well as verbal behaviors are hypothesized to contribute to the etiology, maintenance, and relapse of mental disorders (e.g., Lewinsohn & Gotlib, 1995). Accordingly, social skills training is an important component of treatment for many psychological disorders, and greater understanding of the link between social skills and various forms of psychopathology can lead to advances in psychosocial therapies.

The relationship between nonverbal social skills and psychopathology raises several important questions and issues for basic and applied research. For example, which nonverbal social skills are associated with specific forms of psychopathology? Can one psychiatric disorder be distinguished from another based solely on nonverbal behavior? What do nonverbal social skills tell us about the etiology and treatment of different psychiatric disorders? Despite the early interest in nonverbal aspects of psychopathology, it is only fairly recently that exploration of the relationship between nonverbal social skills and psychopathology has begun.

One difficulty with much of this work has been the lack of a theoretical framework for defining social skills. For the most part, social skills are defined broadly or are conceptualized as general social competence. Moreover, emphasis is often placed on the importance of verbal skills in determining social competence. Yet, research in nonverbal communication has recognized the critical role that nonverbal and emotional communication skills play in notions of social competence (Feldman, Philippot, & Custrini, 1991; Riggio, 1986; Riggio, Messamer, & Throckmorton, 1991; Rosenthal, 1979; Schlundt & McFall, 1985). For example, Riggio (1986, 1989) conceptualizes social skills/competence as composed of three types of basic communication skills that have both verbal and nonverbal forms: sending or encoding ability, receiving or decoding ability, and control or regulating ability (see Table 2.1). Furthermore, the nonverbal domain is dominated by skill in emotional communication because it primarily involves the sending, interpreting, and regulation of emotional messages. This is consistent with popular notions of emotional competence (e.g., Saarni, 1999) and emotional intelligence (e.g., Salovey & Mayer, 1990).

This review focuses on the relation between psychopathology and the nonverbal dimensions of social skills outlined in Riggio's (1986, 1989) model. We review observational and experimental studies that focus on the emotional expressiveness, emotional sensitivity, and emotional control abilities of individuals with psychological disorders. For the sake of parsimony, we concentrate on three distinct psychological disorders for which nonverbal social skills are particularly salient: schizophrenia, major depression, and social anxiety disorder (social phobia). We integrate relevant etiological theories that provide a framework for understanding the relation between

Table 2.1 A Model for Basic Social Skills

Nonverbal Domain

Emotional Expressivity (EE): Emotional expressivity relates to skill in sending/encoding nonverbal and emotional messages, but also includes the nonverbal expression of attitudes, dominance, and interpersonal orientation. Accuracy in expressing felt emotional states is involved in EE.

Emotional Sensitivity (ES): Emotional sensitivity reflects skill in receiving/decoding nonverbal messages as well as attentiveness to nonverbal cues.

Emotional Control (EC): Emotional control is the ability to control and regulate emotional and nonverbal displays. EC also involves the ability to mask felt emotional states and to deliberately portray particular emotions "on cue."

Social/Verbal Domain

Social Expressivity (SE): Social expressivity is skill in verbal expression/encoding and the ability to engage others in social interaction (i.e., skill in attaining, guiding, and maintaining conversations).

Social Sensitivity (SS): Social sensitivity is the ability to decode/interpret others' verbal communications, as well as knowledge of and sensitivity to the norms governing appropriate social behavior. It is related to a social "self-consciousness" that allows persons to monitor their own social behavior and realize its impact on others.

Social Control (SC): Social control is skill in social role playing and in social self-presentation. This skill is also important in guiding the direction and content of communication in social interaction and is the social skill most commonly associated with notions of social competence or social intelligence.

Global Social Skill/Competence (SSI Total): A general indicator of global social competence can be obtained by summing the SSI dimensions. However, a balance among the SSI dimensions is also important in notions of global social skill or competence. Thus, the SSI imbalance score is used in combination with the total score to obtain an indication of global social skill.

Source: From Riggio (1986, 1989).

nonverbal social skills and these disorders.[1] Finally, we summarize our findings and suggest future directions for research on nonverbal social skills and psychopathology.

Emotional Expressiveness

Emotional expressiveness not only is nonverbal sending skill, particularly skill in sending emotional messages, but also includes the expression of attitudes, dominance, and interpersonal orientation (Riggio, 1986, 1989). In addition, this skill reflects ability to express felt emotional states accurately. Individuals who are highly emotionally expressive are animated, emotionally charged, and able to arouse or inspire others based on their ability to transmit feelings. Studies of nonverbal behavior demonstrate that individuals with schizophrenia and major depression show similar deficits in emotional expressiveness (e.g., flattened affect, gaze aversion), whereas mixed results typify studies that examine emotional expressiveness among those with social anxiety disorder.

Schizophrenia, like depression, is characterized by flat affect. Andreasen (1979) found that affective flattening was common among individuals with schizophrenia, yet it was similarly common among individuals with major depression and could not be used to discriminate between the two groups. The salient behavioral components in Andreason's rating system for affective flattening in schizophrenia were paucity of expressive gestures, unchanging facial expressions, lack of vocal inflections, decreased spontaneous movements, and poor eye contact. Subsequent studies also reported that patients with schizophrenia display few facial expressions, minimal gaze, and unusual gestures and postures (Berenbaum, 1992; Gaebel & Wölwer, 1992).

Importantly, recent ethological studies of schizophrenia have included participants who were medication free, ruling out the possibility that nonverbal deficiencies found among individuals with schizophrenia were due to the effects of neuroleptic agents. These studies have shown that, compared to control participants, medication-free individuals with schizophrenia indeed exhibited fewer glances at the interviewer, less prosocial behavior (e.g., smiling), fewer gestures, and fewer body-focused and object-focused movements (Pitman et al., 1987; Troisi, Spalletta, & Pasini, 1998). In adult populations, the nonverbal behavior in those with schizophrenia appears highly similar to that of those with depression, with the exception of unusual gestures and postures sometimes exhibited among individuals with schizophrenia.

Nonverbal behavior may also be a marker in children who later meet criteria for schizophrenia. Based on blind, retrospective analyses of videotapes, Walker, Grimes, Davis, and Smith (1993) reported abnormalities in facial expressions among high-risk children before the onset of schizophrenia. Specifically, there were lower proportions of joy expressions among the total expressions of the preschizophrenic females than among same-sex healthy siblings. However, there were inconsistent differences between preschizophrenic males and their same-sex healthy siblings. Nevertheless, the authors found that both male and female preschizophrenic subjects exhibited more negative affect than their same-sex healthy counterparts. This study suggested that nonverbal deficiencies in expressiveness might be subtle indicators of schizophrenia rather than just a behavioral by-product of schizophrenia.

In addition to flattened facial affect, one of the most common nonverbal behaviors in psychopathology is poor eye contact with other people. Diminished eye contact with other people appears to be the most robust nonverbal index of depression (Hinchliffe, Lancashire, & Roberts, 1971; Rutter, 1973; Waxer, 1974). Additional nonverbal markers of depression include downward curvature of the mouth, downward angling of the head, and lack of head, hand, and body gestures or movements (Jones & Pasna, 1979; Pedersen et al., 1988; Waxer, 1976).

Interestingly, a body of research indicates that facial actions both modulate ongoing emotions and initiate them (for reviews of facial feedback hypotheses, see Adelmann & Zajonc, 1989; McIntosh, 1996). For example, Ekman (1992) had nonclinical participants move certain facial muscles and subsequently report about their mood. Unknown to the participants, they were directed to exhibit facial expressions characteristic of different emotions (e.g., happy and sad). The way participants felt was significantly influenced by whether they had been posing positive or negative emotional expressions. Thus, wearing a sad face might actually make one feel sad.

Nonverbal behavior also appears to be associated with depression in children, although perhaps not to the same extent as for adults. Kazdin, Sherick, Esveldt-Dawson, and Rancurello (1985) found that nonverbal behaviors correlated with the severity of depression for child psychiatric inpatients. For both boys and girls, depression was associated with less facial expressiveness, less head shaking, fewer gestures, fewer body movements, and more tearfulness. In addition, girls demonstrated a negative correlation between depression and eye contact, smiling, intonation, and self-movements. When compared to nondepressed psychiatric patients, however, only facial expressiveness distinguished these groups. Depressed children showed significantly less facial expressiveness during an interview than did nondepressed children. Based on their findings, Kazdin et al. suggested that there is a less robust relationship between depression and nonverbal behavior for children than has been shown in studies of adults.

Observational studies of depressed patients showed that individuals become more emotionally expressive as a result of successful pharmacological and psychological treatments, whereas medication may lead to less emotional expressiveness among individuals with schizophrenia. Schelde and Hertz (1994) described the depressive phase as typified by withdrawal, nonspecific gaze, looking down, little self-activity, little motor activity, and substantial reduction of social interaction. They described the recovery phase as an increase in verbal and nonverbal communication, including looking at others, raising and wrinkling eyebrows, nodding, smiling, laughing, and gesturing. Fisch, Frey, and Hirsbrunner (1983) found that, on recovery, previously depressed patients spent more time in motion, displayed a more complex pattern of movement, and initiated and terminated movement more rapidly than when they were depressed. These observations stand in contrast to studies of the effects of neuroleptic medications for schizophrenia. Schneider et al. (1992) compared a group of previously drug-free patients with schizophrenia and schizophreniform disorder to a similar group of patients who were already receiving medication. After 3 weeks of medication, the previously drug-free group members showed reductions in facial activity and facial expression, whereas there were no changes in the facial behavior of members of the group with already medicated individuals.

Some behavioral analyses of treatment outcome for depressed patients suggest that certain nonverbal behaviors may predict response to antidepressant treatment (Nelson & Charney, 1981; Ranelli & Miller, 1981). However, a number of these studies have found inconsistent or null results (Bouhuys, Beersma, Hoofdakker, & Roossien, 1987; Fossi, Faravelli, & Paoli, 1984), and many are plagued by methodological problems, such as low statistical power and poor construct validity (e.g., Troisi, Pasini, Bersani, Grispini, & Ciani, 1989). Therefore, it is unclear whether response to antidepressant treatment can be predicted by a general level of psychomotor retardation or by specific nonverbal expressive behaviors. Nonetheless, improvement appears to be characterized by a number of nonverbal behaviors that represent more than just a general increase in psychomotor behavior.

Perhaps due only to recent recognition in psychiatric nosology, few studies have focused on specific nonverbal expressive skills among individuals diagnosed with social anxiety disorder (social phobia)—a condition characterized by an excessive fear of being embarrassed, humiliated, or judged negatively in social or performance situations. Using a behavioral rating system of social performance (Social Performance Rating Scale, SPRS), Fydrich, Chambless, Perry, Buergener, and Beazley (1998) compared participants with social anxiety disorder to participants with another anxiety disorder and participants without a history of any psychological disorder.

Heavily weighted by nonverbal expressive behaviors, the five SPRS ratings are gaze or eye contact, vocal quality, speech length, discomfort, and conversation flow. Vocal quality ratings include tonal quality, pitch, clarity, and volume. Discomfort ratings include extremity movements, self-manipulation, facial expression, posture, and gestures. Fydrich et al. (1998) found that trained raters assigned significantly less positive SPRS ratings to the social anxiety disorder group relative to both the anxious and normal control groups, whereas there was no difference between the two control groups.

Using a precursor to the SPRS, Turner, Beidel, Dancu, and Keys (1986) compared individuals with social anxiety disorder to individuals diagnosed with avoidant personality disorder. In addition to differences on self-reported measures of symptom severity, they found that persons with social anxiety disorder were rated more positively on behavioral measures of gaze, tone, and overall skill.

These results are important in light of the overlap between avoidant personality disorder and the generalized subtype of social anxiety disorder (Herbert, Hope, & Bellack, 1992; Holt, Heimberg, Hope, & Liebowitz, 1992; Schneier, Spitzer, Gibbon, Fyer, & Liebowitz, 1991). Like depression and schizophrenia, social anxiety disorder can be characterized by minimal gaze or eye contact. However, whereas major depression and schizophrenia are marked by flat affect and psychomotor retardation, social anxiety disorder may be marked by an agitated response associated with physiological arousal.

Despite these findings, the results of studies comparing individuals with social anxiety disorder to nonanxious individuals in social-evaluative situations have been inconsistent. One study that compared the public speaking of participants with social anxiety disorder to that of nonanxious controls found no difference in observer-rated performance (Rapee & Lim, 1992). Another study found few differences between individuals with social anxiety disorder and nonanxious controls on specific nonverbal behaviors (e.g., eye contact), whereas individuals with social anxiety disorder performed worse on more global measures of performance (Beidel, Turner, & Dancu, 1985). Yet other studies have found that individuals with social anxiety disorder performed significantly worse than nonanxious as well as anxious control groups, particularly when rated on nonverbal dimensions of behavior (Alden & Wallace, 1995; Fydrich et al., 1998). Thus, the few studies of emotional expressiveness in social anxiety disorder have yielded less consistent results than the well-studied nonverbal behaviors in depression and schizophrenia.

Clearly, the relationship between social anxiety disorder and nonverbal social skills is not a simple one. There appear to be some individual differences among individuals that may help explain the conflicting empirical findings. Many individuals with high social anxiety perform very well in social situations, whereas some individuals with little or no social anxiety have social skill deficits (McNeil, Ries, & Turk, 1995). Another potential source of conflicting findings is the different behavioral measures and rating systems used; some focus on specific behavioral skills, whereas others focus more on global perceptions of social competence. Moreover, although many studies exclude participants with a diagnosis of major depression or dysthymia, few control for the level of subclinical depression. Inasmuch as anxiety and depression are substantially overlapping constructs, relatively higher levels of depression could impair emotional expressiveness among some individuals with social anxiety disorder.

Some researchers have suggested that many individuals with social anxiety disorder do not suffer from a deficit in social skills. Rather, individuals with social anxiety disorder who demonstrate poor social performance often do so because of an inhibition of social skills (e.g., Rapee, 1995). Support for this interpretation comes from the observation that individuals with social anxiety disorder report no difficulty whatsoever performing behaviors such as eating, writing, or urinating in private—behaviors that elicit great fear when the individual must do them under the potential scrutiny of other people (Barlow, 1988). This issue becomes more clouded when it deals with behaviors that are necessarily public, such as formal speaking or conversations with strangers.

Along those lines, Alden and Wallace (1995) demonstrated that individuals with social anxiety disorder exhibited more skillful social behavior when their conversational partner engaged in intentionally positive rather than negative social behavior. This suggests that the less skillful social behavior of participants with social anxiety disorder was a function of the context, elicited to some extent by the negative behavior of a confederate, rather than a general skill deficit.

Furthermore, it may be that this aspect of social anxiety disorder is due not to deficits in expressive skills, but to heightened sensitivity to the emotional (i.e., positive versus negative) reactions of others, causing inhibition of expressive behavior when others react negatively. This behavior does not necessarily lead to an unfavorable global evaluation of performance by observers. However, it may contribute to overly negative self-evaluations by individuals with social anxiety disorder (Rapee & Lim, 1992).

In summary, studies of nonverbal behavior show that individuals with schizophrenia and major depression show a similar global restriction of emotional expressiveness, whereas there are no consistent deficits of emotional expressiveness among individuals with social anxiety disorder. Among those with depression and schizophrenia, common deficiencies in emotional expressiveness include restricted facial expressions, minimal eye contact with other people, limited gesturing, and restricted body movements.[2] Downward curvature of the mouth and downward angling of the head are more specific to depression, while unusual gestures and postures are sometimes more specific to schizophrenia. Studies that examined whether individuals with social anxiety disorder exhibited difficulties in emotional expressiveness are mixed. When the focus is on specific nonverbal social skills, it appears that many individuals with social anxiety disorder do make less eye contact and exhibit greater visible discomfort. However, as in depression, this often may be a function of social skill inhibition rather than social skill deficits.

Emotional Sensitivity

Emotional sensitivity is defined as skill in receiving and interpreting the nonverbal communications of others (Riggio, 1986, 1989). Individuals who are emotionally sensitive attend to and accurately interpret the subtle emotional cues of others. Those who are highly emotionally sensitive may be susceptible to becoming emotionally aroused by others, empathetically experiencing their emotional states. Experimental studies indicate that schizophrenia and major depression are associated with a decreased ability to decode nonverbal cues, particularly facial expressions of emotion, with the most profound deficiencies in emotional sensitivity exhibited by individuals with schizophrenia. Some experimental studies also suggest that people with social anxiety may have a heightened emotional sensitivity to angry or critical faces, which may be an underlying cause of why persons with social anxiety disorder appear less socially skilled (i.e., expressive) when interacting with confederates who act negatively toward them (Alden & Wallace, 1995).

Several studies have consistently found that patients with schizophrenia perform significantly worse than healthy controls on emotion recognition and emotion-labeling tasks. For example, Dougherty, Bartlett, and Izard (1974) presented photos of eight basic facial expressions of emotion to female inpatients with schizophrenia and to healthy controls. Patients with schizophrenia were less accurate than controls in labeling and recognizing the emotions; they had particular difficulty recognizing disgust-contempt and shame-humiliation.

Using both facial photographs and nonverbal videotaped scenes, Muzekari and Bates (1977) also found that male and female patients with chronic schizophrenia were less accurate than healthy controls in identifying emotions. Similarly, Cramer, Weegmann, and O'Neil (1989) found that patients with schizophrenia, compared to controls, less accurately judged the emotional content of videotaped scenes of social interactions.

In addition, patients with schizophrenia have more often failed to comment on affect of faces during free responses to videotapes of social interactions and photographs depicting posed emotional expressions (Cramer, Bowen, & O'Neill, 1992; Pilowsky & Bassett, 1980). Studies have also shown that children with schizophrenia, adolescents with schizophrenia, and high-risk children of adults with schizophrenia also exhibit emotion identification deficits (Anthony, 1978; Walker, 1980; Walker, Marwit, & Emory, 1980).

Some interesting literature has focused on how individuals with schizophrenia interpret mixed messages. Mixed messages typically occur when the verbal content of a message is contradicted by such nonverbal behaviors as facial expression, vocal tone, or physical gesture. Newman (1977) compared how male patients with schizophrenia and control participants interpreted mixed messages. It was found that participants with schizophrenia relied more on the verbal channel than the nonverbal channel (i.e., vocal tone) and rated inconsistent messages with a negative vocal component as more confusing than did controls.

Reilly and Muzekari (1979) also examined how mixed messages are interpreted by patients with schizophrenia, "emotionally disturbed" children, healthy adult controls, and healthy child controls. All the participants in this study were male. Healthy adult participants appeared to be influenced by all communication elements (verbal statement, facial expression, vocal tone, and physical gesture) in mixed messages, whereas the other three groups were primarily influenced by words.

In a recent study of both congruent and incongruent affective communications (Davis & Stewart, 2001), participants with paranoid schizophrenia interpreted most communications in a manner consistent with nonclinical and depressed participants. However, in contrast to the other two groups, participants with paranoid schizophrenia interpreted communications with a negative verbal message as virtually devoid of any affect at all. Overall, these results are consistent with findings that individuals with schizophrenia suffer deficits in nonverbal social perception and social judgment (Toomey, Wallace, Corrigan, Schuldberg, & Green, 1997).

Experimental studies suggest that depressed individuals also have difficulty decoding nonverbal facial cues. For example, Giannini, Folts, Melemis, Giannini, and Loiselle (1995) compared 20 clinically depressed males and 20 matched controls, who viewed videotapes of 5 male medical interns participating in gambling trials. The interns attempted to earn variable amounts of money playing at a slot machine. The amount of money at risk was randomly determined to be a nickel, a quarter, or a dollar. Participants in the study were instructed to guess the amount of money at risk based only on nonverbal facial cues. The depressed participants were less accurate than control participants and less accurate than chance.

Additional experimental studies have demonstrated that depression diminishes the ability to decode facial emotion stimuli accurately among adults with affective disorders, including those with bipolar disorder (Cooley & Nowicki, 1989; Gur et al., 1992; Rubinow & Post, 1992). Linking emotional sensitivity to functioning, Hale (1998) found that the judgment of negative emotions (particularly sadness) in both general and ambiguous faces among outpatients with major depression was associated with depression severity at baseline and predicted the persistence of depression after 6 months.

Some studies have directly compared emotional sensitivity skills of individuals with either schizophrenia or major depression. For example, in a well-designed study, Feinberg et al. (1986) used four tasks to compare the ability to process facial stimuli among patients with schizophrenia, patients with major depression, and healthy controls. Two tasks (one with upright and one with inverted photographs of faces) investigated facial identity matching, one task assessed emotion recognition, and one task assessed emotion labeling. Whereas depressed participants performed worse than controls only on the emotion-labeling task, participants with schizophrenia showed deficits on all four tasks and did worse than depressed participants on the emotion recognition and emotion-labeling tasks.

Gessler, Cutting, Frith, and Weinman (1989) compared five groups of individuals on an emotion judgment task and a non-emotion judgment task. The groups included individuals diagnosed with acute schizophrenia, chronic schizophrenia, schizophrenia in remission, and depression, as well as healthy controls. Participants were asked to make a dichotomous (happy or sad) judgment about a set of photographed faces. Subsequently, participants were asked to make a dichotomous (old or young) judgment on a set of photographs chosen from the original pool as a nonemotion task designed to be of equal discrimination difficulty. Although some group differences were not statistically significant due to low power, individuals with acute and chronic schizophrenia appeared to perform equally poorly on the emotion judgment task, whereas individuals with remitted schizophrenia, depressed individuals, and healthy controls performed equally well on the emotion judgment task. Contrary to the predictions of the investigators, individuals with acute schizophrenia, chronic schizophrenia, and depression all exhibited deficits in age judgment when compared to healthy controls; the greatest age judgment deficits were demonstrated by those with acute schizophrenia.

Other experimental studies examining the ability to judge facial affect have found that participants with schizophrenia generally perform worse than participants with affective disorders (Addington & Addington, 1998; Heimberg, Gur, Erwin, Shtasel, & Gur, 1992; Walker, McGuire, & Bettes, 1984), although there are some exceptions (e.g., Zuroff & Colussy, 1986), which may be due to low statistical power and methodological variation. Taken together, however, these studies typically showed a wider range of deficits in emotional sensitivity among individuals with schizophrenia relative to those with depression.

Although it is generally accepted that people with schizophrenia have problems judging the emotional states of others, the underlying mechanisms involved are not well understood. Cramer et al. (1992) have proposed three possibilities: formal thought disorder, selective avoidance of psychological factors, or perceptual/attentional deficits. Based on a study of patients' free responses to videotaped social interactions, Cramer et al. suggested that perceptual or attentional deficits best explained their results. However, they could not rule out thought disorder or limit their findings to schizophrenia inasmuch as there was no psychiatric control group, only a nonclinical control group.

Consistent with the perceptual deficit hypothesis, Frith, Stevens, Johnstone, Owens, and Crow (1983) provided evidence that individuals with schizophrenia do not perceive faces holistically, as do healthy controls. Rather, individuals with schizophrenia seem to process faces as the sum of their parts (i.e., fail to integrate the components of faces) in the same way they process histoform objects. Failure of perceptual integration is a plausible mechanism for the deficits in emotional sensitivity observed in persons with schizophrenia. Nevertheless, as Frith et al. suggested, further study is needed to determine whether such a failure of integration is specific for facial (i.e., socially meaningful) stimuli, or whether it represents a more general perceptual disintegration in schizophrenia.

Other factors that should be considered include poor social learning and the effects of neuroleptic or anticholinergic medications (Morrison, Bellack, & Mueser, 1988). Recently, Whitaker, Deakin, and Tomenson (2001) found that impaired face and nonface visual-spatial function and recognition performance were generally correlated with drug dose among participants with schizophrenia.

On a neurostructural level, right hemisphere dysfunction has been implicated in the pathophysiology of schizophrenia (Cutting, 1990; Morrison et al., 1988). With regard to nonverbal behavior, this structural hypothesis suggests that a neurological impairment in the right cerebral hemisphere could be responsible for deficits in the expression of emotion and the processing of emotional faces. There is evidence that, among nonclinical participants, the right hemisphere plays a selective role in the processing of both faces in general and faces showing emotion (Suberi & McKeever, 1977).

Moreover, there is evidence that right hemisphere damage can cause an impairment of spontaneous emotional gesturing known as motor aprosodia, and such deficits have been documented in some patients with schizophrenia (Murphy & Cutting, 1990). Other studies have shown that patients with right hemispheric damage are usually more impaired than patients with left hemispheric damage or controls on tasks of emotion recognition and/or emotion identification (Benowitz et al., 1983; DeKosky, Heilman, Bowers, & Valenstein, 1980; Etcoff, 1984).

These studies provide some support for the hypothesis that the nonverbal deficits, particularly emotional decoding, seen in patients with schizophrenia relate to structural damage in the right cerebral hemisphere. However, Bruyer (chapter 8, this volume) provides evidence that the neural structures governing facial expression are more specific than the right hemisphere.

Unlike the decreased emotional sensitivity in schizophrenia and depression, social anxiety disorder might be characterized by a specific, heightened emotional sensitivity. While sensitivity to emotions is an adaptive skill, hypersensitivity to negative affect in others can be socially debilitating. Riggio (1986, 1989) asserts that extreme sensitivity to both emotional cues and social cues, particularly in persons who may lack emotional expressiveness and the ability to regulate or control their felt emotional states, can be particularly problematic, leading to withdrawal from and avoidance of social situations.

A handful of interesting studies suggest that individuals with social anxiety disorder may have an attention, recognition, or response bias for critical or angry faces. For example, Lundh and Öst (1996) compared participants with social anxiety disorder to control participants on a task of face recognition. Participants were presented with 20 photos and were asked to judge whether the person in each photo was critical or accepting. After a 5-minute word stem completion task, participants were unexpectedly presented with a recognition task using slightly different photos of the original faces and 60 distractor faces. Although the participants with social anxiety disorder did not rate the persons in the photos as more critical than the control participants did, they did recognize more of the critical than the accepting faces. Conversely, control participants tended to recognize more accepting than critical faces. Lundh and Öst concluded that the participants with social anxiety disorder either had a better memory for critical faces or had a greater tendency to guess that a face had been presented if critical. Unfortunately, the design of this study did not rule out the possibility of such a response bias.

Hansen and Hansen (1988) demonstrated that nonclinical participants more efficiently identify an angry face (versus happy or neutral faces) in a crowd; perhaps this identification is a result of a preattentive, parallel search for signals of direct threat. Mogg and Bradley (1998) suggested that vulnerability to anxiety stems from a lower threshold for appraising threat rather than a bias in the direction of attention deployment (see also Mogg and Bradley, chapter 6, this volume). They conducted a series of studies using various tasks to investigate attentional bias for emotional faces among clinical and nonclinical participants. Like Hansen and Hansen, Mogg and Bradley showed that all participants, whether high or low in anxiety, demonstrated faster detection of threat faces in happy crowds than of happy faces in threat crowds. Moreover, they showed that this effect was more apparent in high- than low-state anxious individuals, suggesting that anxiety facilitates the detection of pictorial threat. Similarly, Mogg and Bradley used other paradigms (e.g., dot probe tasks with facial stimuli) to show that individuals with high anxiety, including those with generalized anxiety disorder, exhibit vigilance for threat faces. Although these studies were not conducted with participants diagnosed with social anxiety disorder, these data shed light on the emotional sensitivity of highly anxious individuals.

Using angry faces as fear-relevant stimuli in a conditioning paradigm, Öhman and colleagues conducted a series of experiments on emotional decoding among nonclinical participants. These studies involved the conditioning of electrodermal or heart rate responses (conditioned responses, CRs) to fear-relevant conditioned stimuli (CSs), using a mild electric shock as an unconditioned stimulus.

Öhman and Dimberg (1978) first compared conditioning to slides of angry, happy, and neutral faces. As predicted, they found that superior conditioning occurred when angry faces were used as CSs relative to happy or neutral faces. Dimberg and Öhman (1983) subsequently showed that the gaze of the angry face was most salient when directed at the target participant. Participants showed greater resistance to extinction when the angry facial expression was directed at them. On the other hand, angry faces looking away were as ineffective as happy faces. Öhman and colleagues (Öhman, 1986; Öhman, Dimberg, & Esteves, 1989) also showed that, following conditioning to angry faces, it is possible to elicit the CR even with very quick (30 ms) unconscious or preattentive presentations of the CS during extinction.

Based on his conditioning studies, Öhman (1986) suggested that there is an evolutionary predisposition for humans to acquire fears of angry, critical, or rejecting faces. According to the preparedness theory of phobias, humans have a biologically based predisposition to fear objects or situations that once threatened the survival of the species throughout its evolutionary history (Mineka & Zinbarg, 1995; Öhman, Dimberg, & Öst, 1985; Seligman, 1971). Thus, individuals who easily developed fears of dangerous objects or situations could have had a selective advantage in the struggle for survival. Furthermore, it is theorized that social anxiety disorder, like specific phobias, develops as a consequence of one or more traumatic conditioning experiences. In partial support of this notion, Öst and Hugdahl (1981) found that 58% of their sample with social anxiety disorder recalled direct traumatic conditioning experiences in the etiology of their phobia.

The gaze aversion demonstrated by individuals with social anxiety disorder also makes sense in light of preparedness theory. Barlow (1988) noted that direct eye contact seems to be very frightening or threatening among our close relatives, the primates. Although this response is greatly altered by contextual and learning factors among humans, experimental evidence shows that angry faces directed at the individual are highly salient. Thus, one can avoid the threat of angry, critical, or rejecting faces by looking away.

In a critical review of experimental literature, McNally (1987) posed some strong challenges to the preparedness theory of phobias. According to preparedness theory, phobias are supposed to be rapidly acquired, irrational, highly resistant to extinction, and differentially associable with stimuli of evolutionary significance (Seligman, 1971). However, McNally indicated that the rate at which phobias are acquired varies widely. He also argued that phobic avoidance is not necessarily irrational in those who fear anxiety and its consequences. Thus, although socially anxious persons recognize they have no physical threat to avoid, they are avoiding the likelihood of becoming extremely anxious in encountering a feared situation.

McNally also showed that, while skin conductance responses established to fear-relevant CSs are highly resistant to extinction in laboratory conditioning, behavioral treatment research demonstrates that "prepared" phobias are eliminated at least as easily as "unprepared" ones, with fears of heights and of animals among the easiest phobias to treat through exposure therapy.

Furthermore, several alternative explanations for the experimental resistance to extinction effect need to be tested. McNally asserted that only one of the original assumptions of preparedness theory remains unaltered by the data and critical analyses: Most phobias are associated with threats of evolutionary significance. Other plausible hypotheses for experimental findings that need to be ruled out are ontogenetic (i.e., cultural) preparedness, stimulus significance (preparedness effects occur because fear-relevant stimuli are more significant than fear-irrelevant stimuli), and CS prepotency (humans are innately predisposed to respond with high levels of attention and arousal, not necessarily fear, to stimuli of evolutionary significance).

In summary, one of the most consistent findings in the area of nonverbal behavior indicates that individuals with schizophrenia have deficiencies in decoding emotional facial expressions (for reviews, see Edwards, Jackson, & Pattison, 2002; Mandal, Pandey, & Prasad, 1998). Moreover, individuals with schizophrenia show greater severity and a broader range of deficits in nonverbal sensitivity when directly compared to individuals with major depression, and these deficits predict broader problems in social functioning (Toomey et al., 1997). In addition, individuals with schizophrenia demonstrate an overreliance on verbal cues in their misperception of mixed messages. Unlike those with schizophrenia, individuals with major depression do not seem to have problems with facial identification tasks; however, they do appear to have difficulty with emotion-labeling tasks. There is little research on emotional sensitivity among individuals with social anxiety disorder. Nonetheless, individuals with social anxiety may have the most specific type of emotional sensitivity—attention, recognition, or possible response bias for angry or critical faces—or perhaps a lower threshold for appraising threat (Mogg & Bradley, 1998).

Emotional Control

Emotional control is the ability to control and regulate emotional and nonverbal displays of behavior. Emotional control includes the ability to convey particular emotions on cue and to hide feelings behind an assumed mask (e.g., laughing appropriately at a joke or putting on a cheerful face to cover sorrow) (Riggio, 1986, 1989). Emotional control also refers to an individual's ability to tolerate and manage negative affect as well as appropriately display positive affect. In contrast, the construct of emotion regulation can refer not only to the regulation of emotions, but also to the regulation of other processes (e.g., attention, memory) by emotions (LeDoux, 1996). In this chapter, we refer to emotional control as the former definition of emotion regulation—the regulation of emotions themselves. Unlike the abundant research in the areas of emotional expressiveness and emotional sensitivity, there has been little empirical research on emotional control within specific diagnostic categories.

Some researchers have suggested that the decrease in emotional expressiveness in schizophrenia is actually a result of the increased need to control internal emotional processes (Ellgring & Smith, 1998). Thus, according to these authors, the flat affect, gaze aversion, and general lack of facial expressiveness seen in schizophrenia is actually related to emotion overregulation. In a fascinating study with bilingual Hispanic patients with schizophrenia (Grand, Marcos, Freedman, & Barroso, 1977), there was a relationship between psychiatric symptom clusters and hand movements of patients during a nondominant-language (English) interview. Hand movements were scored by clinicians from videotaped Spanish and English interviews and examined in relation to structured ratings of psychiatric symptoms. Certain object-focused and body-focused movements increased during the English language interview. Grand et al. theorized that, apart from their communicative value for the listener, hand movements that accompany speech serve an important regulatory and supportive function in the encoding of thought for the speaker. Thus, these authors attributed the increases in hand movements to a combination of psychological stress and verbal encoding stress from the second-language interview.

Furthermore, as in depression, an increase in body-focused touching may be related to attempts to regulate negative affect. Research on deception has shown a similar increase in body-focused touching when people are deceiving as compared to telling the truth, presumably in an attempt to regulate the negative affect associated with lying (Riggio & Friedman, 1983).

Major depression itself could be conceptualized as a disorder of emotion regulation. Gross and Muñoz (1995) suggested an integrative conceptualization of depression as a dysregulation of emotions by which the frequency, intensity, and duration of negative emotions (especially sadness) are increased, and those of positive emotions (e.g., interest and enjoyment) are decreased. This is consistent with Clark and Watson's (1991) model of depression stemming from two higher order factors—the presence of negative affect and the absence of positive affect (i.e., anhedonia).

Sex differences in emotional sensitivity and emotional control may also help explain why more women than men experience depression. Epidemiologic studies show that women are about twice as likely as men to experience unipolar depression (Blazer, Kessler, McGonagle, & Swartz, 1994; Weissman & Olfson, 1995). In terms of nonverbal behavior, women are more emotionally sensitive than men, while men exhibit greater emotional control (e.g., suppress emotional displays better) than women (Hall, 1984; Riggio, 1986). Greater emotional sensitivity and less emotional control may combine to put women at greater risk for depression. Research on nonclinical populations (Riggio, 1986) found positive relationships between emotional sensitivity and both apprehensiveness and private self-consciousness, or an awareness of one's internal states. Thus, women may be more likely to amplify their moods by ruminating about their depressed states and the possible causes of these states, whereas men are more likely to engage in distracting behaviors (as an emotional control strategy) to dampen their mood when depressed (Nolen-Hoeksema, 1987). Greater passive rumination, coupled with the tendency to be more sensitive to emotional cues, can create a depressive risk factor for women regardless of the original cause of depression.

On a broader level, Lewinsohn originally hypothesized that poor social skills played a causal role in the development of depression (Lewinsohn, 1974; Lewinsohn, Weinstein, & Shaw, 1969). Later, Lewinsohn and colleagues refined their theory of depression into an integrative, multifactoral model in which depression is conceptualized as the result of environmentally initiated changes in behavior, affect, and cognitions (Lewinsohn, Hoberman, Teri, & Hautzinger, 1985). In this modified theory, social skills deficits play a role in the maintenance of depression, but no longer represent a primary causal factor.

Segrin (2000) reviewed the empirical support for three different theoretical relationships between social skills deficits and depression: poor social skills as a cause of depression, depression as a cause of poor social skills, and poor social skills as a vulnerability factor in the development of depression. Segrin concluded that there is evidence to support each of these conceptualizations. However, among the 12 longitudinal studies that examined the relationship between poor social skills and depression, the majority failed to support the hypothesis that social skills deficits are an antecedent to depression.

In terms of systematic studies of emotion regulation, Westen, Muderrisoglu, Fowler, Shedler, and Koren (1997) developed an observer-rated Q-sort instrument to assess both the pattern of affect a person habitually experiences (specific emotions and their intensity) and the mechanisms the person uses to regulate them. Westen et al. applied this methodology to study the emotion regulation of individuals with dysthymic disorder. Dysthymic disorder presents with symptoms similar to major depressive disorder. The main difference is that dysthymia is more chronic (minimum of 2 years), and primary symptoms such as dysphoria and anhedonia are experienced with less frequency than in major depression (American Psychiatric Association, 1994). Westen and colleagues found that these individuals with dysthymic disorder tended to dwell on negative events and responded passively to events for which assertiveness would have been more adaptive. However, compared to individuals diagnosed with borderline personality disorder who also showed high levels of depressive symptoms, individuals with dysthymic disorder showed a number of active and effective coping strategies (see Linehan, 1993, for a discussion on emotion regulation in borderline personality disorder).

Although some ethological investigators have suggested that intensive body touching represents "active listening" during interactions with others (e.g., Hale, Jansen, Bouhuys, Jenner, & Hoofdakker, 1997), increased body touching likely plays a role in emotion regulation. As mentioned, some investigators have attempted to predict antidepressive treatment response based on nonverbal behavior; however, these results are inconsistent. In some studies, less body touching was linked to poor treatment response and higher relapse (Bouhuys & Albersnagel, 1992; Hale, Jansen, Bouhuys, &

Hoofdakker, 1997), whereas in at least one other study, more body touching was linked to poor treatment outcome (e.g., Ranelli & Miller, 1981). Still other studies have produced null results (see Bouhuys, chapter 10, this volume, for a discussion of possible explanations for these discrepancies).

Perhaps inconsistencies in this body of literature can be explained by the level of attunement between an interviewer or family member and the individual with depression. For example, Bouhuys and colleagues have found that the more the nonverbal behavior of patients was attuned to the nonverbal behavior of the interviewer, the more favorable was the patients' short-term outcome of depression (Bouhuys & Sam, 2000; Geerts & Bouhuys, 1998; Geerts, Bouhuys, & Hoofdakker, 1996). Thus, to the degree that a depressed individual's nonverbal behavior is attuned to another (which may involve more or less body-focused and other hand movements), this could represent a positive prognosis for treatment outcome. However, persons may be using body-focused touching to soothe themselves rather than because they are in synchrony with their speaking partner (e.g., Grand et al., 1977), and this represents a poorer prognosis for treatment outcome. Clearly, however, more research that explicitly focuses on an individual's ability to control emotion is needed to clarify the role of body-focused touching and other nonverbal behaviors in depression.

Problems in emotional control among individuals with social anxiety disorder can be gleaned from behavioral and physiological assessments. Like individuals with other anxiety disorders, those with social anxiety disorder report physiological symptoms such as sweating, shaking, hot flushes, palpitations, and nausea (Rapee, 1995). Compared to individuals with panic disorder, those with social anxiety disorder are more likely to report blushing, twitching, and stammering (Amies, Gelder, & Shaw, 1983; Solyom, Ledwidge, & Solyom, 1986).

These somatic symptoms suggest difficulties in emotion regulation, particularly because individuals with social anxiety disorder often report embarrassment and distress over their visible signs of anxiety. Avoidance and escape behaviors also implicate problems with emotion regulation. Behavioral assessment tests and self-report measures indicate that many individuals with social anxiety disorder avoid or escape social and performance situations to control feelings of anxiety (McNeil et al., 1995). Such emotional control behaviors may be adaptive in the short term; however, they contribute to maintenance of the disorder in the long run.

In summary, there is very little empirical research that directly assesses emotional control/regulation in psychopathology, and much of what can be considered must be inferred from studies of emotional expressiveness. For example, deficits in emotion regulation may play a key role in the deficits in emotional expressiveness and emotional sensitivity seen in schizophrenia. In addition, the somatic signs of physiological arousal and behavioral avoidance seen in social anxiety disorder may be considered hallmarks of emotional control problems—individuals exhibit these signs and behaviors when they have difficulty tolerating anxiety. Based on the available empirical data, it appears that there are significant individual differences in emotional control that warrant further investigation.

Summary and Conclusion

Nonverbal studies of schizophrenia, major depression, and social anxiety disorder demonstrate that individuals with these disorders show some common and unique deficits in emotional expressiveness, emotional sensitivity, and emotional control. Individuals from all three diagnostic groups tend to avoid eye contact with other people. Both individuals with schizophrenia and those with major depression also tend to show flat affect and psychomotor retardation, whereas individuals with social anxiety disorder tend to show an agitated response associated with physiological arousal. Individuals in all three diagnostic groups also demonstrate difficulties in emotional sensitivity. Individuals with schizophrenia show the most severe deficits in emotional sensitivity, with problems not only labeling emotions, but also recognizing emotional faces. Depressed individuals also show problems with emotion-labeling tasks. Individuals with social anxiety disorder may have the most specific reaction to emotional faces: a possible memory bias for critical, angry, or rejecting faces. With regard to emotional control, there is little empirical data that directly address the ability to regulate emotion within specific disorders. However, problems in emotional control can be inferred from deficiencies in emotional expressiveness. The area of emotion regulation has gained recent interest, and systematic studies of emotional control in psychopathology should be forthcoming.

Unlike emotional expressiveness, to our knowledge, researchers have not examined whether an alleviation of depressive illness leads to improvement in emotional face decoding—a worthy task for future investigations. In a recent study, Penn and Combs (2000) found that the emotion identification skills of persons with schizophrenia can be improved with either contingent monetary reinforcement or promotion of facial feedback. It would be informative to study if such effects are associated with improvements in social functioning among persons with schizophrenia. Likewise, one may examine whether specific interventions for social anxiety disorder diminish the heightened sensitivity to angry or critical faces.

Furthermore, to our knowledge, no experimental studies have asked individuals with schizophrenia, major depression, or social anxiety disorder to mask felt emotions, that is, to try to deceive others regarding their emotional states. Gross and Levenson (1993) examined emotional suppression, defined as the conscious inhibition of emotional expressive behavior while emotionally aroused, in a nonclinical sample. Applying the same methodology to clinical populations would provide more insight into the nature of emotion regulation in persons with psychological disorders.

The study of nonverbal social skills has yielded important information relevant to the diagnosis and treatment of psychological disorders. Proper assessment of psychological disorders depends on the clinician's ability to evaluate nonverbal behavior accurately and reliably. Furthermore, evaluation of nonverbal behavior is typically integrated with other measures to gauge the progress of treatment. Thus, it is important that symptom descriptions of various disorders be based on empirical findings as described in this chapter rather than being based on more subjective clinical impressions. Etiological theories of psychological disorders suggest that deficits in nonverbal behavior are more than residual symptoms; problems in nonverbal social skills contribute to the exacerbation and maintenance of psychological disorders.

Deficiencies in nonverbal social skills are particularly salient to the disorders reviewed in this chapter—schizophrenia, major depression, and social anxiety disorder—because social skills training has been a common component of treatment. Benton and Schroeder (1990) conducted a meta-analysis of social skills training for schizophrenia. They concluded that social skills training has a strong positive impact on behavioral measures of social skill, but only marginal effects for broader ratings of symptoms and functioning among persons with schizophrenia.

Social skills training is one form of behavior therapy, and behavior therapy has been identified as an empirically supported treatment for major depression (DeRubeis & Crits-Christoph, 1998). Social skills training may be the central focus of treatment for depression (e.g., Bellack, Hersen, & Himmelhoch, 1996) or one important component of behavior therapy for depression (Lewinsohn & Gotlib, 1995). Taylor (1996) conducted a meta-analysis of cognitive-behavioral treatments for social anxiety disorder. Taylor found that social skills training was as effective as other treatments, including exposure therapy, cognitive restructuring, and exposure plus cognitive restructuring.

However, it may be argued that the effective component of social skills training lies in the exposure to feared social interactions that is inherent within it (Heimberg, Dodge, & Becker, 1987). Likewise, the effectiveness of social skills training for major depression may, in part, be attributed to the behavioral activation that results from it. Although social skills training is rarely the sole focus of treatment anymore, it nevertheless can constitute an important component of multidimensional treatments for these disorders.

Although beyond the scope of this chapter, nonverbal social skills are important for several other psychological disorders and psychosocial problems (see Linehan, 1993; Nowicki & Duke, 1994). As mentioned, more systematic studies on the way individuals regulate or control their emotions are needed. Fruitful foci for future investigations might also include cross-cultural studies that establish the universality of nonverbal behaviors in psychopathology and more longitudinal studies that examine the etiological link between specific nonverbal social skills and psychological disorders.

Notes

1. We do not provide a comprehensive discussion of etiological models, yet we do attempt to present sound theories that directly address findings from the nonverbal literature. For additional discussions on relevant theories, see Kring and Earnst (chapter 11, this volume) on schizophrenia, Bouhuys (chapter 10, this volume) on major depression, and Mogg and Bradley (chapter 6) on anxiety.

2. See Kring and Earnst (chapter 11, this volume) for interesting results showing that, although individuals with schizophrenia display less observable expressive behavior than do controls, they exhibit comparable or even more microexpressive behavior at an unobservable level.

References

Addington, J., & Addington, D. (1998). Facial affect recognition and information processing in schizophrenia and bipolar disorder. *Schizophrenia Research, 32*, 171–181.

Adelmann, P. K., & Zajonc, R. B. (1989). Facial efference and the experience of emotion. *Annual Review of Psychology, 40*, 249–280.

Alden, L. E., & Wallace, S. T. (1995). Social phobia and social appraisal in successful and unsuccessful social interactions. *Behaviour Research and Therapy, 33*, 497–505.

American Psychiatric Association. (1994). *Diagnostic and statistical manual of mental disorders* (4th ed.). Washington, DC: Author.

Amies, P. L., Gelder, M. G., & Shaw, P. M. (1983). Social phobia: A comparative clinical study. *British Journal of Psychiatry, 142*, 174–179.

Andreasen, N. C. (1979). Affective flattening and the criteria for schizophrenia. *American Journal of Psychiatry, 136*, 944–947.

Anthony, B. (1978). Piagetian egocentrism, empathy and affect discrimination in children at high risk for psychosis. In E. Anthony (Ed.), *The child in his family* (pp. 359–379). New York: Wiley.

Argyle, M. (1981). The contribution of social interaction research to social skill training. In J. D. Wine & M. D. Smye (Eds.), *Social competence* (pp. 261–286). New York: Guilford Press.

Barlow, D. H. (1988). *Anxiety and its disorders: The nature and treatment of anxiety and panic.* New York: Guilford Press.

Beck, A. T. (1987). Cognitive models of depression. *Journal of Cognitive Psychotherapy: An International Quarterly, 1*, 5–37.

Beck, A. T. (1991). Cognitive therapy: A 30-year retrospective. *American Psychologist, 46*, 368–375.

Beidel, D. C., Turner, S. M., & Dancu, C. V. (1985). Physiological, cognitive, and behavioral aspects of social anxiety. *Behaviour Research and Therapy, 23*, 109–117.

Bellack, A. S., Hersen, M., & Himmelhoch, J. M. (1996). Social skills training for depression: A treatment manual. In V. B. Van Hasselt & M. Hersen (Eds.),

Sourcebook of psychological treatment manuals for adult disorders (pp. 179–200). New York: Plenum Press.

Benowitz, L. I., Bear, D. M., Mesalum, M. M., Rosenthal, R., Zaidel, E. & Sperry, R. W. (1983). Nonverbal sensitivity following lateralized cerebral injury. *Cortex, 19*, 5–12.

Benton, M. K., & Schroeder, H. E. (1990). Social skills training with schizophrenics: A meta-analytic evaluation. *Journal of Consulting and Clinical Psychology, 58*, 741–747.

Berenbaum, H. (1992). Posed facial expressions of emotion in schizophrenia and depression. *Psychological Medicine, 22*, 929–937.

Blazer, D. G., Kessler, R. C., McGonagle, K. A., & Swartz, M. S. (1994). The prevalence and distribution of major depression in a national community sample: The National Comorbidity Survey. *American Journal of Psychiatry, 151*, 979–986.

Bouhuys, A. L., & Albersnagel, F. A. (1992). Do interactional capacities based on observed behavior interfere with improvement in severely depressed patients? A longitudinal study. *Journal of Affective Disorders, 25*, 107–116.

Bouhuys, A. L., Beersma, D. G. M., Hoofdakker, R. H. v. d., & Roossien, A. (1987). The prediction of short- and long-term improvement in depressive patients: Ethological methods of observing behavior versus clinical ratings. *Ethology and Sociobiology, 8* (Suppl.), 117–130.

Bouhuys, A. L., & Sam, M. M. (2000). Lack of coordination of nonverbal behaviour between patients and interviewers as a potential risk factor to depression recurrence: Vulnerability accumulation in depression. *Journal of Affective Disorders, 57*, 189–200.

Clark, L. A., & Watson, D. (1991). Tripartite model of anxiety and depression: Psychometric evidence and taxonomic implications. *Journal of Abnormal Psychology, 100*, 316–336.

Cooley, E. I., & Nowicki, S. (1989). Discrimination of facial expressions of emotion by depressed subjects. *Genetic, Social, and General Psychology Monographs, 115*, 449–465.

Cramer, P., Bowen, J., & O'Neill, M. (1992). Schizophrenics and social judgement: Why do schizophrenics get it wrong? *British Journal of Psychiatry, 160*, 481–487.

Cramer, P., Weegmann, M., & O'Neil, M. (1989). Schizophrenia and the perception of emotions: How accurately do schizophrenics judge the emotional states of others? *British Journal of Psychiatry, 155*, 225–228.

Cutting, J. (1990). *The right cerebral hemisphere and psychiatric disorders.* Oxford, England: Oxford University Press.

Davis, P. J., & Stewart, K. D. (2001). Interpretation of congruent and incongruent affective communications in paranoid schizophrenia. *British Journal of Clinical Psychology, 40*, 249–259.

DeKosky, S. T., Heilman, K. M., Bowers, D., & Valenstein, E. (1980). Recognition and discrimination of emotional faces and pictures. *Brain and Language, 9*, 206–214.

DeRubeis, R. J., & Crits-Christoph, P. (1998). Empirically supported individual and group psychological treatments for adult mental disorders. *Journal of Consulting and Clinical Psychology, 66*, 37–52.

Dimberg, U., & Öhman, A. (1983). The effects of directional facial cues on electrodermal conditioning to facial stimuli. *Psychophysiology, 20*, 160–167.

Dougherty, F. E., Bartlett, E. S., & Izard, C. E. (1974). Responses of schizophrenics to expressions of fundamental emotions. *Journal of Clinical Psychology, 30*, 243–246.

Edwards, J., Jackson, H. J., & Pattison, P. E. (2002). Emotion recognition via facial expression and affective prosody in schizophrenia: A methodological review. *Clinical Psychology Review, 22*, 789–832.

Ekman, P. (1992). Facial expressions of emotion: New findings, new questions. *Psychological Science, 3*, 34–38.

Ellgring, H., & Smith, M. (1998). Affect regulation during psychosis. In W. F. Flack, Jr. & J. D. Laird (Eds.), *Emotions in psychopathology: Theory and research* (pp. 323–325). New York: Oxford University Press.

Etcoff, N. L. (1984). Perceptual and conceptual organization of facial emotions: Hemispheric differences. *Brain and Cognition, 3*, 385–412.

Feinberg, T. E., Rifkin, A., Schaffer, C., & Walker, E. (1986). Facial discrimination and emotional recognition in schizophrenia and affective disorders. *Archives of General Psychiatry, 43*, 276–279.

Feldman, R. S., Philippot, P., & Custrini, R. J. (1991). Social competence and nonverbal behavior. In R. S. Feldman & B. Rimé (Eds.), *Fundamentals of nonverbal behavior: Studies in emotion and social interaction* (pp. 329–350). New York: Cambridge University Press.

Fisch, H. U., Frey, S., & Hirsbrunner, H. P. (1983). Analyzing nonverbal behavior in depression. *Journal of Abnormal Psychology, 92*, 307–318.

Fossi, L., Faravelli, C., & Paoli, M. (1984). The ethological approach to the assessment of depressive disorders. *Journal of Nervous and Mental Disease, 172*, 332–341.

Frith, C. D., Stevens, M., Johnstone, E. C., Owens, D. G. C., & Crow, T. J. (1983). Integration of schematic faces and other complex objects in schizophrenia. *Journal of Nervous and Mental Disease, 171*, 34–39.

Fydrich, T., Chambless, D. L., Perry, K. J., Buergener, F., & Beazley, M. B. (1998). Behavioral assessment of social performance: A rating system for social phobia. *Behaviour Research and Therapy, 36*, 995–1010.

Gaebel, W., & Wölwer, W. (1992). Facial expression and emotional face recognition in schizophrenia and depression. *European Archives of Psychiatry and Clinical Neuroscience, 242*, 46–52.

Geerts, E., & Bouhuys, N. (1998). Multi-level prediction of short-term outcome of depression: Non-verbal interpersonal processes, cognitions and personality traits. *Psychiatry Research, 79*, 59–72.

Geerts, E., Bouhuys, N., & Hoofdakker, R. H. v. d. (1996). Nonverbal attunement between depressed patients and an interviewer predicts subsequent improvement. *Journal of Affective Disorders, 40*, 15–21.

Gessler, S., Cutting, J., Frith, C. D., & Weinman, J. (1989). Schizophrenic inability to judge facial emotion: A controlled study. *British Journal of Clinical Psychology, 28*, 19–29.

Giannini, A. J., Folts, D. J., Melemis, S. M., Giannini, M. C., & Loiselle, R. H. (1995). Depressed men's lower ability to interpret nonverbal cues: A preliminary study. *Perceptual and Motor Skills, 81*, 555–560.

Grand, S., Marcos, L. R., Freedman, N., & Barroso, F. (1977). Relation of psycho-pathology and bilingualism to kinetic aspects of interview behavior in schizophrenia. *Journal of Abnormal Psychology, 86*, 492–500.

Griesinger, W. (1876). *Die pathologie und therapie der psychischen krankheiten.* Braunschweig, Germany: Wreden.

Gross, J. J., & Levenson, R. W. (1993). Emotional suppression: Physiology, self-report, and expressive behavior. *Journal of Personality and Social Psychology, 64*, 970–986.

Gross, J. J., & Muñoz, R. F. (1995). Emotion regulation and mental health. *Clinical Psychology: Science and Practice, 2*, 151–164.

Gur, R. C., Erwin, R. J., Bur, R. E., Zwil, A. S., Heimberg, C., & Kraemer, H. C. (1992). Facial emotion discrimination: II. Behavioral findings in depression. *Psychiatry Research, 41*, 241–251.

Hale, W. W., III. (1998). Judgment of facial expressions and depression persistence. *Psychiatry Research, 80*, 265–274.

Hale, W. W., III, Jansen, J. H. C., Bouhuys, A. L., & Hoofdakker, R. H. v. d. (1997). Depression relapse and ethological measures. *Psychiatry Research, 70*, 57–64.

Hale, W. W., III, Jansen, J. H. C., Bouhuys, A. L., Jenner, J. A., & Hoofdakker, R. H. v. d. (1997). Non-verbal behavioral interactions of depressed patients with partners and strangers: The role of behavioral social support and involvement in depression persistence. *Journal of Affective Disorders, 44*, 111–122.

Hall, J. A. (1984). *Nonverbal sex differences: Communication accuracy and expressive style.* Baltimore, MD: Johns Hopkins University Press.

Hansen, C. H., & Hansen, R. D. (1988). Finding the face in the crowd: An anger superiority effect. *Journal of Personality and Social Psychology, 54*, 917–924.

Heimberg, C., Gur, R. E., Erwin, R. J., Shtasel, D. L., & Gur, R. C. (1992). Facial emotion discrimination: III. Behavioral findings in schizophrenia. *Psychiatry Research, 42*, 253–265.

Heimberg, R. G., Dodge, C. S., & Becker, R. E. (1987). Social phobia. In L. Michelson & M. Ascher (Eds.), *Cognitive behavioral assessment and treatment of anxiety disorders* (pp. 280–309). New York: Plenum Press.

Herbert, J. D., Hope, D. A., & Bellack, A. S. (1992). Validity of the distinction between generalized social phobia and avoidant personality disorder. *Journal of Abnormal Psychology, 101*, 332–339.

Hinchliffe, M. K., Lancashire, M., & Roberts, F. J. (1971). A study of eye-contact changes in depressed and recovered psychiatric patients. *British Journal of Psychiatry, 119*, 213–215.

Holt, C. S., Heimberg, R. G., Hope, D. A., & Liebowitz, M. R. (1992). Situational domains of social phobia. *Journal of Anxiety Disorders, 6*, 63–77.

Jones, I. M., & Pasna, M. (1979). Some non-verbal aspects of depression and schizophrenia occurring during the interview. *Journal of Nervous and Mental Disease, 167*, 402–409.

Kazdin, A. E., Sherick, R. B., Esveldt-Dawson, K., & Rancurello, M. D. (1985). Nonverbal behavior and childhood depression. *Journal of the American Academy of Child Psychiatry, 24*, 303–309.

Kraepelin, E. (1913). *Psychiatrie: Ein lehrbuch für studierende und aerzte.* Leipzig, Germany: Barth.

LeDoux, J. (1996). *The emotional brain*. New York: Simon & Shuster.

Lewinsohn, P. M. (1974). A behavioral approach to depression. In R. J. Friedman & M. M. Katz (Eds.), *The psychology of depression: Contemporary theory and research* (pp. 157–185). New York: Wiley.

Lewinsohn, P. M., & Gotlib, I. H. (1995). Behavioral theory and treatment of depression. In E. E. Beckham & W. R. Leber (Eds.), *Handbook of depression* (2nd ed., pp. 352–375). New York: Guilford Press.

Lewinsohn, P. M., Hoberman, H., Teri, L., & Hautzinger, M. (1985). An integrative theory of depression. In S. Reiss & R. Bootzin (Eds.), *Theoretical issues in behavior therapy* (pp. 331–359). New York: Academic Press.

Lewinsohn, P. M., Weinstein, M., & Shaw, D. (1969). Depression: A clinical-research approach. In R. D. Rubin & C. M. Frand (Eds.), *Advances in behavior therapy* (pp. 231–240). New York: Academic Press.

Linehan, M. M. (1993). *Cognitive-behavioral treatment of borderline personality disorder*. New York: Guilford Press.

Lundh, L. G., & Öst, L. G. (1996). Recognition bias for critical faces in social phobics. *Behaviour Research and Therapy, 34,* 787–794.

Mandal, M. K., Pandey, R., & Prasad, A. B. (1998). Facial expressions of emotions and schizophrenia: A review. *Schizophrenia Bulletin, 24,* 399–412.

McIntosh, D. N. (1996). Facial feedback hypothesis: Evidence, implications, and directions. *Motivation & Emotion, 20,* 121–147.

McNally, R. J. (1987). Preparedness and phobias: A review. *Psychological Bulletin, 101,* 283–303.

McNeil, D. W., Ries, B. J., & Turk, C. L. (1995). Behavioral assessment: Self-report, physiology, and overt behavior. In R. G. Heimberg, M. R. Liebowitz, D. A. Hope, & F. R. Schneier (Eds.), *Social anxiety disorder: Diagnosis, assessment, and treatment* (pp. 202–231). New York: Guilford Press.

Mineka, S., & Zinbarg, R. (1995). Conditioning and ethological models of social anxiety disorder. In R. G. Heimberg, M. R. Liebowitz, D. A. Hope, & F. R. Schneier (Eds.), *Social anxiety disorder: Diagnosis, assessment, and treatment* (pp. 134–162). New York: Guilford Press.

Mogg, K., & Bradley, B. P. (1998). A cognitive-motivational analysis of anxiety. *Behaviour Research & Therapy, 36,* 809–848.

Morrison, R. L., Bellack, A. S., & Mueser, K. T. (1988). Deficits in facial-affect recognition and schizophrenia. *Schizophrenia Bulletin, 14,* 67–83.

Murphy, D., & Cutting, J. (1990). Prosodic comprehension and expression in schizophrenia. *Journal of Neurology, Neurosurgery, and Psychiatry, 53,* 727–730.

Muzekari, L. H., & Bates, M. E. (1977). Judgment of emotion among chronic schizophrenics. *Journal of Clinical Psychology, 33,* 662–666.

Nelson, J. C., & Charney, D. S. (1981). The symptoms of major depressive illness. *American Journal of Psychiatry, 138,* 1–13.

Newman, E. H. (1977). Resolution of inconsistent attitude communications in normal and schizophrenic subjects. *Journal of Abnormal Psychology, 86,* 41–46.

Nolen-Hoeksema, S. (1987). Sex differences in unipolar depression: Evidence and theory. *Psychological Bulletin, 101,* 259–282.

Nowicki, S., Jr., & Duke, M. P. (1994). Individual differences in the nonverbal communication of affect: The Diagnostic Analysis of Nonverbal Accuracy Scale. *Journal of Nonverbal Behavior, 18,* 9–35.

Öhman, A. (1986). Face the beast and fear the face: Animal and social fears as prototypes for evolutionary analyses of emotion. *Psychophysiology, 23,* 123–145.

Öhman, A., & Dimberg, U. (1978). Facial expressions as conditioned stimuli for electrodermal responses: A case of "preparedness"? *Journal of Personality and Social Psychology, 36,* 1251–1258.

Öhman, A., Dimberg, U., & Esteves, F. (1989). Preattentive activation of aversive emotions. In T. Archer & L. G. Nilsson (Eds.), *Aversion, avoidance and anxiety; Perspectives on aversively motivated behavior* (pp. 169–199). Hillsdale, NJ: Erlbaum.

Öhman, A., Dimberg, U., & Öst, L. G. (1985). Animal and social anxiety disorder: Biological constraints on the learned fear response. In S. Reiss & R. Bootzin (Eds.), *Theoretical issues in behavior therapy* (pp. 123–175). New York: Academic Press.

Öst, L. G., & Hugdahl, K. (1981). Acquisition of phobias and anxiety response patterns in clinical patients. *Behaviour Research and Therapy, 16,* 439–447.

Pedersen, J., Schelde, J. T. M., Hannibal, E., Behnke, K., Nielsen, B. M., & Hertz, M. (1988). An ethological description of depression. *Acta Psychiatrica Scandinavica, 78,* 320–330.

Penn, D. L., & Combs, D. (2000). Modification of affect perception deficits in schizophrenia. *Schizophrenia Research, 46,* 217–229.

Pilowsky, I., & Bassett, D. (1980). Schizophrenia and the response to facial emotions. *Comprehensive Psychiatry, 21,* 236–244.

Pitman, R. K., Kolb, B., Orr, S. P., deJong, J., Yadati, S., & Singh, M. M. (1987). On the utility of ethological data in psychiatric research. The example of facial behavior in schizophrenia. *Ethology and Sociobiology, 8*(Suppl.), 111–116.

Ranelli, C. J., & Miller, R. E. (1981). Behavioral predictors of amitriptyline response in depression. *American Journal of Psychiatry, 138,* 30–34.

Rapee, R. M. (1995). Descriptive psychopathology of social anxiety disorder. In R. G. Heimberg, M. R. Liebowitz, D. A. Hope, & F. R. Schneier (Eds.), *Social anxiety disorder: Diagnosis, assessment, and treatment* (pp. 41–66). New York: Guilford Press.

Rapee, R. M., & Lim, L. (1992). Discrepancy between self- and observer ratings of performance in social phobics. *Journal of Abnormal Psychology, 101,* 727–731.

Reilly, S. S., & Muzekari, L. H. (1979). Responses of normal and disturbed adults and children to mixed messages. *Journal of Abnormal Psychology, 88,* 203–208.

Riggio, R. E. (1986). Assessment of basic social skills. *Journal of Personality and Social Psychology, 51,* 649–660.

Riggio, R. E. (1989). *Manual for the Social Skills Inventory.* Palo Alto, CA: Consulting Psychologists Press.

Riggio, R. E. (1992). Social interaction skills and nonverbal behavior. In R. S. Feldman (Ed.), *Application of nonverbal behavioral theories and research* (pp. 3–30). Hillsdale, NJ: Erlbaum.

Riggio, R. E., & Friedman, H. S. (1983). Individual differences and cues to decep- tion. *Journal of Personality and Social Psychology, 45*, 899–915.

Riggio, R. E., Messamer, J., & Throckmorton, B. (1991). Social and academic intelligence: Conceptually distinct but overlapping constructs. *Personality and Individual Differences, 12*, 695–702.

Riggio, R. E., Watring, K. P., & Throckmorton, B. (1993). Social skills, social support, and psychosocial adjustment. *Personality and Individual Differ- ences, 15*, 275–280.

Riggio, R. E., & Zimmerman, J. (1991). Social skills and interpersonal relation- ships: Influences on social support and support-seeking. In W. H. Jones & D. Perlman (Eds.), *Advances in personal relationships* (Vol. 2, pp. 133–155). London: Jessica Kingsley.

Rosenthal, R. (Ed.). (1979). *Skill in nonverbal communication: Individual differ- ences.* Cambridge, MA: Oelgeschlager, Gunn, & Hain.

Rubinow, D. R., & Post, R. M. (1992). Impaired recognition of affect in facial expression in depressed patients. *Biological Psychiatry, 31*, 947–953.

Rutter, D. R. (1973). Visual interaction in psychiatric patients. *British Journal of Psychiatry, 123*, 193–202.

Saarni, C. (1999). *The development of emotional competence.* New York: Guil- ford Press.

Salovey, P., & Mayer, J. D. (1990). Emotional intelligence. *Imagination, Cogni- tion and Personality, 9*, 185–211.

Schelde, T., & Hertz, M. (1994). Ethology and psychotherapy. *Ethology and So- ciobiology, 15*, 383–392.

Schlundt, D. G., & McFall, R. M. (1985). New directions in the assessment of social competence and social skills. In L. L. Abate & M. A. Milan (Eds.), *Handbook of social skills training and research* (pp. 22–49). New York: Wiley.

Schneider, F., Ellring, H., Friedrich, J., Fus, I., Beyer, T., Heimann, H., & Himer, W. (1992). The effects of neuroleptics on facial action in schizophrenic pa- tients. *Pharmacopsychiatry, 25*, 233–239.

Schneier, F. R., Spitzer, R. L., Gibbon, M., Fyer, A. J., & Liebowitz, M. R. (1991). The relationship of social anxiety disorder subtypes and avoidant personality disorder. *Comprehensive Psychiatry, 32*, 496–502.

Segrin, C. (2000). Social skills deficits associated with depression. *Clinical Psy- chology Review, 20*, 379–403.

Seligman, M. (1971). Phobias and preparedness. *Behavior Therapy, 2*, 307–320.

Solyom, L., Ledwidge, B., & Solyom, C. (1986). Delineating social phobia. *British Journal of Psychiatry, 149*, 464–470.

Suberi, M., & McKeever, W. F. (1977). Differential right hemispheric memory of emotional and non-emotional faces. *Neuropsychologia, 15*, 757–768.

Taylor, S. (1996). Meta-analysis of cognitive-behavioral treatments for social anxiety disorder. *Journal of Behavior Therapy and Experimental Psychiatry, 27*, 1–9.

Toomey, R., Wallace, C. J., Corrigan, P. W., Schuldberg, D., & Green, M. F. (1997). Social processing correlates of nonverbal social perception in schizo- phrenia. *Psychiatry, 60*, 292–300.

Troisi, A., Pasini, A., Bersani, G., Grispini, A., & Ciani, N. (1989). Ethological predictors of amitriptyline response in depressed outpatients. *Journal of Affective Disorders, 17*, 129–136.

Troisi, A., Spalletta, G., & Pasini, A. (1998). Nonverbal behaviour deficits in schizophrenia: An ethological study of drug-free patients. *Acta Psychiatrica Scandinavica, 97*, 109–115.

Trower, P., Bryant, B., & Argyle, M. (1978). *Social skills and mental health.* Pittsburgh, PA: University of Pittsburgh Press.

Turner, S. M., Beidel, D. C., Dancu, C. V., & Keys, D. J. (1986). Psychopathology of social phobia and comparison to avoidant personality disorder. *Journal of Abnormal Psychology, 95*, 389–394.

Walker, E. (1980). Emotion recognition in disturbed and normal children. *Journal of Child Psychology and Psychiatry and Allied Disciplines, 22*, 263–269.

Walker, E., Marwit, S. J., & Emory, E. (1980). A cross-sectional study of emotion recognition in schizophrenics. *Journal of Abnormal Psychology, 89*, 428–436.

Walker, E., McGuire, M., & Bettes, B. (1984). Recognition and identification of facial stimuli by schizophrenics and patients with affective disorders. *British Journal of Clinical Psychology, 23*, 37–44.

Walker, E. F., Grimes, K. E., Davis, D. M., & Smith, A. J. (1993). Childhood precursors of schizophrenia: Facial expressions of emotion. *American Journal of Psychiatry, 150*, 1654–1660.

Waxer, P. (1974). Nonverbal cues for depression. *Journal of Abnormal Psychology, 83*, 319–322.

Waxer, P. (1976). Nonverbal cues for depth of depression: Set versus no set. *Journal of Consulting and Clinical Psychology, 44*, 493.

Weissman, M. M., & Olfson, M. (1995). Depression in women: Implications for health care research. *Science, 269*, 799–801.

Westen, D., Muderrisoglu, S., Fowler, C., Shedler, J., & Koren, D. (1997). Affect regulation and affective experience: Individual differences, group differences, and measurement using a Q-sort procedure. *Journal of Consulting and Clinical Psychology, 65*, 429–439.

Whitaker, J. F., Deakin, J. F., & Tomenson, B. (2001). Face processing in schizophrenia: Defining the deficit. *Psychological Medicine, 31*, 499–507.

Zuroff, D. C., & Colussy, S. A. (1986). Emotion recognition in schizophrenic and depressed inpatients. *Journal of Clinical Psychology, 42*, 411–417.

3

Of Butterflies and Roaring Thunder

Nonverbal Communication in Interaction and
Regulation of Emotion

ARVID KAPPAS AND JEAN DESCÔTEAUX

Emotional expression is often understood as a readout of an individual's affective state, as linked to specific action tendencies and reflecting changes in action readiness, or as simply social motivations. However, there is also the belief that emotional expressions serve regulatory functions for the affective state of the individual, for the affective state of the interaction partner(s), and for the interaction itself. Because of the complexity of this tapestry of entwined processes, it is not surprising that the promise of using emotional expressions for the analysis of individual transient states or of interindividual differences, for the diagnosis of pathologies, or for analysis of the progress of therapies has not yet been fulfilled to the satisfaction of most researchers or practitioners.

In this chapter, we discuss the "meaning" of nonverbal behavior, specifically facial actions, as it relates to intrapersonal processes and to the regulatory aspects of nonverbal communication for the individual and in dyadic interaction. We highlight problems with current notions that we view as "myths" and propose a model to illustrate the interactive and dynamic nature of affect regulation in a social context, the superlens model of affective communication.

If the notion of therapy for any organismic dysfunction entails two main components, diagnosis and treatment, then what is really needed is a "machine with two buttons." The first button performs the diagnosis; the second button delivers the best treatment. After the two buttons are pressed, the patient leaves, hopefully in a better state than when he or she arrived. An advanced model of this machine might even make the diagnosis button superfluous, and only one button would be needed, which would perform both functions.

Unfortunately, there is no such machine, and most likely, there will not be any such thing in the near future. Instead, communication between the patient and the care provider(s) performing diagnosis and treatment must be relied on. While this state of affairs is common for any sort of therapy, it is most relevant for psychotherapy. In this case, the role of communication is manifold for diagnostic and for treatment purposes. However, regardless of the particular setting of the therapy, the communicative processes involved are specific instances of very general communication systems. Similarly, the relationship between a patient or client and the therapist is nothing but a special instance of human social relationships.

Obviously, accuracy of diagnosis and treatment efficiency are multidimensional constructs and relate not only to validity and outcome, but also to cost in terms of time and resources. It is safe to say, independent of the specific problem, client, therapist, or type of therapy, that in real life there is no single process element that is optimal or that could not use improvement. Given the central role of communication for the therapy process, it appears logical that one way to optimize therapy would be better understanding of the communication process itself. Hence, as therapy is only a special form of communication and a special case of a social relation, what is known about communication and social relations in general and, subsequently, how a therapeutic setting differs from the general form must be specified. Thus, the purpose of this chapter is not specific recommendations on how to facilitate communication or how to improve a particular therapy, but to provide a current account of basic knowledge that is relevant for an understanding of the communicative and relational processes in therapy.

What must be frustrating for the reader who wants concrete advice is that the understanding of communication and interactional processes is in constant flux. For example, the interpretation of the "meaning" of nonverbal communication, an important element in many psychotherapeutic exchanges, has changed markedly in the last few decades. Obviously, as always, the situation seems more complex than if presented 20 years earlier. To make matters worse, the situation will surely be judged even more complex 20 years from now. Yet, as our models grow more complex, they also start to describe better "what is going on." Simplifications of these processes might be convenient, but they might also lead to wrong conclusions about what is going on in a particular interaction.

So what is known? Sophisticated and innovative research has reinforced the belief that nonverbal communication is the cradle of all forms of communication and of social cognition (Rochat & Striano, 1999). At the same time, it is clear that the development of language does not render nonverbal communication redundant or superfluous. Verbal and nonverbal communication together form the basis of dyadic communication, in which the participants form an integrated system for information exchange. While this information might refer to abstract concepts or objects, there is always information about the sender that is contained and that can be extracted.

The sender's affective states and social motivations can influence verbal and nonverbal behaviors and can and will be interpreted as such both consciously and outside awareness (Patterson, Foster, & Bellmer, 2001). It is unproductive to think of ourselves as "television sets" that constantly emit things we cannot control or things that we want to project. But, undoubtedly, at times we do emit such signals, voluntarily and involuntarily. Some of these displays are strategic, while others are not.[1] Similarly, regardless of whether we do actually emit such signals, an interaction partner might interpret any nonverbal behavior as signals. One of the more problematic aspects of understanding nonverbal communication in such a context is that not only the presence of a behavior may be relevant, but also the relative absence of a behavior. In interaction, behaviors always take their effect in a context of expectations and representations. The impact of context can be conscious, but it does not need to be.

Nonverbal behaviors not only serve as signs or symptoms, but also are likely to have a regulatory effect in a complex feedback system within the individual and within the dyad or group (Kappas, 1991). Aspects related to reciprocity and synchronization may also serve maintenance functions for relationships and can be symptomatic of their current state. Hence, there can be multiple functions of each action, and there can be multiple consequences of an ongoing or subsequent interaction.

As relationships are never static, there is a dynamic aspect in the impact of behaviors in interaction. For example, a given event can push the representation of context in the minds of the interactants in a particular direction and hence influence the interpretation (the meaning) of subsequent actions or lead to the reinterpretation of previous interactions. Because of the complex interplay of intraindividual and interindividual consequences of expressive behaviors, it is difficult to estimate the impact of a particular event.

Given that (emotional) communication in interaction forms a complex dynamic system, it is possible that even a seemingly insignificant and singular event becomes significant in shifting the state of the system as a whole in one or another direction. In this sense, a laugh, a frown, or a stone-faced visage might, in an analogy, resemble the flapping of the wings of a butterfly, which could (theoretically) shift an unstable weather system in one or the other direction (Gleick, 1987). In communication, this might mean creating a sense of trust or confidence or of mistrust and reproach. Here, it is relevant to understand that such a shift might be a conscious interpretation or simply take the form of a "gut feeling" (see also Krause, Steimer-Krause, Merten, & Burkhard, 1998; Patterson et al., 2001).

In this chapter, we outline the state of knowledge regarding several aspects of nonverbal communication and at the same time debunk common notions or, more provocatively, myths that have permeated the discussion on the potential or actual role of nonverbal communication for clinical diagnosis and therapy.

The Myth of Emotional Facial Expression: It Does Not Only Express Emotion

The myth of emotional facial expression can be paraphrased: Facial expressions reflect emotional states. Hence, facial activity measurement can be used to assess emotional states. This knowledge can be used for diagnosis of patients, for whom it is crucial to understand their feelings. Measuring facial activity is particularly interesting because it can be interpreted as a parallel stream of behavior that allows understanding of how the patient feels about what is being said by the patient or by the patient's interaction partner. It is even possible to assess the patient's emotional state when the patient is unaware of his or her feelings.

The belief that facial activity is linked to emotion states has a long history within science and within popular belief. Particularly, the publication of Darwin's book, *The Expression of the Emotions in Man and Animals* (1872/1998), had a major impact on the role of emotional expressions for research on emotion and largely reinforced the commonly held belief that there is a link between emotions and expressive behavior. Milestone research, particularly by Ekman and colleagues, has cemented the common representation that faces express emotions. However, essentially all of the involved researchers, including Darwin and Ekman, have usually maintained a view that is far more differentiated than the distilled version that has resulted from endless summarizing and synthesizing in secondary and tertiary literature.

In fact, facial behavior and other nonverbal behaviors are assumed to be influenced not only by emotion, but also by a host of other factors, including motivations, social context, and cultural conventions (e.g., "display rules," Ekman, 1982; Ekman & Friesen, 1969; Kappas, 1999). In addition, there are other nonaffective processes that influence facial behavior, such as mastication, speech, or respiration. Kappas (1999) suggested consideration of these influences as parallel and concurrent source streams that are combined through coupling, decoupling, and inhibition of decoupling to produce facial output. Hence, it would only be possible to deduce from facial behavior the emotional state of an expressor if these states would produce unique signatures that could not be produced or masked by the other factors.[2] However, this does not seem to be the case. To evaluate the relevant empirical evidence, two underlying assumptions or hypotheses must be clearly distinguished: (a) There is a set of emotional states that can be differentiated, and all of them or some possess unique signatures; (b) for each or some of the signatures, it is known whether they can be produced by any of the other factors (see also Kappas, 2003).

There are three major schools of thought regarding the sets of emotional states that we talk about here (see Russell & Fernández-Dols, 1997). The basic emotions view assumes that there is a small and limited set of emotions that are characterized by signature expressions (Ekman, 1982, 1992a, 1992b, 1994a, 1994b). In contrast, the appraisal view assumes that emotional states are the consequence of affective information processing, that there are expressive concomitants of this information processing or its outcomes, and that some facial patterns are the sum or product of a pattern of appraisal outcomes that relate to specific emotion labels (Scherer, 1992, 1993; Smith & Scott, 1997). Finally, the dimensional view holds that emotional states are fundamentally differentiated on a small number of dimensions, such as valence and activation, and that facial activity is linked to these dimensions (Russell, 1994, 1997).[3]

While the appraisal view could be interpreted as a special case of the dimensional view, there are differences in that the appraisal view makes specific assumptions on how the emotional states come about (through the appraisal process), and that there are functional links between particular molecular changes of facial activity and the adaptational requirements associated with a particular evaluation of the relationship of an individual and the individual's goals and needs in a particular situation or event.

To us, there appears to be a clear difference in the specificity of predictions among these three views, with the basic emotions view being the most clearly defined and the dimensional view the least clear, as far as testable predictions are concerned. This specificity cuts both ways. While the assumption that there exists only a small set of emotions facilitates the research process, it also implies that there are many states that will not be measured or interpreted that would still be labeled affective by appraisal researchers or dimensional theorists (see Oster, Hegley, & Nagel, 1992; Sayette, Cohn, Wertz, Perrott, & Parrott, 2001). On the other hand, in a model that is simply based on valence and activation, each state can be "interpreted."

Space limitations do not allow discussion of each of the basic emotions, each appraisal dimension, or each affective dimension and whether there seem to be clear signatures that can be related to them; surprisingly, it is not even necessary. Taking the second hypothesis (whether factors other than emotion could produce the same signatures) into account, the discussion is easy and surprisingly short. There is no evidence and no claim that there are any facial actions that could be measured to index an affective state in a general dimensional framework, or in an appraisal framework, that could not also be due to other factors, such as voluntary movement.

If facial behavior cannot be relied on as a unique signature for a particular emotional state, its applied use in a therapeutic context as an unbiased indicator of that state is low. For example, several studies have shown that the activation of the corrugator supercilii muscle, which contracts the eyebrows and pulls them down, is associated with the valence of the current affective state—there is increased tension if the state is negative and decreased tension if the state is positive (e.g., Cacioppo, 2001; Cacioppo, Petty, Losch, & Kim, 1986). However, there are many processes, voluntary or not, that can produce increases and decreases in the activation of this muscle. Hence, based on muscle activation alone, it is not possible in a specific case to deduce, in an individual, that the individual was in a positive or negative state.

Of course, it cannot be excluded that there is a particular type of corrugator activation that is indeed a unique signature of affective valence. Such a signature could reveal itself with more sophisticated analyses, such as taking the dynamics into account or the coaction with other muscles (see also Cacioppo & Tassinary, 1990). At present, there is no such knowledge (see also Tassinary & Cacioppo, 1992).

As far as basic emotions are concerned, the situation appears a bit better. There are indications that "felt joy" can be distinguished from other joy expressions (Ekman, 1997; Ekman, Davidson, & Friesen, 1990; Ekman & Friesen, 1982; Ekman, Friesen, & O'Sullivan, 1988; Ekman & O'Sullivan, 1992; Frank, Ekman, & Friesen, 1993; Hess, Kappas, McHugo, Kleck, & Lanzetta, 1989). However, these findings might apply only to specific contexts, and less is known regarding differences between felt and unfelt anger, disgust,[4] sadness, or contempt. Unless there is a specific reason to assume that identifying felt joy in the therapeutic interaction will be a major benefit, it cannot be recommended that the clinician buy a coder's manual and assume the same diagnostic benefits as, for example, from using a well-established inventory for depression or the like.

This volume testifies to the richness of research that is currently addressing these issues, and it might be only a matter of years until a different recommendation could be made; given the current state of knowledge, measures of facial behavior, or other nonverbal behaviors, cannot be considered unbiased indicators of affective states outside controlled (clinical or other) research contexts. Yet, this seemingly pessimistic assessment does not translate to a general rejection of the usefulness of measuring nonverbal behaviors in a clinical context. We believe that there is much interesting material for the clinician as far as research and application is concerned, as we show in the following sections.

The Myth of the Meaningless Facial Expression: It Is Potentially a Rich Source of Information About the Sender

Having argued that the meaning of facial expression is unclear because there are factors other than emotions that might produce the same patterns, we want to make it clear that, for the clinician, there might still be much useful information to be found in the face. First, facial behavior might reflect action tendencies or action readiness (Frijda, 1986; Frijda, Kuipers, & ter Schure, 1989) or social motivations (Fridlund, 1994, 1997; Hess, Banse, & Kappas, 1995; Jakobs, Manstead, & Fischer, 1999a, 1999b; Timmers, Fischer, & Manstead, 1998). These determinants of facial behavior are probably intrinsically even more proximal to the relational structure of the dyad than the emotional state discussed above and are of interest.[5] If the face or other nonverbal communication channels is a rich source of information that relates directly to the relational aspect of the patient-clinician dyad, interest in measuring this type of behavior is particularly high.

For example, it is known that emotional expressions, whether facial or vocal, are the product of spontaneous and voluntary influences (Kappas, Hess, & Scherer, 1991; Rinn, 1991). It is known to be difficult to assess whether a particular emotional expression is spontaneous or voluntary, but it can be assumed that both voluntary and spontaneous influences are linked to the relationship between the two interactants and the context, such as the content of the concurrent conversation. If the question of interpreting whether nonverbal behavior information conveys information regarding the emotional state of a person is enlarged to whether nonverbal behavior conveys information regarding the sender's role in the context of the conversation (and the expressions shown are part of this role), then the reality of dyadic communication in a clinical context is arguably closer.

At this point, there are two different approaches to understanding the meaning of nonverbal behavior—one is primarily driven by theory and the other primarily by empirical observation. This book testifies to the state of both approaches. It is clear that there is much promise in using nonverbal behavior as a tool in the diagnostic and therapeutic context, but it must be clear that progress must be linked to the realization that the critical information might not be the emotional state of the client or patient as such.

While little is known about specific and discriminating signatures of emotional states, much less is known whether there are signatures that relate to specific action tendencies or social motivations. Again, this is not to say that there are no such signatures, but they are not known, so they cannot be used concretely in the process of diagnosis or therapy. Given that there is reason to believe that processes such as action tendencies or social motivations are highly relevant for understanding the "functioning" of the patient and that nonverbal communication is also undoubtedly interpreted in these terms by therapists, even at times if this is in a nonsystematic or naive fashion, more research is urgently needed to establish a solid foundation for the analysis and interpretation of nonverbal cues for such purposes. Evidently, many of the criticisms raised concerning the interpretation of nonverbal behaviors as indicators of affective states can be applied to the notion of nonverbal behaviors as markers of action tendencies or social motivations. Furthermore, it would be foolish to assume that nonverbal behaviors could not be linked to any or all of these processes in particular circumstances.

Essentially, at this point, it is necessary to step back and question the interpretations regarding the relationships of internal states and psychological processes and overt nonverbal behavior. Care must be taken in developing means to tease these influences apart, and an open mind must be kept as to alternative explanations for a given nonverbal behavior, whether it is interpreted in a clinical or in a research context.

We believe that the link of nonverbal behaviors and intrapersonal processes is more complex than any single construct (such as "emotion," "action tendency," or "social motivation") could encompass. This holds particularly true if, as we believe, nonverbal behaviors also serve a variety of interpersonal regulatory functions. We hold that an appreciation of the richness of influences on nonverbal behavior can only be reached by a dialectic approach to intrapersonal and interpersonal determinants and effects.

The Myth of Ping-Pong Communication: It Is a Dynamic Net of Concurrent Interactive Processes

One of the common misconceptions of nonverbal communication is to think of communication as a sequential process in which two (or more) interactants take separate turns being sender and receiver. The notion that conversations are such a give-and-take process is reinforced by a cursory glance at transcripts of communications, but even here it becomes obvious that, at times, there are concurrent utterances. In fact, as soon as the verbal domain is left, it becomes obvious that a dyad is in fact a closely knit net of concurrent mutual exchanges across several nonverbal channels. At the same time, each participant is both sender and receiver (Kappas, 1991; Patterson, 1995; see also Patterson, 1999).

We believe that communication, whether dyadic or not, has the potential to expand the interpersonal boundaries of information processing to form an entity that can be studied in its own right. In this sense, the communicative unit (e.g., dyad) allows distributed affective information processing that transcends the single brain of the individual (see also the concepts of social shared cognition, Manstead & Fischer, 2001, and interpersonally distributed cognition, Parkinson, 2001). We argue here that, functionally, there is not only the level of intrapersonal affective processing, but also some processing that is relevant to the individual that is actually performed in the brain of the interaction partner. The conventional notion of the physical boundaries of two interacting individuals is not denied, but is seen as one possible approach to understanding (dyadic) communication.

A distributed affective information processing view would not insist on this conventional separation. Instead, the dyad is seen as a qualitatively different entity or unit. The functional characteristics of the individual within that unit could then be used in the context of clinical diagnosis and treatment. The goal of these processes is not only to exchange information, but also to regulate the affective state. The next sections outline mechanisms relevant to this process, such as motor mimicry, facial feedback, and empathy, as well as a conceptual model, the superlens. Finally, a hypothetical example of some of these processes in a therapeutic setting is presented.

Distributed Affective Information Processing

To illustrate the notion of distributed affective information processing, it is best to take an example from early human ontogeny. Current thinking regarding how emotions are elicited converges on the notion that an organism, when confronted with a particular situation or event, performs an evaluation or appraisal as to whether there is an implication for the personal well-being, the needs, and goals of the individual, and whether the individual has the means to deal with or adapt to this situation (see Scherer, Schorr, & Johnstone, 2001).

Little is known regarding the details of this appraisal process as such, including identification of the underlying processes and where they occur in the brain (Kappas, 2001). However, it is plausible to assume that this type of appraisal could occur at multiple levels. For example, appraisal can be assumed to be at a sensory motor level, at which the evaluation of a stimulus is hardwired; at a schematic level, which is based on learned knowledge; and at a conceptual level, which is based on ad hoc conceptual processing and on learned knowledge (Leventhal & Scherer, 1987). Hence, if a baby is confronted with a painful stimulus, a loud sound, or a bright flash of light, an evaluation can occur because no learned knowledge is necessary to process the relevance of the stimulus since all of these stimuli are intrinsically negative or aversive. Particular people and objects quickly acquire importance for the baby through knowledge representations that will be activated when these stimuli are again encountered.

But what happens when a stimulus is encountered that is novel, but not intrinsically pleasant or unpleasant? In these cases, if the caregiver is present, a quick exchange of gaze can be observed. In fact, it has been shown that the facial expression of the caregiver in this context determines the behavior of infants. This process is often referred to as *social referencing* (Feinman, 1982; Sorce, Emde, Campos, & Klinnert, 1985).

One interpretation of social referencing implies that the knowledge representation in the brain of the caregiver was requested by the infant to complete the internal evaluation regarding the specific significance of the novel object. It is as if, because no appropriate knowledge was activated sufficiently in the brain of the child, there is a consequent behavior to check for knowledge in the functional external extension of the infant—the caregiver. This type of information exchange is fundamentally different from mere observation of features and reflection thereof because it is social and interactive in nature. The infant sends a request, and the caregiver replies with the relevant information. It is because of this that this type of intersubjectivity is considered the cradle of social cognition (Rochat & Striano, 1999) and perhaps of cognition in general (see also Tarabulsy, Tessier, & Kappas, 1996).

As the infant gets older, the fuzzy boundaries of the self crystallize, and intersubjectivity can take on different forms. However, the notion of distributed affective information processing in the adult exists and has a long history in scientific psychology (Hatfield, Cacioppo, & Rapson, 1994). For example, Lipps (1907) argued that the state of an interaction partner becomes known through a process that involves mimicry of the other's facial expression and facial feedback that can influence the observer's affective state (see Pigman, 1995; Wallbott, 1991). This empathic process relies on a dyadic link that recruits automatic subprocesses such as motor mimicry and facial feedback. While the direct evidence for this type of process is meager (Blairy, Herrera, & Hess, 1999; Hess, Philippot, & Blairy, 1998; Kappas, Hess, & Banse, 1992), there is good evidence that the subprocesses involved (motor mimicry and facial feedback) exist and function in the hypothesized fashion.

Motor Mimicry

As far as motor mimicry is concerned, there is new evidence of the existence of so-called mirror neurons that are activated in the context of specific motor actions, whether they are observed or performed by the individual (Rizzolatti & Arbib, 1998). Rizzolatti and Arbib argued that these mirror neurons are the basis of imitative behavior that is possibly the cradle of speech acquisition and production. While the natural tendency of these neurons is to fire when a relevant behavior is observed, the organism learns to inhibit the imitative movement over time, and the action of these neurons is considered the origin of a visuomotor priming effect (Craighero, Fadiga, Rizzolatti, & Umilta, 1998; Craighero, Fadiga, Umilta, & Rizzolatti, 1997; Rizzolatti & Arbib, 1998).

It is relevant in this context that it has been demonstrated that infants show reliable imitation of facial actions, some of which correspond to the stereotypical emotion prototypes proposed by the emotions view (Bjorklund, 1987; Kaitz, Meschulach-Sarfaty, Auerbach, & Eidelman, 1988; Meltzoff & Moore, 1977). As the infants grow older, the tendency to imitate decreases.

We hypothesize that the imitative mode of facial action generation is decoupled from the facial behavior output stream, and the decoupling is only inhibited in specific social situations, such as in interaction with friends (see also Hess et al., 1995; Kappas, 1999). For example, contagion of emotional expressions, such as laughter, seems to be moderated by the relationship between the interactants (Banse, Hess, & Kappas, 1993).

Similarly, Hatfield, Cacioppo, and Rapson (1994) reported that the expressions of the persons who are significant for us tend to be imitated more closely, and that expressions are synchronized more tightly with those we appreciate or love. Bernieri (1988) found that the degree of synchrony between two people's expressions determines the intensity of their emotional rapport. Prior feelings experienced toward an actor and the imitator's goal toward the interaction may also exert a strong influence on the type of emotional contagion produced.

For example, McHugo, Lanzetta, Sullivan, Masters, and Englis (1985) observed that supporters of then-President Reagan were matching the valence of his facial expressions while viewing a videotape of one of his speeches; his opponents, on the contrary, were only responding to the president's mimics with negatively valenced expressions (although it appears that they also tended to imitate the president's expressions, but to a much lower degree; see also Smith, McHugo, & Kappas, 1996). Englis, Vaughan, and Lanzetta (1981) also showed that competing individuals may synchronize their expressions with each other, suggesting the presence of an emotional rapport, but these expressions may be opposite, as is the case when an individual smiles at the mistakes of an opponent (see also Way & Masters, 1996). Krause, Steiner-Krause, Merten, and Burkhard (1998) repeatedly found that, in interactions within "normal" subject populations, the emotional facial expressions shown corresponded better to the supposed emotional state of the interaction partner rather than to that of the subject (see Krause et al., 1998).[6]

By and large, most of these results are not inconsistent with Frijda's (1986) action tendency theory. This theory states that "interactive expressions" are produced automatically and involuntarily in response to emotional stimuli and reflect action tendencies, such as the desire to be receptive and attentive to someone or the desire to get rid of a difficulty or to conquer something.

Facial Feedback

One pathway by which motor mimicry is supposed to modulate ongoing emotional states is facial feedback (Hatfield et al., 1994; Levenson, 1996). The notion that the degree to which facial activity is inhibited or amplified has an impact on the underlying state goes back at least to Darwin (1872/ 1998). Initial attempts to show such effects empirically produced ambiguous results. The situation was aggravated by the fact that the term facial feedback was also used for two other supposed processes, namely, that simply making a face elicits an emotion, and that there can be no emotion in the complete absence of any facial expression (Ellsworth & Tourangeau, 1981; Tourangeau & Ellsworth, 1979).

However, more recently, there have been a number of independent studies addressing the methodological concerns voiced regarding the initial studies (Hess, Kappas, McHugo, Lanzetta, & Kleck, 1992; Kappas, 1989; Strack, Martin, & Stepper, 1988). These newer attempts could clearly show the moderating effect of facial expression, and the consensus currently is that there is such an effect, but that its size is small (Adelmann & Zajonc, 1989; Levenson, 1996; Manstead, 1988; Matsumoto, 1987; McIntosh, 1996). Furthermore, there is also some evidence that posing particular patterns of facial activation can introduce subjective and physiological components of emotion (Ekman, Levenson, & Friesen, 1983; Levenson, Carstensen, Friesen, & Ekman, 1991; Levenson, Ekman, & Friesen, 1990). However, there are still arguments as to the interpretation of these generative effects of posing facial expressions (e.g., Boiten, 1996; Levenson & Ekman, 2002).

So, while the effect of facial feedback seems real, the question is whether it can have any relevant function in emotion regulation given that it is rather weak. Here it is relevant that there might be emotions for which facial feedback is more effective than for others (e.g., amusement but not disgust; Kappas, 1989). But independent of the potential emotion specificity of feedback effects is the issue to what degree effect size is a valid indicator of relevance in dynamic systems.

Research in systems dynamics and, particularly, more recently on so-called chaotic behavior of complex systems has shown that there exists a sensitive dependence on initial conditions (Gleick, 1987), particularly if a system is characterized by feedback loops and delayed feedback conditions. This effect has been popularized as the butterfly effect. Simulations of weather systems have shown that minute differences in the initial conditions of the model can lead to increasingly large differences in the predicted weather pattern over time. Hence, the popular notion that the beating of a butterfly's wings in Beijing could influence the weather in New York and make a difference as to whether a thunderstorm might hit the city or pass it by.

The sensitive dependence on initial conditions has been shown in different domains and is an accepted effect in the context of complex dynamic systems. It is here that our conception of communication becomes relevant. If nonverbal communication is studied by measuring, for example, facial behavior of an isolated subject reacting to emotion-eliciting slides, the effort is doomed to fail to capture the complexity of ongoing dyadic communication. There is a difference in assuming that communication is a ping-pong mode of sending and receiving and acknowledging the interaction between both participants. In this case, interaction is not to be confused with statistical interaction, but refers to dynamic interaction with mutual and internal feedback processes.

The Superlens Model of Communication

Kappas (1991) proposed the superlens model of communication to capture this complexity. Figure 3.1 shows a current version of this model. Here,

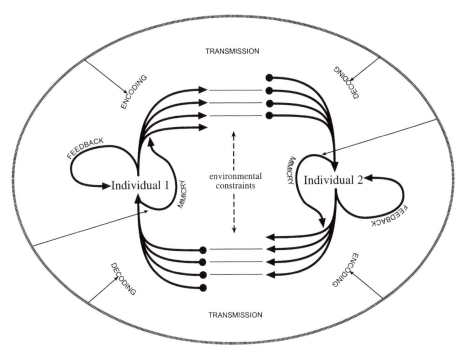

TRANSMISSION

ENCODING

DECODING

FEEDBACK

MIMICRY

MIMICRY

environmental
constraints

Individual 1

Individual 2

FEEDBACK

DECODING

ENCODING

TRANSMISSION

social context + cultural conventions

Fig. 3.1 Superlens model of dyadic communication. (After Kappas, 1991.)

two people interact. They externalize (encode) internal states in multiple communication channels.

It is relevant here that these states refer not only to emotions as such, but also to action tendencies and social motivations. Furthermore, the channels are to some degree, but rarely completely, redundant. Encoding is subject to social context and cultural conventions. Even within a single channel, such as facial activity, there are differential influences regarding the coupling and decoupling of source stream influences (voluntary components, involuntary affective/motivational components, and nonaffective components such as speaking, breathing, mastication, etc.; Kappas, 1999).

Transmission is influenced by environmental constraints, such as distance, viewing angle (Kappas, Hess, Barr, & Kleck, 1994), lighting conditions, or noise. Consequently, there are aspects of nonverbal behavior that are never perceived or that are biased as a function of these environmental constraints. The attribution of the sender state through the receiver is in fact an attribution process that occurs at multiple levels (see also Patterson et al., 2001).

It is known, for example, that prototypical facial expressions of emotion are "recognized" extremely rapidly (Kirouac & Doré, 1983, 1984), and this is even possible without conscious awareness, as indicated by specific physiological reactions to masked facial stimuli (Esteves, Dimberg, & Öhman, 1995; Morris, Öhman, & Dolan, 1998; Parra, Esteves, Flykt, & Öhman, 1997). The word *recognized* is in quotation marks because, in many cases, the criterion is not to attribute how a person feels, but to indicate which state is supposed to be depicted by a facial stimulus.

To clarify this distinction, if the picture is actually a synthetic picture or a cartoon, it is known that the image does not display a human being while a certain emotional state is present, yet researchers will ask what emotion is expressed by the (schematic or realistic) face. The model shows a line that adds to the attribution process, but is not linked to transmitted signals from the sender. It represents the influence of stereotypes that lead to the false perception of cues that were, in fact, not present (Kappas, 1997; Kappas et al., 1991).

The model also depicts feedback processes, which potentially modulate the underlying state, and it shows mimicry processes linked to perceiving the other. Note that, as discussed, mimicry processes are modulated by social context. All relations are mirrored to illustrate the concurrent nature of communication in both directions. In addition to the intra- and interpersonal regulation of the affective states of the interactants, there is also the structural regulation of the interaction itself (e.g., turn-taking) that occurs naturally in the concurrent "dance" between them.

Multiple Levels of Empathy

Distributed affective information processing as implied by the superlens model does not rely only on automatic processing of nonverbal cues. Indeed, there are different concepts of empathy, and most of them include not only the aforementioned automatic processes, but also others. For example, authors such as Hoffman (1982) have suggested that people may also link the affective indices they perceive in the other person's expressions to their own memories of some closely related affective experience. For example, a little girl may start to cry after witnessing a young boy who just cut his finger and now bleeds heavily; witnessing such an event may activate the memory of a past experience during which she, too, had cut her finger badly. Thus, the type of process postulated here is not so much a function of sensory motor information processing as schematic/conceptual processing, to use Leventhal and Scherer's (1987) terms.

Others have suggested that people tend to use "role playing" in their attempts at being empathic, that is, trying to put oneself virtually in the role and perspective of the other person in a given context (Feshback, 1975; Hoffman, 1982). However, the role of affective processes in this type of mechanism is less clear: Role playing may induce an affective subjective experience in the person who tries to be empathic (via sensory motor or schematic/conceptual processes), or it may simply provide the person with a cognitive context that enables the person to understand better the sequence of actions and the goals reached within the original situation (a more cognitive and conceptual hypothesis, such as the one put forward by Karniol, 1982).

Whereas many recent conceptions of empathy (Feshback, 1975; Hoffman, 1982; Karniol, 1982) result from research efforts that have been conducted within a developmental framework, they find an echo in prior theoretical notions advanced by clinicians such as Reik (1948), who proposed a four-step model to explain the empathic process. He described this process as moving from

1. An instinctive imitative activity and relaxation of conscious controls upon becoming absorbed by the object of empathy, through
2. Introjection of the other person in ourselves, and the consequent
3. "Reverberation" or "resonance" between the internalized feelings of the other and evocations of our own experience and imaginings, to
4. Deliberate withdrawal and psychological distancing to effect clear differentiation of the self and the other person in the final phase (see Katz, 1963).

So, in sum, most authors, whether from a developmental or clinical background, postulate that automatic processes are involved in the first stages of the empathic process, such as sensory-motor feedback and schematic/memory effects, which are in most cases followed by more conscious, cognitive, or conceptual mechanisms in an effort to treat or use the reverberation in a constructive way within the relationship (see also Levenson, 1996).

A Psychodynamic Perspective of Empathy and Affect Regulation in a Communicative Framework

Direct links can be made between the communication and regulation notions presented above and psychotherapy. On the methodological level, for instance, psychotherapy-related concepts support the idea of using the dyad as the most important unit of analysis when studying affective interactions (real or imagined). To illustrate this point, we report three examples drawn from the psychodynamic tradition. First, the proponents of object relations theories state that most "peak" affects are linked with particular representations of the self in relation to a significant other (e.g., see Kernberg, 1996; for a discussion of object relations theories, see Greenberg & Mitchell, 1983). Second, some instruments designed to analyze narratives involving the self in interaction with others, such as Luborsky's core conflictual relationship themes, emphasize the intended desire a person has toward an other and, most importantly, the anticipated response of this other and the corresponding counterreaction of the self (Luborsky & Crits-Christoph, 1990). Finally, the frequently cited defense mechanism of projective identification postulates that the individual who is interacting with the defensive person is pressured to feel and behave according to the image that is projected on him (Grinberg, 1979; Kernberg, 1975; Ogden, 1979). Thus, in one way or another, these theories, instruments, and mechanisms emphasize the self-other dyad when referring to affects or emotions.

Evidently, researchers and clinicians need not confine their analyses to the dyadic level. As the superlens model suggests (see Fig. 3.1), an analysis of emotionally charged events at both individual and dyadic levels is likely to aid in understanding the clinically relevant dynamics between the two interactants. Thus, this partial emphasis on individual processes highlights the importance of relying on more intrapsychic psychotherapy concepts.

We believe that the idea of "defense mechanism" is particularly relevant in this context as it is related to affective regulation. Initially, defense mechanisms were thought to be used by the ego as a means of defense against the unacceptable wishes of the id (Freud, 1923/1961, 1926/1959). Later contributions have somewhat broadened the domain of influence of these mechanisms by acknowledging the regulating effect they may have on affects as well (Freud, 1949).

Interestingly, although unconscious by definition, defense mechanisms have recently been linked with coping mechanisms, which are considered by some to be a more conscious version of the former ones (Plutchik, 1998; but see also Westen, 1998, for the limitations of this conscious/unconscious distinction). For example, according to Plutchik (1998), "Denial may be an unconscious ego defense, while its derivative, minimization, may be a conscious way of handling a frustrating situation by minimizing its relative importance" (p. 373). Thus, whether we refer to unconscious defense mechanisms or their more conscious coping counterparts, intrapsychic concepts such as these should aid in understanding affect regulation.

Some links may also be found between empathy and some psychodynamically related concepts. For instance, in terms of relational processes, psychodynamically oriented theories put strong emphasis on the transference and countertransference exchanges that occur within the therapeutic setting. Transference is usually defined as an unconscious relational process that reactivates in the present some internal representations of significant others from the past, with the basis of these representations constructed in childhood. By definition, the activated representations do not correspond to reality and induce in the person the affective states, wishes, attitudes, and other relational tendencies that were once experienced in contact with the object (Freud, 1912/1958, 1914/1958; Kernberg, 1996; Racker, 1968). While transference is usually reserved for the patient's biased perceptions, countertransference is used in reference to the therapist. In its classical form, it designates the therapist's unconscious response to the patient's transference (Freud, 1910/1958, 1912/1958, 1915/1958); more recent conceptions have it represent the total emotional reaction of the therapist to the patient, including both conscious and unconscious components (Kernberg, 1965; Racker, 1968; Winnicott, 1949).

Following these definitions, it is reasonable to assume that mimicry, synchronization, and empathic activities on the part of the therapist lead to countertransference. On the other side, the person of the therapist, whether real or imagined, activates certain schematic processes in the patient that bias the patient's perceptions and push the patient toward thinking, feeling, and behaving in ways that are related to his or her past. In a way, during these transference episodes, the patient becomes "synchronized" with the distorted image or perception of the therapist and reacts in ways that are either empathic or counterempathic, depending on the valence of the patient's corresponding attitudes (see the discussion above of the reactions of those who watched a speech made by President Reagan).[7]

Now, how do concepts such as motor mimicry, synchronization of expressive behavior, facial feedback, empathy, transference and countertransference, and defense and coping mechanisms work in concert during actual interpersonal processes? To answer this question, it must be taken into account that some of these may function as causative agents, some as affective regulators, or even some as both. Moreover, while all interactions take place in a given environment, in a context in which the interactants have prior expectations and goals for the interaction, and under the influence of cultural conventions, the specific situation is likely to exert a moderator influence on the relative importance of each of the factors enumerated above.

Obviously, the study of every possible link that may exist between these factors is beyond the scope of this chapter. In addition, not enough is yet known about these mechanisms to complete such a task. Consequently, we present here a hypothetical example to show how and when these mechanisms could be involved during an interaction and how they may be interrelated. Of course, this example is highly speculative. Nonetheless, based on our research and clinical experience, we believe it offers a fairly plausible representation of how things might occur in reality.

In this example, a patient suffering from a borderline personality disorder (American Psychiatric Association, 1994) is meeting her female therapist for the second time. Generally, such patients are characterized by huge and intense oscillations in the valence of their emotional reactions. It is also well known that the relative lack of structure of the therapeutic setting and the relative proximity to and intimacy with the therapist make these patients highly uncomfortable. Related to these intimacy issues is an unconscious fear of being abandoned, an outcome they tend to avoid at all costs. As a consequence, they frequently enter into acute negative transference episodes very early in treatment (Kernberg, 1975; Kernberg, Selzer, Koenigsberg, Carr, & Appelbaum, 1989).

Thus, in our example, our borderline patient readily finds herself facing an important person toward whom she tends to maintain a predominantly negative attitude. In the other chair is a therapist who is motivated to help her. To repeat an earlier citation (point 1 described above, Reik, 1948; see also Katz, 1963), the therapist is thus prepared to "relax her conscious controls and become absorbed by the object of her empathy." This can be viewed as setting the "initial conditions" of a complex system, as described earlier in reference to the butterfly effect (Gleick, 1987).

Now, let us assume that, at a certain point, the therapist is engaged in a cognitive effort aimed at disentangling some rather contradictory verbal content of the patient. While doing so, she is likely to frown, a sign that appears to be associated with intense concentration or deep reflexive activity (Smith, 1989). In our example, this constitutes the seemingly insignificant event that will shift the whole system. Indeed, frowning not only is associated with concentration, but also is a constituent of most negative emotional expressions (Smith & Scott, 1997). With their well-known sensitivity to possible rejecting cues in others (Gabbard, 1994; Kernberg, 1975), borderline patients are very likely to pick up on this kind of expression.

Two parallel mechanisms may arguably come into play at this point. First, since the therapist is important to her, our patient may automatically imitate her expression, but given her prior negative attitude toward the therapist, she may add more negative components to it, the feedback of which might slightly increase her negative affective attitude. Second, under the pressure of her already present tendency toward negative transference, a schema associated with the angry faces of significant others may become activated in the mind of the patient, the activation of which will further bias her perceptions or thought contents. Furthermore, the activation of such a schema is likely to create or increase the negative affective subjective experience of the patient, a consequence that has been suggested by some authors (Jenkins & Oatley, 1998; Magai & Hunziker, 1998).

At this point, it might be argued that the mechanisms invoked are too complex, and that the whole scenario would be better explained as a skeptical patient who interprets negatively the cues expressed by the therapist. In our opinion, this version, although offering the advantage of providing a catchy descriptive theme, reduces the richness of the tapestry of interacting mechanisms and does not provide as many opportunities for generating testable hypotheses. Thus, we consider the former version more valuable.

Given this increase in the intensity of her negative affective experience, the patient is likely to use strategies to regulate its intensity. In these circumstances, a mechanism frequently relied on by borderline patients is the defense of projective identification. According to Sandler (1987), "What one wants to get rid of in oneself can be disposed of by projective identification, and through controlling the object one can then gain the unconscious illusion that one is controlling the unwanted and projected aspect of the self" (p. 20). Thus, following this scenario, the patient is likely to project a rejecting angry face toward the person of the therapist, whom she will subsequently try to control to become less distressed by the whole situation. As in the preceding paragraph, we prefer this explanation to one based on a simple bias in perception since it may provide, in our view, better understanding of the mechanisms involved. Then the patient's statements will most probably reflect this attempt at controlling the therapist, as depicted in her words to the effect that the therapist has no business knowing about this or that intimate aspect of her relationships. But, what is even more important is that projective identification tends to force the negative role on the other person, who, especially if the person is trying to be empathic, will feel pressured to adopt and enact it (Grinberg, 1979; Ogden, 1979).

Although the constituent microscopic mechanisms of this process are not yet known, it is highly likely that mimicry, synchronization, and schematic components are involved. Whatever the case, the therapist might likely react in either of two ways. In the first scenario, the therapist, being even more puzzled and irritated by this whole situation, frowns more intensely and begins to show signs of slight anger. Most probably, this reaction will increase the patient's distress; the patient will then try to exert stricter control over the interaction. If not interrupted, this feedback loop will increase the negative affective experience of both interactants, which given borderline patients' tendency to regulate their affect behaviorally (Westen, 1998), is likely to push the patient to yell in hate at the therapist before leaving and slamming the door behind her. This scenario will probably have repeated what usually happens in the life of the patient when such circumstances arise.

In contrast, if the therapist is able to observe her role at the beginning of the enaction (i.e., becomes aware of her countertransference reactions), the intensity of her affective experience will diminish, the ability to make objective judgments will increase, and she will be in a position to make an interpretation to the patient to the effect that the patient is acting the way she is because she is afraid that the therapist might get angry with her and not want her anymore as a patient. In these circumstances, the patient will either deny the whole thing or recognize the truth of the interpretation; more often than not, it will diminish the threat feared by the patient and regulate her affective experience and behavior.

Obviously, this example is rather simplistic and does not render justice to all the thought contents and regulation mechanisms that might be created or triggered in the minds of both interaction partners. However, given space constraints, we believe it sums the essence of what we want to illustrate.

Conclusion

Using nonverbal communication in a clinical context to aid diagnosis and research is probably a more formidable task than was previously thought.

Current knowledge regarding the processes involved continues to reinforce the idea that there is much relevant information in nonverbal aspects of communicative processes. However, the point of having identified clear signatures for processes that have been traditionally associated with nonverbal behavior, such as emotional states, has not yet been reached. There is reason to believe that there are other factors influencing nonverbal behavior, such as action tendencies and social motivations. These might also be very interesting to understand, but even less is known about signatures of these components contributing to nonverbal behavior.

Are measures of nonverbal behavior useful as diagnostic tools in the context of therapy? There has been a waxing and waning of enthusiasm on the usefulness of including nonverbal behaviors in the diagnostic and therapeutic process. However, it should become obvious that the evolution of theories in this domain does not simply reflect the periodical and repetitive swing of a pendulum, with the extremes being assumptions that facial actions are always influenced by affective states on the one hand and the notion that there is no relationship between emotions and facial activity on the other hand. In fact, the theoretical development in this context might best be seen as a spiral that evolves toward a more and more sophisticated understanding of the relationship of facial activity and emotions in a social context.

Yet, we are far from understanding the underlying mechanisms. As research in this area becomes more diverse, ranging from the role of specific neurons such as mirror neurons (Rizzolatti & Arbib, 1998), to the role of facial expressions for nonhuman primates (Miller, Banks, & Ogawa, 1964; Parr, 1999; Parr, Hopkins, & de Waal, 1998), to physiological and behavioral changes when observing facial activity (Kappas et al., 1992; Levenson, 1996), it must be realized that no single approach will be sufficient to tackle the issue of the relationship of emotion, expression, and regulation.

Social neuroscience has provided a paradigmatic framework that can guide the development of a program of basic research necessary to understand the full complexity of nonverbal behavior in interaction (Cacioppo & Berntson, 1992; Cacioppo, Berntson, & Crites, 1996). Following this approach, it is necessary to acknowledge that social interactions can, and should, be described at multiple levels of organization, from cellular to social. Events at any level of organization can be the consequence of one or more processes at that level, as well as at other levels. Furthermore, there can be complex interactions of processes at any or all levels.

Acknowledging the multilevel nature of the dyadic interaction that is typical in clinical settings has two consequences: (a) It must be considered that the individuals and the dyad together form a complex system with multiple feedback loops; hence, there is the potential of the system to react in nonlinear ways to specific events in the interactive stream, and these effects cannot be estimated based on research outside dyadic interactions. (b) Variables related to the interaction itself become potentially more interesting than trying to link specific expressions to underlying states of the sender (see Merten & Krause, chapter 5, this volume).

Emotion regulation is at the same time an intrapersonal and an interpersonal process. It occurs at multiple levels and includes automatic and voluntary processes. It does not appear appropriate to treat these regulation processes as mutually exclusive, such as contrasting cognitive and sensory motor modes of empathy, but rather to consider the possibility that all of these occur in parallel and influence each other. Some of these processes might be more susceptible to social context than others. It is here, the point at which there is a critical difference between dyadic communication in a clinical context and "everyday" communication, that the relationship between patient or client and therapist changes much more rapidly than in other types of communication. This change is a function of the therapy and not only of passing time. Hence, we expect that those phenomena that are sensitive to social context, from the intensity and type of expression shown, to the modulating effects of mimicry or countermimicry, are differentially relevant over the course of the therapy. These hypotheses clearly need to be tested as they follow logically from basic research on nonverbal communication, but have not traditionally been considered in a clinical context.

As knowledge regarding dynamic systems increases, examples in various domains show that a small change can indeed have a large impact on a given system. Effects become causes of other effects, and those in turn create feedback cascades that do not lend themselves to an analysis based on the notion of static cause-effect relationships. However, whether this view describes the reality of human interaction is not known today.

As tempting as these analogies are, they remain hypotheses unless there is empirical support. It is here that studies are needed not only in the laboratory, but also in applied contexts, such as in psychotherapy. The development of knowledge and its application likely will need to go hand in hand because meaningful events are more likely to occur in meaningful interactions.

According to current thinking in emotion theory, there are essentially no emotions if there is "nothing at stake" (Smith, 1993). This implies that, while basic research is needed to understand emotion in communication, there is a need to study such processes in truly emotional contexts. Thus, clinicians should not wait until theorists will finally provide a comprehensive model of nonverbal behavior and emotion in communication, but should take an active role in building it. Meanwhile, it appears prudent to be cautious in using nonverbal behaviors as indicators of affective or motivational states, beliefs, attitudes, or the state of the relationship in which these behaviors occurred.

Notes

1. Fridlund argues that strategic use does not require intention and need not be conscious. Hence, there is no correspondence between a strategic versus a

nonstrategic dichotomy and a voluntary versus an involuntary distinction (Kappas, Bherer, & Thériault, 2000).

2. A good discussion of problems of inference relevant in the present context can be found in Cacioppo and Tassinary (1990).

3. We do not consider the extreme position of the behavioral ecology view (Fridlund, 1994) that there is no relation between facial behavior and emotion because the emotion concept in this case would be irrelevant.

4. There are some indications that spontaneous and deliberate expressions of disgust differ in regard to timing, but it is not clear to what degree these differences would occur also in conversation (Hess & Kleck, 1990, 1994). Judges were not able to identify correctly the felt and false disgust expressions.

5. Obviously, it can be argued that a particular emotion in a particular context reflects the relationship between both partners in the dyad. For example, a contempt expression could be interpreted as representing a particular attitudinal stance toward the other. However, the named theorists argue that the expressive behavior is a direct function of the action tendency or the social motivation and is not necessarily mediated by the emotional state "contempt."

6. This pattern can break down if one of the two interaction partners is suffering, for example, from schizophrenia; in this case, the patient's facial displays correspond better to his own supposed emotional state than to that of his or her interaction partner.

7. Interestingly, classical psychoanalytic therapy (patient lying on a couch) avoids eye-to-eye contact between therapist and patient. In this type of setting, processes based on facial mimicry are not available for empathic, transference, or countertransference purposes. It is likely that other channels, such as the nonverbal characteristics of the voice, become more important.

References

Adelmann, P. K., & Zajonc, R. B. (1989). Facial efference and the experience of emotion. *Annual Review of Psychology, 40*, 249–280.

American Psychiatric Association. (1994). *Diagnostic and statistical manual of mental disorders* (4th ed.). Washington, DC: Author.

Babad, E., Bernieri, F. J., & Rosenthal, R. (1989). Nonverbal communication and leakage in the behavior of biased and unbiased teachers. *Journal of Personality and Social Psychology, 56*, 89–94.

Banse, R., Hess, U., & Kappas, A. (1993). Friendship facilitates contagious laughter. *Psychophysiology, 30*, S15.

Bernieri, F. J. (1988). Coordinated movement and rapport in teacher-student interactions. *Journal of Nonverbal Behavior, 12*, 120–138.

Bjorklund, D. F. (1987). A note on neonatal imitation. *Developmental Review, 7*, 86–92.

Blairy, S., Herrera, P., & Hess, U. (1999). Mimicry and the judgment of emotional facial expressions. *Journal of Nonverbal Behavior, 23*, 5–41.

Boiten, F. (1996). Autonomic response patterns during voluntary facial action. *Psychophysiology, 33*, 123–131.

Cacioppo, J. T. (2001, October). *Reflections on Nicolaus Copernicus, Thomas Kuhn, and Sir Arthur Eddington.* Paper presented at the Forty-First Annual

Meeting of the Society for Psychophysiological Research, Montreal, Quebec, Canada.

Cacioppo, J. T., & Berntson, G. G. (1992). Social psychological contributions to the decade of the brain: The doctrine of multilevel analysis. *American Psychologist, 47*, 1019–1028.

Cacioppo, J. T., Berntson, G. G., & Crites, S. L. J. (1996). Social neuroscience: Principles of psychophysiological arousal and response. In E. T. Higgins & A. W. Kruglanski (Eds.), *Social psychology: Handbook of basic principles* (pp. 72–101). New York: Guilford Press.

Cacioppo, J. T., Petty, R. E., Losch, M. E., & Kim, H. S. (1986). Electromyographic activity over facial muscle regions can discriminate the valence and intensity of affective reactions. *Journal of Personality and Social Psychology, 50*, 260–268.

Cacioppo, J. T., & Tassinary, L. G. (1990). Psychophysiology and psychophysiological inference. In J. T. Cacioppo & L. G. Tassinary (Eds.), *Principles of psychophysiology* (pp. 3–33). Cambridge, England: Cambridge University Press.

Craighero, L., Fadiga, L., Rizzolatti, G., & Umilta, C. (1998). Visuomotor priming. *Visual Cognition, 5*, 109–125.

Craighero, L., Fadiga, L., Umilta, C., & Rizzolatti, G. (1997). Evidence for visuomotor priming effect. *Neuroreport: An International Journal for the Rapid Communication of Research in Neuroscience, 8*, 347–349.

Darwin, C. (1998). *The expression of the emotions in man and animals: Definitive edition* (P. Ekman, Ed.). Oxford, England: Oxford University Press. (Original work published 1872)

Ekman, P. (Ed.). (1982). *Emotion in the human face* (2nd ed.). Cambridge, England: Cambridge University Press.

Ekman, P. (1992a). Are there basic emotions? *Psychological Review, 99*, 550–553.

Ekman, P. (1992b). An argument for basic emotions. *Cognition and Emotion, 6*, 169–200.

Ekman, P. (1994a). All emotions are basic. In P. Ekman & R. J. Davidson (Eds.), *The nature of emotion: Fundamental questions* (pp. 15–19). New York: Oxford University Press.

Ekman, P. (1994b). Strong evidence for universals in facial expressions: A reply to Russell's mistaken critique. *Psychological Bulletin, 115*, 268–287.

Ekman, P. (1997). Afterword: Smiles when lying. In P. Ekman & E. Rosenberg (Eds.), *What the face reveals: Basic and applied studies of the spontaneous expression using the Facial Action Coding System (FACS)* (pp. 215–216). New York: Oxford University Press.

Ekman, P., Davidson, R. J., & Friesen, W. V. (1990). The Duchenne smile: Emotional expression and brain physiology II. *Journal of Personality and Social Psychology, 58*, 342–353.

Ekman, P., & Friesen, W. V. (1969). The repertoire of nonverbal behavior: Categories, origins, usage, and coding. *Semiotica, 1*, 49–98.

Ekman, P., & Friesen, W. V. (1982). Felt, false, and miserable smiles. *Journal of Nonverbal Behavior, 6*, 238–252.

Ekman, P., Friesen, W. V., & O'Sullivan, M. (1988). Smiles when lying. *Journal of Personality and Social Psychology, 54*, 414–420.

Ekman, P., Levenson, R. W., & Friesen, W. V. (1983). Autonomic nervous system activity distinguishes among emotions. *Science, 221*, 1208–1210.

Ekman, P., & O'Sullivan, M. (1992). Who can catch a liar? *American Psychologist, 46*, 913–920.

Ellsworth, P. E., & Tourangeau, R. (1981). On our failure to disconfirm what nobody ever said. *Journal of Personality and Social Psychology, 40*, 363–369.

Englis, B. G., Vaughan, K. B., & Lanzetta, J. T. (1981). Conditioning of counterempathic responses. *Journal of Experimental Social Psychology, 18*, 375–391.

Esteves, F., Dimberg, U., & Öhman, A. (1995). Automatically elicited fear: Conditioned skin conductance responses to masked facial expressions. *Cognition and Emotion, 8*, 393–413.

Feinman, S. (1982). Social referencing in infancy. *Merrill Palmer Quarterly, 28*, 445–470.

Feshback, N. D. (1975). Empathy in children: Some theoretical and empirical considerations. *The Counseling Psychologist, 4*, 25–30.

Frank, M. G., Ekman, P., & Friesen, W. V. (1993). Behavioral markers and recognizability of the smile of enjoyment. *Journal of Personality and Social Psychology, 64*, 83–93.

Freud, A. (1949). *Le moi et les mécanismes de défense* [The ego and the mechanisms of defense]. Paris: Presses Universitaires de France.

Freud, S. (1958). The future prospects of psycho-analytic therapy. In J. Strachey (Ed.), *The standard edition of the complete psychological works of Sigmund Freud* (Vol. 11, pp. 139–151). London: Hogarth Press. (Original work published 1910)

Freud, S. (1958). The dynamics of transference. In J. Strachey (Ed.), *The standard edition of the complete psychological works of Sigmund Freud* (Vol. 12, pp. 99–108). London: Hogarth Press. (Original work published 1912)

Freud, S. (1958). Remembering, repeating and working through. In J. Strachey (Ed.), *The standard edition of the complete psychological works of Sigmund Freud* (Vol. 12, pp. 147–156). London: Hogarth Press. (Original work published 1914)

Freud, S. (1958). Instincts and their vicissitudes. In J. Strachey (Ed.), *The standard edition of the complete psychological works of Sigmund Freud* (Vol. 14, pp. 117–140). London: Hogarth Press. (Original work published 1915)

Freud, S. (1959). Inhibitions, symptoms, and anxiety. In J. Strachey (Ed. and Trans.), *The standard edition of the complete psychological works of Sigmund Freud* (Vol. 20, pp. 75–175). London: Hogarth Press. (Original work published 1926)

Freud, S. (1961). The ego and the id. In J. Strachey (Ed. and Trans.), *The standard edition of the complete psychological works of Sigmund Freud* (Vol. 19, pp. 1–66). London: Hogarth Press. (Original work published 1923)

Fridlund, A. (1994). *Human facial expression: An evolutionary view.* San Diego, CA: Academic Press.

Fridlund, A. J. (1997). The new ethology of human facial expressions. In J. A. Russell & J. M. Fernández-Dols (Eds.), *The psychology of facial expression* (pp. 103–129). Cambridge, England: Cambridge University Press.

Frijda, N. H. (1986). *The emotions.* Cambridge, England: Cambridge University Press.

Frijda, N. H., Kuipers, P., & ter Schure, E. (1989). Relations among emotion, appraisal, and action readiness. *Journal of Personality and Social Psychology, 57,* 212–228.

Gabbard, G. O. (1994). *Psychodynamic psychiatry in clinical practice: The* DSM-IV *edition.* Washington, DC: American Psychiatric Press.

Gleick, J. (1987). *Chaos: Making of a new science.* New York: Penguin.

Greenberg, J. R., & Mitchell, S. A. (1983). *Object relations in psychoanalytic theory.* Cambridge, MA: Harvard University Press.

Grinberg, L. (1979). Countertransference and projective counteridentification. In L. Epstein & A. Feiner (Eds.), *Countertransference* (pp. 169–191). New York: Jason Aronson.

Hatfield, E., Cacioppo, J. T., & Rapson, R. L. (1994). *Emotional contagion.* Cambridge, England: Cambridge University Press.

Hess, U., Banse, R., & Kappas, A. (1995). The intensity of facial expression is determined by underlying affective state and social situation. *Journal of Personality and Social Psychology, 69,* 280–288.

Hess, U., Kappas, A., McHugo, G. J., Kleck, R. E., & Lanzetta, J. T. (1989). An analysis of the encoding and decoding of spontaneous and posed smiles: The use of facial electromyography. *Journal of Nonverbal Behavior, 13,* 121–137.

Hess, U., Kappas, A., McHugo, G. J., Lanzetta, J. T., & Kleck, R. E. (1992). The facilitative effect of facial expression on the self-generation of emotion. *International Journal of Psychophysiology, 12,* 251–265.

Hess, U., & Kleck, R. E. (1990). Differentiating emotion elicited and deliberate emotional facial expressions. *European Journal of Social Psychology, 20,* 369–385.

Hess, U., & Kleck, R. E. (1994). The cues decoders use in attempting to differentiate emotion-elicited and posed facial expressions. *European Journal of Social Psychology, 24,* 367–381.

Hess, U., Philippot, P., & Blairy, S. (1998). Facial reactions to emotional facial expressions: Affect or cognition? *Cognition and Emotion, 12,* 509–531.

Hoffman, M. L. (1982). Development of prosocial motivation. In N. Eisenberg (Ed.), *The development of prosocial behavior* (pp. 218–231). New York: Academic Press.

Jakobs, E., Manstead, A. S. R., & Fischer, A. H. (1999a). Social motives and emotional feelings as determinants of facial displays: The case of smiling. *Personality and Social Psychology Bulletin, 25,* 424–435.

Jakobs, E., Manstead, A. S. R., & Fischer, A. H. (1999b). Social motives, emotional feelings, and smiling. *Cognition and Emotion, 13,* 321–345.

Jenkins, J. M., & Oatley, K. (1998). The development of emotion schemas in children: Processes that underlie psychopathology. In W. F. Flack & J. D. Laird (Eds.), *Emotions in psychopathology: Theory and research* (pp. 45–56). New York: Oxford University Press.

Kaitz, M., Meschulach-Sarfaty, O., Auerbach, J., & Eidelman, A. (1988). A reexamination of newborn's ability to imitate facial expression. *Developmental Psychology, 24,* 3–7.

Kappas, A. (1989). *Control of emotion.* Unpublished doctoral thesis, Dartmouth College, Hanover, NH.

Kappas, A. (1991). The illusion of the neutral observer: On the communication of emotion. *Cahiers de Linguistique Française de l'Université de Genève, 12,* 153–168.

Kappas, A. (1997). The fascination with faces: Are they windows to our soul? *Journal of Nonverbal Behavior, 21,* 157–161.

Kappas, A. (1999, September). *Reconceptualizing the influence of social context on facial displays: Towards a new view of display rules.* Paper presented at the Eighth European Conference on Facial Expression—Measurement and Meaning, Saarbrücken, Germany.

Kappas, A. (2001). A metaphor is a metaphor is a metaphor: Exorcising the homunculus from appraisal theory. In K. R. Scherer, A. Schorr, & T. Johnstone (Eds.), *Appraisal processes in emotion: Theory, methods, research* (pp. 157–172). New York: Oxford University Press.

Kappas, A. (2003). What facial activity can and cannot tell us about emotions. In M. Katsikitis (Ed.), *The human face: Measurement and meaning* (pp. 215–234). Dordrecht: Kluwer Academic Publishers.

Kappas, A., Bherer, F., & Thériault, M. (2000). Inhibiting facial expressions: Limitations to the voluntary control of facial expressions of emotion. *Motivation and Emotion, 24,* 259–270.

Kappas, A., Hess, U., & Banse, R. (1992). Skin conductance reactions to dynamic facial expressions revisited: Empathic responding or information processing? *Psychophysiology, 29,* S42.

Kappas, A., Hess, U., Barr, C. L., & Kleck, R. E. (1994). Angle of regard: The effect of vertical viewing angle on the perception of facial expressions. *Journal of Nonverbal Behavior, 18,* 263–280.

Kappas, A., Hess, U., & Scherer, K. R. (1991). Voice and emotion. In R. S. Feldman & B. Rimé (Eds.), *Fundamentals of nonverbal behavior* (pp. 200–238). Cambridge, England: Cambridge University Press.

Karniol, R. (1982). Settings, scripts, and self-schemata: A cognitive analysis of the development of prosocial behavior. In N. Eisenberg (Ed.), *The development of prosocial behavior* (pp. 251–278). New York: Academic Press.

Katz, R. L. (1963). *Empathy: Its nature and uses.* New York: Free Press.

Kernberg, O. F. (1965). Notes on countertransference. *Journal of the American Psychoanalytic Association, 13,* 38–56.

Kernberg, O. F. (1975). *Borderline conditions and pathological narcissism.* New York: Jason Aronson.

Kernberg, O. F. (1996). A psychoanalytic theory of personality disorders. In J. F. Clarkin & M. F. Lenzenweger (Eds.), *Major theories of personality disorders* (pp. 106–140). New York: Guilford Press.

Kernberg, O. F., Selzer, M. A., Koenigsberg, H. W., Carr, A. C., & Appelbaum, A. H. (1989). *Psychodynamic psychotherapy of borderline patients.* New York: Basic Books.

Kirouac, G., & Doré, F. Y. (1983). Accuracy and latency of judgment of facial expressions of emotions. *Perceptual and Motor Skills, 57,* 683–686.

Kirouac, G., & Doré, F. Y. (1984). Judgment of facial expressions of emotion as a function of exposure time. *Perceptual and Motor Skills, 59,* 147–150.

Krause, R., Steimer-Krause, E., Merten, J., & Burkhard, U. (1998). Dyadic interaction regulation, emotion, and psychopathology. In W. F. J. Flack & J. D. Laird (Eds.), *Emotions in psychopathology: Theory and research* (pp. 70–80). New York: Oxford University Press.

Levenson, R. W. (1996). Biological substrates of empathy and facial modulation of emotion: Two facets of the scientific legacy of John Lanzetta. *Motivation and Emotion, 20,* 185–204.

Levenson, R. W., Carstensen, L. L., Friesen, W. V., & Ekman, P. (1991). Emotion, physiology, and expression in old age. *Psychology and Aging, 6,* 28–35.

Levenson, R. W., & Ekman, P. (2002). Difficulty does not account for emotion-specific heart rate changes in the directed facial action task. *Psychophysiology, 39,* 397–405.

Levenson, R. W., Ekman, P., & Friesen, W. V. (1990). Voluntary facial action generates emotion-specific autonomic nervous system activity. *Psychophysiology, 27,* 363–384.

Leventhal, H., & Scherer, K. (1987). The relationship of emotion to cognition: A functional approach to a semantic controversy. *Cognition and Emotion, 1,* 3–28.

Lipps, T. (1907). Das Wissen von fremden Ichen [The knowledge of other selves]. In T. Lipps (Ed.), *Psychologische Untersuchungen Vol. 1: Bewußtsein und Gegenstände* (Vol. 1, pp. 694–722). Leipzig, Germany: W. Engelmann.

Luborsky, L., & Crits-Cristoph, P. (1990). *Understanding transference: The core conflictual relationship method.* New York: Basic Books.

Magai, C., & Hunziker, J. (1998). "To bedlam and part way back": Discrete emotions theory and borderline symptoms. In W. F. Flack & J. D. Laird (Eds.), *Emotions in psychopathology: Theory and research* (pp. 380–393). New York: Oxford University Press.

Manstead, A. S. R. (1988). The role of facial movement in emotion. In H. L. Wagner (Ed.), *Social psychophysiology: Theory and clinical application* (pp. 105–129). Chichester, England: Wiley.

Manstead, A. S. R., & Fischer, A. H. (2001). Social appraisal: The social world as object of and influence on appraisal processes. In K. R. Scherer, A. Schorr, & T. Johnstone (Eds.), *Appraisal processes in emotion: Theory, methods, research* (pp. 221–232). New York: Oxford University Press.

Matsumoto, D. (1987). The role of facial response in the experience of emotion: More methodological problems and a meta-analysis. *Journal of Personality and Social Psychology, 52,* 759–768.

McHugo, G. J., Lanzetta, J. T., Sullivan, D. G., Masters, R. D., & Englis, B. G. (1985). Emotional reactions to a political leader's expressive displays. *Journal of Personality and Social Psychology, 49,* 1513–1529.

McIntosh, D. N. (1996). Facial feedback hypotheses: Evidence, implications, and directions. *Motivation and Emotion, 20,* 121–147.

Meltzoff, A. N., & Moore, M. K. (1977). Imitation of facial and manual gestures by human neonates. *Science, 198*(4312), 74–78.

Miller, R. E., Banks, J. H. J., & Ogawa, N. (1964). Role of facial expression in "cooperative-avoidance conditioning" in monkeys. *Journal of Abnormal and Social Psychology, 67,* 24–30.

Morris, J. S., Öhman, A., & Dolan, R. J. (1998). Conscious and unconscious emotional learning in the human amygdala. *Nature, 393*, 467–470.

Ogden, T. H. (1979). On projective identification. *International Journal of Psycho-Analysis, 60*, 357–373.

Oster, H., Hegley, D., & Nagel, L. (1992). Adult judgments and fine-grained analysis of infant facial expressions: Testing the validity of a priori coding formulas. *Developmental Psychology, 28*, 1115–1131.

Parkinson, B. (2001). Putting appraisal in context. In K. R. Scherer, A. Schorr, & T. Johnstone (Eds.), *Appraisal processes in emotion: Theory, methods, research* (pp. 173–186). New York: Oxford University Press.

Parr, L. A. (1999, March 26–27). *Emotional communication: A chimpanzee's perspective.* Paper presented at the Emory Cognition and Development Project Symposium on Emotion in Communication, Emory University, Atlanta, GA.

Parr, L. A., Hopkins, W. D., & de Waal, F. B. M. (1998). The perception of facial expressions in chimpanzees (*Pan troglodytes*). *Evolution in Communication, 2*, 1–23.

Parra, C., Esteves, F., Flykt, A., & Öhman, A. (1997). Pavlovian conditioning to social stimuli: Backward masking and the dissociation of implicit and explicit cognitive processes. *European Psychologist, 2*, 106–117.

Patterson, M. L. (1995). Invited article: A parallel process model of nonverbal communication. *Journal of Nonverbal Behavior, 19*, 3–29.

Patterson, M. L. (1999). The evolution of a parallel process model of nonverbal communication. In P. Philippot, R. S. Feldman, & E. J. Coats (Eds.), *The social context of nonverbal behavior* (pp. 317–347). New York: Cambridge University Press.

Patterson, M. L., Foster, J. L., & Bellmer, C. D. (2001). Another look at accuracy and confidence in social judgments. *Journal of Nonverbal Behavior, 25*, 207–219.

Pigman, G. W. (1995). Freud and the history of empathy. *International Journal of Psychoanalysis, 76*, 237–256.

Plutchik, R. (1998). Emotions, diagnoses and ego defenses: A psychoevolutionary perspective. In W. F. Flack & J. D. Laird (Eds.), *Emotions in psychopathology: Theory and research* (pp. 367–379). New York: Oxford University Press.

Racker, H. (1968). *Transference and countertransference.* New York: International Universities Press.

Reik, T. (1948). *Listening with the third ear: The inner experience of a psychoanalyst.* New York: Farrar, Strauss.

Rinn, W. E. (1991). Neuropsychology of facial expression. In R. S. Feldman & B. Rimé (Eds.), *Fundamentals of nonverbal behavior* (pp. 3–30). Cambridge, England: Cambridge University Press.

Rizzolatti, G., & Arbib, M. A. (1998). Language within our grasp. *Trends in Neurosciences, 21*, 188–194.

Rochat, P., & Striano, T. (1999). Social-cognitive development in the first year. In P. Rochat (Ed.), *Early social cognition* (pp. 3–31). Mahwah, NJ: Erlbaum.

Russell, J. A. (1994). Is there universal recognition of emotion from facial expressions? A review of the cross-cultural studies. *Psychological Bulletin, 115*, 102–141.

Russell, J. A. (1997). Reading emotions from and into faces: Resurrecting a dimensional-contextual perspective. In J. A. Russell & J. M. Fernández-Dols (Eds.), *The psychology of facial expression* (pp. 295–320). Cambridge, England: Cambridge University Press.

Russell, J. A., & Fernández-Dols, J. M. (Eds.). (1997). *The psychology of facial expression.* Cambridge, England: Cambridge University Press.

Sandler, J. (Ed.). (1987). *Projection, identification, projective identification.* Madison, CT: International Universities Press.

Sayette, M. A., Cohn, J. F., Wertz, J. M., Perrott, M. A., & Parrott, D. J. (2001). A psychometric evaluation of the Facial Action Coding System for assessing spontaneous expression. *Journal of Nonverbal Behavior, 25,* 167–185.

Scherer, K. R. (1992). What does a facial expression express? In K. T. Strongman (Ed.), *International review of studies on emotion* (Vol. 2, pp. 139–165). New York: Wiley.

Scherer, K. R. (1993). Neuroscience projections to current debates in emotion psychology. *Cognition and Emotion, 7,* 1–41.

Scherer, K. R., Schorr, A., & Johnstone, T. (Eds.). (2001). *Appraisal processes in emotion: Theory, methods, research.* New York: Oxford University Press.

Smith, C. A. (1989). Dimensions of appraisal and physiological response in emotion. *Journal of Personality and Social Psychology, 56,* 339–353.

Smith, C. A. (1993). Evaluations of what's at stake and what I can do. In B. C. Lowe & S. E. Kahn (Eds.), *Women, work, and coping: A multidisciplinary approach to work place stress* (pp. 238–265). Montreal, Canada: McGill-Queen's Press.

Smith, C. A., McHugo, G. J., & Kappas, A. (1996). Epilogue: Overarching themes and enduring contributions of the Lanzetta Research. *Motivation and Emotion, 20,* 237–253.

Smith, C. A., & Scott, H. S. (1997). A componential approach to the meaning of facial expressions. In J. A. Russell & J.-M. Fernández Dols (Eds.), *New directions in the study of facial expression* (pp. 229–254). Cambridge, England: Cambridge University Press.

Sorce, J. F., Emde, R. N., Campos, J., & Klinnert, M. D. (1985). Maternal emotional signalling: Its effects on the visual cliff behavior of 1-year-olds. *Developmental Psychology, 21,* 195–200.

Strack, F., Martin, L. L., & Stepper, S. (1988). Inhibiting and facilitating conditions of the human smile: A nonobtrusive test of the facial feedback hypothesis. *Journal of Personality and Social Psychology, 54,* 778–777.

Tarabulsy, G. M., Tessier, R., & Kappas, A. (1996). Contingency detection and the contingent organization of behavior in interactions: Implications for socioemotional development in infancy. *Psychological Bulletin, 120,* 25–41.

Tassinary, L. G., & Caciiopo, J. T. (1992). Unobservable facial actions and emotion. *Psychological Science, 3,* 28–33.

Timmers, M., Fischer, A. H., & Manstead, A. S. R. (1998). Gender differences in motives for regulating emotions. *Personality and Social Psychology Bulletin, 24,* 974–985.

Tourangeau, R., & Ellsworth, P. C. (1979). The role of facial response in the experience of emotion. *Journal of Personality and Social Psychology, 37,* 1519–1531.

Wallbott, H. G. (1991). Recognition of emotion from facial expression via imitation? Some indirect evidence for an old theory. *British Journal of Social Psychology, 30,* 207–219.

Way, B. M., & Masters, R. D. (1996). Political attitudes: Interactions of cognition and affect. *Motivation and Emotion, 20,* 205–236.

Westen, D. (1998). Affect regulation and psychopathology: Applications to depression and borderline personality disorder. In W. F. Flack & J. D. Laird (Eds.), *Emotions in psychopathology: Theory and research* (pp. 394–406). New York: Oxford University Press.

Winnicott, D. W. (1949). Hate in the countertransference. *International Journal of Psycho-analysis, 30,* 69–74.

4

Changes in Nonverbal Behavior During the Development of Therapeutic Relationships

LINDA TICKLE-DEGNEN AND ELIZABETH GAVETT

To achieve the goals of therapy, therapist and client bond together through attitude, emotion, and action. From Freud's (1914/1924) early theorizing on transference and rapport, to client-centered conceptions of the curative aspects of therapist interpersonal attitudes and behaviors (Rogers, 1957), to interactional models of counseling (Claiborn & Lichtenberg, 1989; Tracey, 1993) and developments in the specification of the therapeutic alliance (Andrusyna, Tang, DeRubeis, & Luborsky, 2001; Gelso & Carter, 1985; Horvath & Luborsky, 1993; Luborsky, 1994), it has become increasingly clear that at least two types of bond characterize successful therapeutic relationships. These types of bond are rapport and the working alliance.[1] Rapport is formed as therapist and client grow to like one another, and the client experiences the therapist as genuinely warm, understanding, and supportive. The working alliance is formed as the therapist and client collaborate with one another to achieve a common goal, and both experience a sense of shared responsibility for the work on therapeutic tasks involved in achieving that goal.

Evidence suggests that the critical development of the two types of bond often is achieved early in therapy. Self-reported feelings of rapport and working alliance measured in the third to seventh sessions have been found to be predictive of the speed of client improvement (Svartberg, Seltzer, & Stiles, 1998) and of therapy outcome months later (Horvath 2001; Martin, Garske, & Davis, 2000). Beyond this evidence, very little is known about the bonding process, particularly about changes in behavior indicative of this process. The small amount of research that has explored behavior has focused on speech content rather than nonverbal behavior, despite the known phylogenetic and ontogenetic primacy of nonverbal behavior in the establishment of affiliative and cooperative human relations (Segerstråle & Molnár, 1997). To understand better how successful and unsuccessful therapeutic relationships develop, there must be more research about changes in both the nonverbal and the verbal behavior of therapists and their clients.

The primary purpose of this chapter is to propose a model that can organize previous research findings and guide future investigations about the role of nonverbal behavior in the development of therapeutic relationships. The chapter has four sections. The first section specifies three nonverbal components of rapport and the working alliance. The second section describes a model of how these three components change as the therapeutic relationship develops. The third section gives an example of how this model of change can be applied to the study of therapeutic dyads. We report the findings of a study of six speech and language therapy dyads over the course of eight weekly therapy sessions. The fourth section addresses the use of the three-period model in clinical research and practice.

Nonverbal Behavior Signs of Rapport and the Working Alliance

The research on nonverbal behavior and rapport suggests that there are three basic nonverbal components of rapport, regardless of type of relationship: attentiveness, positivity-negativity, and coordination (see Tickle-Degnen & Rosenthal, 1990, 1992, for a review).[2] First, rapport is marked by the degree to which individuals in an interaction have focused attention on one another. This attentiveness, indicated by the position and orientation of the sensory receptors—eyes, ears, and body—enables individuals to receive information from one another and signals readiness and interest in receiving this information.

Second, rapport is marked by the degree to which individuals are responding positively and negatively to one another. Positive behaviors such as smiling and moving closer to another, even when within adequate range to receive information from the other, signal enjoyment, liking, and, minimally, a readiness to do no harm. Alternatively, negative behaviors such as disgust and hostility expressions signal dislike and readiness to hurt the other person, at least emotionally.

Third, rapport is marked by the degree to which the individuals coordinate their behavior with one another. Coordination involves rapid, primarily unconscious, processes of interpersonal influence and adaptation (Burgoon, Stern, & Dillman, 1995; Cappella, 1996; Chartrand & Bargh, 1999) and may result in the convergence of individuals' thoughts or emotions (Hatfield, Cacioppo, & Rapson, 1994). It is indicated by similarity in behavior, such as matched leg and arm positions, or by the synchronized timing and rhythm of behavior, such as almost simultaneous shifts in leg and arm positions.

Attentiveness, positivity-negativity, and coordination can be conceptualized as nonverbal components of the working alliance as well as rapport. Table 4.1 demonstrates how nonverbal behavior morphology and signal meaning would vary across the two types of bonds. For rapport, nonverbal behavior is interpersonally focused. It indicates the readiness to receive information about the other's identity, the evaluative response to interaction with the other, and the mutual influence and adaptation of each person in relation to their identities, interpersonal thoughts, and emotions. For the working alliance, nonverbal behavior is task focused, indicating processes underlying the achievement of task goals (Patterson, 1983). Attentiveness behavior indicates readiness to receive information relative to performing and completing a task, positivity and negativity behavior indicate a response to task performance and mastery, and coordination indicates the mutual influence and adaptation of each person in relation to performing the task.

Tasks can be internally or externally focused, and, as summarized in Table 4.1, the nonverbal behavior associated with the working alliance will have different forms (or morphology) during these two types of tasks. Internally focused tasks require the members of a dyad to make face-to-face contact to exchange information. These types of tasks occur commonly in verbally mediated therapies, such as counseling and speech therapy. They also occur in close relationships, as when spouses are having a conversation to try to solve a family problem or among coworkers during business meetings. Externally focused tasks require the members of the dyad to pay attention to objects and stimuli outside the interpersonal interaction. These types of tasks occur commonly in therapies that use objects, manual activities, or physical exercise, such as play therapy and physical rehabilitation. They also occur during human relations in education, sports, and manual occupation settings.

Table 4.1 shows that the morphology of behavior associated with the working alliance is highly similar to that for rapport, especially during internally focused tasks when there is face-to-face contact. Although the behavior is highly similar, the meaning of the signal differs. When people are attentive to one another to find out about one another's interpersonal feelings, their behavior is related to rapport. When they are attentive to find out technical or task-related information, their behavior is related to the working alliance. Similarly, positivity-negativity behavior that is a response to the other's personhood is a signal of rapport, while the morphologically similar behavior that occurs in response to a particular task is a signal of the working alliance.

Bänninger-Huber (1992) used Ekman and Friesen's (1978) Facial Action Coding System to examine smiles and other behavior in one brief moment-to-moment sequence of interaction during a psychoanalytic therapy session. Her description exemplifies the complexity of distinguishing positivity-negativity behavior that signals rapport from that which signals the

Table 4.1 Morphology and and Signal Meaning of Nonverbal Behavior Components of Rapport and the Working Alliance

Nonverbal Behavior	Rapport	Working Alliance	
		Internally Focused Task: Task performance requires information from persons in dyad	Externally Focused Task: Task performance requires information from environment external to dyad
	Knowledge about each other's identity requires information from persons in dyad		
Attentiveness			
Morphology	Physical orientation of sense organs to receive information from person in dyad	Physical orientation of sense organs to receive information from person in dyad	Physical orientation of sense organs to receive information from environment external to persons in dyad
Meaning	Signals reception of information about who other person is a readiness to send information about self to other person	Signals reception of task information from other person and readiness to send task information to other person	Signals reception of task information from external source
Positivity-negativity			
Morphology	Expressions of positive and negative emotions	Expressions of positive and negative emotions during task performance	Expressions of positive and negative emotions during task performance
Meaning	Signals emotional response to other person	Signals emotional response to task performance	Signals emotional response to task performance
Coordination			
Morphology	Similarity and timing of the dyad members' behavior	Similarity and timing of the dyad members' behavior during task performance	Similarity and timing of the dyad members' behavior during the task performance
Meaning	Signals degree of mutual influence and adaptation in relation to personal identities	Signals degree of mutual influence and adaptation of persons in relation to task	Signals degree of mutual influence and adaptation of persons and environment in relation to task

working alliance in internally focused tasks. First, in the interaction sequence, the client produced a feigned smile that Bänninger-Huber interpreted as an indication of a desire to be understood and accepted by the therapist (rapport). Next, the therapist produced a miserable smile that appeared to indicate a mix of empathy for the client (rapport) as well as an attempt to control the emotional course of the sequence (working alliance). Finally, both demonstrated genuine smiles, suggesting they were satisfied with the outcomes of successfully dealing with the client's negative emotions (working alliance). A transition from an internally to an externally focused task would have occurred if the therapist and client had finished their session by pulling out and looking over their calendars to confirm the next appointment date. The working alliance would have been demonstrated by the simultaneous focus of their visual attention on their separate calendars.[3]

Changes in Nonverbal Behavior During the Development of Rapport and the Working Alliance

What the example from Bänninger-Huber (1992) demonstrates is that the role of nonverbal behavior in the development of therapeutic relationships is best understood through the simultaneous mapping of two parameters of change: (a) changes in the morphology and patterning of nonverbal behavior and (b) changes in the signal meaning and relationship function of the behavior. This section describes a model that supports simultaneous mapping of these parameters of change. Furthermore, the model can be applied to therapeutic tasks that are either internally or externally focused.

It is generally agreed that the development of rapport is a prerequisite for the development of a working alliance (Gelso & Carter, 1985; Horvath & Luborsky, 1993). Therapist and client must first have a basic understanding of the other as a person, trust one another, and value the identities proffered before they start to work as an effective functioning unit to achieve the goals of therapy. Given this premise, we divide the time course of the development of the therapeutic relationship into three periods that represent the primary signal meanings or functions of nonverbal behavior extant in each period: the development of rapport, the development of the working alliance, and the maintenance of a working relationship. Table 4.2 summarizes the functions of nonverbal behavior across the three periods. We recognize that relationship is emergent from transactions between individuals, and patterns of change can be highly idiosyncratic and fluid in many respects (Altman, 1993; Baxter & Montgomery, 1997). Nonetheless, the delineation of periods of change is useful for guiding the description and study of that change.

In the first relationship period, nonverbal behavior provides stronger signals relevant to rapport than the working alliance. In the second period, nonverbal behavior provides equally strong signals for both types of bonds.

Table 4.2 Functions of Nonverbal Behavior Across Three Periods of Relationship

	Relationship Period		
Nonverbal Behavior	1, Development of Rapport	2, Development of the Working Alliance	3, Ongoing Working Relationship
Attentiveness	Gather information about one another	Learn the tasks of therapy	Regulate change via the gathering of information
Positivity and negativity	Display cooperative intent and friendliness	Express emotion in support of and response to task mastery	Regulate change via emotions
Coordination	Regulate and influence interpersonal involvement	Develop a working relational culture	Regualte change via inteprersonal influence and adaptation processes

In the third period, signal strength may cycle or vary as therapist and client work to maintain their relationship through the difficult challenges that confront them. Behavior in all periods is hypothesized to signal the status of the therapeutic alliance (defined as the strength of the rapport and working alliance bonds) and to function as a support or impediment to the development of the alliance.

To support the model, we draw on a broad base of relationship literature, encompassing therapy relationships (primarily those in psychotherapy, but also those in medicine and rehabilitation) and close relationships (parent-child, friendship, and marriage). The literature on therapy relationships is informative about bonding processes when individuals have an asymmetric status relative to one another, their relationship is expected to be time and location limited, and one individual receives the other's services for payment. One limitation of this body of literature is that it has tended to be one sided rather than relational in its focus, studying either the therapist or the client, and focused more on outcomes than process.

The literature on close relationships is informative because researchers in this area have tended, especially recently, to study the dyad as a relational unit and have focused on change and stability processes involved in relationship formation and maintenance. The application of the literature on close relationships to the understanding of therapeutic relationships is predicated on the view that (a) there are some overlapping features between the two types of relationship, such as emotional intensity and shared experience (Derlega, McIntyre, Winstead, & Morrow, 2001; Winstead & Derlega, 1994); (b) individuals' interactional patterns in therapy were learned in close relationships (Safran, Crocker, McMain, & Murray, 1990; Tracey, 1993); and (c) human relationships of all types share fundamental nonverbal processes of affiliation and cooperation.

First Period: The Development of Rapport

Nonverbal behavior serves many functions in the first encounters that people have with one another (Patterson, 1983). Three functions are central to the establishment of rapport: gathering information about one another, displaying cooperative intent and friendliness, and regulating and influencing interpersonal involvement.

Attentiveness Behavior: Gathering Information
About One Another

In the first encounter, the paths of separate individuals with separate histories are just now crossing. The kind of knowledge that they have of one another is based on presupposition from the sparse identity information that each holds of the other. They know their roles, "therapist" and "client," and have sets of expectations, overlapping or not, about which behaviors and goals are appropriate for these roles. The problem with this information is that it is largely conjecture and minimally experience based. Therefore, during the first encounter, a primary function of communication is to gather experience-based information about one another's identities. People learn information through interacting with one another very quickly, within the first minute of the encounter (Ambady, Bernieri, & Richeson, 2000).

One means by which people so rapidly gather information is by vigilantly attending, through visual and auditory regard, to cues of identity. This vigilance at a first encounter may have its roots in our phylogenetic past. When animals encounter one another at a distance, their first behavior is sensory attentiveness. They gather information and cautiously make their movements while assuming protective positioning, like a crouch (Darwin 1872/1965). In humans, there appear to be similar information-gathering stances. A client who views the therapist as a potential source of serious personal benefit or harm may be particularly vigilant (DiMatteo, Prince, & Hays, 1986). The client is seeking information to answer the question, Is this person someone who is kind, who understands me, who I can trust, with whom I can work, and who can help me? The therapist, on the other hand, may be vigilant not so much out of personal benefit or threat as out of the service-based role of gathering information about the client's identity particularly related to a presenting problem (Schindler, Hohenberger-Sieber, & Hahlweg, 1989). The therapist seeks to answer the question, Is this person someone who I can value, who I can understand, who will trust me, with whom I can work, and who I can help?

Positivity and Negativity Behavior: Displaying Cooperative Intent and Friendliness

The maintenance of an atmosphere of friendliness is highly important in this exchange of information. Again, roots of the management of friendly, positive behavior appear to be found in our phylogenetic past. According to a biological evolutionary perspective, all relationships that require mutual cooperation to achieve beneficial outcomes for individuals begin with bidirectional signals of intent to do no harm and to cooperate (Preuschoft & van Hooff, 1997). These signals are communicated very quickly through posturing and facial expressions.

The positivity behavior of first encounters is highly stereotypical and influenced by norms associated with politeness and social roles. Through polite friendly behaviors, people create smooth interaction and simultaneously offer their identities as valuable and likeable (Clark, Pataki, & Carver, 1996; DePaulo, 1992; Goffman, 1959). In early interactions, occupational therapists who express negativity openly have lower rapport with their colleagues and are rated less positively by their clinical supervisors than individuals who do not express negativity openly (Tickle-Degnen & Puccinelli,

1999). Even in the first encounters of psychotherapy, when it is appropriate for clients to disclose negative feelings (Winstead & Derlega, 1994), reciprocal friendly interaction usually occurs (Thompson, Hill, & Mahalik, 1991; Tracey, 1993). This reciprocal friendliness is thought to be fundamental for establishing therapeutic rapport (Tickle-Degnen & Rosenthal, 1992; Tracey, 1993).

The emphasis on normative displays and rule- or role-bound behavior may create a disjunction between feelings and behavior in the first encounter. This disjunction has been described as a difference in the manifest versus latent levels of the communicated messages (e.g., Tracey, 1993). At the manifest level, the therapist and client accept the overt, strategically managed friendly behavior as the message that is being communicated, implicitly recognizing the importance of accepting messages of cooperative intent at this early stage. Latent messages are covertly rather than overtly expressed, are difficult for uninformed observers to decode, and constitute the unique needs and interpersonal styles of the communicators. The client may feel anxiety yet attempt to manage its expression through a smile. To the sensitive observer, the latent message of anxiety may reveal itself in the morphology of a false smile (Ekman & Keltner, 1997). Later in the relationship, the therapist and client would start to communicate overtly about feelings such as anxiety or anger that were latent in the first encounters.

Coordination Behavior: Regulating and Influencing Interpersonal Involvement

Individuals' behaviors show matched patterning and mutual adaptation very rapidly within the first encounter regardless of whether the relationship is casual, close, or therapeutic (Cappella, 1981, 1996; Gilbert, 1993; Street, 1984). Parent-infant studies (Crown, Feldstein, Jasnow, Beebe, & Jaffe, 2001; Lester, Hoffman, & Brazelton, 1985; Papoušek & Papoušek, 1997) suggest that there are innate pressures for individuals to adapt their interaction patterns to one another for survival, information gathering, and synchronization of cooperative activity (Burgoon et al., 1995).

Researchers who study behavioral adaptation refer to the coordination process as having patterning that is tight and rigid versus loose and flexible (Burgoon et al., 1995; Cappella, 1996; Gottman, 1979; Warner, Malloy, Schneider, Knoth, & Wilder, 1987; Watzlawick, Bavelas, & Jackson, 1967). Although the construct of tightness of patterning (Bernieri & Rosenthal, 1991) is in a formative stage of specification, it may have important ramifications for understanding changes in nonverbal behavior over the development of relationships. Synchrony and some degree of tightness are necessary for effective communication and signify bonding (Bernieri, Reznick, & Rosenthal, 1988; Warner, 1992). The degree of tightness in adult-infant coordination has been found to predict infant attachment and cognition outcomes (Jaffe, Beebe, Feldstein, Crown, & Jasnow, 2001). Excessively tight coordination may be due to one or both persons' high degree of responsiveness to the other and may reflect an effort to overcome problematic interaction.

Studies of initial encounters among peers are supportive of this interpretation. For example, Honeycutt (1989) showed how an individual expecting to interact with an unfriendly stranger was more talkative during the encounter with that stranger than someone expecting to interact with a friendly stranger. LaFrance and Ickes (1981) found that posture sharing was negatively associated with rapport in a study of a first encounter among peers. They suggested that the postural sharing might have been indicative of effort to establish rapport rather than indicative of its actual establishment. Similarly, Cappella (1996) found that strangers were more likely to adapt their speech turn-taking to one another than were well-acquainted individuals, suggesting that there was a "hyperpoliteness" (p. 382) operating in initial encounters.

In psychotherapy, as in peer encounters, there appears to be an optimal level of coordination that forms the basis for effective interaction. For example, Kritzer and Valenti (1990) found that there was a sustained level of synchronized therapist-client movement from the beginning to the end of a first encounter with therapists who had been rated as interpersonally skilled. With therapists who had been rated less skilled, synchronization at the beginning of the encounter was equal to that of the dyads with the more skilled therapists, but it declined as the encounter progressed. The researchers did not attempt to determine whether synchronization was achieved by the therapist adapting to client behavior or by the client adapting to therapist behavior.

Lichtenberg et al. (1998) studied directionality of interpersonal influence during therapy. They calculated the degree to which client verbal behavior predicted subsequent therapist verbal behavior (a high prediction indicated that the therapist adapted to the client) versus the degree to which therapist behavior predicted subsequent client behavior (a high prediction indicated the client adapted to the therapist). Dyads with ultimately unsuccessful outcomes compared to those with successful outcomes were characterized by tighter coordination, with the therapist adapting more to the client than vice versa. Other research has shown this type of coordination to occur in the earliest encounters of therapy, mostly with maladjusted clients (Dietzel & Abeles, 1975; Tracey, 1993). One explanation for these findings is that therapists, because of their higher level of interpersonal skill, are more capable of adapting than are clients (Tracey, 1993). This explanation, however, has yet to be tested.

The Second Period: The Development of the Working Alliance

After the first encounter, individuals have a common, if short, shared history and have experience-based information about one another's identities and a sense of whether they will be able to cooperate. Their focus on dealing with the tasks and goals intensifies over the next few encounters while their rapport continues to develop.[4] Through a process of exploration, they learn together what exactly it is they are trying to accomplish and how they will guide their actions and manage their emotions to accomplish it. The task-related functions of nonverbal behavior in this second period are the following: learning the tasks of therapy, responding to task and success failure, and developing a working relational culture.

Attentiveness Behavior: Learning the Tasks of Therapy

The tasks of therapy that are internally focused (see Table 4.1) require therapist and client to learn how to focus attention on different channels of communication—the voice, face, body—to accurately interpret the meaning of one another's interpersonal behavior. Their empathic accuracy with one another should increase over time as each verifies with the other the validity of his or her interpretations (Marangoni, Garcia, Ickes, & Teng, 1995).

For example, a client may feel anxious when talking about a particular topic. The therapist may note this anxiety through the client's voice or bodily behavior and comment about it. Over time, the therapist may learn that it is more effective to focus most of the time on a client's bodily movement than facial expressions to learn about the client's anxiety. The client, on the other hand, will learn that dealing with unspoken anxiety is one of the tasks of therapy, and that certain types of therapist behavior indicate that the therapist is trying to ascertain whether the client is feeling anxious. Eventually, the client might say, "Yes, you're right, I am feeling anxious!" before the therapist says a word about the client's feelings. Just as has been shown to occur in marital couples (Noller, 1992; Thomas, Fletcher, & Lange, 1997), therapist and client have learned the idiosyncratic meaning of one another's behavior through the gradual training of their focus of attention.

Similarly, the tasks of therapy that are externally focused require therapist and client to learn how to attend to different features of the environment that are critical for task performance (Tickle-Degnen & Coster, 1995). For example, a therapist learns which toys effectively capture a child client's interest by watching the child's exploration around a playroom. The therapist may choose to support the child's skilled use of a particular toy by directing the child's attention to critical features. Speech, gaze direction, and pointing serve to draw the child's attention: "It makes noise if you press this button here." Attention-directing behavior occurs in any context in which an expert is coaching a novice in the successful completion of a task, whether the novice is an infant, child (Papoušek & Papoušek, 1997; Rogoff, 1990), or adult (Burke, 1986).

Positivity and Negativity Behavior:
Expressing Emotions in Support of
and Response to Task Mastery

With the fading of the social norm of friendliness and the need to create favorable impressions and the turning of the therapist's attention to a latent level of communication, affect may fluctuate more freely in this period than in the first encounters. Behavior may become more congruent with feelings. Nonetheless, expressions of warmth and personal intimacy continue to be important to the development of the therapeutic relationship. The client's developing sense of trust reduces anxiety (Ben Sira, 1988) that impedes task exploration (White, 1959) and effective problem solving (Lyubomirsky & Nolen-Hoeksema, 1995; Schwartz & Clore, 1996).

In dyads successfully building a working alliance, there would be genuine expressions of happiness when the client achieves a new insight, solves a problem, or learns a new skill. There would be expressions of reassurance seeking, frustration, or attempts to control negative emotions when the client struggles or fails during the performance of a therapeutic task. The genuine (Duchenne) smile may be a hallmark of successful performance in both internally and externally focused tasks that involve either children or adults (e.g., Bänninger-Huber, 1992; Schneider, 1997). It is likely that there are additional nonverbal markers of "good moments" in therapy, such as "a voice quality that is active, alive, energetic, fresh, spontaneous, and vibrant" (Mahrer & Nadler, 1986, p. 12).

Coordination Behavior: Developing a Working
Relational Culture

The shared experience of the client and therapist accrues over therapy sessions, and from this experience it is likely that a "relational culture" emerges (Wood, 1982). Montgomery's (1994) description of the emergence of a relational culture in close relationships is similar to what may happen in therapy: "The partners work out more and more ways of relating that are particularly effective for them and them alone" (p. 73). The difference between the relational cultures of therapy and close relationships is that the one in therapy is more task oriented. It is specifically a working relational culture, defined by tasks that are initiated, continued, and terminated solely to achieve the goal of improving the health and well-being of the client through the services provided by the therapist (Winstead & Derlega, 1994). Therapy has the asymmetrical character of a parent-child relationship rather than the symmetrical character of a friendship between peers.

Although the therapeutic relationship may remain asymmetrical in character throughout its course, there may be gradual reduction in this asymmetry over time. For example, there might be gradual lessening of the restriction that the client unilaterally discloses intimate information. The therapist may begin occasionally to disclose intimate information about his or her personal life, albeit within the constraints of ethical standards that are part of the working culture of therapy. Likewise, the tight coordination that may be created by the therapist conforming to the behavior of the client in the first period of the relationship may start to ease in the second period. The interaction may be perceived as less effortful and more comfortable.

Some therapeutic dyads may negotiate the path into a working consensus about the tasks and goals of therapy more easily than others do. The path might be easier when the therapist clearly articulates reasonable goals to the client and unambiguously and systematically offers or tries out tasks that have clear relevance to these goals. It is possible that therapists who perform their particular therapeutic technique more consistently are able to convey more clearly to the client how the client is to collaborate, which goals are to be achieved, and which tasks are to be used. Luborsky et al. (1985) found that the "purity" of therapists' application of techniques was positively associated with the alliance and predicted therapy outcomes. Although nonverbal behavior in relation to technical purity has not been investigated, purity might be indicated by low degrees of hesitation, consistent attentiveness patterns, and high degrees of expressed confidence.

The Third Period: The Ongoing Working Relationship

The hard work of therapy begins once a working bond exists. There have been recent advances in the understanding of the dynamic nature of stability in close relationships that clarify how relationships are sustained. These advances may help shed light on how therapeutic relationships are sustained until goals are reached. The character of interpersonal interaction over time appears to fluctuate in a cyclical manner in response to the dialectical needs of individuals to have intimate disclosure, affiliation, and collaboration on the one hand and to have privacy, solitude, and autonomy on the other (Altman, 1993; Baxter & Montgomery, 1997). In addition, people act in ways that can hurt their relationships: They ignore, get angry with, or misjudge one another. These interactive "errors" must be followed by "repairs," such as renewed attention, humor, or apologies if relationships are to survive or function in a healthy manner (Gottman, 1994; Tronick, 1990).

Engagement-disengagement cycles and error-repair processes may operate in therapy as they do in close relationships, but research in this area is only beginning. One primary difference between therapy and close relationships is that the therapist and client are more likely than close relationship partners to engage in metacommunication, that is, to communicate about these natural communication processes (Watzlawick et al., 1967). Furthermore, the therapist, unlike a spouse or a friend, may consciously and systematically use these processes to guide the client into a new insight, a higher level of maturity, or a new personhood (e.g., Safran et al., 1990).

The problem inherent in maintaining an ongoing relationship is that these processes involve forces that can weaken the relational bond and can lead to an unanticipated dissolution of the bond.

One formidable task of therapy during this period is to maintain a dynamic stability in the therapeutic relationship despite pressures of dissolution. The functions of nonverbal behavior during this period are the following: regulating change via the exchange of information, regulating change via emotions, and regulating change via interpersonal influence and adaptation processes.

Attentiveness Behavior: Regulating Change via the Exchange of Information

During the ongoing period of the therapeutic relationship, the client and therapist are focused on exchanging information during tasks designed to address the client's problems and limitations directly. To move the client forward toward therapeutic goals, these tasks challenge the client's identity, emotions, and abilities. One of the therapist's challenges is to manage the quality, timing, intensity, and duration of the exchange of information to encourage change in the client, yet not cause emotional, cognitive, or physical exhaustion and subsequent withdrawal from the tasks.

Research findings suggest that the more time spent in the direct exchange of information, the better the therapeutic process and outcomes. Henry, Schacht, and Strupp (1986) found better outcomes among psychotherapy clients who spent more time disclosing and less time "walling off" and avoiding than among clients who spent less time disclosing and more time avoiding. Ambady, Koo, Rosenthal, and Winograd (2002) found better health outcomes among geriatric clients whose physical therapists were less distancing in their behavior and more expressively engaged with the client. In a study of married couples and their therapists, de Roten, Darwish, Stern, Fivaz-Depeursinge, and Corboz-Warnery (1999) found that triads with the strongest self-reported alliances spent more time engaging with one another rather than disengaging, whereas those with the weakest alliances spent more time in the reverse pattern. Engagement was demonstrated through faces and bodies directed internally toward the center of the triad and disengagement through faces or bodies oriented away from one another.

There was a promising indication in the study by de Roten et al. (1999) that therapy researchers are starting to explore the sequential timing and cyclical nature of engagement processes within a session. The researchers tentatively found that the triads with the strongest alliances demonstrated a more predictable engagement-disengagement pattern than those with the weakest alliances. Those with the strongest alliances maintained a body formation of engagement over a relatively long period of time, then crossed over into a disengagement pattern for a short period of time, followed by a return to an engagement pattern. The weaker alliances showed less predictable patterns of sequence. These findings suggest that there are cycles of interpersonal attentiveness within psychotherapy sessions that are indicative of hard work just as there are cycles of attentiveness found in other types of effortful cognitive and externally focused tasks (e.g., Meadowcroft, 1996).

Research on close relationships suggests that there are engagement-disengagement cycles not only within encounters, but also across encounters over time. For example, VanLear (1991) found that the personal disclosures of individuals in new and long-term friendships and romantic relationships cycled between openness and closedness. The amplitude of cycles was higher, that is more extreme, in long-term than new relationships and in deteriorating than stable relationships. VanLear suggested that there may be a higher degree of revelation during the periods of openness, but no difference in restraint during the periods of closedness, in long-term compared to new relationships. In deteriorating compared to stable relationships, there may be greater candor regarding dissatisfaction during periods of openness and more guarded disclosures during periods of closedness.

It is unknown whether similar types of cycles would be found in therapeutic relationships and, if they were found, whether dialectical processes such as those found in close relationships were the basis for these cycles. Factors that make therapy a unique form of relationship would affect cyclical processes. These factors include the formalized periodicity of contact and noncontact built into the therapy appointment schedule, the unilateral disclosure of intimate information by the client, and the commitment to work on the client's rather than the therapist's problems.

Positivity and Negativity Behavior: Regulating Change via Emotions

Since individuals in a stable relationship feel that their bond to one another is relatively secure, they are likely to express their emotions in a genuine, unguarded manner. This genuineness enables intimacy to deepen. Yet certain forms of it can weaken the bond. In particular, open and unregulated negativity in the form of hostility, disgust, and belittlement, all of which indicate disparagement of the other's enduring attributes and identity, have been found in poorly functioning marriages (Gottman, 1979, 1994; Gottman & Levenson, 2002) and in therapeutic sessions that have poor outcomes (Henry et al., 1986). Negativity in the form of anger or sadness that is a reaction to a particular situation or a transitory behavior in the other appears to be less likely to weaken the bond.

It has been found in research on close relationships that individuals in stable relationships have many strategies for maintaining and repairing their bonds with one another. For example, they interrupt negative sequences of interaction by not reciprocating negativity and work to prevent or repair the damage of these sequences through expressions of affection and affiliation (Dindia & Baxter, 1987; Gottman, 1994; Guerrero, Jones, & Burgoon, 2000; Rusbult, Verette, Whitney, Slovik, & Lipkus, 1991; Stafford & Canary, 1991; Tronick, 1990).

In observational studies of therapy sessions, Safran et al. (1990; Safren & Muran, 2000) found an "alliance rupture and resolution" process in psychotherapy that is analogous to the error-repair process in close relationships. They defined an alliance rupture as an impairment or fluctuation in the strength of the alliance. It typically occurs when a client indirectly and passively expresses negative feelings toward the therapist, often through nonverbal behavior. For example, the client may withdraw from interaction or have a sarcastic tone of voice. To resolve the rupture successfully, the therapist usually metacommunicates with the client about the interaction and relationship issues underlying the client's feelings, empathizes with the client, and helps the client to directly express the negative feelings in a mature manner.

Ruptures could occur during either an internally or externally focused task. A client who has partial paralysis of his or her arm secondary to a stroke may experience repeated frustration in trying to grasp a cup during occupational therapy. The client may give up on the task, perceive the goal of being able to grasp an object as worthless, and call into question the therapist's expertise or the value of therapy. The therapist must note the building frustration expressed in the client's behavior and work with the client to repair the alliance rupture to continue rehabilitation.

Although negative emotionality events may have a higher probability of occurring past the earliest encounters of therapy, the evidence suggests that the overriding emotional tone of successful therapy is a positive one (Ambady et al., 2002; Thompson et al., 1991), just as it is in high-functioning close relationships (Gottman, 1994). There is conflicting evidence regarding the pattern of change in overall positivity over the course of therapy. Thompson et al. (1991) found no variation in verbal friendliness over time. However, Hentschel and Bijleveld (1995), who measured positivity dimensions of rapport and the working alliance from videotapes, found a gradual increase over time.

Coordination Behavior: Regulating Change via Interpersonal Influence and Adaptation Processes

There appears to be a reorganization of interpersonal coordination after the initial establishment of rapport and the working alliance. This reorganization is often characterized as interpersonal conflict (e.g., Horvath & Luborsky, 1993) or instability (Tracey, 1993). The evidence is inconsistent about the exact form this reorganization takes (see Mallinckrodt, 1997, for a review). For example, while some have found systematic changes in friendliness and dominance patterns of verbal coordination from earlier to later therapy sessions (e.g., Dietzel & Abelese, 1975; Tracey, 1993), others have not (e.g., Thompson et al., 1991). It is difficult to interpret the overall implications of these studies, however, because the measures of verbal behavior were different in every study, although all were based on complementarity models of interpersonal interaction (e.g., Strong et al., 1988).

It may be better to conceptualize reorganization as a multidimensional rather than unidimensional process. Tracey (1993) recognized this multidimensionality in his stage theory of therapeutic change; he theorized that coordination of positivity behavior would follow a different path than coordination of negativity behavior. This multidimensionality has been difficult to measure. Fortunately, there are signs that reliable and valid multidimensional methods are emerging.

Hentschel and Bijleveld (1995) conducted a particularly illuminating study of two cases, each consisting of nearly 30 treatment sessions. The study had several strengths not demonstrated in typical studies of change in relationship patterns over time. The authors analyzed videotapes rather than simply audiotapes or transcripts. Furthermore, they used validated measures of dimensions of rapport and the working alliance: the Penn Helping Alliance Scales (Alexander & Luborsky, 1986) and Therapeutic Alliance Rating Scales (Marziali, Marmar, & Krupnik, 1981). Finally, they applied time series modeling to the data to determine (a) dimensions of coordination found in each of the two cases and (b) how patterns of coordination measured in the different dimensions changed over time.

Two dimensions of coordination were found in each case. The first dimension was related to the working alliance. It involved the coordination of therapist intervention strategies (e.g., giving support or pushing the client) and client self-presentations and confidence reactions (e.g., separation of feeling and behavior, self-confidence, or resistance). In this dimension there was a "swinging" pattern over time, and based on our visual inspection of the graphed results, the swinging appears to have had the highest frequency between the 3rd and 15th sessions, especially in one of the dyads (i.e., the "Bernese" dyad).

The second dimension was related to rapport. It involved the coordination of therapist intervention strategies (e.g., giving support or not giving a critique) with client positive attitude, liking, and joint effort. The researchers found a gradual increase in this liking dimension over the entire course of therapy. The different shapes of the two trajectories suggest that reorganization of interpersonal coordination may have different temporal patterns dependent on the component of rapport or working alliance that is examined.

Summary of the Literature Regarding Changes in the Morphology and Function of Nonverbal Behavior Over Time

The literature on relationships suggests that, over time, attentiveness behavior in the therapeutic relationship transitions from indicating a focus on the interpersonal to task aspects of interaction. Over time, individuals fine-tune their focus of attention as they learn which features of their partners and the tasks require their attention. Stable relationships may show cycles of engagement and disengagement.

Positive and negative behavior may become more congruent with actual emotions and feelings over time. The expression of negative emotions is more likely once rapport is established. This expression has the potential of creating a rupture in the alliance. In stable relationships, signs of resolution follow signs of rupture.

With the initiation of a therapeutic relationship, the behavior of individuals may be tightly coordinated. Behavioral patterns at first influenced by the client may gradually give way to patterns influenced more by the therapist, particularly in dyads with the most skillfully conducted therapy. There may be a period of reorganization of interpersonal behavior as individuals in a stable relationship move to tasks that are challenging to both the therapist and client.

A Study of Nonverbal Behavior and the Development of Therapeutic Relationships

The three-period model accommodates and organizes findings from studies of a wide range of relationships because it is based on general dimensions of nonverbal behavior that are fundamental to all human interaction: Individuals attend, respond affectively, and adapt to one another. Furthermore, the temporal aspect of the model is based on a construct, the therapeutic alliance, that describes bonding functions and processes that underlie many types of task-oriented, collaborative human relationships. Given that there is very little direct empirical evidence for how nonverbal behavior changes during the development of therapeutic relationships, it is reasonable to conduct future research using constructs that are at the level of fundamental and general ("nonspecific") processes of human interaction. There is no question that therapy differs from other forms of relationship, that therapeutic relationships differ across discipline and subdiscipline, and that each therapeutic encounter is unique in some respect. It is highly likely that these differences would create unique patterns of nonverbal behavior on some level. Yet, at this formative stage of knowledge, there is a need for exploring and describing generalized patterns of behavior. Once there is some agreement that patterns can be measured validly and reliably across therapeutic contexts, tests of theories of specific and unique factors can be conducted.

In this spirit of exploring general patterns of nonverbal behavior across the development of therapeutic relationships, we conducted an observational study of novice speech and language therapists and their first clients. The primary question was whether the three-period model could be used to explain changes in patterns of nonverbal behavior across therapy sessions. The videotapes of six dyads were available for the first 8 of 12 scheduled weekly 45-min sessions. All therapists were female and received intense supervision during the period of the study. All clients were either elementary- or middle-school-aged children who were being treated for speech disorders (difficulty articulating different sounds) or language disorders (understanding and using language in everyday life). The tasks used to treat speech disorders tended to be internally focused because the therapist was doing skill training that often required the child to watch the therapist's face and mouth. The tasks used to treat language disorders involved internal focus (e.g., carrying on a conversation with the therapist) or external focus (e.g., reading and doing homework with the therapist).

After each session, each therapist completed self-report items associated with the therapeutic alliance, including ratings of rapport with the client (mutual enjoyment, interest in, and responsiveness to one another) and of feelings related to success during the session. The rating of success was used as an indirect measure of the dyad's working alliance.[5] Videoclips were taken from the beginning, middle, and end segments of each session and were shown to judges, who rated the behavior of each participant on items related to attentiveness and positivity. From these rated items, each therapist and client received an attentiveness score and a positivity score, ranging from low (0) to high (8). In addition, the "match" between therapist and client attentiveness was calculated by taking the absolute difference of the individual attentiveness scores of the two dyad members. Likewise, a match score for positivity behavior was also calculated.[6]

The Association Between Therapeutic Alliance and Nonverbal Behavior at Each Time

On examination of the graphs and basic descriptive analyses, it appeared that the first session was different from Sessions 2, 3, and 4, which appeared to be different from Sessions 5, 6, 7, and 8. Subsequent analyses continued to validate these three groupings of sessions into three periods and appeared to support the conclusion that there were changing functions of nonverbal behavior across these periods. Table 4.3 summarizes the valence and magnitude of the associations between nonverbal behavior and the therapists' ratings of rapport and success for each of the three periods. These associations appear to be consistent with the three-period model of change.

The pattern of associations in the first period suggests that nonverbal behavior was more indicative of rapport than therapeutic success. Rapport was higher in dyads in which both participants had low and matched degrees of attentiveness, yet higher levels of positivity. The participants were not highly engaged with one another but were friendly. Their behavior may have been reflective of an easy comfort with one another as they began

Table 4.3 Valence and Magnitude of the Associations Between Therapist-Client Nonverbal Behavior and Therapist Ratings of the Rapport and Therapeutic Success at Three Periods

	Period 1		Period 2		Period 3	
	Rapport	Success	Rapport	Success	Rapport	Success
Attentiveness						
Therapist	(– –)	0	(–)	(+)	(– –)	(–)
Client	(– –)	(– – –)	(–)	(–)	(+)	(++)
Match	(++)	0	(–)	(–)	(+++)	(+++)
Positivity						
Therapist	(++)	(+)	(+)	(+++)	(– –)	(– –)
Client	(+)	0	0	(+)	(–)	(– –)
Match	0	0	(+++)	(++)	(– – –)	(– –)

Note. N = 6 dyads. Because the sample size was small, the associations are merely suggestive. Period 1 = Session 1; Period 2 = Sessions 2–4; Period 3 = Sessions 5–8.
(+++) = large positive correlation ($r \geq .50$); (++) = moderate positive correlation ($.30 \geq r > .50$); (+) = small positive correlation ($.10 \geq r > .30$); 0 = no relationship ($-.10 > r > .10$); (–) = small negative correlation ($-.30 > r \geq -.10$); (– –) = moderate negative correlation ($-.50 > r \geq .30$); (– – –) = large ngative correlation ($r \leq -.50$).

therapy. Rapport was lower in dyads that had a higher, yet mismatched, level of attentiveness and lower levels of positivity. This pattern suggests that the participants were vigilant, but not necessarily in a mutually coordinated manner, perhaps suggestive of difficulty connecting to one another interpersonally.

The pattern of associations in the second period suggests that nonverbal behavior was equally indicative of rapport and success. Positivity, more than attentiveness, was a signal of the strength of the therapeutic alliance. Rapport and therapeutic success were higher in dyads that had higher levels of positivity behavior, particularly as expressed by the therapist, and in which therapist and client had matched levels of positivity. During this intense period of learning and exploration for the therapist and client, this higher and coordinated positivity would suggest that the therapist and client were mutually experiencing mastery. Rapport and therapeutic success were lower in dyads that had lower levels and unmatched positivity, suggesting less coordinated experience of mastery.

Moving from the second to the third period, there was a striking reversal in the valence of most of the associations between nonverbal behavior and the therapeutic alliance. In particular, client attentiveness and its match to therapist attentiveness were negative correlates of the alliance in the second period, albeit weak ones, yet they were strong positive correlates of the alliance in the third period. Furthermore, therapist positivity and its match to client positivity were strong positive correlates of the alliance in the second period and equally strong negative correlates in the third period. In the third period, clients were more attentive, yet less positive, indicating a serious attention to task in the higher alliance dyads. Therapists were more matched to the client's level of attentiveness in these dyads compared to the lower alliance dyads, yet less matched in positivity. Note the striking similarity between the lower alliance dyads in this third period with the higher alliance dyads in the second period. Perhaps the lower alliance dyads were taking longer to establish a therapeutic alliance than the higher alliance dyads that had moved on to serious, sustained therapeutic work.

Changes in Nonverbal Behavior Across Periods in Dyads with Secure and Insecure Alliances

The results shown in Table 4.3 describe differences between dyads at each time period. They do not show change as it occurred within the dyads across time. This section reports changes in nonverbal behavior within dyads that appeared to have secure alliances versus those that had insecure alliances. We begin by describing how dyads were categorized according to the strength of their alliances.

Although there were no client ratings of the therapeutic alliance in this study, an inspection of the data suggested, as others have found (Frieswyk et al., 1986; Horvath & Luborsky, 1993), that client involvement and affective response to therapy were fundamental to understanding the therapeutic alliance. Three types of dyads emerged in relation to client nonverbal attentiveness and positivity. Table 4.4 provides descriptive information about the three types of dyads: Insecure Alliance Type I, Insecure Alliance Type II, and Secure Alliance. The key distinguishing factor between the insecure and secure types of dyads was the degree of client attentiveness averaged across the entire eight sessions. The secure dyads ($n = 2$) had clients who were highly attentive and moderately positive in their behavior. The insecure dyads ($n = 4$) had clients who were less attentive. The insecure dyads were broken down further according to average client positivity behavior. The Type I dyads ($n = 2$) had clients whose behavior was low in positivity, and the Type II dyads ($n = 2$) had clients whose behavior was high in positivity.

There were other distinctions as well. Therapists in secure dyads demonstrated moderate levels of attentiveness and positivity and reported therapeutic alliances of high strength. Therapists in Type I insecure dyads demonstrated low levels of attentiveness and positivity and reported alliances of moderate strength. Therapists in Type II insecure dyads demonstrated high levels of attentiveness and positivity and reported alliances of relatively lower strength. Patterns of "tightness" of coordination, that is, the

Table 4.4 Description of Dyads According to Strength of Alliance

	Dyad Type		
	Insecure Alliance Type 1	Insecure Alliance Type II	Secure Alliance
Nonverbal attentiveness			
Therapist	Low	High	Moderate
Client	Low	Low	High
Match	Tight	Loose	Tight
Nonverbal positivity			
Therapist	Low	High	Moderate
Client	Low	High	Moderate
Match	Tight	Loose	Loose
Therapist ratings			
Rapport	Moderate	Low	High
Success	Moderate	Low	High
Client characteristics			
Gender	Male/female	Male/female	Male/female
Age	Middle school	Elementary	Elementary/middle
Disorder	Language	Language	Speech

degree of match between client and therapist behavior, also appeared to vary across the types of dyad.

Finally, the secure dyads were treating clients for speech disorders, and the insecure dyads were treating clients for language disorders. Clinical supervisors reported that novice therapists, like the ones in this study, often feel more confident learning to treat speech than language disorders. Treatment for speech disorders involves step-by-step behavioral procedures for changing clients' physical movements, and change in client skill is, at times, immediately observable. Treatment for language disorders, on the other hand, incorporates procedures that are not as easy to operationalize behaviorally; the emphasis is on changing client symbol systems, and change in client skill is often not easy to observe.

One speculation is that the strength of the alliance and nonverbal behavior patterns of these dyads were related to the types of tasks and challenges involved in the performance of the two types of therapy. On the other hand, there appeared to be qualitative differences in the friendliness and ease of interaction of individuals within secure compared to insecure dyads, with these differences seemingly unexplained by the type of therapy being con-

ducted. This observation is in line with the findings of some other researchers (e.g., Horvath & Symonds, 1991; Krupnik et al., 1996; Salvio, Beutler,
Wood, & Engle, 1992), who found therapeutic alliance to operate somewhat,
although not entirely, independently of specific therapeutic tasks and procedures used in various forms of psychotherapy.

Levels of client attentiveness and positivity were graphed across the
three relationship periods to determine if there were distinguishing temporal patterns among the three types of dyad. Figure 4.1 shows the trajectories
of client attentiveness across sessions. The most notable feature of the figure is the "bubble" shape formed by the trajectories. The clients started
with the same level of attentiveness in the first session, but then during the
second period varied considerably. In the third period, there was a convergence of the attentiveness of the clients. This increase in variance between
the dyads and then a decline was a consistent pattern across all measures,
but was most pronounced in client attentiveness.

Figure 4.2 shows a similar bubble shape for client positivity. However,
client positivity appears to be more varied across dyads and across all three
periods. The behavioral variance that occurred in the second period among
the dyads may have been due to differences in the ability of the therapist
and client to form a working alliance. By the eighth session, all dyads appeared to have achieved a relatively high level of client attentiveness, if not
equally high levels of client positivity.

Figures 4.3 and 4.4 show changes in the therapist-client match of attentiveness and positivity, respectively. The match of behavior in the insecure
dyads plunged in the second period and appeared to recover in the third
period. The match of behavior in the secure dyads, however, was relatively
high across the second period and plunged in the third period. Matched
behavior in the second period may have signaled that the secure dyads
were successfully achieving a working relational culture, and once into the
hard work of the third period, the need for explicit behavioral coordination
was no longer required in the secure dyads. It is possible that the therapists
in the secure dyads during the third period were actually disengaging a bit
from the client, allowing the client to exercise initiative and autonomy in
carrying out the therapeutic tasks.

Study Summary

What is informative about this study of speech and language therapists is
that there appears to be a systematic change of nonverbal behavior across
time that was related to the development of the therapeutic alliance. In
summary, the findings were as follows:

1. Nonverbal behavior in the first period appeared to signal rapport
   more than the working alliance. In the second and third periods,
   however, nonverbal behavior appeared to signal both rapport and

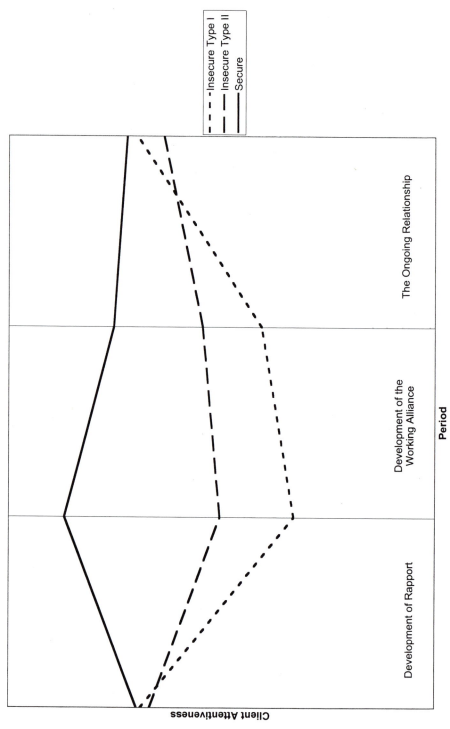

Period

Development of Rapport | Development of the Working Alliance | The Ongoing Relationship

Client Attentiveness

- - - - Insecure Type I
——— Insecure Type II
———— Secure

Fig. 4.1 Changes in client attentiveness over three periods of relationship for each of three types of dyad.

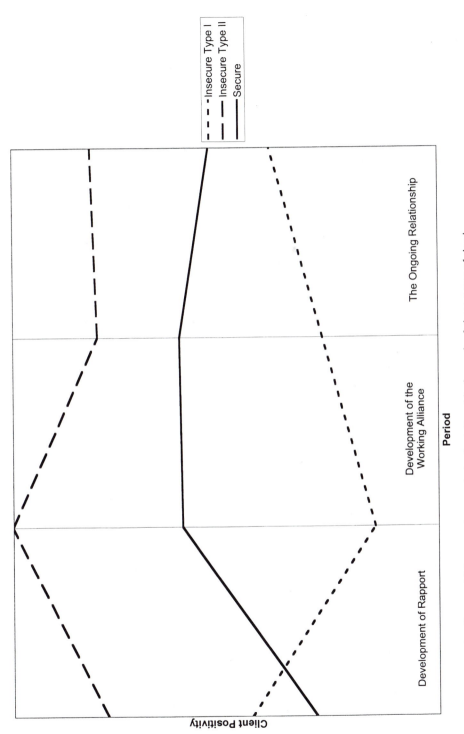

Fig. 4.2 Changes in client positivity over three periods of relationship for each of three types of dyad.

Legend:
- Insecure Type I
- Insecure Type II
- Secure

Y-axis: Client Positivity

X-axis: Period
- Development of Rapport
- Development of the Working Alliance
- The Ongoing Relationship

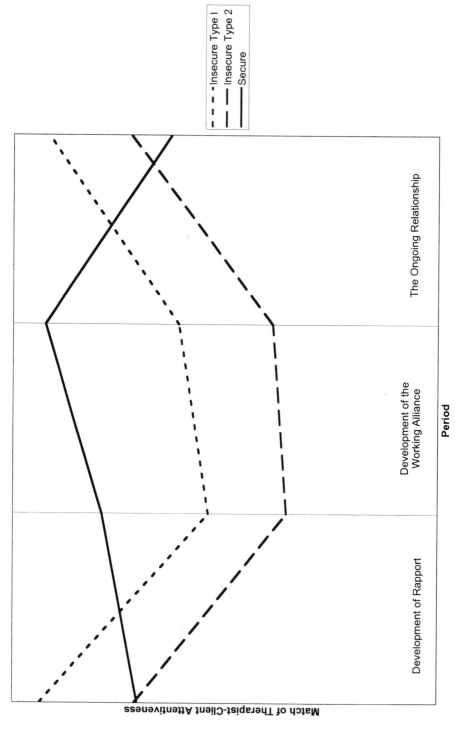

Fig. 4.3 Changes in match of therapist-client attentiveness over three periods of relationship for each of three types of dyad.

100

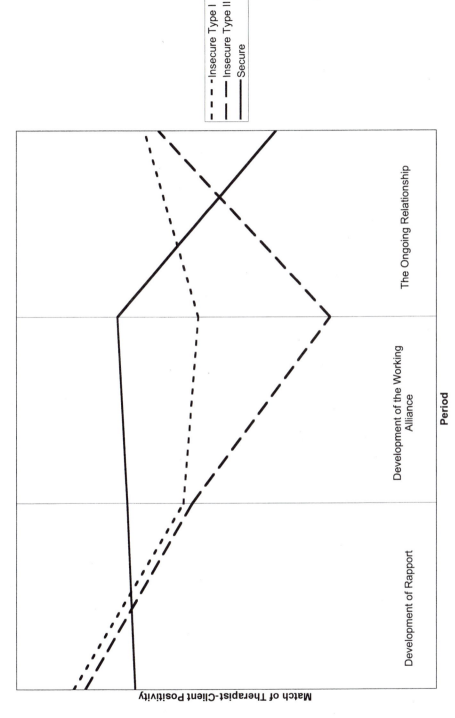

Fig. 4.4 Changes in match of therapist-client positivity over three relationship periods for each of three types of dyad.

the working alliance. In addition, the three types of nonverbal behavior appeared to capture important changes in the alliance.

2. The associations between nonverbal behavior and the therapeutic alliance were complex. Attentiveness, positivity, and coordination showed reversals of valence in their associations with the alliance ratings over time. This finding suggests that it is invalid to assume that attentiveness, positivity, and coordination are always positive correlates of the alliance.

3. During the middle period, levels of nonverbal behavior varied considerably across the dyads, more so than in the other two periods. This finding suggests that this period may be characterized by considerable exploration as individuals develop a relational culture that works best for their particular dyad. The third period appeared to be one of stabilization in the alliance. Since the final four sessions of therapy were not analyzed, it is not possible to determine whether this apparent stabilization continued, declined, decreased, or cycled.

This study was exploratory, descriptive, and limited in many respects. For example, like most studies of therapeutic change, the sample size was small, and the entire course of therapy was not examined. In addition, sequential and time series analyses could not be applied to the data because of the restricted sampling of nonverbal behavior. As a consequence, it was not possible to identify patterns of influence, particularly the degree to which therapists were adapting to the client and vice versa, nor was it possible to identify whether there were cyclical patterns. One other important limitation was that we did not simultaneously track changes in nonverbal behavior and changes in the contextual features of the interaction (e.g., whether the task was internally or externally focused at each clip). Such tracking would have given us more information about the meaning and function of nonverbal behavior over time.

Conclusion

The literature and study presented here suggest that the period model of the therapeutic alliance is a valid one. There appear to be systematic changes in behavior associated with the development of the alliance over time. There also appears to be a period of rapid change and variability in relationships. Study designs that are based on the assumption that the alliance is associated with a single linear path of change in nonverbal behavior may incorrectly conclude that nonverbal behavior does not demonstrate a systematic relationship to the alliance. The use of temporal designs and statistical methods for analyzing complex, dynamic, within-dyad interpersonal coordination will reduce the likelihood of invalid conclusions (Gottman, 1995; Hentschel & Bijleveld, 1995; Warner, 1998).

Despite methodological advances, the role of nonverbal behavior in the development of relationships may continue to be more difficult to study in therapeutic relationships than in close relationships. Compared to close relationships, therapeutic relationships are rarer, and they are more difficult to access because of a formalized system to protect the rights and privacy of clients. Even if access is gained, researchers must take precautions not to interfere with the therapy process or client rights. Videotaping, the best method for collecting nonverbal behavior data, may be too invasive in many therapeutic contexts.

As a result of these factors, it will continue to be important for knowledge development in the field of therapeutic relationships to be informed by knowledge development in the field of close relationships. This condition is not an unreasonable one given that human relations of all types share patterns of nonverbal behavior that appear to be derived from phylogenetic and ontogenetic origins.

The three-period model has potential clinical application beyond its use as a research tool. It may serve to sensitize therapists to the importance of their own and their clients' nonverbal behavior in the development of the therapeutic relationship. With this sensitivity, therapists are more likely to be able to track the strength of their therapeutic alliances, manage the interpersonal aspects of therapy with more skill, and act quickly to repair any ruptures that threaten the alliance.

Acknowledgments

We thank the student therapists, clients, and speech and language clinical supervisors of the Boston University Rehabilitation Services for participating in the study reported in this chapter. The study was funded by a Boston University Sargent College Accelerated Research Award granted to the first author.

Notes

1. The terms *rapport, working alliance*, and *therapeutic alliance* have been used in many different and overlapping ways in the therapeutic literature (Horvath & Luborsky, 1993). We chose to use rapport and working alliance for the lower-level constructs representing two types of bonds involved in a higher, more general construct, the therapeutic alliance. Rapport has been called the liking bond (Gelso & Carter, 1985) of the "real" (versus "unreal" transference) relationship, Type I signs of the helping alliance (Luborsky, 1994), and the therapeutic bond (Greenberg, Rice, & Elliot, 1993). The working alliance has been called the working bond (Gelso & Carter, 1985), Type II signs of the helping alliance (Luborsky, 1994), and task collaboration (Greenberg et al., 1993). A third type of bond is also often discussed, especially in the psychodynamic literature: the transference relationship or the unreal relationship. This third type of bond is not discussed here.

2. Tickle-Degnen and Rosenthal (1990, 1992) treated positive and negative behaviors as two poles of a single dimension. Here we treat these behaviors

as falling on separate yet related dimensions that have different interpersonal implications (DePaulo, 1992; Tracey, 1993; Watson, Clark, & Tellegen, 1988).

3. Individuals can shift rapidly from internal to external focus during the course of a single interpersonal interaction or be simultaneously internally and externally focused (as when people are listening to one another while visually attending to an external object). Furthermore, we have limited our description of rapport only to internally focused conditions, primarily because we believe it likely that most of rapport-related interaction in therapy is of this sort. However, it is possible for rapport to occur as an externally focused condition as well, for example, such as when a client comes to a session with photographs from a vacation with the intent of showing them to the therapist simply out of friendship and liking.

4. In our discussion, we describe therapy as consisting of at least several sessions about an hour long. The periods that we propose need not be delimited by number of sessions that have taken place, but rather can be thought of as shrinking or expanding based on the overall expected course of therapy. It is entirely possible that the length of time required to develop the first two periods of the therapeutic alliance is a function of (a) the length of time that the individuals anticipate being together, (b) the degree of bonding and intimacy required to achieve therapeutic goals, and (c) the complexity of the tasks and goals. Depending on these factors, Periods 1 and 2 theoretically could occur entirely within the first encounter or endure for several encounters. There has been little research, however, directed at understanding the time frame of the development of the therapeutic alliance based on these factors.

5. The study was designed primarily to study the rapport bond and not to require the child clients to evaluate their therapists. Therefore, more direct measures of the working alliance and ratings by the clients were not collected. It seemed reasonable to assume that the therapists' feelings of success were influenced by the engagement of the clients in the tasks of therapy and, therefore, were related to the working alliance.

6. Three to five clips, 15 s long, were taken from the beginning, middle, and end segments of each session. Clips were randomly placed in four master stimulus tapes and shown to different sets of approximately 10 judges each. Sound was turned off. The judges could see only the therapist or the client, and the judges made 8-point ratings on 10 scales after viewing each clip. Correlational and principal component analyses demonstrated that two components accounted for variation among the scales; subsequently, the items falling on each component were averaged to create attentiveness and positivity scores for each participant. The attentiveness score was created from the item attentive, and the following items, all reversed: withdrawn, lethargic, and distracted. The positivity score was created from the items playful, happy, animated, relaxed, stiff (reversed), and serious (reversed). Negative affective scales were not included in this study because of the low probability of these highly supervised sessions showing negative affectivity. The effective interrater reliability of the attentiveness score was .76 and of the positivity score was .82. Several types of coordination scores were calculated by comparing therapist and client attentiveness and positivity scores (e.g., correlations, difference scores, progressive change in difference scores within a session). Only the results from the absolute value of difference scores (reversed to become "match" variables) are presented

in this chapter because they were the ones most clearly correlated with therapist ratings of the alliance. In general, the higher degree of match, the "tighter" the coordination demonstrated in the other coordination scores.

References

Alexander, L. B., & Luborsky, L. (1986). The Penn Helping Alliance Scales. In L. S. Greenberg & W. M. Pinsof (Eds.), *The psychotherapeutic process: A research handbook* (pp. 325–366). New York: Guilford Press.

Altman, I. (1993). Dialectics, physical environments, and personal relationships. *Communication Monographs, 60,* 26–34.

Ambady, N., Bernieri, F. J., & Richeson, J. A. (2000). Toward a histology of social behavior: Judgmental accuracy from thin slices of the behavioral stream. *Advances in Experimental Social Psychology, 32* 201–271.

Ambady, N., Koo, J., Rosenthal, R., & Winograd, C. H. (2002). Physical therapists' nonverbal communication predicts geriatric patients' health outcomes. *Psychology & Aging, 17,* 443–452.

Andrusyna, T. P., Tang, T. Z., DeRubeis, R. J., & Luborsky, L. (2001). The factor structure of the Working Alliance Inventory in cognitive-behavioral therapy. *Journal of Psychotherapy Practice & Research, 10,* 173–178.

Bänninger-Huber, E. (1992). Prototypical affective microsequences in psychotherapeutic interaction. *Psychotherapy Research, 2,* 291–306.

Baxter, L. A., & Montgomery, B. M. (1997). Rethinking communication in personal relationships from a dialectical perspective. In S. Duck (Ed.), *Handbook of personal relationships* (2nd ed., pp. 305–350). New York: Wiley.

Ben-Sira, Z. (1988). Affective behavior and perceptions of health professionals. In D. S. Gochman (Ed.), *Health behavior* (pp. 305–317). New York: Plenum.

Bernieri, F. J., Reznick, J. S., & Rosenthal, R. (1988). Synchrony, pseudosynchrony, and dissynchrony: Measuring the entrainment process in mother-infant interactions. *Journal of Personality and Social Psychology, 54,* 243–253.

Bernieri, F. J., & Rosenthal, R. (1991). Interpersonal coordination: Behavior matching and interactional synchrony. In R. Feldman & R. Rime (Eds.), *Fundamentals of nonverbal behavior* (pp. 401–432). Cambridge, England: Cambridge University Press.

Burgoon, J. K., Stern, L. A., & Dillman, L. (1995). *Interpersonal adaptation: Dyadic interaction patterns.* Cambridge, England: Cambridge University Press.

Burke, J. (1986). Interacting plans in the accomplishment of a practical activity. In D. E. Ellis & W. A. Donahue (Eds.), *Contemporary issues in language and discourse processes* (pp. 203–222). Hillsdale, NJ: Erlbaum.

Cappella, J. N. (1981). Mutual influence in expressive behavior: Adult-adult and infant-adult dyadic interaction. *Psychological Bulletin, 89,* 101–132.

Cappella, J. N. (1996). Dynamic coordination of vocal and kinesic behavior in dyadic interaction: Methods, problems, and interpersonal outcomes. In J. H. Watt & C. A. VanLear (Eds.), *Dynamic patterns in communication processes* (pp. 353–386). Thousand Oaks, CA: Sage.

Chartrand, T. L., & Bargh, J. A. (1999). The chameleon effect: The perception-behavior link and social interaction. *Journal of Personality & Social Psychology, 76,* 893–910.

Claiborn, C. D., & Lichtenberg, J. W. (1989). Interactional counseling. *The Counseling Psychologist, 17,* 355–453.

Clark, M. S., Pataki, S. P., & Carver, V. H. (1996). Some thoughts and findings on self-presentation of emotions in relationships. In G. J. O. Fletcher & J. Fitness (Eds.), *Knowledge structures in close relationships: A social psychological approach* (pp. 247–274). Mahwah, NJ: Erlbaum.

Crown, C. L., Feldstein, S., Jasnow, M. D., Beebe, B., & Jaffe, J. (2001). The cross-modal coordination of interpersonal timing: Six-week-old infants' gaze with adults' vocal behavior. *Journal of Psycholinguistic Research, 30,* 1–23.

Darwin, C. (1965). *The expression of emotions in man and animals.* Chicago: University of Chicago Press. (Original work published 1872)

DePaulo, B. M. (1992). Nonverbal behavior and self-presentation. *Psychological Bulletin, 111,* 203–243.

Derlega, V. J., McIntyre, R., Winstead, B. A., & Morrow, G. (2001). A preliminary study of an attraction-barrier model of patients' commitment and responses to dissatisfaction in psychotherapy. *Psychotherapy: Theory, Research, Practice, Training, 38,* 283–296.

de Roten, Y., Darwish, J., Stern, D. J., Fivaz-Depeursinge, E., & Corboz-Warnery, A. (1999). Nonverbal communication and alliance in therapy: The body formation coding system. *Journal of Clinical Psychology, 55,* 425–438.

Dietzel, C. S., & Abeles, N. (1975). Client-therapist complementarity and therapeutic outcomes. *Journal of Counseling Psychology, 22,* 264–272.

DiMatteo, M. R., Prince, L. M., & Hays, R. (1986). Nonverbal communication in the medical context: The physician-patient relationship. In P. D. Blanck, R. Buck, & R. Rosenthal (Eds.), *Nonverbal communication in the clinical context* (pp. 74–98). University Park, PA: Pennsylvania State University Press.

Dindia, K., & Baxter, L. A. (1987). Strategies for maintaining and repairing marital relationships. *Journal of Social and Personal Relationships, 4,* 143–158.

Ekman, P., & Friesen, W. V. (1978). *Manual for the Facial Action Coding System.* Palo Alto, CA: Consulting Psychologists Press.

Ekman, P., & Keltner, D. (1997). Universal facial expressions of emotion: An old controversy and new findings. In U. Segerstråle & P. Molnár (Eds.), *Nonverbal communication: Where nature meets culture* (pp. 27–46). Mahwah, NJ: Erlbaum.

Freud, S. (1924). On the history of the psycho-analytic movement. In J. Riviere (Trans.), *Collected papers* (Vol. 1, pp.287–359). London: Hogarth. (Original work published 1914)

Frieswyk, S. H., Allen, J. G., Colson, D. B., Coyne, L., Gabbard, G. O., Horwitz, L., & Newsom, G. (1986). Therapeutic alliance: Its place as a process and outcome variable in dynamic therapeutic research. *Journal of Consulting and Clinical Psychology, 54,* 32–38.

Gelso, C. J., & Carter, J. A. (1985). The relationship in counseling and psychotherapy: Components, consequences, and theoretical antecedents. *The Counseling Psychologist, 13,* 155–243.

Gilbert, D. A. (1993). Reciprocity of involvement activities in client-nurse interactions. *Western Journal of Nursing Research, 15,* 674–689.

Goffman, E. (1959). *The presentation of self in everyday life.* Garden City, NY: Doubleday/Anchor.

Gottman, J. M. (1979). *Marital interactions: Experimental investigations.* New York: Academic.

Gottman, J. M. (1994). *What predicts divorce? The relationship between marital processes and marital outcomes* (pp. 409–440). Hillsdale, NJ: Erlbaum.

Gottman, J. M. (1995). *The analysis of change.* Mahwah, NJ: Erlbaum.

Gottman, J. M., & Levenson, R. W. (2002). A two-factor model for predicting when a couple will divorce: Exploratory analyses using 14-year longitudinal data. *Family Process, 41,* 83–96.

Greenberg, L. S., Rice, L. N., & Elliott, R. (1993). *Facilitating emotional change: The moment-by-moment process.* New York: Guilford Press.

Guerrero, L. K., Johnes, S. M., & Burgoon, J. K. (2000). Responses to nonverbal intimacy change in romantic dyads: Effects of behavioral valence and degree of behavioral change on nonverbal and verbal reactions. *Communication Monographs, 67,* 325–346.

Hatfield, E., Cacioppo, J. T., & Rapson, R. L. (1994). *Emotional contagion.* Paris: Cambridge University Press.

Henry, W. P., Schacht, T. E., & Strupp, H. H. (1986). Structural analysis of social behavior: Application to a study of interpersonal process in differential psychotherapeutic outcome. *Journal of Counseling and Clinical Psychology, 54,* 27–31.

Hentschel, U., & Bijleveld, C. C. J. H. (1995). It takes two to do therapy: On differential aspects in the formation of therapeutic alliance. *Psychotherapy Research, 5,* 22–32.

Honeycutt, J. M. (1989). Effects of preinteraction expectancies on interaction involvement and behavioral responses in initial interaction. *Journal of Nonverbal Behavior, 13,* 25–36.

Horvath, A. O. (2001). The alliance. *Psychotherapy: Theory, Research, Practice, Training, 38,* 365–372.

Horvath, A. O., & Luborsky, L. (1993). The role of the therapeutic alliance in psychotherapy. *Journal of Counseling and Clinical Psychology, 61,* 561–573.

Horvath, A. O., & Symonds, B. D. (1991). Relation between working alliance and outcome in psychotherapy: A meta-analysis. *Journal of Counseling Psychology, 38,* 139–149.

Jaffe, J., Beebe, B., Feldstein, S., Crown, C. L., & Jasnow, M. D. (2001). Rhythms of dialogue in infancy: Coordinated timing in development. *Monographs of the Society for Research in Child Development, 66,* vi–131.

Kritzer, R., & Valenti, S. S. (1990, March). *Rapport in therapist-client interactions: An ecological analysis of the effects of nonverbal sensitivity and interactional synchrony.* Paper presented at the 61st annual meeting of the Eastern Psychological Association, Philadelphia, PA.

Krupnik, J. L., Sotsky, S. M., Simmens, S., Moyer, J., Elkin, I., Watkins, J., & Pilkonis, P. A. (1996). The role of the therapeutic alliance in psychotherapy and pharmacotherapy outcome: Findings in the National Institute of Mental Health Treatment of Depression Collaborative Research Program. *Journal of Consulting and Clinical Psychology, 64,* 532–539.

LaFrance, M., & Ickes, W. (1981). Posture mirroring and interactional involvement: Sex and sex typing effects. *Journal of Nonverbal Behavior, 5,* 139–154.

Lester, B. M., Hoffman, J., & Brazelton, T. B. (1985). The rhythmic structure of mother-infant interaction in term and preterm infants. *Child Development,* *56*, 15–27.

Lichtenberg, J. W., Wettersten, K. B., Mull, H., Moberly, R. L., Merkley, K. B., & Corey, A. T. (1998). Relationship formation and relational control as correlates of psychotherapy quality and outcome. *Journal of Counseling Psychology, 45*, 322–337.

Luborsky, L. (1994). Therapeutic alliances as predictors of psychotherapy outcomes: Factors explaining the predictive success. In A. Horvath & L. Greenberg (Eds.), *The working alliance—Theory, research, and practice* (pp. 38–50). New York: Wiley.

Lyubomirsky, S., & Nolen-Hoeksema, S. (1995). Effects of self-focused rumination on negative thinking and interpersonal problem solving. *Journal of Personality and Social Psychology, 69*, 176–190.

Mahrer, A. R., & Nadler, W. P. (1986). Good moments in psychotherapy: A preliminary review, a list, and some promising research avenues. *Journal of Consulting and Clinical Psychology, 54*, 10–15.

Mallinckrodt, B. (1997). Interpersonal relationship processes in individual and group psychotherapy. In S. Duck (Ed.), *Handbook of personal relationships* (2nd ed., pp. 671–694). New York: Wiley.

Marangoni, C., Garcia, S., Ickes, W., & Teng, G. (1995). Empathic accuracy in a clinically relevant context. *Journal of Personality and Social Psychology, 68*, 854–869.

Martin, D. J., Garske, J. P., & Davis, M. K. (2000). Relation of the therapeutic alliance with outcome and other variables: A meta-analytic review. *Journal of Consulting & Clinical Psychology, 68*, 438–450.

Marziali, E., Marmar, C., & Krupnick, J. (1981). Therapeutic alliance scales: Development and relationship to psychotherapy outcome. *American Journal of Psychiatry, 138*, 361–364.

Meadowcroft, J. M. (1996). Attention span cycles. In J. H. Watt & C. A. VanLear (Eds.), *Dynamic patterns in communication processes* (pp. 255–276). Thousand Oaks, CA: Sage.

Montgomery, B. M. (1994). Communication in close relationships. In A. L. Weber & J. H. Harvey (Eds.), *Perspectives on close relationships* (pp. 67–87). Boston: Allyn & Bacon.

Noller, P. (1992). Nonverbal communication in marriage. In R. S. Feldman (Ed.), *Applications of nonverbal behavioral theories and research* (pp. 31–59). Hillsdale, NJ: Erlbaum.

Papoušek, H., & Papoušek, M. (1997). Preverbal communication in humans and the genesis of culture. In U. Segerstråle & P. Molnár (Eds.), *Nonverbal communication: Where nature meets culture* (pp. 87–108). Mahwah, NJ: Erlbaum.

Patterson, M. L. (1983). *Nonverbal behavior: A functional perspective.* New York: Springer-Verlag.

Preuschoft, S., & van Hooff, J. (1997). The social function of "smile" and "laughter": Variations across primate species and societies. In U. Segerstråle & P. Molnár (Eds.), *Nonverbal communication: Where nature meets culture* (pp. 171–190). Mahwah, NJ: Erlbaum.

Rogers, C. (1957). The necessary and sufficient conditions of therapeutic change. *Journal of Consulting Psychology, 21*, 95–105.

Rogoff, B. (1990). *Apprenticeship in thinking.* New York: Oxford University Press.

Rusbult, C. E., Verette, J., Whitney, G. A., Slovik, L. F., & Lipkus, I. (1991). Accommodation processes in close relationships: Theory and preliminary empirical evidence. *Journal of Personality and Social Psychology, 60,* 53–78.

Safran, J. D., Crocker, P., McMain, S., & Murray, P. (1990). The therapeutic alliance rupture as a therapy event for empirical investigation. *Psychotherapy, 27,* 154–165.

Safran, J. D., & Muran, J. C. (2000). Resolving therapeutic alliance ruptures: Diversity and integration. *Journal of Clinical Psychology, 56,* 233–243.

Salvio, M., Beutler, L. E., Wood, J. M., & Engle, D. (1992). The strength of the therapeutic alliance in three treatments for depression. *Psychotherapy Research, 2,* 31–36.

Schindler, L., Hohenberger-Sieber, E., & Hahlweg, K. (1989). Observing client-therapist interaction in behaviour therapy: Development and first application of an observational system. *British Journal of Clinical Psychology, 28,* 213–226.

Schneider, K. (1997). Development of emotions and their expression in task-oriented situations in infants and preschool children. In U. Segerstråle & P. Molnár (Eds.), *Nonverbal communication: Where nature meets culture* (pp. 109–130). Mahwah, NJ: Erlbaum.

Schwarz, N., & Clore, G. L. (1996). Feelings and phenomenal experiences. In E. T. Higgins & A. W. Kruglanski (Eds.), *Social psychology: Handbook of basic principles* (pp. 433– 465). New York: Guilford Press.

Segerstråle, U., & Molnár, P. (Eds.) (1997). *Nonverbal communication: Where nature meets culture.* Mahwah, NJ: Erlbaum.

Stafford, L., & Canary, D. J. (1991). Maintenance strategies and romantic relationship type, gender, and relational characteristics. *Journal of Social and Personal Relationships, 8,* 217–242.

Street, R. L. (1984). Speech convergence and speech evaluation in fact-finding interviews. *Human Communication Research, 11,* 139–169.

Strong, S. R., Hills, H. I., Kilmartin, C. T., DeVries, H., Lanier, K., Nelson, B. N., Strickland, D., & Meyer, III, C. W. (1988). The dynamic relations among interpersonal behaviors: A test of complementarity and anticomplementarity. *Journal of Personality and Social Psychology, 54,* 798–810.

Svartberg, M., Seltzer, M. H., & Stiles, T. C. (1998). The effects of common and specific factors in short-term anxiety-provoking psychotherapy: A pilot process-outcome study. *Journal of Nervous and Mental Disease, 186,* 691–696.

Thomas, G., Fletcher, G. J. O., & Lange, C. (1997). On-line empathic accuracy in marital interaction. *Journal of Personality and Social Psychology, 72,* 839–850.

Thompson, B. J., Hill, C. E., & Mahalik, J. R. (1991). A test of the complimentary hypotheses in interpersonal theory of psychotherapy: Multiple case comparisons. *Psychotherapy, 28,* 572–579.

Tickle-Degnen, L., & Coster, W. (1995). Therapeutic interaction and the management of challenge during the beginning minutes of sensory integration treatment. *The Occupational Therapy Journal of Research, 15,* 122–141.

Tickle-Degnen, L., & Puccinelli, N. (1999). The nonverbal expression of negative emotions: Peer and supervisor responses to occupational therapy students' emotional attributes. *Occupational Therapy Journal of Research, 19,* 18–39.

Tickle-Degnen, L., & Rosenthal, R. (1990). Target article: The nature of rapport and its nonverbal correlates. *Psychological Inquiry, 1,* 285–293.

Tickle-Degnen, L., & Rosenthal, R. (1992). Nonverbal aspects of therapeutic rapport. In R. S. Feldman (Ed.), *Applications of nonverbal behavioral theories and research* (pp. 143–164). Hillsdale, NJ: Erlbaum.

Tracey, T. J. (1993). An interpersonal stage model of the therapeutic process. *Journal of Counseling Psychology, 40,* 396–409.

Tronick, E. Z. (1990). The development of rapport. *Psychological Inquiry, 1,* 322–323.

VanLear, C. A. (1991). Testing a cyclical model of communicative openness in relationship development: Two longitudinal studies. *Communication Monographs, 58,* 337–361.

Warner, R. M. (1992). Speaker, partner and observer evaluations of affect during social interaction as a function of interaction tempo. *Journal of Language and Social Psychology, 11,* 253–266.

Warner, R. M. (1998). *Spectral analysis of time-series data.* London: Guilford Press.

Warner, R. M., Malloy, D., Schneider, K., Knoth, R., & Wilder, B. (1987). Rhythmic organization of social interaction and observer ratings of positive affect and involvement. *Journal of Nonverbal Behavior, 11,* 57–74.

Watson D., Clark, L. A., & Tellegen, A. (1988). Development and validation of brief measures of positive and negative affect: The PANAS Scales. *Journal of Personality and Social Psychology, 54,* 1063–1070.

Watzlawick, P., Bavelas, J. B., & Jackson, D. D. (1967). *Pragmatics of human communication: A study of interactional patterns, pathologies, and paradoxes.* New York: Norton.

White, R. W. (1959). Motivation reconsidered: The concept of competence. *Psychological Review, 66,* 297–333.

Winstead, B. A., & Derlega, V. J. (1994). The therapy relationship. In A. L. Weber & J. H. Harvey (Eds.), *Perspectives on close relationships* (pp. 325–339). Boston: Allyn & Bacon.

Wood, J. (1982). Communication and relational culture: Bases for the study of human relationship. *Communication Quarterly, 30,* 75–83.

5

What Makes Good Therapists Fail?

JÖRG MERTEN AND RAINER KRAUSE

What Makes Mental Disorders So Persistent?

There is a broad consensus that the rate of spontaneous remission of mental disorders is remarkably low (Grawe, 1992). Considering the tremendous amount of suffering involved, this is a paradox. Why should any reasonable person so intensely insist on self-harm or harming others? Once this point is reached, concepts like repetition-compulsion, maladaptive patterns (Luborsky, 1977), schemata (Horowitz, 1997), or even the death drive (Eissler, 1971) are discussed. The focus of the discussion is on the behavior and on mental representations of the patient. Such concepts are sufficient if they are broad enough to include the social partners of the patient in the repetition-compulsion. The results we report demonstrate how the longevity of mental disorders is related to a high level of stability in internal feelings and the unconscious behavior of the patient's social partner.

Patients with specific psychological disorders establish specific relationship patterns. They enact these unconsciously and with the majority of the people with which they interact. Relationship patterns not only comprise a specific manner of expression, but also include the specific reactions of social partners (Frisch, Schwab, & Krause, 1995; Krause, 1982; Krause, Steimer-Krause, Merten, & Ullrich, 1998; Schulz, 2000; Schwab, Merten, & Krause, 1997; Steimer-Krause, Krause, & Wagner, 1990).

One of the ways in which the implementation of a relationship pattern can be achieved is by inducing the social partner to show specific affects (Krause, 1990) or an action readiness (Frijda, 1986). Several studies supplied evidence for this assumption. For example, in one study, dyadic interactions between severely disordered patients (suffering from paranoid schizophrenia or severe psychosomatic syndromes like ulcerative colitis) and healthy subjects were videotaped, and their facial behavior was analyzed. In both samples, healthy subjects reduced their affective expression toward the level of the patients (Krause, 1998; Steimer-Krause, 1996). In a different group, patients suffering from low back pain—related to unconscious conflicts or, in psychoanalytic terms, from a conversion neurosis—also talked to healthy subjects. Neither patients nor healthy subjects showed reduction of facial expression. On the contrary, there was an excess of facial affective microreactions, especially of those with conflicting natures.

A dimension that might be helpful in understanding these results is the structure of personality. According to Rudolf (1993), structure is the enduring pattern of the self in relation to others. This interaction pattern is described in the frames of self-perception, self-governance, defense, object perception, communication, and attachment. All these functions are influenced by the amount of reflective functioning or mentalization. These concepts were developed by Fonagy, Target, Steele, and Steele (1998) and have the following meaning:

> the active expression of a psychological capacity intimately related to the representation of the self. . . . Reflective functioning involves both a self-reflective and an interpersonal component that ideally provides the individual with a well-developed capacity to distinguish inner from outer reality, pretend from real modes of functioning, intra personal mental and emotional processes from interpersonal communication. (p. 4)

A measure that has been validated sufficiently and that aims at similar functions is the OPD (operationalized psychodynamic diagnostics; OPD Working Group, 2001). It was developed by a German clinical and research team and now has been translated into English. It also measures deficiencies in the capabilities to build distinct mental representations of the self, of significant objects, and of the feelings experienced (Fonagy, 1991; Fonagy & Target, 1998; Schulz, 2000). OPD distinguishes among four different qualities of structural personality organization: good, moderate, low, and disorganized.

At the moment, two studies have supplied evidence for the relationship between OPD ratings and facial affective behavior. A group of patients with low-to-moderate quality of structural personality organization was characterized by a reduction of facial behavior (Schulz, 2000), while a group of patients with moderate quality displayed as many facial expressions as healthy subjects (Merten & Brunnhuber, 2002). The latter study showed fewer negative emotions. Subjects with good quality structural personality organization and with a high capacity for reflective functioning showed few connections between facial expressions and emotional experience. The frequency of negative facial affects like anger, contempt, and disgust positively correlated with the emotional experience of joy (Hufnagel, Krause,

Steimer-Krause, & Wagner, 1993). However, in the case of low-structured subjects, frequencies of negative facial affects, such as contempt and disgust, were congruently correlated to negative feelings.

To understand the conditions of congruent and noncongruent connections, a context analysis of facial expression was performed (Merten, 2002). It showed that partners of healthy subjects attributed the facial affect of the subjects to the mental objects about which they were talking and thinking, while in the case of patients with reduced capacity for mentalization, facial displays of contempt and disgust were expressions of genuine self-regulatory emotions that were directly related to the social partner with whom the patient was interacting. These two functions of facial affective signs can be disentangled by contextual gazing and speaking. Facial affective signs related to the social partner occur in gazing and speaking contexts that differ from those related to objects that are not present (Merten, 1997). Thus, negative facial displays of healthy subjects most often occur in the context of verbal comments and use objects as referents, while those of low-structured patients do not show this kind of relationship.

Negative affects that are not tied to verbal comments disturb the regulation of the relationship. In dyads with subjects of low structural personality organization, they merely serve as an interactive emblematic sign for the actual social partner. A deficiency in the quality of relationships of low-structured subjects is indicated by a dramatically reduced display of negative affects like anger, contempt, and disgust during mutual gazing; this reduction goes far beyond the usual reduction of well-structured subjects (Merten, 1997). In dyads with patients with a low OPD rating and a low capacity for mentalization, only 3% to 6% of negative affects were shown during mutual gazing. This corresponded to 21% to 29% of the total sampling time. In dyads with well-structured subjects, 17% of the negative affects were shown during mutual gazing. This amounted to 35% of the total observation time. Well-structured subjects can afford to do so because of the above-mentioned linkage of negative affects to verbal content and because they initiate a positive relationship by mutual smiling during mutual gazing, something that is utterly missing in the other group. This type of interaction allows the display of many negative affects during mutual gazing without weakening the relationship. Outside observers do not attribute hostility, but liveliness, high cathexis, interest, and engagement to the dyad.

It can be concluded that essential parts of a maladaptive relationship pattern consist of unconscious affective interactions. They give way to object and self-representations and to feelings that characterize the specific unconscious intersubjective field of a dyad (Benecke, Krause, & Merten, 2000). Qualitatively distinct patterns are related to the structural personality variables mentioned.

Implementation of the Maladaptive Relationship Pattern in the Intersubjective Field

Returning to the psychotherapeutic process, it is difficult to attribute the longevity of these problems to the patient alone. The enactment of the repetition-compulsion has to be understood as a social undertaking to which at least two individuals contribute. Patients, as well as healthy individuals, preconsciously anticipate the further development of the ongoing interaction through cognitive-affective modeling (Bänninger-Huber, 1992, 1996; Krause, 1997; Patterson, 1991). Subjects build and modify models that comprise cognitive-affective mental representations of the way they experience themselves and their social partners and the way they would like to behave toward each other. Cognitive-affective models of patients can be characterized by specific conflicts (e.g., a wish for intimacy and at the same time the fear of it) that will directly influence the kind of relationship that can be established. In the case of schizophrenic patients, for example, a conflict between intimacy and distance is predominant, and they enact this conflict in the intersubjective field by unconsciously inducing social partners to behave in a reserved manner.

One mechanism to entrap a social partner into behaving in accordance with an unconscious conflict is called *projective identification*. According to Ogden (1988), this process, which consists of three phases, includes a transfer of unbearable parts of the self-representation to the object representation, which is a purely mental process. In the next phase, the social partner is unconsciously induced to experience the unbearable internal feelings by means of a preconscious social manipulation. Now, these unbearable states can be controlled and experienced by watching the other managing the situation, which is also a move from passivity to activity (Porder, 1991). Merten (1996) and Steimer-Krause (1996) showed empirically how the second phase of projective identification is implemented by means of nonverbal behavior. Similar processes take place in psychotherapeutic interactions; they constitute the emotional quality of the intersubjective field and of the therapeutic relationship, which is the most important aspect of the therapeutic bond.

Relationship of the Emotional Quality of a Therapeutic Relationship to Therapeutic Outcome

In the search for relevant unconscious behavior responsible for therapeutic change, we compared facial affective behavior of patients and therapists to that of healthy subjects in "everyday" interactions. Essential differences between psychotherapeutic and everyday interactions included a reduction in the overall facial affectivity of patients and therapists. In addition, joy and disgust were displayed less by both patients and therapists. At the same time, simultaneous Duchenne smiles (indicative of positive emotional quality of relationships) were considerably less common. Healthy subjects in everyday interactions showed three times more simultaneous Duchenne smiles than patients and therapists. Patients and therapists also displayed less contempt than healthy subjects in everyday interactions, but patients showed contempt twice as much as therapists. Fear and surprise, usually rare events, were more often shown by patients in the psychotherapeutic situation. The therapists also showed more surprise than subjects in everyday interactions.

To interpret the reduction of simultaneous smiling as an indicator of a less-positive relationship seems peculiar since, from the vantage point of the layperson and from most empirical research, a positive therapeutic relationship is considered the most important predictor of psychotherapy outcome (Orlinsky, Grawe, & Parks, 1994). But, this seeming contradiction can be clarified by studying the conceptualization of the emotional quality of the therapeutic relationship and the ways of measuring it. Besides differing considerably (Orlinksky et al., 1994), the studies are often inadequate from a conceptual point of view (Krause, 1997). Henry, Strupp, Schact, and Gaston (1994), following Gaston (1990), distinguished four components of the therapeutic alliance: (a) the working alliance, (b) the affective bond of the patient to the therapist, (c) the empathic understanding and involvement of the therapist, and (d) mutual agreement on goals and tasks of the therapy. Orlinsky et al. (1994) distinguished task-oriented teamwork from the social-emotional aspect of the therapeutic alliance. The social-emotional aspect is subdivided into communicative contact and mutual affect.

To yield empirical evidence for the importance of these aspects, Orlinsky et al. (1994) performed a meta-analysis of studies that investigated psychotherapeutic process and outcome. The above-mentioned aspects of "communicative contact" and "mutual affect" yielded high effect sizes on therapeutic outcome. This is the case, although the original studies were heterogeneous, in respect to the procedures used to operationalize and measure aspects of the therapeutic alliance. One of the flaws of the meta-analysis is that, in the end, it is not clear which of the specific aspects of the therapeutic alliance process correlated with the therapeutic outcome. For instance, Orlinsky et al. (1994) used terms like "mutual affect" or "reciprocal affirmation," but the empirical findings subsumed differed enormously in respect to operationalization. A study by Collins et al. (1985) was subsumed under reciprocal affirmation, but what was actually observed was the extent to which affective exchange between patients in the waiting room occurred as reported by the staff on one item of the Ward Atmosphere Scale (Moos, 1974).

Taking into account the studies described above, it can be concluded that the therapeutic relationship is important, but the personal, social-emotional side of it needs further and objective scrutinization to enrich the knowledge of its interactive components. Communicative contact and mutual affect, introduced by Orlinsky et al. (1994) as categories, are promising, but the analysis of the primary studies is disappointing in the sense that emotions and reciprocity in process were only unsatisfactorily investigated, and there actually was no study in which objective means to analyze the affective behavior of therapist and patient were used.

Curative Factors of the Therapeutic Relationship

It is presumed that the above-mentioned findings on nonverbal interaction styles, implementation of relationship patterns, and adaptation of social partners describe dyadic processes that are of major interest with respect to psychotherapeutic processes. It is assumed that those therapists who are not submitting themselves unconsciously to the adaptation patterns the patients normally impose on their partners are successful. In doing so, the therapist stops a vicious circle by disproving the dreaded expectations of the patient. This can happen even if the therapist is not aware of doing so since these processes take place on the level of micromomentary nonverbal behavior, which is hardly controllable (Ekman, 1985).

To add empirical evidence, 11 patients were selected by 11 therapists according to their capacity to get through the design of the study. Nevertheless, all of them were severely disordered; 9 had been treated before without success. The therapists of cognitive-behavioral, psychoanalytic, and client-centered theoretical orientation were very experienced. They treated the patients in a brief psychotherapy setting of 15 h, during which the therapists and their patients were videotaped by two cameras.

Facial affective behavior in the first therapy sessions was related to therapeutic outcome, which was assessed by both patient and therapist. Facial behavior of the therapists did not exhibit any differences that could be related to differences in their theoretical orientation. Facial behavior depends more on individual characteristics or dyadic adaptation processes than on theoretical orientation.

In dyadic interactions between two healthy persons, the most frequent facial affective event is felt happiness. This was not the case with the patients. Most of them showed mainly contempt, disgust, or anger as the most frequent emotion. In the following, we call the affect with the highest proportion *leitaffekt* according to the metaphor of the leitmotiv. For example, a patient with a borderline diagnosis showed 363 facial activities in the first session; 40% of these activities could not be interpreted. The rest were 1 genuine happiness expression, 11 interest or curiosity, and 187 negative affects, 82% of which were disgust. Therefore, disgust was this patient's leitaffekt. Following the patient's narrations, his most important wish was to be loved and to be liked. A conflict could be assumed between the conscious wish and its implementation on the level of microaffects. Therefore, a negative leitaffekt was considered an indicator of a dysfunctional interactive and self-regulatory process, and a negative relation to therapeutic outcome was assumed. However, neither the affective valence of the leitaffekt of the patient nor its frequency correlated significantly with one of the outcome measures.

On the other hand, in line with the above-mentioned results for adaptation, therapists who adapted their facial affective behavior to that of the patients and in this way became involved in the relationship pattern of the patient did have a poor therapeutic outcome. The relative frequency of the leitaffekt of the therapist correlated negatively with the therapist's own outcome rating, which usually was given half a year later ($r = -.63$, $p < .05$, $N = 11$). Therapists who displayed high amounts of a single facial affect during the first session rated their therapeutic outcome as "worse" after the 15th session; this was independent of the type of leitaffekt they displayed. This could be interpreted as a consequence of the implementation of a maladaptive repetitive pattern, which reduced the normal variance of affectivity.

This hypothesis was supported by the fact that the therapist's frequent expression of anger, contempt, and disgust was positively correlated with the therapist's own outcome rating ($r = .81$, $p = .003$, $N = 11$) and with the change assessment scores of a questionnaire for symptoms (FBL; Fahrenberg, 1975; $r = .54$, $p = .11$, $N = 10$) as long as they were different from that of the patient. Therefore, a well-balanced proportion of positive and negative emotions is a necessary condition for positive therapeutic outcome. The proportion of felt happiness of patients and negative affects of therapists correlated with all three outcome measures (Table 5.1). In therapies in which the patient expressed many positive affects and in which there were only a few negative affects on behalf of the therapist, outcome was worse. Successful therapists compensated for the surplus of positive affects with their own negative affects.

To understand more about the process behind these correlational figures, two single-case analyses of 15 sessions of psychoanalytic focal treatments,

Table 5.1 Facial Affective Behavior and Therapeutic Outcome

	Outcome Perspective		
Predictor	Therapist	Patient	Combined
%$Leitaffekt_T$	−.63*		
Negative affects$_T$	+.81*		
Happy felt$_P$/negative affects$_T$	−.64*	−.55$^+$	−.76*

Spearman correlation: *$p < .05$, $^+p < .10$; %$Leitaffekt_T$, relative frequency of the $Leitaffekt$; Happy felt$_P$/negative affects$_T$, proportion of patient's happy felt expression and therapist's negative affects.

one case leading to success, the other leading to a negative outcome, were conducted (Merten, Ullrich, Anstadt, Krause, & Buchheim, 1996). In the less successful case, an unresolved conflict of the therapist fitted into the problem of the patient, leading to the consequence that both patient and therapist enacted it in the unconscious affective realm, leading to a negative outcome. The internal problem was that the therapist could not tolerate his own aggressive feelings. This was implanted in expressing an abundance of mutual liking displayed by mutual smiling and much positive reciprocity. In the successful therapy, compensatory affective behavior prevailed. The therapist showed negative emotions, while the patient smiled (Krause & Merten, 1999; Merten, 2001).

The correlations between frequencies of facial affects and therapeutic outcome reported above do not cover the actual implementation of maladaptive relationship patterns. The actual implementation takes place on the level of dyadic emotional patterns of patient and therapist as they occur simultaneously or within a short temporal distance. Emotional patterns describe individual and dyadic emotional processes as they appear in facial affective behavior of patient and therapist. They also contain information about emotional self-regulatory processes as well as about the quality of relationship regulation between patient and therapist.

Application of definitions and properties of emotional patterns provided by Merten (1996) and a mathematical algorithm to detect "hidden real-time patterns" by Magnusson (1996) revealed that dyadic patterns of Duchenne smiles (that is, genuine joy expressions that appear simultaneously or almost simultaneously in the interaction) occurred in nearly all therapies, whereas no pattern of negative affects for both participants was found. Therefore, motor mimicry of facial affective behavior—as far as it is detected by our measurement tools (Friesen & Ekman, 1984)—only takes place in the case of the positive emotion of happiness.

In cases for which negative affects are part of a dyadic pattern, the negative affect was compensated by a social smile or a Duchenne smile of the partner. In addition, several therapy-specific patterns describe the implementation of core psychodynamic conflicts. To give an example, a patient with a conflict between attachment and separation wishes engaged in much positive facial affective behavior with the therapist, but also displayed a pattern of anger, followed by an expression of fear that could be matched directly to the conflict of the patient. This and other cases are described elsewhere in detail (Anstadt, Merten, Ullrich, & Krause, 1997; Krause, 1998; Merten, 2001; Merten et al., 1996).

Table 5.2 shows the correlations between characteristics of emotional patterns in different therapies and therapeutic outcome. A major result is that the frequency of dyadic emotional patterns correlates negatively with therapeutic outcome in all three perspectives, and the maximum complexity of the patterns also correlates negatively in the same manner.

Table 5.2 Correlations Between Facial Affective Behavior
and Therapeutic Outcome

	Outcome Perspective		
Predictor	Therapist	Patient	Combined
Maximum complexity of patterns	−.69*	−.43	−.68[+]
Number of dyadic patterns	−.58[+]	−.81*	−.75*
Simultaneous Duchenne smiles	−.63*		

Spearman correlations: *$p < .05$, [+]$p < .10$.

A specific subcategory of emotional patterns is that composed of the simultaneous appearance of a Duchenne smile in both interaction partners. From the perspective of the therapist rating (Table 5.2), the frequency of these smiles was significantly negatively correlated with therapeutic outcome. In addition, we found a curvilinear quadratic relation between the frequency of mutual smiling initiated by the therapist and therapeutic outcome ($P = .038$, $b^2 = -.64$). Therapies in which there was not even one incident of positive mutual smiling initiated by the therapist were rated on a medium level of outcome. In therapies with deterioration or the patient dropped out, we found more than four incidents of mutual smiling initiated by the therapist. The therapies with the highest outcome rate were between the two cases.

It can be concluded that the implementation of relationship patterns is indicated, in general, by high frequencies and high complexity of dyadic patterns and also by the presence of too many patterns of positive emotions from both interaction partners. Furthermore, this kind of implementation was correlated with negative therapeutic outcome.

If the therapist becomes involved in the maladaptive relationship pattern and if this is not resolved during the course of treatment, the dreaded pattern will be repeated and further reinforced. This assumption was confirmed by the following results. In therapies with better outcome, conflict indicators were augmented to a certain point in treatment and tended to decrease in later sessions. Indicators for bad outcome were high complexity in dyadic relationship patterns and predominance of conflict indicators in the last session. In these cases, therapists were unable to recognize or resolve the maladaptive relationship pattern in which they were involved.

Summary

The high stability of mental disorders is attributed to a successful unconscious implementation of maladaptive relationship patterns in everyday interactions. This process is understood as a dyadic interaction in which both subjects, the healthy person as well as the patient, contribute. As a consequence, the facial affective behavior of the healthy subject changes and becomes more similar to that of the patient than to that of healthy subjects interacting with each other. Dyadic interactions between healthy subjects are characterized by much of positive and negative facial affective behavior by both partners, while dyads of patients with low structural personality organization or diminished reflective capacities and healthy subjects typically exhibit a single negative leitaffekt on both sides.

Psychotherapeutic interactions differ from everyday interactions between healthy subjects mainly in respect to these adaptation phenomena. Experienced therapists, regardless of their theoretical orientation, were emotionally withholding, at least in their facial affect display. Emotion-specific differences were found in the expression of emotions like joy, contempt, and disgust, which were reduced. On the other hand, surprise and fear were shown with higher frequency than in everyday interactions. The increase of surprise indicates that new and potentially conflictive information has to be assimilated. The increase of fear signals this conflict and triggers the onset of defense mechanisms that can hamper the process of therapeutic change.

The reduction of joy in the psychotherapeutic interactions analyzed in our study was attributed not only to illness of the patient, but to an emotional absence in most therapists. In regard to the implementation of maladaptive relationship patterns in therapeutic relationships, dyadic aspects of facial affective behavior are special indicators of the affective bond and meaningful predictors of therapeutic outcome.

The leitaffekt of patients in the first therapy session did not correlate—nor did any other variable of the facial affective behavior—with any outcome perspective. Facial affective behavior and dyadic variables of the therapist were found to be much more related to outcome perspectives than facial affective behavior of patients. Therefore, an important finding is that the therapist's facial affective behavior is an especially useful predictor of therapeutic outcome. What characterizes most successful therapists is the absence of a single, high-frequency leitaffekt. From another perspective, we might say that therapeutic failure is related to a loss of variability in the therapist's expressive regulatory system.

Results related to facial affective behavior in patients and therapists, their significance for the affective bond, and their relation to therapeutic outcome can be summarized in the following manner. A therapist's differential negative facial expressiveness seems to be a necessary condition for a problem-oriented therapeutic process. However, the therapist's negative affects can be indicators of different psychological contents: They can be reactions to the patient's actual behavior or its narratives, but they can also be tied to the behavior of protagonists talked about in the narratives. In both cases, they represent important starting points for the understanding of the patient's problems, which are centered on affective conflicts with others, themselves, or the therapist.

Successful implementation of maladaptive relationship patterns is indicated by many emotional dyadic patterns and the high complexity of these patterns. Although a certain number of dyadic patterns are characteristic and necessary for all dyadic interactions, large numbers in therapeutic interactions imply the danger of conflictive involvement of the therapist. Large quantities of positive local reciprocity are particular predictors of bad outcome; nevertheless, a certain amount of reciprocity is necessary to establish an affective bond between patient and therapist. In this manner, some of the experienced therapists were able to handle much negative expressiveness in their patients. Displays of positive affects by the patients are also crucial for the therapeutic process and have to be managed. The more successful therapists did this in a compensatory fashion. The less successful ones reacted more often reciprocally and even initiated positive reciprocity several times.

The concept of leitaffekt and the variables centered on it integrate most of these considerations. An outstanding positive leitaffekt on the side of the therapist indicates a behavior that is more similar to everyday interactions with healthy partners than a problem-oriented one in therapy. An intensely negative leitaffekt by the therapist can be overwhelming and can totally hinder the establishment of a positive relationship. Consequently, facial affective behavior functions as an indicator of a good relationship balance in successful therapists and can be considered as the result of a compromise between negative affective involvement and positive affiliation.

References

Anstadt, T., Merten, J., Ullrich, B., & Krause, R. (1997). Affective dyadic behavior, core conflictual relationship themes and treatment outcome. *Psychotherapy Research, 7*(4), 397–417.

Bänninger-Huber, E. (1992). Prototypical affective microsequences in psychotherapeutic interaction. *Psychotherapy Research, 2*, 291–306.

Bänninger-Huber, E. (1996). *Mimik-Uebertragung-Interaktion. Die Untersuchung affektiver Prozesse in der Psychotherapie* [Facial expression, transference, interaction. The investigation of affective processes in psychotherapy]. Bern, Switzerland: Huber.

Benecke, C., Krause, R., & Merten, J. (2000). On the constitution of the intersubjective field. *Psychotherapie, 5*(2), 73–80.

Collins, J. F., Ellsworth, R. B., Casey, N. A., Hyer, L., Hickey, R. H., Schoonover, R. A., Twemlow, S. W., & Nesselroade, J. R. (1985). Treatment characteristics of psychiatric programs that correlate with patient community adjustment. *Journal of Clinical Psychology, 41*, 299–308.

Eissler, K. R. (1971). Death drive, ambivalence, and narcissism. *Psychoanalytic Study of the Child, 26*, 25–78.

Ekman, P. (1985). *Telling lies*. New York: Norton.

Fahrenberg, J. (1975). Die Freiburger Beschwerdeliste FBL [Freiburger Symptom List]. *Zeitschrift für Klinische Psychologie, 4*, 79–100.

Fonagy, P. (1991). Thinking about thinking: Some clinical and theoretical considerations in the treatment of a borderline patient. *International Journal of Psychoanalysis, 72*, 639–656.

Fonagy, P., & Target, M. (1998). Mentalization and changing aims of child psychoanalysis. *Psychoanalytic Dialogues, 8*, 87–114.

Fonagy, P., Target, M., Steel, H., & Steele, M. (1998). *Reflective functioning manual*. Version V for application to adult attachment interviews. (Available from: Prof. P. Fonagy, Psychoanalysis Unit, Subdepartment of Clinical Health Psychology, University College of London, Gower Street, London WC 1E 6BT.)

Friesen, W. V., & Ekman, P. (1984). *EMFACS-7; Emotional Facial Action Coding System*. Unpublished manual.

Frijda, N. H. (1986). *The emotions*. Cambridge, England: Cambridge University Press.

Frisch, I., Schwab, F., & Krause, R. (1995). Affektives Ausdrucksverhalten gesunder und an Colitis erkrankter männlicher und weiblicher Erwachsener. *Zeitschrift für Klinische Psychologie, 24*, 230–238.

Gaston, L. (1990). The concept of the alliance and its role in psychotherapy. *Psychotherapy, 27*, 143–153.

Grawe, K. (1992) Psychotherapieforschung zu Beginn der neunziger Jahre [Psychotherapy research at the beginning of the modern era]. *Psychologische Rundschau, 3*, 132–162.

Henry, H., Strupp, W., Schacht, T., & Gaston, L. (1994). Process and outcome in psychotherapy—Noch einmal. In S. L. Garfield & A. E. Bergin (Eds.), *Handbook of psychotherapy and behavior change* (4th ed., pp. 467–508). New York: Wiley.

Horowitz, M. J. (1997). *Formulation as a basis for planning psychotherapy treatment*. Washington DC: American Psychiatric Press.

Hufnagel, H., Krause, R., Steimer-Krause, E., & Wagner, G. (1993). Facial expression and introspection within different groups of mental disturbances. In J. W. Pennebaker & H. C. Traue (Eds.), *Emotion, inhibition and health* (pp. 164–178). Göttingen, Germany: Huber & Hogrefe.

Krause, R. (1982). A social psychological approach to the study of stuttering. In C. Fraser & K. R. Scherer (Eds.), *Advances in the social psychology of language* (pp. 77–122). Cambridge, England: Cambridge University Press.

Krause, R. (1990). Psychodynamik der Emotionsstörungen [Psychodynamics of mental disorders]. In K. R. Scherer (Ed.), *Psychologie der Emotionen. Enzyklopädie der Psychologie* (pp. 630–705). Themenbereich C, Theorie und Forschung, Serie IV, Motivation und Emotion, Band 3, Psychologie der Emotion. Göttingen, Germany: Hogrefe.

Krause, R. (1997). *Allgemeine psychoanalytische Krankheitslehre. Band 1: Grundlagen* [General psychoanalytic theory of mental disorders. Part 1: Basics]. Stuttgart, Germany: Kohlhammer.

Krause, R. (1998). *Allgemeine psychoanalytische Krankheitslehre. Band 2: Mod-*

elle [General psychoanalytic theory of mental disorders. Part 2: Models]. Stuttgart, Germany: Kohlhammer.

Krause, R., & Merten, J. (1999). Affects, regulation of relationship, transference and countertransference. *International Forum of Psychoanalysis, 8,* S.103–S.114.

Krause, R., Steimer-Krause, E., Merten, J., & Ullrich, B. (1998). Dyadic interaction regulation, emotion and psychopathology. In W. Flack & J. Laird (Eds.), *Emotions and psychopathology: Theory and research* (pp. 70–80). New York: Oxford University Press.

Luborsky, L. (1977). Measuring a pervasive structure in psychotherapy: The core conflictual relationship theme method. In N. Freedman & N. Grand (Eds.), *Communicative structures and psychic structures* (pp. 367–395). New York: Plenum Press.

Magnusson, M. S. (1996). Hidden real-time patterns in intra- and inter-individual behavior: Description and detection. *European Journal of Psychological Assessment, 12,* 112–123.

Merten, J. (1996). *Affekte und die Regulation nonverbalen, interaktiven Verhaltens* [Affects and the regulation of nonverbal, interactive behavior]. (Strukturelle Aspekte mimisch-affektiven Verhaltens und die Integration von Affekten in Regulationsmodelle). Bern, Switzerland: Peter Lang.

Merten, J. (1997). Facial-affective behavior, mutual gaze and emotional experience in dyadic interactions. *Journal of Nonverbal Behavior, 21,* 179–201.

Merten, J. (2001). *Beziehungsregulation in Psychotherapien. Maladaptive Beziehungsmuster und der therapeutische Prozeß* [Relationship regulation in psychotherapies. Maladaptive patterns and the therapeutic process]. Stuttgart, Germany: Kohlhammer.

Merten, J. (2002). Context analysis of facial affective behavior in clinical populations. In M. Katsikitis (Eds.), *The human face: Measurement and meaning* (pp 131–147). Dordrecht, The Netherlands: Kluwer.

Merten, J., & Brunnhuber, S. (2002). Emotional expression and relationship-regulation in psychodynamic interviews with patients suffering from a somatoform pain disorder. *Psychopathology.* Manuscript submitted for publication.

Merten, J., Ullrich, B., Anstadt, T., Krause, R., & Buchheim, P. (1996). Emotional experiencing and facial expression in the psychotherapeutic-process and its relation to treatment outcome. A pilot-study. *Psychotherapy Research, 6,* 198–212.

Moos, R. H. (1974). *Evaluating treatment environments: A social ecological approach.* New York: Wiley.

Ogden, T. H. (1988). On projective identification. *International Journal of Psychoanalysis, 60,* 357–373.

OPD Working Group. (2001). *Operationalized Psychodynamic Diagnostics (OPD).* Seattle, OR: Hogrefe.

Orlinsky, D., Grawe, K., & Parks, B. (1994). Process and outcome in psychotherapy—Noch einmal. In S. L. Garfield & A. E. Bergin (Eds.), *Handbook of psychotherapy and behavior change* (4th ed., pp. 270–376). New York: Wiley.

Patterson, M. L. (1991). A functional approach to nonverbal exchange. In

R. S. Feldman & B. Rime (Eds.), *Fundamentals of nonverbal behavior* (pp. 458–495). New York: Cambridge University Press.

Porder, M. S. (1991). Projective identification: An alternative hypothesis. *Psychoanalytic Quarterly, 56,* 431–451.

Rudolf, G. (1993). Die Struktur der Persönlichkeit [The structure of personality]. In G. Rudolf (Ed.), *Psychotherapeutische Medizin* (pp. 55–83). Stuttgart, Germany: Enke.

Schulz, S. (2000). *Affektive Indikatoren struktureller Störungen* [Affective indicators of structural disorders]. Doctoral dissertation published at http://www.dissertation.de.

Schwab, F., Merten, J., & Krause, R. (1997). Expressiveness in dyadic communication. In A. Vingerhoets, F. van Bussel, & J. Boelhouwer (Eds.), *The (non) expression of emotions in health and disease* (pp. S.211–S.221). Tilburg, The Netherlands: Tilburg University Press.

Steimer-Krause, E. (1996). *Übertragung, Affekt und Beziehung. Theorie und Analyse nonverbaler Interaktionen schizophrener Patienten* [Transference, affect and relationship. Theory and analysis of nonverbal interactions of schizophrenic patients]. Bern, Switzerland: Peter Lang.

Steimer-Krause, E., Krause, R., & Wagner, G. (1990). Interaction regulations used by schizophrenic and psychosomatic patients. Studies on facial behavior in dyadic interactions. *Psychiatry: Interpersonal and Biological Processes, 53,* 209–228.

PART II

NONVERBAL BEHAVIOR
IN NEGATIVE LIFE EVENTS

6

Selective Processing of Nonverbal Information in Anxiety

Attentional Biases for Threat

KARIN MOGG AND BRENDAN P. BRADLEY

Role of Selective Attention in Anxiety

Selective attention is a fundamental aspect of information processing. Our sense organs are continuously impinged on by a vast amount of information, including images, sounds, and sensations, and attentional mechanisms allow us to select specific sources of sensory information for further analysis. Although our senses may be capable of simultaneously processing information from various different sources, we are limited in our actions as it is often difficult for us to respond effectively to more than one source of information at a time.

Thus, as Allport (1989) pointed out, a crucial function of attention is "selection-for-action," which is of fundamental biological importance in allowing us to direct our behavior in an adaptive and coordinated manner. For example, it is helpful in terms of survival value that there is a mechanism which allows us to shift our gaze rapidly to the location of a potential threat in our surroundings, so that we can analyze the scene to take appropriate action, such as fight or flight. Attentional mechanisms allow us to disengage from whatever we are currently doing and to orient us toward relevant or important cues in the environment. Thus, selective attention plays a key role in mediating a wide range of biologically important behaviors, including searching for food and evading danger, as well as other goal-directed actions. Selective attention is clearly a nonverbal process insofar as it is not specific to any particular stimulus or response modality. Indeed, one of the most overt indicators of the focus of selective attention is a nonverbal behavior, the direction of eye gaze, that is, what we look at.

In this chapter, we will take a fairly broad perspective of the role of nonverbal information processing in anxiety. We examine attentional biases as reflected by various nonverbal indices (e.g., performance on visuospatial tasks, shifts of gaze) and, more importantly, focus on attentional biases for different types of nonverbal threat stimuli, including not only angry facial expressions, but also phobia-related pictures (e.g., spiders) and scenes of death and disaster (although we also briefly outline some background research using word stimuli).

Recent cognitive theories have proposed that attentional processes play a critical role in causing and maintaining clinical anxiety states (e.g., Eysenck, 1992; Mathews, 1990; Williams, Watts, MacLeod, & Mathews, 1988, 1997). These theoretical views build on earlier cognitive models of emotion put forward by Beck and Bower in the late 1970s and early 1980s (e.g., Beck, 1976; Bower, 1981). Beck proposed that cognitive representations of threat-related information are activated in anxiety, and that these "danger schemata" act as a filter on information processing. Consequently, anxious individuals have a processing bias that favors threat-related stimuli; that is, they selectively perceive, attend to, and remember threatening information.

Bower's (1981) associative network model of emotion similarly predicts anxiety-congruent biases in all aspects of information processing, including selective attention, memory, and reasoning, although the underlying mechanism is presumed to be different. According to Bower, each emotion is represented as a node in an associative memory network in which it is linked with other representations, such as memories of events. Activation of an emotion node, such as the anxiety node, would lead to increased accessibility of mood-congruent material, which in turn would result in selective processing of threat-related information in anxious individuals.

These cognitive models of anxiety have important clinical implications. For example, according to Beck's (1976) schema model, if the threat-related processing bias can be neutralized by cognitive therapy, this should lead to a reduction in a person's anxiety levels. Indeed, this view has been supported by controlled treatment trials, which showed that cognitive therapy is effective for clinical anxiety (e.g., Butler, Fennell, Robson, & Gelder, 1991).

These theoretical developments also stimulated a considerable amount of research interest in cognitive biases in anxiety. Two tasks have been widely used to examine attentional biases: the modified Stroop color-naming task and the visual probe task. In the former, words are displayed in different colors, and participants are asked to name the color as quickly as possible and to ignore the word meaning. Color-naming speed provides an index of how much processing resources are allocated to the word content. Anxious patients typically take longer to name the colors of threatening words than they take for the colors of neutral words in comparison with normal controls (e.g., Mathews & MacLeod, 1985; review by Williams, Mathews & MacLeod, 1996), which is consistent with an attentional bias to threat.

The visual probe task is based on research by Posner and colleagues, which indicated that the speed of manual responses to visual probes provides an index of visual attention (e.g., Posner, Snyder, & Davidson, 1980). That is, people are generally faster in responding to a probe stimulus (e.g., a small dot) that is presented in an attended, rather than unattended, region of a visual display. In MacLeod, Mathews, and Tata's (1986) version of the visual probe task, a series of word pairs is presented, with one word above the other on each trial. For some pairs, one word is threat related and the other neutral. Each word pair is presented relatively briefly (e.g., 500 ms), and when it disappears, a dot appears in the position just occupied by one of the words. Participants press a key in response to the dot probe. Anxious patients are faster to respond to probes that replace threat words than neutral words, indicating an attentional bias for threat information (e.g., MacLeod et al., 1986; Mogg, Bradley & Williams, 1995).

Research using these tasks has shown attentional biases in a wide range of anxiety disorders, including simple phobia, panic disorder, social phobia, and generalized anxiety disorder (e.g., Mathews & MacLeod, 1985; Mattia, Heimberg, & Hope, 1993; McNally, Riemann, & Kim, 1990; Watts, McKenna, Sharrock, & Trezise, 1986). Such findings of anxiety-related attentional biases seem supportive of the schema and network theories. But, by the late 1980s, findings also emerged that were problematic for these theories, such as failures to find anxiety-related biases in memory (e.g., Mogg, Mathews, & Weinman, 1987). Consequently, revised cognitive theories were put forward that proposed that anxiety-related biases do not influence all aspects of processing, but that they instead operate primarily in preattentive and attentional processes (e.g., Eysenck, 1992; Mathews & MacLeod, 1994; Williams et al., 1988).

According to Williams et al. (1988), individuals who are vulnerable to anxiety (i.e., those with high trait anxiety) are characterized by a permanent tendency to be vigilant for threat. Moreover, their tendency to direct attention toward threat will become more apparent as their level of stress increases (or as the threat value of the stimulus increases). In contrast, individuals who are low in trait anxiety will show the opposite pattern of attentional bias; that is, they have a tendency to direct their attention away from threat. These biases (i.e., vigilance in high trait anxiety, avoidance in low trait anxiety) are presumed to operate preattentively. That is, the biases are found in very early, automatic aspects of information processing, before information has entered conscious awareness. Williams et al. revised their theory in 1997 to update it using concepts and terminology from the parallel distributed processing model of Cohen, Dunbar, and McClelland (1990). Despite these modifications, the fundamental assumptions of the model remained largely the same; that is, individuals who are prone to be vigilant for threat have increased vulnerability to anxiety.

Williams et al.'s (1988, 1997) model appeared to be very helpful in accommodating a considerable amount of evidence of attentional biases from both clinical and nonclinical studies of anxiety. This included not only the findings of vigilance for threat-related words in generally anxious patients, noted above, but also evidence that such biases operate for subliminally presented threat stimuli. For example, on the modified Stroop task, individuals with generalized anxiety disorder show impaired color-naming performance on trials with subliminal threat words (i.e., words that are presented very briefly and masked so that individuals are unaware of their presence) (e.g., Bradley, Mogg, Millar, & White, 1995; Mogg, Bradley, Williams, & Mathews, 1993). In addition, on the visual probe task, individuals with generalized anxiety disorder are relatively faster, compared with controls, to detect probes that replace briefly presented, masked threat words (e.g., Mogg et al., 1995). Each of these findings is consistent with a preattentive bias for threat in clinical anxiety (i.e., a bias that operates outside awareness).

With regard to nonclinical studies, attentional biases for threat-related words are not often found in individuals within the normal population who have high levels of trait anxiety unless these individuals are under stress. For example, MacLeod and Mathews (1988) found no difference in attentional bias between high and low trait anxious students when the students were tested on the visual probe task several months before their end-of-year examinations, when their current anxious mood was normal. However, 1 week before their examinations, when their anxious mood state was increased, students with high trait anxiety showed greater vigilance for exam-related threat words (e.g., "failure"), whereas those with low trait anxiety showed an opposite trend to be avoidant of exam-related threat words.

A similar pattern of results was obtained by Mogg, Bradley, and Hallowell (1994); that is, high trait anxious students became more vigilant for threat words under exam stress, while there was a trend for low trait anxious students to become more avoidant. MacLeod and Rutherford (1992) found, using the modified Stroop task, that high trait anxious students under exam stress showed greater interference in color-naming performance for threat words than neutral words, but only when the words were presented subliminally. Despite some inconsistencies (see Mogg & Bradley, 1998, for more detailed discussion), such findings seem largely consistent with Williams et al.'s (1988, 1997) theoretical view that, when experiencing stressful life events, individuals who are vulnerable to anxiety have an automatic tendency to be vigilant for threat.

The experimental work described so far used single words as stimuli. Indeed, this is a limitation of much research into cognitive biases in emotional disorders. Such reliance on the use of word stimuli introduces several potential difficulties. First, single words have relatively mild threat value and so are not likely to be very informative about processing biases for more highly emotional material. Second, because this work has largely ignored processing of nonverbal information, it is unclear whether anxiety-related biases operate more generally for other forms of threat stimuli, such as pictorial scenes. Third, single words do not seem very representative of direct sources of threat in the environment, and so it would seem useful to investigate attentional biases in anxiety while using more naturalistic and ecologically valid types of threat stimuli.

A major risk of an experimental strategy that relies excessively on word stimuli is that the cognitive theories that are based on this work may only have explanatory value for a relatively restricted class of mild threat stimuli. There have also been further theoretical developments that provide persuasive grounds for using nonverbal stimuli in the study of attentional biases. Öhman's (1993, 1996) model of fear and anxiety is important in emphasizing, from an evolutionary perspective, the adaptive value of a cognitive mechanism for detecting threat. For an organism to respond effectively to threats in the environment, it is important that the threat should be rapidly detected and located, and that physiological systems are activated to facilitate energy-demanding flight and defense responses.

According to Öhman's model, it is proposed that automatic, preattentive processes play an important role in mediating vulnerability to fears and phobias. That is, fear responses are initiated by automatic, stimulus-analysis mechanisms, which operate prior to awareness and are sensitive to biologically prepared aversive stimuli (e.g., spiders, angry faces). When fear-relevant stimuli are detected by these preattentive mechanisms, autonomic anxiety responses are automatically triggered (e.g., increased heart rate and sweating), and these fear responses can occur independent of awareness of the threat stimulus. Moreover, once a threat stimulus is detected by the preattentive mechanisms, the focus of attention is automatically shifted to its location.

Öhman's model emphasizes the importance of biologically prepared stimuli in triggering automatic threat feature detectors, which may help explain why some studies have difficulty in reliably demonstrating attentional biases for threat words (e.g., Wenzel & Holt, 1999); we return to this point again below. Indeed, Öhman's model directly predicts that pictorial representations of innate threat stimuli (e.g., angry faces, snakes, spiders, blood-injury [BI] scenes) would be particularly effective in automatically capturing attention and triggering anxiety responses. Given the importance of examining attentional biases for nonverbal stimuli, at this point we describe some recent findings from studies that investigated selective attention to threat pictures.

Biases in Selective Attention to Emotional Faces

We modified the visual probe task to examine attentional biases for threatening faces (Bradley et al., 1997). A series of photographs of face pairs was presented, with the faces in each pair presented side by side for 500 ms. The facial expressions were threatening (i.e., angry or hostile), happy, or neutral (see Fig. 6.1 for an example). Our first two nonclinical studies indicated emotion-congruent attentional biases as nondysphoric individuals (who had low levels of depression and anxiety) showed greater avoidance of threat faces, relative to happy or neutral faces, compared with dysphoric individuals (Bradley et al., 1997). However, it was not clear from these initial studies whether avoidance of threat faces was associated with low levels of depression, anxiety, or negative affect in general (Watson & Clark, 1984). In a subsequent nonclinical study, we preselected volunteers on their trait anxiety scores (to obtain better separated high and low trait anxiety groups) and also included two exposure durations for the face stimuli (500 and 1,250 ms) to examine the time course of the attentional bias (Bradley, Mogg, Falla, & Hamilton, 1998). Results showed that high trait anxious individuals were more vigilant for threat faces relative to happy faces across both exposure durations. A subsequent study, which used only the 500-ms duration, replicated this finding of vigilance for angry faces in high trait anxiety (Mogg & Bradley, 1999b).

The above studies examined attentional biases for faces in nonclinical anxiety, and we were also interested to see whether similar biases existed for clinical anxiety. Consequently, we investigated these biases in generalized anxiety disorder using the visual probe task with threatening, happy, and neutral faces shown for two exposure durations: 500 and 1,250 ms (Bradley, Mogg, White, Groom, & de Bono, 1999). Anxious patients showed greater vigilance for threat faces relative to neutral faces compared with normal controls. This effect did not vary as a function of exposure duration. Anxious patients also showed increased vigilance for happy faces, but this was only significant in the second half of the task. As the biases for threat and happy faces appeared to develop over a different time frame, this suggests that different underlying mechanisms may be responsible. For exam-

Fig. 6.1 Example of a face pair showing threatening and neutral expressions. Copyright Brendan Bradley and Karin Mogg, 2000. Reprinted with permission.

ple, the threat bias may be mediated by relatively automatic processes involved in initial orienting of attention, whereas the bias for positive faces in clinical anxiety may depend on later strategic processes.

We carried out another series of three experiments to examine whether the bias for threat faces does indeed operate in early, preattentive processes (i.e., independently of awareness) (Mogg & Bradley, 1999a). In these visual probe studies, the face pairs were presented very briefly (ranging from 14 to 34 ms), followed by a pattern mask, and then the probe stimulus appeared after the offset of the mask. The results of two experiments were consistent with a preattentive bias for threat faces. That is, individuals were faster to respond to probes occurring in the spatial location of masked threat rather than neutral faces, consistent with the automatic capture of their attention by subliminal threat cues. Interestingly, this effect was most apparent in the left visual field, which was suggestive of right hemisphere involvement. Furthermore, one of these experiments (Experiment 3) indicated that the bias for masked threat faces was greater in high than low trait anxious individuals. However, one experiment in this series did not show evidence of a preattentive bias, although this may have been due to the awareness of the faces being less well restricted in that study.

We then conducted another experiment (Mogg & Bradley, 2002), which had two main aims: to examine whether our previous evidence of an anxiety-related bias for masked threat faces (Mogg & Bradley, 1999a, Experiment 3) could be replicated and to assess the relationship between the preattentive bias and measures of trait and social anxiety. One might expect that angry faces are a more salient stimulus for the concerns of socially anxious individuals, relative to those with more generalized anxious concerns. The results indicated that anxious individuals were faster to respond to probes replacing masked threat than neutral faces, and that this preattentive bias for threat appeared to be primarily a function of high levels of social anxiety and social avoidance rather than trait anxiety. The bias was also more apparent when threat faces were presented in the left visual field, which is compatible with our previous findings and also seems consistent with other evidence suggesting right hemisphere dominance in processing of threat (e.g., Christianson, Saisa, & Silfvenius, 1995).

Another task that has been used to examine attentional biases for angry faces is the pop-out task. This task involves presenting, on each trial, an array of pictures of faces in which one of the faces differs from the others in terms of its emotional expression. For example, in an array of 12 faces, there may be a picture of an angry face in a "crowd" of happy faces. Participants are required to detect the discrepant face in the array as quickly as possible. Using this task, Byrne and Eysenck (1995) found that high trait anxious individuals showed enhanced detection of angry faces rather than happy faces. Gilboa-Schechtman, Foa, and Amir (1999) also found vigilance for threat faces on a pop-out task, as patients with generalized social phobia showed enhanced detection of angry faces compared to happy target faces in arrays of neutral faces. So these studies provide further evidence of an anxiety-related attentional bias for angry faces.

The findings of preattentive and attentional biases for angry faces, described above, were obtained from tasks in which the biases were inferred from manual reaction time data. However, we have also been concerned to use more direct and naturalistic experimental methods, which have greater ecological validity; so we carried out several eye movement studies to examine the direction of gaze in response to emotional faces.

In our first eye movement study (Bradley, Mogg, & Millar, 2000), we monitored participants' direction of gaze while they completed a visual probe task in which the stimuli included angry, sad, happy, and neutral faces shown for 500 ms. The manual response time (RT) data showed greater vigilance for threat faces, relative to neutral faces, in those with high and medium levels of state anxiety, but not in those with low state anxiety. This attentional effect in the RT data did not seem to depend on eye movements as many participants did not shift their gaze during the display of the faces. This reflects a well-established distinction between covert attention shifts and overt eye movements; that is, it is possible to attend to a stimulus without necessarily directly looking at it, although in many everyday situations, we do generally tend to look at what we attend to (Klein, Kingstone, & Pontefract, 1995). However, for those who made frequent eye movements to the faces, there was a consistent relationship between the probe RT and eye movement measures of vigilance for negative faces relative to positive faces. Thus, the RT measure of attentional bias on the visual probe task, using faces shown for 500 ms, appears to provide a valid index of the direction of initial orienting to emotional face stimuli.

Our second eye movement study investigated attentional biases for emotional faces in generalized anxiety disorder and depressive disorder (Mogg, Millar, & Bradley, 2000). We again used the visual probe task, in which the faces were shown for 1,000 ms. Results showed that individuals with generalized anxiety disorder (without depressive disorder) were more likely to look first toward threat faces rather than neutral faces compared with normal controls and those with depressive disorder. They also shifted their gaze more quickly toward threat faces, rather than away from them, relative to the other two groups. The manual RT data did not show a significant bias in this study. This may have been due to the RT measure being obtained 1 s after the onset of the face display, which is long enough to allow more than one shift of attention to the faces, and so the RT bias measure at 1 s may not be very sensitive to automatic, initial orienting processes. In contrast, the eye movement data provided clear evidence of a bias of initial orienting to nonverbal threat stimuli in clinical generalized anxiety.

Despite the demanding nature of eye movement studies, we encourage their wider use given the ecological validity of using direction of gaze as a measure of attentional bias. For example, there is currently some debate about whether individuals with high social anxiety have a different pattern of attentional bias for angry faces compared with the pattern of those with high generalized anxiety (Clark, 1999; Mansell, Clark, Ehlers, & Chen, 1999). This issue highlights the need for additional evidence from converging measures of attentional bias to help clarify whether discrepant findings might be due to methodological differences between studies or whether they do reflect different patterns of bias in different types of anxiety.

Attentional Biases for Phobia-Related Stimuli: Spiders

There is growing evidence of attentional biases in spider-fearful individuals; for example, evidence comes from studies using the emotional Stroop task with spider-related words (e.g., Watts et al., 1986) and also with spider pictures (Kindt & Brosschot, 1997; Lavy & van den Hout, 1993). In addition, this processing bias appears to be increased by high state anxiety (Chen, Lewin, & Craske, 1996) and reduced by treatment (Lavy, van den Hout, & Arntz, 1993; van den Hout, Tenney, Huygens, & de Jong, 1997). However, some researchers (e.g., de Ruiter & Brosschot, 1994; Thorpe & Salkovkis, 1997) have questioned the value of the emotional Stroop task due to its dubious ecological validity and potential interpretative difficulties. For example, interference in color-naming threat words might reflect vigilance for threat, or it might instead reflect an effortful attempt to avoid processing threat material.

Other tasks have sometimes failed to provide evidence of attentional biases in spider-fearful individuals, such as a distraction task used by Merckelbach, Kenemans, Dijjsktra, and Schouten (1993) and the visual probe task using spider-related words as stimuli (Wenzel & Holt, 1999). Such negative findings may be explained by methodological variables, including the type of threat stimulus and its exposure duration. As noted, there are theoretical grounds (e.g., Öhman, 1996) for predicting that such attentional biases would be particularly apparent for spider pictures, rather than for spider-related words (e.g., web, hairy), because pictures provide a closer match with naturalistic, biologically prepared fear stimuli (i.e., real-life spiders). In addition, a key function of the cognitive mechanisms responsible for the bias is presumed to be the rapid, automatic detection of threat, and so it would seem important to use tasks that are particularly sensitive to these processes.

For example, on the visual probe task, the stimuli are presented in pairs, and the attentional bias measure is obtained from response times to probes that replace one of the stimuli. Thus, the RT bias measure reflects which stimulus is being attended to at the offset of the stimulus pair. As noted above, a bias in initial orienting to threat should be more evident at shorter stimulus exposure durations because these provide less opportunity for shifts of attention between the two members of the stimulus pair before the probe appears. With longer stimulus durations (e.g., 1 s or longer), attention may shift between the members of the stimulus pair, and so the RT bias measure taken under these conditions may not necessarily reflect which stimulus initially captured attention.

We examined the time course of attentional biases for spider pictures in a pictorial version of the visual probe task (Mogg & Bradley, 2003). The stimuli included pairs of photographs of spiders and cats; these were shown for 200, 500, or 2,000 ms. The results supported the prediction of greater vigilance for spider stimuli in individuals who were fearful of spiders, compared with those with low spider fear, at the shortest exposure duration of 200 ms. The attentional bias in the high-fear group reduced as stimulus exposure duration increased, with no significant biases found in the longer exposure conditions. These findings do indeed suggest that fear-relevant stimuli initially capture attention, but that this attentional bias is not maintained over time.

These findings may help to explain the mixed pattern of findings from studies of attentional biases for fear-related stimuli as they suggest that evidence of attentional biases depends critically on the type of task used. Thus, an attentional bias may be revealed using fear-relevant pictures with relatively short exposure conditions, but not when using fear-relevant words with longer durations (Mogg & Bradley, 2003, vs. Wenzel & Holt, 1999). This would seem entirely consistent with cognitive models of fear and anxiety, which predict that attentional biases should be most readily found for biologically prepared stimuli (i.e., pictorial representations of innate threats) shown under conditions that are optimally sensitive to processes involved in initial orienting to and rapid detection of threat (Öhman, 1996).

Biases in Selective Attention to Highly Aversive Pictorial Scenes

Research using nonverbal stimuli has also been used to compare predictions from two different cognitive models of anxiety. According to Williams et al.'s (1988, 1997) view, attentional biases for threat reflect vulnerability to anxiety; and as stimulus threat value increases, high trait anxious individuals should become more vigilant, and low trait individuals more avoidant, of threat. However, according to an alternative "cognitive-motivational" view, a key cognitive factor underlying vulnerability to anxiety is a tendency to overestimate stimulus threat value rather than the attentional bias per se (Mogg & Bradley, 1998). The latter model suggests that the attentional bias instead largely depends on whether a stimulus is evaluated as threatening, such that stimuli which are evaluated as having high threat value have a general tendency to capture attention. These different theoretical views lead to different predictions about the effect of stimulus threat value on attentional bias: Williams et al.'s (1997) model predicts that high-threat stimuli should provoke vigilance in high trait anxious people and avoidance in low trait individuals, whereas Mogg and Bradley's (1998) view predicts that all individuals, including those with low trait anxiety, should be more vigilant for high-threat stimuli than for mild threat stimuli.

It is difficult to test these predictions with word stimuli because these have relatively mild threat value. So, we carried out two experiments using the visual probe task, in which stimulus threat value was manipulated by selecting high and mild threat pictorial scenes (Mogg et al., 2000). The high-threat pictures included photographs such as those of mutilated bodies and a woman being attacked, while the mild-threat pictures included scenes such as soldiers with a tank and a man behind bars. The results from both studies indicated a main effect of stimulus threat value on attentional bias. That is, as stimulus threat value increased, avoidance of threat decreased and vigilance for threat increased. This effect was found even with low trait anxious individuals, consistent with the cognitive-motivational view. Thus, vigilance for threat stimuli does not seem to be, in itself, a sign of vulnerability to anxiety because it is found in people who are not anxiety prone if the threat value of the stimulus is sufficiently high.

One reason why it is of interest to compare these two cognitive models is that they have different implications for treatments for anxiety. Williams et al.'s (1988, 1997) model assumes that the attentional bias for threat is a key factor underlying susceptibility to anxiety, and so it follows that treatment should try to neutralize this bias, for example, by attentional retraining. On the other hand, Mogg and Bradley's (1998) model suggests that it should be more effective for therapy to target those processes involved in valence evaluation. Indeed, consistent with this view, a key aim of cognitive therapy, which is widely used for anxiety disorders, is to help anxious individuals reappraise anxiety-triggering stimuli and situations and to replace fearful evaluations of events with more positive and safety-oriented appraisals (e.g., Beck, Emery, & Greenberg, 1986).

Research using highly emotional pictorial scenes has also been used to address a somewhat different theoretical issue, which concerns the time course of attentional biases. As noted, there is considerable evidence that anxious individuals attend selectively to threat stimuli, and that this bias occurs in preattentive processes and initial orienting. However, several studies have indicated that threat material does not seem to be recalled better by anxious or fearful individuals, which seems surprising given that information which is preferentially attended to is typically better remembered (e.g., Mogg et al., 1987; Nugent & Mineka, 1994; Watts, Tresize, & Sharrock, 1986). One possible explanation is a "vigilant-avoidant" pattern of bias in anxiety (e.g., Mogg et al., 1987) by which anxious individuals initially direct their attention to threat, but then try to avoid detailed processing of it in an attempt to minimize their discomfort. This pattern of bias could be important in maintaining anxiety states because anxious individuals would be more likely to identify potentially threatening events, whereas subsequent cognitive avoidance would interfere with habituation or objective evaluation of them, which in turn would contribute to a failure of emotional processing (Rachman, 1980).

To examine the time course of attentional biases, we used the visual probe task with a variety of stimulus exposure durations and stimulus materials. In a nonclinical study using threat words, individuals with higher levels of state anxiety scores showed greater vigilance for threat words shown for 100 ms, with similar trends at 500 and 1,500 ms (Mogg, Bradley, de Bono, & Painter, 1997). In studies using angry faces, discussed above, we found evidence of anxiety-related vigilance that did not significantly vary across the two stimulus durations of 500 and 1,250 ms in either nonclinical high trait anxiety (Bradley et al., 1998) or in generalized anxiety disorder (Bradley et al., 1999). So these studies using relatively mild threat stimuli, such as words and photographs of faces, suggest that the bias in initial orienting to threat is not significantly counteracted by subsequent avoidance strategies (at least for the durations observed).

Our spider fear study indicated that attentional vigilance was evident for spider pictures at 200 ms in the high-fear group, but was not apparent at the longer exposure durations of 500 or 2,000 ms (Mogg & Bradley, 2003). This suggests that the fear-relevant stimuli initially captured attention, but that the attentional bias was not maintained over time. However, this study also found no evidence that initial vigilance was followed by avoidance of threat. Indeed, none of these studies found avoidance of threat at the longer stimulus durations of 1 s or longer. One possible explanation is that avoidance strategies may only be apparent for highly emotional stimuli that induce an aversive mood state, and the stimuli used in these studies did not elicit sufficient anxiety to reveal the hypothesized vigilance-avoidance pattern.

We examined this in a visual probe study by using high-threat pictorial scenes (e.g., person being attacked with knife, mutilated corpse) paired with neutral scenes, in which the stimulus pairs were presented for either 500 or 1,500 ms (Mogg, Bradley, Miles, & Dixon, in press). Our main hypothesis was that high anxious individuals will show enhanced initial orienting to high-threat scenes (i.e., vigilance at 500 ms), but avoidance of high threat at the longer exposure duration of 1,500 ms. As the high-threat pictures had a preponderance of scenes depicting attack, injury, death, and mutilation, we also assessed BI fear and trait anxiety in our sample of participants as we suspected that BI fear may be a more specific predictor of attentional biases for these stimuli rather than an index of general anxiety proneness. The results showed that, when the sample was divided into high and low trait anxiety groups, high-trait anxious individuals were more vigilant for high-threat scenes at the shorter exposure duration (500 ms). Furthermore, when the sample was reallocated to groups on the basis of BI fear scores, individuals with high BI fear showed vigilance for high-threat scenes at 500 ms and avoidance of them at 1,500 ms, which is consistent with expectation from the vigilance-avoidance hypothesis.

This pattern of initial vigilance for highly aversive information, followed by avoidance, is of potential clinical significance because it may promote the conditions under which sensitization, rather than extinction (or fear reduction), takes place (Marks, 1987). Consequently, it may play an important role in the maintenance of excessive fear and anxiety. If so, this suggests it would be therapeutically helpful to target specifically this subsequent cognitive avoidance because avoidant processing (following initial orienting) may impede an individual's ability to reevaluate the threat stimulus and to reappraise it as less threatening. Thus, secondary avoidance strategies may interfere with cognitive treatment interventions.

Conclusions

Experimental research that clarifies the precise nature of information processing biases in nonclinical and clinical anxiety is likely to be helpful not only in contributing to the understanding of the processes that may cause or maintain anxiety, but also in suggesting more effective methods of treatment. We adopted a somewhat broad perspective on the role of nonverbal processes in psychopathology. We argue that it is important for research into cognitive theories of anxiety to give greater consideration to processing of nonverbal threat information rather than relying primarily on single-word stimuli. It is also important to examine attentional responses to different types of nonverbal stimuli, including not only pictures of emotional facial expressions, but also other types of pictorial threats, such as phobia-related pictures (e.g., spiders) and scenes of death and disaster.

Failure to adopt such a wide perspective may result in the development of cognitive theories of anxiety that are incomplete and that lack general explanatory value, if, for example, they only pertain to a relatively restricted class of threat stimuli. For example, preliminary findings using word stimuli suggested that vigilance for threat was only found in nonclinical anxiety when individuals were under stress. However, more recent findings from tasks using nonverbal stimuli (e.g., angry faces) indicate anxiety-related vigilance under normal (no-stress) conditions. Thus, contrary to the suggestion from early research using word stimuli, the presence of stress does not seem to be necessary for eliciting vigilance in normal (i.e., nonclinical) individuals if more biologically prepared, nonverbal threat stimuli are used.

Finally, research into attentional biases in emotional disorders may progress more effectively if there is greater use of experimental methods that directly observe nonverbal behaviors, which provide a naturalistic, ecologically valid index of attentional orienting, such as direction of gaze.

Acknowledgments

Preparation of this chapter and much of the research reported here was supported by the Wellcome Trust (51076). Karin Mogg is a Wellcome Senior Research Fellow in Basic Biomedical Science.

References

Allport, A. (1989) Visual attention. In M. I. Posner (Ed.), *Foundations of cognitive science*. Cambridge, MA: MIT Press.

Beck, A. T. (1976). *Cognitive therapy and the emotional disorders*. New York: International Universities Press.

Beck, A. T., Emery, G., & Greenberg, R. C. (1986). *Anxiety disorders and phobias: A cognitive perspective*. New York: Basic Books.

Bower, G. H. (1981). Mood and memory. *American Psychologist, 36*, 129–148.

Bradley, B. P., Mogg, K., Falla, S. J., & Hamilton, L. R. (1998). Attentional bias for threatening facial expressions in anxiety: Manipulation of stimulus duration. *Cognition and Emotion, 12*, 737–753.

Bradley, B. P., Mogg, K., & Millar, N. (2000). Overt and covert orienting of attention to emotional faces in anxiety. *Cognition and Emotion, 14*, 789–808.

Bradley, B. P., Mogg, K., Millar, N., Bonham-Carter, C., Fergusson, E., Jenkins, J., & Parr, M. (1997). Attentional biases for emotional faces. *Cognition and Emotion, 11*, 25–42.

Bradley, B. P., Mogg, K., Millar, N., & White, J. (1995). Selective processing of negative information: Effects of clinical anxiety, concurrent depression, and awareness. *Journal of Abnormal Psychology, 104*, 3, 532–536.

Bradley, B. P., Mogg, K., White, J., Groom, C., & de Bono, J. (1999). Attentional bias for emotional faces in generalised anxiety disorder. *British Journal of Clinical Psychology, 38*, 267–278.

Butler, G., Fennell, M., Robson, P., & Gelder, M. (1991). Comparison of behaviour therapy and cognitive behaviour therapy in the treatment of generalised anxiety disorder. *Journal of Consulting and Clinical Psychology, 59*, 167–175.

Byrne, A., & Eysenck, M. W. (1995). Trait anxiety, anxious mood and threat detection. *Cognition and Emotion, 9*, 549–562.

Chen, E., Lewin, M. R., & Craske, M. G. (1996). Effects of state anxiety on selective processing of threatening information. *Cognition and Emotion, 10*, 225–240.

Christianson, S. A., Saisa, J., & Silfvenius, H. (1995). The right hemisphere recognises the bad guys. *Cognition and Emotion, 9*, 309–324.

Clark, D. M. (1999). Anxiety disorders: Why they persist and how to treat them. *Behaviour Research and Therapy, 37*, 5–27.

Cohen, J., Dunbar, K., & McClelland, J. (1990). On the control of automatic processes: A parallel distributed processing account of the Stroop effect. *Psychological Review, 97*, 332–361.

de Ruiter, C., & Brosschot, J. F. (1994). The emotional Stroop interference in anxiety: Attentional bias or cognitive avoidance. *Behaviour Research and Therapy, 32*, 315–319.

Eysenck, M. W. (1992). *Anxiety: The cognitive perspective.* Hove, England: Erlbaum.

Gilboa-Schechtman, E., Foa, E. B., & Amir, N. (1999). Attentional biases for facial expressions in social phobia: The face-in-the-crowd paradigm. *Cognition and Emotion, 13*, 305–318.

Kindt, M., & Brosschot, J. F. (1997). Phobia-related cognitive bias for pictorial and linguistic stimuli. *Journal of Abnormal Psychology, 106*, 644–648.

Klein, R., Kingstone, A., & Pontefract, A. (1995). Orienting of visual attention. In K. Rayner (Ed.), *Eye movements and visual cognition* (pp. 46–65). New York: Springer-Verlag.

Lavy, E., & van den Hout, M. (1993). Selective attention evidenced by pictorial and linguistic Stroop tasks. *Behaviour Therapy, 24*, 645–657.

Lavy, E., van den Hout, M., & Arntz, A. (1993). Attentional bias and spider phobia: Conceptual and clinical issues. *Behaviour Research and Therapy, 31*, 17–24.

MacLeod, C., & Mathews, A. (1988). Anxiety and the allocation of attention to threat. *Quarterly Journal of Experimental Psychology, 40*, 653–670.

MacLeod, C., Mathews, A., & Tata, P. (1986). Attentional bias in emotional disorders. *Journal of Abnormal Psychology, 95*, 15–20.

MacLeod, C., & Rutherford, E. M. (1992). Anxiety and the selective processing of emotional information: Mediating roles of awareness, trait and state variables, and personal relevance of stimulus materials. *Behaviour Research and Therapy, 30*, 479–491.

Mansell, W., Clark, D. M., Ehlers, A., & Chen, Y. P. (1999). Social anxiety and attention away from emotional faces. *Cognition and Emotion, 13*, 673–690.

Marks, I. M. (1987). *Fears, phobias and rituals.* Oxford, England: Oxford University Press.

Mathews, A. (1990). Why worry? The cognitive function of anxiety. *Behaviour Research and Therapy, 28*, 455–468.

Mathews, A., & MacLeod, C. (1985). Selective processing of threat cues in anxiety states. *Behaviour Research and Therapy, 23*, 563–569.

Mathews, A., & MacLeod, C. (1994). Cognitive approaches to emotion and emotional disorders. *Annual Review of Psychology, 45*, 25–50.

Mattia, J. I., Heimberg, R. G., & Hope, D. A. (1993). The revised Stroop color-naming task in social phobics. *Behaviour Research and Therapy, 31*, 305–314.

McNally, R. J., Riemann, B. C., & Kim, E. (1990). Selective processing of threat cues in panic disorder. *Behaviour Research and Therapy, 28*, 407–412.

Merckelbach, H., Kenemans, J. L., Dijkstra, A., & Schouten, E. (1993). No attentional bias for pictorial stimuli in spider-fearful subjects. *Journal of Psychopathology and Behavioral Assessment, 15*, 197–206.

Mogg, K., & Bradley, B. P. (1998). A cognitive-motivational analysis of anxiety. *Behaviour Research and Therapy, 36*, 809–848.

Mogg, K., & Bradley, B. P. (1999a). Orienting of attention to threatening facial expressions presented under conditions of restricted awareness. *Cognition and Emotion, 13*, 713–740.

Mogg, K., & Bradley, B. P. (1999b). Some methodological issues in assessing attentional biases for threatening faces in anxiety: A replication study using a modified version of the probe detection task. *Behaviour Research and Therapy, 37*, 595–604.

Mogg, K., & Bradley, B. P. (2002). Selective orienting to masked threat faces in social anxiety. *Behavior Research and Therapy, 40*, 1403–1414.

Mogg, K., Bradley, B. P., de Bono, J., & Painter, M. (1997). Time course of attentional bias for threat information in non-clinical anxiety. *Behaviour Research and Therapy, 35*, 297–303.

Mogg, K., Bradley, B. P., & Hallowell, N. (1994). Attentional bias to threat: Roles of trait anxiety, stressful events, and awareness. *Quarterly Journal of Experimental Psychology, 47A*, 841–864.

Mogg, K., Bradley, B. P., Miles, F., & Dixon, R. (in press). Time course of attentional bias for threat scenes: Testing the vigilance-avoidance hypothesis. *Cognition and Emotion.*

Mogg, K., Bradley, B. P., & Williams, R. (1995). Attentional bias in anxiety and depression: The role of awareness. *British Journal of Clinical Psychology, 34*, 17–36.

Mogg, K., Bradley, B. P., Williams, R., & Mathews, A. (1993). Subliminal processing of emotional information in anxiety and depression. *Journal of Abnormal Psychology, 102*, 304–311.

Mogg, K., & Bradley, B. P. (2003). *Time course of attentional bias for pictorial stimuli in spider-fearful individuals.* Manuscript in preparation.

Mogg, K., Mathews, A., & Weinman, J. (1987). Memory bias in clinical anxiety. *Journal of Abnormal Psychology, 96*, 94–98.

Mogg, K., McNamara, J., Powys, M., Rawlinson, H., Seiffer, A., & Bradley, B. P. (2000). Selective attention to threat: A test of two cognitive models. *Cognition and Emotion, 14*, 375–399.

Mogg, K., Millar, N., & Bradley, B. P. (2000). Biases in eye movements to threatening facial expressions in generalised anxiety disorder and depressive disorder. *Journal of Abnormal Psychology, 109*, 695–704.

Nugent, K., & Mineka, S. (1994). The effect of high and low trait anxiety on implicit and explicit memory tasks. *Cognition and Emotion, 8*, 147–163.

Öhman, A. (1993). Fear and anxiety as emotional phenomena: Clinical phenomenology, evolutionary perspectives, and information processing mechanisms. In M. Lewis & J. M. Haviland (Eds.), *Handbook of emotions* (pp. 511–536). New York: Guilford Press.

Öhman, A. (1996). Preferential preattentive processing of threat in anxiety: Preparedness and attentional biases. In R. M. Rapee (Ed.), *Current controversies in the anxiety disorders* (pp 253–290). New York: Guilford Press.

Posner, M. I., Snyder, C. R., & Davidson, B. J. (1980). Attention and the detection of signals. *Journal of Experimental Psychology: General, 109*, 160–174.

Rachman, S. (1980). Emotional processing. *Behaviour Research and Therapy, 18*, 51–60.

Thorpe, S., & Salkovskis, P. (1997). Information processing in spider phobics: The Stroop colour naming test may indicate strategic but not automatic attentional bias. *Behaviour Research and Therapy, 35*, 131–144.

van den Hout, M., Tenney, N., Huygens, K., & de Jong, P. (1997). Preconscious processing bias in specific phobia. *Behaviour Research and Therapy, 35*, 29–34.

Watson, D., & Clark, L. A. (1984). Negative affectivity: The disposition to experience aversive emotional states. *Psychological Bulletin, 96*, 465–490.

Watts, F., McKenna, F. P., Sharrock, R., & Trezise, L. (1986). Colour-naming of phobia-related words. *British Journal of Psychology, 77*, 97–108.

Watts, F., Tresize, L., & Sharrock, R. (1986). Processing of phobic stimuli. *British Journal of Clinical Psychology, 25*, 253–261.

Wenzel, A., & Holt, C. S. (1999). Dot probe performance in two specific phobias. *British Journal of Clinical Psychology, 38*, 407–410.

Williams, J. M. G., Mathews, A., & MacLeod, C. (1996). The emotional Stroop task and psychopathology. *Psychological Bulletin, 120*, 3–24.

Williams, J. M. G., Watts, F. N., MacLeod, C., & Mathews, A. (1988). *Cognitive psychology and emotional disorders*. Chichester, England: Wiley.

Williams, J. M. G., Watts, F. N., MacLeod, C., & Mathews, A. (1997). *Cognitive psychology and emotional disorders* (2nd ed.). Chichester, England: Wiley.

7

The Social and Functional Aspects of Emotional Expression During Bereavement

GEORGE A. BONANNO AND ANTHONY PAPA

Much of the early theory and research on emotion focused on intrapsychic processes related to the experience and physiology of emotion or on the role played by emotion in broader self-regulatory and motivational processes. As researchers turned their attention increasingly toward nonverbal expressions, particularly toward expressions of emotion in the face, the social aspects of emotion became apparent (e.g., Tomkins, 1962). A core assumption of most contemporary accounts of emotion is that the expression of emotion influences an individual's adaptation to both significant life events and the social milieu (Barrett & Campos, 1987; Bowlby, 1980; Ekman, 1992; Keltner & Kring, 1998; Lazarus, 1991).

A particularly promising context from which to examine the social and functional aspects of nonverbal emotional expression is midlife conjugal bereavement. The death of a spouse is often considered to be one of the most difficult stressor events a person might endure (e.g., Holmes & Rahe, 1967). This may be particularly important when such a loss occurs prematurely, during midlife (Bonanno & Keltner, 1997).

In this chapter, we first provide some background by considering the distinction between the constructs of grief and emotion. Next, we review traditional concepts of emotion and bereavement and then turn to more recent conceptualizations of bereavement from a social functional perspective. We review the empirical evidence in support of the social functional view of emotion during bereavement, with particular emphasis on the interpersonal consequences and how these might influence or interact with supports in the bereaved person's social environment. In the remainder of the chapter, we take a closer look at the theoretical and empirical literature on social support processes in aversive life events and attempt to integrate these views with the social functional approach to emotional expression.

Differentiating Grief and Emotion

Few would argue that grief is a highly emotionally charged experience that shares features with several basic emotions, particularly sadness (Lazarus, 1991). The similarities between grief and emotion have caused some investigators to describe grief as a form of emotion (Averill & Nunley, 1993; Stearns & Knapp, 1996). A closer analysis, however, reveals a number of key differences between the two constructs. Bonanno (2001; Bonanno & Kaltman, 1999) has outlined four such differences. First, emotion and grief involve different temporal experiences. Emotions are by definition ephemeral, typically lasting seconds and only occasionally longer (Ekman, 1984; Izard, 1977), whereas grief is a markedly more enduring state that persists in most bereaved individuals for several months up to several years (Bonanno & Kaltman, 2001).

Second, although the process of mourning is most commonly associated with sadness, the death of a loved one also evokes a wide range of other emotions, including other negative emotions, such as anger, contempt, hostility, fear, and guilt (Abraham, 1924; Belitsky & Jacobs, 1986; Bonanno & Keltner, 1997; Bonanno, Mihalecz, & LeJeune, 1999; Bowlby, 1980; Cerney & Buskirk, 1991; Kavanagh, 1990; Lazare, 1989; Osterweis, Solomon, & Green, 1984; Raphael, 1983), and genuinely positive emotions related to amusement, happiness, and pride (Bonanno, Mihalecz, et al., 1999; Bonanno & Keltner, 1997; Keltner & Bonanno, 1997; Shuchter & Zisook, 1993).

Third, different meaning structures appear to characterize each phenomenon. Emotions involve relatively simple, brief, and proximal appraisals of harm or benefit, of coping potential, and of the interaction of these processes with motivational states relevant to the immediate situation (Frijda, 1993; Lazarus, 1991; Roseman, Antoniou, & Jose, 1996; Scherer, 1993). However, emotional responses may even occur in the absence of these simple cognitive appraisals. There is now compelling evidence that the chemical and physical responses associated with basic emotions, such as fear, can be triggered solely in response to rapid, automated, subcortical processing of crude perceptual information (LeDoux, 1989, 1996). In contrast, the meaning structures associated with grief can involve the entire life span, as well as major aspects of the past and present, of identity, and of beliefs about the world (Bonanno, 1997; Bonanno & Kaltman, 1999; Schwartzberg & Janoff-Bulman, 1991) and future (Horowitz et al., 1997; Lehman, Wortman, & Williams, 1987; Shuchter & Zisook, 1993).

Fourth, emotion and grief tend to evoke different coping responses. Emotion is closely bound to short-term coping responses that target the immediate psychological or physical state. Emotion and coping appear to be so intimately related, in fact, that coping has been described as a mediator of emotion (Folkman & Lazarus, 1988, 1990). The coping efforts associated with grieving, in contrast, are typically aimed at much more long-term concerns, such as calming the repeated experiences of emotional distress and the concrete disruptions in social roles, economic situation, and familial configuration (Bonanno & Keltner, 1997; Izard, 1977; Lazarus, 1991; Shuchter & Zisook, 1993; Stroebe & Stroebe, 1987).

In summary, emotions are relatively ephemeral; vary greatly in their form; are tied to relatively simple, proximal appraisals of the immediate situational context; and are closely bound to short-term coping responses. In contrast, grief is usually considerably longer in duration; encompasses a variety of emotional responses; interacts with broader and longer term meaning structures; and tends to require relatively longer term coping responses. For these reasons, in the research we describe below, we compared emotional processes associated with a loss (as measured by their immediate, situation-bound manifestations, e.g., facial expressions of emotion) with grief symptoms (as measured by structured clinical interviews designed to assess participants' level of psychological functioning over longer periods of time, e.g., difficulty concentrating during the past month).

The Traditional Grief Work Perspective on Emotion and Bereavement

Until recently, conceptions of emotion during bereavement were based largely on the traditional view that recovery from the death of a loved one necessitates that the bereaved survivor work through the cognitive and emotional meanings of the loss (Belitsky & Jacobs, 1986; Bowlby, 1980; Cerney & Buskirk, 1991; Deutsch, 1937; Freud, 1917/1957; Horowitz, 1986; Lazare, 1989; Lindemann, 1944; Marris, 1958; Osterweis et al., 1984; Parkes & Weiss, 1983; Rando, 1984; Raphael, 1983; Sanders, 1993; Worden, 1991). Key to this perspective is the assumption that grief-related emotions generally need to be expressed. For example, bereavement theorists have assumed almost without question that grieving individuals "have a need to express their responses to a loss or death" (Corr, Nabe, & Corr, 1994, p. 199), and that the "emotional expression of inner experience is a highly adaptive means of coping with the painful aspects of grief" (Shuchter & Zisook, 1993, p. 33). Not surprisingly, great emphasis has been placed on the "natural release of affects related to the loss" (Raphael, 1983, p. 368) and, for many bereavement theorists, the "expression of grieving affects" (Raphael, 1983, p. 368) is seen as a central component of the recovery process.

The traditional emphasis on expressing grief-related emotion has centered primarily on negative emotions, particularly anger and hostility (Belitsky & Jacobs, 1986; Bowlby, 1980; Cerney & Buskirk, 1991; Lazare,

1989; Raphael, 1983). Interestingly, grief work theorists have been relatively silent on the possible role of positive emotions during bereavement. In fact, references to positive emotions are virtually nonexistent in the bereavement literature.

What, then, does the grief work perspective suggest about expressing positive emotions during bereavement? Although speculation on this point is somewhat tenuous (Bonanno, 2001), it can be argued that theorists espousing a traditional grief work view would see expressing positive emotions as a kind of denial that disrupts or impedes the proper work of mourning. There is some evidence to support this supposition. Consider, for example, Sanders's (1979) categorization of a "denial group" of bereaved individuals, based on their responses to self-report scales, as "determined optimists" (p. 238). Denial during bereavement has also been associated with exaggerated positive or "idealized" representations of the deceased (Raphael, 1983). Bowlby (1980) also described a form of "disordered mourning" in which there is a prolonged absence of grieving despite "tell-tale signs that the bereaved person has in fact been affected and that his mental equilibrium is disturbed" (p. 153). Among the tell-tale signs indexed were the positive emotions of pride and cheerfulness, as well as optimism and the appearance of being "in good spirits" (p. 156).

The Social and Functional Perspective on Emotion During Bereavement

Although the grief work perspective has been widely endorsed in the bereavement literature (Stroebe & Stroebe, 1987), it has yet to generate convincing empirical support (Bonanno & Kaltman, 1999). Indeed, much of the recent evidence on emotion during bereavement actually contradicts the grief work perspective and appears to be much more consistent with social functional approaches to emotion (Barrett & Campos, 1987; Bonanno & Keltner, 1997; Bowlby, 1980; Darwin, 1872; Ekman, 1992; Keltner, 1995; Keltner & Haidt, 2001; Lazarus, 1991).

From a social functional perspective, emotions are universal, inherited behavioral response programs that have evolved as solutions to persistent, fundamental threats to survival (Keltner & Haidt, in press). This perspective further assumes that emotions evolved as solutions to both intrapersonal and interpersonal challenges (Barrett & Campos, 1987; Bonanno & Keltner, 1997; Darwin, 1872; Ekman, 1992; Keltner & Buswell, 1997; Levenson, 1994). Emotions organize intrapersonal functioning by serving as a vehicle by which situation-specific behavioral patterns, such as the anger or flight responses, are activated and by coordinating different types of response systems (e.g., experiential, behavioral, and physiological response systems). Emotions influence interpersonal functioning by fostering quick and effective communication among members of the species and by evoking responses in others that help maintain the social order and intimate relationships.

Negative Emotions

Emotion theorists have tended to parse basic negative emotions based largely on their unique adaptive and functional relevance. We consider these distinctions here for two emotions, anger and sadness, typically associated with bereavement. Anger is generally thought to externalize blame, mobilize resources, and help ward off attack by communicating the readiness to defend the self. In contrast, sadness is unrelated to blame, but appears to foster reflection, resignation, and acceptance and evokes sympathy and helping responses in others (Izard, 1977, 1992; Lazarus, 1991; Stearns, 1993). Expressing anger during bereavement may be adaptive in some situations (i.e., by externalizing blame or mobilizing resources), and there may be specified situations for which the defense from either real or perceived attack is a genuine need. Similarly, expressing sadness during bereavement may help to focus thoughts on coping with the concrete difficulties associated with the loss (e.g., changes in financial status) and might serve as a useful signal to others of the need for comfort or assistance.

It is difficult to imagine how the repeated or intensified expressions of these emotions, as suggested by the traditional grief work perspective, would promote recovery. Indeed, from a social functional point of view, the persistent and intense expression of negative emotions often leads to untoward personal and social consequences (Keltner, Ellsworth, & Edwards, 1993; Keltner, Moffitt, & Stouthamer-Loeber, 1995; Lemerise & Dodge, 1993; Levenson & Gottman, 1983; Watson & Clark, 1984; Watson & Pennebaker, 1989). Persistent or intense expressions of anger, for example, threaten to damage interpersonal relationships and undo social supports (Cole & Zahn-Waxler, 1992; Keltner et al., 1993). In fact, in many cultures expressions of anger during bereavement are viewed as potential dangers to the social fabric of the larger community and hence are actively discouraged (Archer, 1999; Rosenblatt, Walsh, & Jackson, 1976). Similarly, prolonged or intensified sadness has been associated with withdrawal, despair, and the elicitation of rejection from others (Ellsworth & Smith, 1985; Lazarus, 1991). One can easily imagine how prolonged expressions of sadness after a loss would wear on those in the bereaved person's immediate social environment. We consider these issues again below.

From a social functional perspective on emotion during bereavement, there are clear advantages to minimizing or otherwise regulating the expression of negative emotions (Bonanno & Keltner, 1997). Minimizing negative emotions during bereavement, for instance, would facilitate attempts to continue to function in areas of personal importance, such as performing in the workplace or caring for dependents (Shuchter & Zisook, 1993; Stroebe & Stroebe, 1987). It is also likely that minimizing or regulating the expression of negative emotions would help to free resources for coping with the myriad concrete problems associated with conjugal loss, such as adjusting to changes in the family configuration or changes in economic status.

Positive Emotions and Laughter

The traditional grief work perspective on emotion during bereavement has all but ignored the possible role played by positive emotions (Bonanno, 1999b). Although positive emotions are frequently discussed by emotion theorists, compared to the well-developed literature on negative emotions, the functional and social relevance of positive emotions are far less well developed. Lazarus, Kanner, and Folkman (1980) noted that positive emotions serve adaptive functions as breathers that both temporarily free a person from the stress of an experience and allow pleasurable diversionary activity; these are sustainers that foster the persistence of coping efforts and restorers that replenish damaged or depleted resources or foster the development of new resources. Several theorists have noted the important social function played by positive emotions such as amusement (Provine, 1992; Ruch, 1993). In the specific context of coping with bereavement, however, Bonanno and Keltner (1997) proposed that positive emotions might serve an important social function by "increasing continued contact with and support from important people in the bereaved person's social environment" (p. 134).

Empirical Studies of Nonverbal Emotional Expression During Bereavement

Despite the relative prominence given to emotional expression in traditional perspectives on bereavement, nonverbal forms of emotional expression have received remarkably little research attention. Some of the only empirical evidence available comes from a set of recent studies conducted in our own lab. These studies used three different methodological approaches. One approach involved the comparison of subjective "felt" experience with a measure of autonomic arousal. A second involved measurement of facial expressions of emotion. The third approach involved the comparison of facial expressions of emotion with simultaneous, "on-line" expressions of emotion-related appraisal coded from narrative transcripts. We examine each of these approaches in turn below.

Affective-Autonomic Response Dissociation

Emotion theorists generally agree that emotions are not single unitary phenomena, but rather manifest in multiple response modalities, including the

subjective felt experience, cognitive processes, visceral-physiological reactions, and expressive-behavioral reactions (Buck, 1988; Ekman, 1992; Izard,
1977, 1992; Lang, 1979; Leventhal, 1984, 1991). Although these different
forms of emotional responding are generally thought to occur in loosely
coupled emotion response "programs," it is also widely acknowledged that
different types of emotional responses may occur partially independent
from one another. Emotion may be expressed at one response channel, for
example and be absent, or even contradicted, at another response channel
(Bonanno, Keltner, Holen, & Horowitz, 1995; Buck, 1988; Ekman, 1992;
Izard, 1977, 1992; Lang, 1979; Lang, Kozak, Miller, Levin, & McLean, 1980;
Levenson, 1994; Leventhal, 1984, 1991; Schwartz, Fair, Greenberg, Freedman, & Klerman, 1974; Schwartz, Fair, Salt, Mandel, & Klerman, 1976).

One form of emotional response dissociation that has received considerable empirical attention is the dissociation between the subjective experiences of distress and physiological arousal. This type of response dissociation, commonly referred to as affective-autonomic response dissociation,
occurs when relatively little negative emotion is experienced, despite
evidence of increased physiological arousal, during potentially stressful situations (Bonanno et al., 1995; Newton & Contrada, 1992; Weinberger,
Schwartz, & Davidson, 1979). Affective-autonomic dissociation is generally
assumed to be a marker of emotional avoidance (Bonanno & Singer, 1990;
Krohne, 1992; Lazarus, 1966; Newton & Contrada, 1992).

Evidence for the construct validity of affective-autonomic response dissociation as a measure of emotional avoidance comes from several sources.
Affective-autonomic dissociation has shown high test-retest reliability over
an 8-month interval (Bonanno et al., 1995) and has been consistently observed among individuals categorized as repressive copers (Asendorpf &
Scherer. 1983; Newton & Contrada, 1992; Weinberger et al., 1979; Weinberger & Davidson, 1994). Repressors, in turn, have shown a general ability
to selectively attend away from threatening information (Bonanno, Davis,
Singer, & Schwartz, 1991; Fox, 1993). Further, when informed of their elevated levels of arousal, repressors have been reported to doubt the accuracy
of the autonomic equipment rather than revise their subjective appraisals
(Weinberger & Davidson, 1994). Affective-autonomic dissociation has also
been found to correlate with clinical ratings of the avoidance of emotional
awareness (Bonanno et al., 1995) and is evidenced regardless of whether
participants report on their subjective experience after a stressful event or
on a continuous basis (Brosschot & Janssen, 1998).

To examine the relationship of affective-autonomic response dissociation to long-term functioning during bereavement, Bonanno et al. (1995)
asked middle-aged, conjugally bereaved adults to talk about their prior relationship with their deceased spouses and their reactions to the loss of that
relationship at the 6-month point in bereavement. Autonomic arousal and
subjective ratings of negative emotion were obtained from the interview

and then combined to form the affective-autonomic dissociation score (for a detailed description of the calculation of the affective-autonomic dissociation score, see Bonanno et al., 1995).

From a traditional grief work perspective, individuals who show emotionally avoidant behaviors, such as affective-autonomic dissociation, while discussing their recent loss could be expected to show relatively intense or chronic grief reactions. Importantly, traditional grief work theorists have assumed that avoidant behaviors, such as affective-autonomic dissociation, may be effective in reducing distress over the short term, but that these behaviors can only temporarily forestall the grieving process, and, consequently, that grief will eventually manifest in the form of a delayed increase in symptoms (Deutsch, 1937; Horowitz, 1976; Osterweis et al., 1984; Parkes & Weiss, 1983; Rando, 1992; Raphael, 1983; Sanders, 1993; Worden, 1991).

In contrast, from a social functional perspective on emotion, the dissociation of emotional arousal might serve an adaptive function during bereavement. Reduced awareness of distress can be viewed as a normative behavioral response based in the evolutionary advantage of the organism being able to respond to many different stimuli on many different levels (Ledoux, 1989, 1996). This may be particularly adaptive during bereavement, as noted above, because it allows increased attention to concrete problems associated with the loss or to care for dependent others (Shuchter & Zisook, 1993). Transient shifts away from painful emotions would also foster well-being more generally by helping to lessen the emotional impact of the loss (Stroebe & Stroebe, 1987).

The results were consistent with the social functional view and contradicted the traditional grief work perspective. Individuals showing affective-autonomic response dissociation tended to show the mildest level of grief symptoms (e.g., dysphoria, trouble sleeping, difficulty accepting the reality of the loss) across 25 months of bereavement perspective (Bonanno et al., 1995; Bonanno, Znoj, Siddique, & Horowitz, 1999). Further, the association between affective-autonomic dissociation and reduced grief symptoms remained significant when initial levels of grief were statistically controlled (Bonanno, Znoj, et al., 1999). There was an association between affective-autonomic response dissociation and increased somatic complaints at the initial 6-month point in bereavement. However, this association was no longer evident at 14- and 25-month follow-ups. In addition, affective-autonomic dissociation was unrelated to the frequency of visits to medical professionals (Bonanno, Znoj, et al., 1999). Thus, affective-autonomic dissociation appears to be an effective means of coping with grief-related symptoms. Although there was some initial cost in elevated somatic complaints, this cost appeared to be relatively short lived and outweighed by the overall benefit of reduced levels of distress (Bonanno et al., 1995).

Facial Expressions of Emotion

Although there are a number of different types of nonverbal expression that might be considered (e.g., tone of voice, posture), there are at least three reasons why facial expressions of emotion are an optimal measure for investigating the consequences of emotion expression during bereavement. First, facial expressions are the primary means by which humans communicate emotion (Bowlby, 1980; Darwin, 1872; Ekman, 1992; Tomkins, 1962). Second, there exist well-validated methods to code facial expressions reliably for a number of basic emotions. Third, social and functional accounts of emotion are arguably most well developed in the literature on facial expressions.

Accordingly, Bonanno and Keltner (1997) coded facial expressions of negative and positive emotions from videotaped interviews of the same conjugally bereaved participants used in the affective-autonomic dissociation studies discussed above. Consistent with the social functional perspective, facial expressions of anger, contempt, disgust, fear, and a negative expression composite, coded from videotapes at 6 months postloss, were each positively correlated with grief at 14 months postloss. Of particular interest was the fact that facial expressions of anger were the most robustly associated with increased grief at 14 months and were still correlated with increased grief at the 25-month point in bereavement. These findings are of particular interest because the expression of anger, perhaps more than any other emotion, is encouraged by grief work theorists (Belitsky & Jacobs, 1986; Cerney & Buskirk, 1991). Further, the relationship of negative emotional expression to increased grief remained significant when both the initial correlations among grief, facial expressions of emotion, and self-reported emotion were statistically controlled.

To illustrate better the mediating role of facial expressions of negative emotion in relation to grief course, we graphed the change in grief symptoms over time for participants who showed the least facial expression of negative emotion (the lower 25% of the distribution) and participants who showed the most facial expression of negative emotion (upper 25% of the distribution). As can be seen in Fig. 7.1, although the low negative emotion group tended to have less grief initially relative to the high negative emotion group, there were still a number of highly grieved participants in each group. Most important for our concerns here, bereaved participants with relatively high levels of initial grief who expressed low levels of negative emotion showed steady declines in grief across time. In contrast, bereaved participants with relatively high levels of initial grief who expressed high levels of negative emotion tended to stay high in grief across the 25 months studied.

The findings for positive emotions were also consistent with the social functional perspective on emotion during bereavement. Laughter and smil-

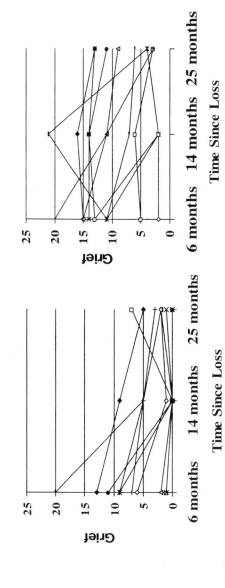

Fig. 7.1 Grief course for bereaved individuals who showed either low or high facial expressions of negative emotion at 6 months postloss.

ing during the bereavement interview were each correlated with reduced grief at 14 and 25 months postloss. As with negative emotions, these correlations tended to remain significant when initial grief and self-reported emotion were controlled. Importantly, these data show important differences between genuine or "Duchenne" laughter and smiles and non-Duchenne or polite expressions. Duchenne expressions are distinguished from non-Duchenne or polite expressions by their inclusion of movement of the orbicularis occuli muscles around the eyes (Duchenne de Boulogne, 1862). In previous studies, these muscle movements have been linked to genuine positive emotion and to positive interpersonal consequences, whereas non-Duchenne expressions do not show these relations (e.g., Frank, Ekman, & Friesen, 1993). Similarly, in the Bonanno and Keltner (1997) study, only Duchenne laughs and smiles were associated with self-reported positive emotion, and only Duchenne laughs and smiles were meaningfully associated with outcome.

Bonanno and Keltner (1997) concluded that the role of positive emotions during mourning creates an "appropriate corollary to the common observation of social isolation and loneliness as intrinsic features of severe grief reactions" (p. 134). Of particular interest to the concerns of this chapter, Keltner and Bonanno (1997) subsequently provided further evidence for the social benefits of laughter during bereavement. In this study, the conjugally bereaved participants who had shown Duchenne laughter while talking about their loss also evaluated their lost relationship as better adjusted on an independent questionnaire assessment and were found to be less ambivalent about other important people currently in their lives.

To explore further the possible social benefits of laughter during bereavement, Keltner and Bonanno (1997) also showed untrained observers videotapes with the sound turned off of the bereaved participants. The observers were informed that the videotapes contained footage of bereaved individuals talking about their loss, and the observers were instructed to provide their honest reactions to the videotapes. Using this approach, it was found that bereaved participants who had laughed during the interview were less likely to evoke frustration in the observers relative to bereaved participants who did not laugh. In addition, and consistent with previous evidence for the social contagion effect of laughter (Hatfield, Cacioppo, & Rapson, 1992; Provine, 1992), the observers also reported experiencing more positive emotion when they viewed bereaved laughers compared to bereaved individuals who did not laugh during the interview. Although the somewhat artificial, short-term nature of this procedure suggests the need for interpretive caution (e.g., how people respond to a videotape may be quite different from how they react to a series of interpersonal encounters over time), at minimum these findings provide preliminary evidence for the immediate social benefits of laughter during bereavement.

The Coherence of Facial Expressions of Emotion

In the previous sections, we discussed the experience and expression of emotions during bereavement, with particular emphasis on the benefits of minimizing or dissociating negative grief-related emotions and accentuating positive grief-related emotions. These findings raise interesting questions about the relative coherence of emotion and the differences in emotional experience and expression across responses systems. In this section, we consider these questions more directly in the context of several widely held assumptions about the coherence of facial expressions of emotion. Specifically, we consider the assumption that facial expressions of emotion show event-response coherence and between-systems coherence (Bonanno & Keltner, in press).

Event-response coherence pertains to the assumption that facial expressions of specific emotions occur in response to compatible appraisal patterns. For instance, the facial muscle movements associated with anger are assumed to follow events that generate appraisals of injustice (Lazarus, 1991; Oatley & Jenkins, 1996), whereas facial muscle movements associated with sadness are assumed to follow events that generate appraisals of irrevocable loss (Lazarus, 1991; Smith & Lazarus, 1993). Bonanno and Keltner (in press) examined event-response coherence during bereavement by first coding participants' narrative discourse for emotion-related appraisal patterns based on Lazarus's (1991) theory of appraisal. They then examined whether facial expressions of anger, sadness, and Duchenne laughter and smiling occurred at approximately the same time as comparable appraisal components. A contingency analysis was employed to control for the base rate occurrence of the facial and appraisal patterns.

Between-systems coherence pertains to the assumption that facial expressions of emotion occur in coordination with other emotion response systems. A particularly interesting aspect of between-systems coherence is the assumption, advanced by a number of emotion theorists, that the experience of emotion is most pronounced when multiple emotion-response systems operate concurrently (D'Amasio, 1994; Ekman, 1992; Ortony & Turner, 1990). To investigate this aspect of between-systems coherence, Bonanno and Keltner (in press) examined whether the self-reported emotional experience for a given emotion was greater among participants who had previously exhibited event-response coherence for that emotion (i.e., exhibited a facial expression and narrative appraisal components of the same emotion concurrently) compared to participants who had not exhibited event-response coherence for the emotion.

The results supported both types of coherence for the two negative emotions, anger and sadness. The findings for laughter and smiling were more complex, but generally were consistent with previous work highlighting the unique qualities of these two different types of facial display. In addition, the laughter findings also suggested several additional implications. In the earlier study, Keltner and Bonanno (1997) reported that individuals who laughed while describing their loss were also more likely to evidence affective-autonomic response dissociation. This finding, which Keltner and Bonanno termed "laughter-as-dissociation," was consistent with previous work associating laughter with the adoption of a novel perspective, with the experience of gaining insight into an undesirable, unexpected, or dangerous situation and in general with the shift toward more positive states (Martin & Lefcourt, 1983; Rothbart, 1973). Based on the laughter-as-dissociation hypothesis, Bonanno and Keltner (in press) subsequently made the prediction that laughter would also be more likely to occur while bereaved participants were describing events related to appraisals of negative emotions, particularly appraisals associated with anger (Tomkins, 1984). Again, the results supported this prediction.

The occurrence of laughter in the context of anger also suggests a broader social function. In this case, laughter might serve as a conciliatory gesture to counteract a potential rupture in the social exchange related to anger. The maintenance of interpersonal support is a crucial concern during distressing periods, such as bereavement (Cohen & Wills, 1985). Both anger and laughter are primarily interpersonal emotions (Averill, 1982; Campos, Campos, & Barrett, 1989; Lemerise & Dodge, 1993; Provine & Fischer, 1989). However, anger threatens to undo social support by signaling to others the externalization of blame, the mobilization of defensive resources, and the readiness to attack (Izard, 1977; Lazarus, 1991). Not surprisingly, anger during bereavement is viewed across many different cultures as a dangerous and inappropriate response that should be regulated or dampened (Mandelbaum, 1959; Rosenblatt, 1993).

In contrast, laughter is associated with enhanced social relations and the evocation of positive emotional responses in others across a range of situational contexts (Hatfield et al., 1992; Provine, 1992; Vinton, 1989; Westfeld, 1993). Further, in contrast to the action-readiness of anger, laughter is typically accompanied by a relaxed posture, reduced muscle tone, and the temporary inability to respond (Fried, Wilson, MacDonald, & Behnke, 1998; Ruch, 1993). Thus, in the context of verbal discourse that communicates anger, laughter signals the speaker's willingness and ability to counteract the potential for aggression and to restore and maintain a more pro-social exchange (Keltner & Bonanno, 1997; Malatesta, 1990).

Further Reflections on the Interpersonal Consequences of Dysphoric Emotion

When considered together, the theory and research reviewed in the previous sections strongly suggest the possibility that there may be a social benefit to minimizing the expression of negative emotions and accentuating the expression of positive emotions, including laughter, during bereavement. By the same token, the intensified and persistent expression of negative emotions, and the failure to take advantage of the salutary impact of positive emotions, may engender a social cost during bereavement.

One explanation for the possible social costs of persistently and intensely expressing negative emotions during bereavement is suggested by a body of research on the role of depression and dysphoria in social interactions (Coyne, 1976; Strack & Coyne, 1983). Dysphoria and depression are highly comorbid with grief and trauma reactions (American Psychiatric Association, 1994; Horowitz et al., 1997). In terms of the interpersonal effects of dysphoria, Coyne and colleagues argued that others find the emotive behavior of depressive and dysphoric people aversive and in turn guilt provoking. This causes the potential supporter to try to reduce the aversive behaviors and alleviate personal guilt by use of ineffectual, nongenuine reassurance and support.

Above, we reviewed the literature to suggest that the persistent and intensified expression of anger and sadness during bereavement would tax the bereaved person's social support system and possibly cause damage to important interpersonal relationships. Similarly, Coyne and colleagues proposed that continued exposure to expressions of dysphoric mood will tend to lead potential supporters to reject and avoid a depressive and dysphoric person. Importantly, however, it is the dysphoric person's response to this rejection and avoidance that finally exacerbates this untoward cycle. In this view, the dysphoric person perceives this rejecting/avoidant response of others and, in a further attempt to gain the much-needed support, responds by acting with increasingly depressive mannerisms. In effect, the response dysphoric individuals evoke in others reinforces and stimulates their depressive/dysphoric symptoms and primes a schema of hypersensitivity to rejection (Coyne, 1976; Strack & Coyne, 1983). These effects have been found in the reactions of both strangers and close family members (Coyne et al., 1987; Howes & Hokanson, 1979) and are associated with higher levels of psychological distress and suppressed immune system functioning for the supporter (Coyne et al., 1987; Kiecolt-Glaser, Glaser, Shuttleworth, & Dyer, 1987).

This cost may explain unwillingness on the part of potential supporters to engage in interactions with those in need. Lehman, Ellard, and Wortman (1986) asked bereaved participants which kinds of support attempts were helpful or unhelpful and compared their responses to those of a sample of potential support providers. What is most interesting about this study is that responses by the control participants about what kinds of support would be useful corresponded highly with those of the bereaved. Yet, given that the pool of potential supporters clearly indicated knowledge of what would be helpful, the bereaved still reported having received a high degree of unhelpful support attempts. Lehman et al. (1986) speculated that the

potential supporters' anxiety about interacting with a person who has experienced a crisis, and the possibility that they may contribute to another
distress, may lead them to act in an automatic or ritualized way. An alternative explanation, more consistent with the interpersonal theory of dysphoria, is that the response patterns of the support recipients in these interactions only allow the potential supporter to respond partially to their needs
or to respond in a superficial manner.

Theoretical and Clinical Implications

The findings reviewed in this chapter suggest a number of implications,
both at the level of general emotion theory and at the more specific level
of possible clinical interventions with bereaved individuals. One obvious
implication is that bereaved individuals who manage to control or minimize their expression of grief-related emotion should be encouraged to continue to do so or, at the very least, not discouraged from doing so. If this
seems an oversimplification, it should be considered that such advice runs
decidedly counter to widespread acceptance of the traditional assumption
that failing to express grief-related emotions is somehow maladaptive or
destined to result eventually in a delayed grief reaction. Indeed, this assumption has persisted despite the fact that delayed grief has yet to be demonstrated empirically, even in studies that have directly assessed the
phenomenon (Bonanno & Field, 2001).

Perhaps a more pressing implication is that bereaved individuals who
do engage in intense and repeated expressions of negative grief-related
emotions need to find ways to alleviate or short-circuit these responses.
Somewhat ironically, since the bereavement literature has focused so much
on the importance of the "expression of grieving affects" (Raphael, 1983,
p. 368), there have been relatively few attempts to understand how grief-
related emotions may be circumvented. One obvious mean by which this
might be undertaken is to encourage distraction behaviors and strategies.
The usefulness of distraction in the aftermath of an untoward event was
demonstrated in a study of the individuals who had endured the Loma
Prieta earthquake in the San Francisco Bay area of California (Nolen-
Hoeksema & Morrow, 1991). In this study, individuals who focused on their
thoughts and feelings regarding the earthquake experienced negative emotions for longer periods of time than did individuals who tended to distract
themselves by engaging in other activities.

A similar implication is suggested by the finding, reviewed above, that
affective-autonomic response dissociation was linked to reduced grief over
time (Bonanno et al., 1995; Bonanno, Znoj, et al., 1999). Although there is
no direct evidence associating this type of response with distraction, it
seems likely that affective-autonomic dissociation comes about either by a
shift in attention away from the undesired emotion or by the instigation of

a competing emotional or distraction response that overrides the undesired emotion (Bonanno, 2001). Further, there is indirect support for this relationship. As mentioned, numerous studies have now shown that affective-autonomic response dissociation is evidenced most frequently among individuals categorized as repressive copers (Asendorpf & Scherer, 1983; Newton & Contrada, 1992; Weinberger et al., 1979; Weinberger & Davidson, 1994), and these individuals, in turn, have shown a general ability to selectively attend away from threatening information (Bonanno et al., 1991; Fox, 1993). More important, repressive copers have also reported more distracting thoughts during stressful cognitive tasks (Bonanno et al., 1991).

Minimizing or dissociating the experience of negative emotion is one way to minimize the expression of negative grief-related emotions. As part of the more general assumption of emotional coherence, emotion theorists have long assumed that the experiential and expressive components of emotion are highly concordant. However, the relationship between these processes is not yet well established. Although researchers have reported modest correlations between facial expressions and self-reports of emotion (e.g., Rosenberg & Ekman, 1994), nonsignificant relations between these different types of emotional responding have also been reported (Fernandez-Dols, Flor, Pilar, & Ruiz-Belda, 1997). Indeed, the premise of emotional response dissociation is predicated on the assumption that different channels of emotional responding, while generally coordinated, may often be activated in a manner that is at least partially independent (Izard, 1990, 1992; Lang, Levin, Miller, & Kozak, 1983; Leventhal, 1991; Newton & Contrada, 1992). This situation is compounded by the fact that emotional experience involves the added consideration of variations in language, which tends to introduce further discrepancies across response channels. Together, these considerations suggest that the experience and expression of emotion are perhaps best thought of as loosely coupled or correlated responses that show a moderate but inconsistent degree of coherence (Lang, 1979; Rosenberg & Ekman, 1994; Tomkins, 1962).

Another important distinction is between minimizing and suppressing the expression of negative emotion. Whereas minimizing the expression of negative emotion has been found to be salutary during bereavement, the overt suppression of negative grief-related emotions is likely to prove less effective. Gross and Levenson (1993, 1997) found that the attempt to suppress negative emotions in response to emotionally evocative films had little impact on the subjective experience of negative emotion (in this case, disgust and sadness), but was associated with increased physiological arousal. Although longitudinal data were not collected, it was argued that repeated attempts to suppress emotional expression may have long-term health consequences (Gross, 1998). Gross and Levenson (1997) further speculated that emotional suppression might utilize cognitive resources and reduce the individual's ability to process the situation emotionally. More important, and relevant to the question of social support discussed above, they speculated that emotional inhibition strategies that are inflexible and indiscriminant may limit social partners' ability to discern and respond in an appropriate manner, a point also emphasized by interpersonal theories of depression (Holahan, Moos, & Bonin, 1999; Sacco, 1999).

When positive emotions are considered, the most compelling implication is that genuine laughter appears to help the bereaved. As obvious and common-sense-filled as this assertion may seem, to a large extent it flies in the face of traditional bereavement theory, which has tended to ignore positive emotions or to view them with suspicion as close relatives of denial. Indeed, perhaps owing to the historical dominance of the traditional grief work approach to bereavement, many well-intentioned people in a bereaved person's social environment, not only friends and relatives, but also counselors, physicians, and therapists, may assume the need to honor the deceased and the pain of loss with somber reassurances. In contrast, however, the findings reviewed in this chapter suggest that warm support coupled with the encouragement to laugh may be equally important, if not imperative.

These findings also suggest, however, that forced expressions of positive emotion would do little good. Indeed, Keltner and Bonanno (1997) reported that non-Duchenne laughter was inversely associated with observers' inclinations to offer comfort to the bereaved, suggesting that forced laughter may actually carry adverse social consequences by dissuading potential support providers.

Despite this caveat, there are numerous ways that people may increase the likelihood that they or other people will laugh. For instance, bereaved individuals might be encouraged to go out with friends and "laugh a little," to read something funny, or to go see a funny movie (Bonanno, 1999b). It is also worth recalling, however, Bonanno and Keltner's (in press) finding that laughter during bereavement occurred most consistently in the context of verbal discussions of anger. In other words, laughter does not require positive contexts in order to occur. Thus, rather than struggling to create a purely positive atmosphere, it may be most helpful to allow bereaved persons to experience and communicate their negative reactions, if they so desire, while at the same time making it clear that it is permissible, if not desirable, to shift away from that negative content with a good laugh (Bonanno, 1999b).

Limitations and Directions for Future Research

It is tempting to extrapolate further from the findings reviewed in this chapter. However, it is essential to note that these findings suffer from several important methodological limitations. Perhaps the most significant limitation is that most of the findings reviewed in this chapter come from the same research participants in the same longitudinal bereavement project. A related limitation is that these data were obtained from bereaved individuals from a specific age group, middle age, who had sustained one type of loss, the death of a spouse. Bereaved individuals from different age ranges or suffering different types of losses might have shown a different set of results. A third point is that most of the emotion data were obtained at a single point in bereavement, 6 months after the death had occurred. It would have been interesting, and perhaps indicative of other relationships between emotion and outcome, had the emotion variables been measured at earlier or later periods in bereavement or across multiple dates.

These limitations underscore an imperative need for continued empirical investigation of the role of emotion in bereavement. One avenue for further research is to examine the role of expressing or minimizing grief-related emotions across different cultural contexts. Discrete emotion theorists generally agree that human emotions serve similar functions and tend to be expressed and understood in a similar manner in all cultures (Ekman, 1992; Ekman, Friesen, & Ellsworth, 1972; Izard, 1971, 1994). However, the "display rules" of a particular culture will guide when, in what particular contexts, and to what extent each emotion may be expressed, suppressed, or masked (Ekman, 1993). The ways that culture influences bereaved individuals' construal of grief, or of their social roles while grieving, will undoubtedly interact with emotion (Averill & Nunley, 1993).

As noted, anger is viewed across many cultures as a potentially volatile, even dangerous, emotion that must be controlled, regulated, or avoided during bereavement. Nonetheless, cultures also differ with respect to the specific rules that govern when or to what extent, if at all, it is socially acceptable to express grief-related anger (Mandelbaum, 1959; Rosenblatt, 1993). Comparative research on the facial behavior of bereaved individuals across different cultures will help answer whether the findings we describe in this chapter (i.e., the inverse association between facial expressions of negative emotions and long-term grief outcome) do in fact generalize to other cultures outside that in the United States.

Finally, further exploration of the role of laughter during bereavement will greatly enhance our understanding of this important phenomenon and the salutary role it appears to play in helping people recover from loss. Like nonverbal emotional expression in general, laughter offers particularly promising avenues for cross-cultural investigation because it obviates the necessity of accounting for language differences. In addition, however, laughter offers the unique advantage of allowing for distinctions between Duchenne and non-Duchenne expressions. Because Duchenne expressions have been consistently tied to genuine positive emotion (Frank et al., 1993; Keltner & Bonanno, 1997) and because they appear to be relatively difficult to produce by volition alone (Duchenne de Boulogne, 1862), they offer a particularly strong nonverbal measure of positive emotion, one that might be used to illuminate important cultural differences or similarities.

Conclusion

In this chapter, we reviewed recent empirical advances in studying the role of nonverbal displays of emotion in bereavement. We adopted a social functional perspective on emotion to understand these findings. The social functional perspective offered several distinct advantages. Foremost among these was that it provided workable operational definitions and a clear, empirically derived set of predictions from which to guide subsequent empirical investigation. This is contrasted against the more traditional grief work approach to bereavement, which lacks theoretical specificity and thus has proved difficult to operationalize for application to an empirical context (Bonanno, 1999a; Stroebe & Stroebe, 1993).

In examining the role of emotion and its social consequences within specific contexts such as bereavement, the social functional perspective also offers the advantage of linking the phenomenon of grieving with the broader body of theoretical and empirical literatures of emotion and evolutionary theory within an implicitly social context. As such, the social functional approach makes possible new insights into the ways that both positive and negative emotion during bereavement may interact with one's social network that may ultimately influence the severity and duration of grief course.

References

Abraham, K. (1924). A short study of the development of the libido; viewed in the light of mental disorders. In K. Abraham (Ed.), *Selected papers on psychoanalysis* (pp. 418–501). London: Hogarth Press.

American Psychiatric Association. (1994). *Diagnostic and statistical manual of mental disorders* (4th ed.). Washington, DC: Author.

Archer, J. (1999). *The nature of grief: The evolution and psychology of reactions to loss.* New York: Routledge.

Asendorpf, J. B., & Scherer, K. R. (1983). The discrepant repressor: Differentiation between low anxiety, high anxiety, and repression of anxiety by autonomic-facial-verbal patterns of behavior. *Journal of Personality and Social Psychology, 45,* 1334–1346.

Averill, J. R. (1982). *Anger and aggression: An essay on emotion.* New York: Springer-Verlag.

Averill, J. R., & Nunley, E. P. (1993). Grief as an emotion and as a disease: A social-constructionist perspective. In M. S. Stroebe, W. Stroebe, & R. O. Hansson (Eds.), *Handbook of bereavement: Theory, research, and intervention* (pp. 367–380). Cambridge, England: Cambridge University Press.

Barrett, K. C., & Campos, J. J. (1987). Perspectives on emotional development II: A functionalist approach to emotions. In J. D. Osofsky (Ed.), *Handbook of infant development* (2nd ed., pp. 555–578). New York: Wiley-Interscience.

Belitsky, R., & Jacobs, S. (1986). Bereavement, attachment theory, and mental disorders. *Psychiatric Annals, 16,* 276–280.

Bonanno, G. A. (1997, July). *Examining the "grief work" approach to bereavement*. Paper presented at the 5th International Conference on Grief and Bereavement, Washington, DC.

Bonanno, G. A. (1999a). Factors associated with the effective accommodation to loss. In C. Figley (Ed.), *The traumatology of grieving* (pp. 37–52). Washington, DC: Taylor & Francis.

Bonanno, G. A. (1999b). Laughter and bereavement. *Bereavement Care, 18,* 19–22.

Bonanno, G. A. (2001). Grief and emotion: Comparing the grief work and social-functional perspectives. In M. Stroebe, W. Stroebe, R. O. Hansson, & H. Schut (Eds.), *New handbook of bereavement: Consciousness, coping, and care* (pp. 493–516). Cambridge, England: Cambridge University Press.

Bonanno, G. A., Davis, P. J., Singer, J. L., & Schwartz, G. E. (1991). The repressor personality and avoidant information processing: A dichotic listening study. *Journal of Research in Personality, 25,* 386–401.

Bonanno, G. A., & Field, N. P. (2001). Predicting the first five years of bereavement. I: The question of delayed grief. *American Behavioral Scientist, 44,* 798–806.

Bonanno, G. A., & Kaltman, S. A. (1999). Toward an integrative perspective on bereavement. *Psychological Bulletin, 125,* 760–776.

Bonanno, G. A., & Kaltman, S. (2001). The varieties of grief experience. *Clinical Psychology Review, 21,* 705–734.

Bonanno, G. A., & Keltner, D. (1997) . Facial expressions of emotion and the course of bereavement. *Journal of Abnormal Psychology, 106,* 126–137.

Bonanno, G. A., & Keltner, D. (in press). The coherence of emotion systems: Comparing "on-line" measures of appraisal and facial expression and self-report. *Cognition and Emotion.*

Bonanno, G. A., Keltner, D., Holen, A., & Horowitz, M. J. (1995). When avoiding unpleasant emotion might not be such a bad thing: Verbal-autonomic response dissociation and midlife conjugal bereavement. *Journal of Personality and Social Psychology, 46,* 975–989.

Bonanno, G. A., Mihalecz, M. C., & LeJeune, J. T. (1999). The core appraisal and emotion themes of conjugal loss. *Motivation and Emotion, 23,* 175–201.

Bonanno, G. A., & Singer, J. L. (1990). Repressive personality style: Theoretical and methodological implications for health and pathology. In J. L. Singer (Ed.), *Repression and dissociation* (pp. 435–470). Chicago: University of Chicago Press.

Bonanno, G. A., Znoj, H. J., Siddique, H., & Horowitz, M. J. (1999). Verbal-autonomic response dissociation and adaptation to midlife conjugal loss: A follow-up at 25 months. *Cognitive Therapy and Research, 23,* 605–624.

Brosschot, J. F., & Janssen, E. (1998). Continuous monitoring of affective-autonomic response dissociation in repressors during negative emotional stimulation. *Personality and Individual Differences, 25,* 69–84.

Bowlby, J. (1980). *Loss: Sadness and depression (Attachment and loss, Vol. 3).* New York: Basic Books.

Buck, R. (1988). *Human motivation and emotion* (2nd ed.). New York: Wiley.

Campos, J. J., Campos, R. G., & Barrett, K. (1989). Emergent themes in the study of emotional development and emotion regulation. *Developmental Psychology, 25,* 394–402.

Cerney, M. W., & Buskirk, J. R. (1991). Anger: The hidden part of grief. *Bulletin of the Menninger Clinic, 55,* 228–237.

Cohen, S., & Wills, T. A. (1985). Stress, social support, and the buffering hypothesis. *Psychological Bulletin, 98,* 310–357.

Cole, P. M., & Zahn-Waxler, C. (1992). Emotional dysregulation in disruptive behavior disorders. In D. Cicchetti & S. L. Toth (Eds)., *Rochester symposium on developmental psychopathology, Vol. 4: Developmental perspectives on depression* (pp. 173–210). Rochester, NY: University of Rochester Press.

Corr, C. A., Nabe, C. M., & Corr, D. M. (1994). *Death and dying, life and living.* Pacific Grove, CA: Brooks/Cole.

Coyne, J. C. (1976). Depression and the response of others. *Journal of Abnormal Psychology, 85,* 186–193.

Coyne, J. C., Kessler, R. C., Tal, M., Turnbull, J., Wortman, C. B., & Greden, J. F. (1987). Living with a depressed person. *Journal of Consulting and Clinical Psychology, 55,* 347–352.

D'Amasio, A. R. (1994). *Descartes' error: Emotion, reason, and the human brain.* New York: Putnam.

Darwin, C. (1872). *The expression of emotion in man and animals.* London: Murray.

Deutsch, H. (1937). Absence of grief. *Psychoanalytic Quarterly, 6,* 12–22.

Duchenne de Boulogne, G. B. (1862). *The mechanism of human facial expression* (R. A. Cuthbertson, Trans.). New York: Cambridge University Press.

Ekman, P. (1984). Expression and the nature of emotion. In K. Scherer & P. Ekman (Eds.), *Approaches to emotion* (pp. 319–344). Hillsdale, NJ: Erlbaum.

Ekman, P. (1992). Are there basic emotions? *Psychological Review, 99,* 550–553.

Ekman, P. (1993). Facial expression and emotion. *American Psychologist, 48,* 384–392.

Ellsworth, P. C., & Smith, C. A. (1985). From appraisal to emotion: Differences among unpleasant feelings. *Motivation and Emotion, 12,* 271–302.

Ekman, P., Friesen, W. V., & Ellsworth, P. (1972). Emotion in the human face: Guidelines for research and an integration of findings. Elmsford, NY: Pergamon.

Fernandez-Dols, J. M., Flor, S., Pilar, C., & Ruiz-Belda, M.-A. (1997). Are spontaneous expressions and emotions linked? An experimental test of coherence. *Journal of Nonverbal Behavior, 21,* 163–177.

Folkman, S., & Lazarus, R. S. (1988). Coping as a mediator of emotion. *Journal of Personality and Social Psychology, 54,* 466–475.

Folkman, S., & Lazarus, R. S. (1990). Coping and emotion. In N. L. Stein, B. Leventhal, & T. Trabasso (Eds)., *Psychological and biological approaches to emotion* (pp. 313–332). New York: Erlbaum.

Fox, E. (1993). Allocation of visual attention and anxiety. *Cognition and Emotion, 7,* 207–215.

Frank, M., Ekman, P., & Friesen, W. V. (1993). Behavioral markers and recognizability of the smile of enjoyment. *Journal of Personality and Social Psychology, 64*, 83–93.

Freud, S. (1957). Mourning and melancholia. In J. Strachey (Ed.), *The standard edition of the complete psychological works of Sigmund Freud* (Vol. 14, pp. 152–170). London: Hogarth Press. (Original work published 1917)

Fried, I., Wilson, C. I., MacDonald, K. A., & Behnke, E. J. (1998). Electric current stimulates laughter. *Nature, 39*, 650.

Frijda, N. H. (1993). The place of appraisal in emotion. *Cognition and Emotion, 7*, 357–387.

Gross, J. J. (1998). Antecedent- and response-focused emotion regulation: Divergent consequences for experience, expression, and physiology. *Journal of Personality & Social Psychology, 74*, 224–237.

Gross, J. J., & Levenson, R. W. (1993). Emotional suppression: Physiology, self-report, and expressive behavior. *Journal of Personality and Social Psychology, 64*, 970–986.

Gross, J. J., & Levenson, R.W. (1997). Hiding feelings: The acute effects of inhibiting negative and positive *emotion. Journal of Abnormal Psychology, 106*, 95–103.

Hatfield, E., Cacioppo, J. T., & Rapson, R. (1992). Primitive emotional contagion. In M. S. Clark (Ed.), *Review of personality and social psychology* (Vol. 14, pp. 151–177). Newbury Park, CA: Sage.

Holahan, C. J., Moos, R. H., & Bonin, L. A. (1999). Social context and depression: An integrative stress and coping framework. In T. Joiner & J. C. Coyne (Eds.), *The interactional nature of depression: Advances in interpersonal approaches*. Washington, DC: APA.

Holmes, T., & Rahe, R. (1967). The social readjustment scale. *Journal of Psychosomatic Research, 11*, 213–218.

Horowitz, M. J. (1986) *Stress response syndromes*. Northvale, NJ: Aronson.

Horowitz, M. J., Siegel, B., Holen, A., Bonanno, G. A., Milbrath, C., & Stinson, C. H. (1997). Diagnostic criteria for complicated grief disorder. *American Journal of Psychiatry, 154*, 904–910.

Howes, M. J., & Hokanson, J. E. (1979). Conversational and social responses to depressive interpersonal behavior. *Journal of Abnormal Psychology, 88*, 625–634.

Izard, C. (1990). Facial expressions and the regulation of emotion. *Journal of Personality and Social Psychology, 58*, 487–498.

Izard, C. E. (1977). *Human emotions*. New York: Plenum.

Izard, C. E. (1992). Basic emotions, relations among emotions, and emotion-cognition relations. *Psychological Review, 99*, 561–564.

Izard, C. E. (1994). Innate and universal facial expressions: Evidence from developmental and cross-cultural research. *Psychological Bulletin, 115*, 288–299.

Kavanagh, D. G. (1990). Towards a cognitive-behavioral intervention for adult grief reactions. *British Journal of Psychiatry, 157*, 373–383.

Keltner, D. (1995). Signs of appeasement: Evidence for the distinct displays of embarrassment, amusement, and shame. *Journal of Personality and Social Psychology, 68*, 441–454.

Keltner, D., & Bonanno, G. A. (1997). A study of laughter and dissociation: Distinct correlates of laughter and smiling during bereavement. *Journal of Personality and Social Psychology, 73*, 687–702.

Keltner, D., & Buswell, B. N. (1996). Evidence for the distinctiveness of embarrassment, shame, and guilt: A study of recalled antecedents and facial expressions of emotion. *Cognition and Emotion, 10*, 155–171.

Keltner, D., & Buswell, B. N. (1997). Embarrassment: Its distinct form and appeasement functions. *Psychological Bulletin, 122*, 250–270.

Keltner, D., Ellsworth, P. C., & Edwards, K. (1993). Beyond simple pessimism: Effects of sadness and anger on social perception. *Journal of Personality and Social Psychology, 64*, 740–752.

Keltner, D., & Haidt, J. (2001). Social functions of emotions. In T. J. Mayne & G. A. Bonanno (Eds.), *Emotions: Current issues and future directions. Emotions and social behavior* (pp. 192–213).

Keltner, D., & Kring, A. M. (1998). Emotion, social function, and psychopathology. *Review of General Psychology, 2*, 320–342.

Keltner, D., Moffitt, T., & Stouthamer-Loeber, M. (1995). Facial expressions of emotion and psychopathology in adolescent boys. *Journal of Abnormal Psychology, 104*, 644–652.

Kiecolt-Glaser, J. K., Glaser, R., Shuttleworth, E. C., & Dyer, C. S. (1987). Chronic stress and immunity in family caregivers of Alzheimer's disease victims. *Psychosomatic Medicine, 49*, 523–535.

Krohne, H. W. (1992). Vigilance and cognitive avoidance as concepts in coping research. In H. W. Krohne (Ed.), *Attention and avoidance strategies in coping with aversiveness* (pp. 19–50). Göttingen, Germany: Hograth & Huber.

Lang, P. J. (1979). Language, image, and emotion. In P. Pliner, K. R. Blankstein, & J. M. Spigel (Eds.), *Perception of emotion in self and others* (Vol. 5). New York: Plenum Press.

Lang, P. J., Kozak, M. J., Miller, G. A., Levin, D. N., & McLean, A. (1980). Emotional imagery: Conceptual structure and pattern of somato-visceral response. *Psychophysiology, 17*, 179–192.

Lang, P. J., Levin, D. N., Miller, G. A., & Kozak, M. J. (1983). Fear behavior, fear imagery, and the psychophysiology of emotion: The problem of affective response integration. *Journal of Abnormal Psychology, 92*, 276–306.

Lazare, A. (1989). Bereavement and unresolved grief. In A. Lazare (Ed.), *Outpatient psychiatry: Diagnosis and treatment* (2nd ed., pp. 381–397). Baltimore, MD: Williams & Wilkins.

Lazarus, R. S. (1966). *Psychological stress and the coping process.* New York: Oxford University Press.

Lazarus, R. S. (1991). *Emotion and adaptation.* New York: Oxford University Press.

Lazarus, R. S., Kanner, A. D., & Folkman, S. (1980). Emotions: A cognitive-phenomenological analysis. In R. Plutchik & H. Kellerman (Eds.), *Theories of emotion. Emotions: Theory, research, and experience* (Vol. 1, pp. 189–217). New York: Academic Press.

LeDoux, J. (1989). Cognitive-emotional interactions in the brain. *Cognition and Emotion, 3*, 267–289.

LeDoux, J. (1996). *The emotional brain.* New York: Simon & Schuster.

Lehman, D. R., Ellard, J. H., & Wortman, C. B. (1986). Social support for the bereaved: Recipients' and providers' perspectives on what is helpful. *Journal of Consulting and Clinical Psychology, 54*, 438–446.

Lehman, D. R., Wortman, C. B., & Williams, A. F. (1987). Long-term effects of losing a spouse or child in a motor vehicle crash. *Journal of Personality and Social Psychology, 52*, 218–231.

Lemerise, E. A., & Dodge, K. A. (1993). The development of anger and hostile interactions. In M. Lewis & J. M. Haviland (Eds.), *Handbook of emotions* (pp. 537–546). New York: Guilford Press.

Levenson, R. W. (1994). Human emotion: A functional view. In P. Ekman & R. J. Davidson (Eds.), *The nature of emotion: Fundamental questions* (pp. 123–126). New York: Oxford University Press.

Levenson, R. W., & Gottman, J. M. (1983). Marital interaction: Physiological linkage and affective exchange. *Journal of Personality and Social Psychology, 45*, 587–597.

Leventhal, H. (1984). A perceptual-motor theory of emotion. In L. Berkowitz (Ed.), *Advances in experimental social psychology* (Vol. 17, pp. 117–182). New York: Academic Press.

Leventhal, H. (1991). Emotion: Prospects for conceptual and empirical development. In R. G. Lister & H. J. Weingartner (Eds.), *Perspectives on cognitive neuroscience* (pp. 325–348). Oxford, England: Oxford University Press.

Lindemann, E. (1944). Symptomatology and management of acute grief. *American Journal of Psychiatry, 101*, 1141–1148.

Lundin, T. (1984). Long-term outcome of bereavement. *British Journal of Psychiatry, 145*, 434–428.

Malatesta, C. Z. (1990). The role of emotions in the development and organization of personality. In R. A. Thompson (Ed.), *Nebraska Symposium on Motivation, Vol. 36. Sociomotivational development* (pp. 1–56). Lincoln: University of Nebraska Press.

Mandelbaum, D. G. (1959). Social uses of funeral rites. In H. Feifel (Ed.), *The meaning of death* (pp. 189–217). New York: McGraw-Hill.

Marris, P. (1958). *Widows and their families*. London: Routledge and Kegan Paul.

Martin, R. A., & Lefcourt, H. M. (1983). The sense of humor as a moderator of the relation between stressors and moods. *Journal of Personality and Social Psychology, 45*, 1313–1324.

Newton, T. L., & Contrada, R. J. (1992). Repressive coping and verbal-autonomic response dissociation: The influence of social context. *Journal of Personality and Social Psychology, 62*, 159–167.

Nolen-Hoeksema, S., & Morrow, J. (1991). A prospective study of depression and posttraumatic stress symptoms after a natural disaster: The 1989 Loma Prieta earthquake. *Journal of Personality and Social Psychology, 61*, 115–121.

Oatley, K., & Jenkins, J. M. (1996). *Understanding emotions*. Cambridge, MA: Blackwell.

Ortony, A., & Turner, T. J. (1990). What's basic about basic emotions? *Psychological Review, 97*, 363–384.

Osterweis, M., Solomon, F., & Green, F. (Eds.). (1984). *Bereavement: Reactions, consequences, and care*. Washington, DC: National Academy Press.

Parkes, C. M., & Weiss, R. S. (1983). *Recovery from bereavement*. New York: Basic Books.

Provine, R. R. (1992). Contagious laughter: Laughter is a sufficient stimulus for laughs and smiles. *Bulletin of the Psychonomic Society, 30*, 1–4.

Provine, R. R., & Fischer, K. R. (1989). Laughing, smiling, and talking: Relation to sleeping and social context in humans. *Ethology, 83*, 295–305.

Rando, T. A. (1984). *Grief, dying and death: Clinical interventions for caregivers*. Champaign, IL: Research Press.

Rando, T. A. (1992). The increasing prevalence of complicated mourning: The onslaught is just beginning. *Omega—Journal of Death & Dying, 26*, 43–59.

Raphael, B. (1983). *The anatomy of bereavement*. New York: Basic Books.

Roseman, I. J., Antoniou, A. A., & Jose, P. E. (1996). Appraisal determinants of emotion: Constructing a more accurate and comprehensive theory. *Cognition and Emotion, 10*, 241–277.

Rosenberg, E. L., & Ekman, P. (1994). Coherence between expressive and experimental systems in emotion. *Cognition and Emotion, 8*, 201–229.

Rosenblatt, P. C. (1993). Grief: The social context of private feelings. In. M. S. Stroebe, W. Stroebe, & R. O. Hansson (Eds.), *Handbook of bereavement: Theory, research, and intervention* (pp. 102–111). Cambridge, England: Cambridge University Press.

Rosenblatt, P. C., Walsh, R. P., & Jackson, D. A. (1976). *Grief and mourning in the cross-cultural perspective*. New Haven, CT: Human Relations Area Files Press.

Rothbart, M. L. (1973). Laughter in young children. *Psychological Bulletin, 80*, 247–256.

Ruch, W. (1993). Exhilaration and humor. In M. Lewis & J. M. Haviland (Eds.), *The handbook of emotion* (pp. 605–616). New York: Guilford Press.

Sacco, W. P. (1999). A social-cognitive model of interpersonal processes in depression. In T. Joiner & J. C. Coyne (Eds.), *The interactional nature of depression: Advances in interpersonal approaches*. Washington, D.C.: APA.

Sanders, C. M. (1979). The use of the MMPI in assessing bereavement outcome. In C. S. Newmark (Ed.), *MMPI: Clinical and research trends* (pp. 223–247). New York: Praeger.

Sanders, C. M. (1993). Risk factors in bereavement outcome. In M. S. Stroebe, W. Stroebe, & R. O. Hansson (Eds.), *Handbook of bereavement: Theory, research, and intervention* (pp. 255–267). New York: Cambridge University Press.

Scherer, K. R. (1993). Studying the emotion-antecedent appraisal process: An expert system approach. *Cognition and Emotion, 7*, 325–355.

Schwartz, G. E., Fair, P. L., Greenberg, P. S., Freedman, M., & Klerman, J. L. (1974). Facial electromyography in the assessment of emotion. *Psychophysiology, 11*, 237.

Schwartz, G. E., Fair, P. L., Salt, P., Mandel, M. R., & Klerman, J. L. (1976). Facial muscle patterning to affective imagery in depressed and nondepressed subjects. *Science, 192*, 489–491.

Schwartzberg, S. S., & Janoff-Bulman, R. (1994). Grief and the search for meaning: Exploring the assumptive worlds of bereaved college students. *Journal of Social and Clinical Psychology, 10*, 270–288.

Shuchter, S. R., & Zisook, S. (1993). The course of normal grief. In M. S. Stroebe,

W. Stroebe, & R. O. Hansson (Eds.), *Handbook of bereavement: Theory, research, and intervention* (pp. 23–43). Cambridge, England: Cambridge University Press.

Smith, C. A., & Lazarus, R. S. (1993). Appraisal components, core relational themes, and the emotions. *Cognition and Emotion, 7,* 223–269.

Stearns, C. Z (1993). Sadness. In M. Lewis & J. M. Haviland (Eds.), *Handbook of emotions* (pp. 547–561). New York: Guilford Press.

Stearns, P. N., & Knapp, M. (1996). Historical perspectives on grief. In R. Harre & W. G. Parrott (Eds.), *The emotions: Social, cultural, and biological dimensions* (pp. 132–150). Thousand Oaks, CA: Sage.

Strack, S., & Coyne, J. C. (1983). Social confirmation of dysphoria: Shared and private reactions to depression. *Journal of Personality and Social Psychology, 44,* 798–806.

Stroebe, W., & Stroebe, M. S. (1993). Determinants of adjustment to bereavement in younger widows and widowers. In M. S. Stroebe, W. Stroebe, & R. O. Hansson (Eds.), *Handbook of bereavement: Theory, research, and intervention* (pp. 208–226). New York: Cambridge University Press.

Stroebe, W., & Stroebe, M. S. (1987). *Bereavement and health.* Cambridge, England: Cambridge University Press.

Tomkins, S. S. (1962). *Affect, imagery, consciousness (Vol. 1): The positive affects.* New York: Springer.

Tomkins, S. S. (1984). Affect theory. In K. Scherer & P. Ekman (Eds.), *Approaches to emotion* (pp. 163–195). Hillsdale, NJ: Erlbaum.

Vinton, K. L. (1989). Humor in the work place: Is it more than telling jokes? *Small Group Behavior, 20,* 151–166.

Watson, D. & Clark, L. A. (1984). Negative affectivity: The disposition to experience aversive emotional states. *Psychological Bulletin, 96,* 465–490.

Watson, D., & Pennebaker, J. W. (1989). Health complaints, stress, and distress: Exploring the central role of negative affectivity. *Psychological Review, 96,* 234–254.

Weinberger, D. A., & Davidson, M. N. (1994). Styles of inhibiting emotional expression: Distinguishing repressive coping from impression management. *Journal of Personality, 62,* 587–613.

Weinberger, D. A., Schwartz, G. E., & Davidson, J. R. (1979). Low-anxious and repressive coping styles: Psychometric patterns of behavioral and physiological responses to stress. *Journal of Abnormal Psychology, 88,* 369–380.

Westfeld, G. E. (1993). The adaptive value of humor and laughter. *Ethnology and Sociobiology, 14,* 141–169.

Worden, J. W. (1991). *Grief counseling and grief therapy: A handbook for the mental health practitioner.* New York: Springer.

Zisook, S., Devaul, R. A., & Click, M. A. (1982). Measuring symptoms of grief and bereavement. *American Journal of Psychiatry, 139,* 1590–1593.

8

Impairments of Facial Nonverbal Communication After Brain Damage

RAYMOND BRUYER

This chapter focuses on deficits in nonverbal behavior resulting from brain damage and on their study within the framework of cognitive neuropsychology. More specifically, the target is facial nonverbal behavior (for a recent neuropsychological overview of other communicative movements, see Feyereisen, 1999).

This chapter is structured as follows. First, the importance of the face as a substrate of nonverbal communication is briefly outlined. Then, it is shown that certain types of brain damage can disrupt very specific features of facial communication, sometimes leading to psychopathological behavior patterns. The neuropsychological analysis of these deficits has been a major basis for the construction of current cognitive models of face processing; these models are summarized in the third section. The chapter then returns to the two main functions subserved by face processing: recognition of facial identity and nonverbal communication. In this fourth part, the contribution of current neuropsychological studies, particularly modern techniques of functional brain imaging in normal subjects, is examined. In the fifth and final section, a bridge is established among electrophysiological studies in nonhuman species, neuroimaging experiments in normal subjects, and neuropsychological observations, that is, the three roots of cognitive neuroscience. In addition, a link also is made with studies in cognitive psychology.

The Face as a Medium of Nonverbal Communication

Inside the human visual environment, faces are fascinating stimuli due to the amount of information they convey. First, the face is the major visual cue that gives access to the identity of other people. Second, the face is the site of many important signals, probably not involved in the recognition of people, some of them crucial for nonverbal communication. Thus, when seeing faces—even unknown faces—the viewer is usually able to discriminate female from male gender, children from adults and elderly people, or Caucasians from Africans and Asians; lipreading can also improve understanding of speech, and with regard to nonverbal communication, the perceiver is able to recognize facial emotional expressions and to detect the direction of gaze of the person met.

It is worth emphasizing the impressive perceptual abilities involved in these operations. First, all faces share an identical visual structure because they are exemplars of a single category (the human face); thus, very precise perceptual processes are required to allow the operations mentioned above. Second, the picture of a given face is rarely stable. Indeed, this picture changes constantly from one moment to the next—in pose, expression, distance, lighting. It changes at a relatively slow rate, by the addition or removal of spectacles, of a beard, or of a moustache and by alterations in haircut or hairstyle. Finally, it is modified even more slowly by the structural effects of aging. Fortunately, the viewer is equipped with perceptual devices by which invariant features are detected so that a single stable representation is derived from each individual face and stored in long-term memory.

Given this state of affairs, it is not surprising to observe two corollaries. On the one hand, virtually all humans are experts in face processing, and this ability seems to be at work very early fromshortly after birth, even if it improves during infancy and childhood. On the other hand, since the 1970s, face processing has become a field of intensive research not only in (cognitive) psychology, but also in neuropsychology, neurophysiology, engineering, and artificial intelligence, as well as in some specific applied activities, such as the army, police, law, banks, and so on. Several recent books offer a comprehensive overview of these studies (Alley, 1988; Bruce, 1988; Bruce & Burton, 1992; Bruce, Cowey, Ellis, & Perrett, 1992; Bruce & Humphreys, 1994; Bruce & Young, 1998; Bruyer, 1986; Davies, Ellis, & Shepherd, 1981; Ellis, Jeeves, Newcombe, & Young, 1986; Johnson & Morton, 1991; Kanwisher & Moscovitch, 2000; Rhodes, 1996; Rhodes & Zebrowitz, 2002; Valentine, 1995; Wenger & Townsend, 2001; Young, 1998; Young & Ellis, 1989a); obviously, many book chapters and review articles can also be consulted.

The catalogue of skills broadly summarized above is that of normal, healthy people. However, brain damage can specifically affect some of these abilities, sometimes leading to psychopathological patterns.

Specific Deficiencies of Facial Nonverbal Communication After Brain Damage

Methodological Consideration

As a method of cognitive psychology, the purpose of cognitive neuropsychology is to contribute to the fractionation of cognitive processes (e.g., face recognition) into more elementary subcomponents. Its major tool is called *double dissociation* (see Shallice, 1988). Thus, to establish that two hypothesized subcomponents (A and B) are really distinct from each other—or dissociable—cognitive neuropsychologists attempt to find two conditions (a and b) so that A-and-only-A is impaired by a-and-only-a, and B-and-only-B is impaired by b-and-only-b. In the field of neuropsychology, the two searched conditions will usually be two different brain-damaged patients or groups of patients. Double dissociations are preferred to simple dissociations (i.e., A-and-only-A is impaired by-a-and-only-a, or B-and-only-B is impaired by b-and-only-b) because the latter picture could only reveal that A and B are, in fact, two states or levels of the same subcomponent A or B (for instance, two levels of difficulty).

Given the individual differences in cognitive processing plus the major individual differences in the effects of brain injuries, current cognitive neuropsychologists prefer to investigate single cases instead of samples of brain-damaged patients (i.e., subjects a and b instead of groups a and b) (Caramazza, 1986; Caramazza & Martin, 1983; Shallice, 1979).

The next section illustrates such a fractionation (see Fig. 8.1). First, a series of single-case studies is reported to document empirically the cognitive model by several dissociations.

A Panel of Clinical Neuropsychological Patterns

Mr. W., a 54-year-old male farmer, suffered from a bilateral occipital vascular brain accident (Bruyer et al., 1983). Following this stroke, he was unable to visually identify familiar and famous faces, a condition called *prosopagnosia* (agnosia for faces). The deficit was very selective: (a) Mr. W. was able to identify persons by cues other than their faces; (b) he was able to visually recognize his livestock; and (c) he performed normally in many tasks designed to assess his abilities to process faces, particularly the processing of facial emotional expressions. In addition, his deficit was limited to conscious recognition, although signs of covert recognition were evidenced.

Covert face recognition (see Bruyer, 1991, or Young, 1994, for reviews) means that the patient does not recognize explicitly, overtly, or consciously the faces seen, while indirect or nonverbal reactions testify implicit, covert, or unconscious recognition. This was observed in the case of Mr. W. Indeed, when invited to try to learn the names of famous-but-unrecognized faces, Mr. W. was able to learn when the true name was used (e.g., the name François Mitterand for photographs of Mitterand), but failed when a false name was used (e.g., the name Ronald Reagan for photographs of John F. Kennedy). Behavioral and physiological (electrodermal responses, brain-evoked potentials) signs of covert recognition have been evidenced in other prosopagnosic patients, but it is worth noting that not all prosopagnosics display such signs.

As far as facial identity is concerned, it is worth mentioning psychiatric behavioral patterns called *delusional misidentification syndromes*. These syndromes involve deviation from normal recognition of people: the belief that the perceived person is the double of a known person (Capgras's syndrome; Capgras & Reboul-Lachaux, 1923), the belief that a familiar person is disguised as another (Frégoli syndrome; Courbon & Fail, 1927), or the belief that the physical appearance of some people may change radically to correspond to the appearance of someone else (intermetamorphosis syndrome; Courbon & Tusques, 1932). The discussion returns to these syndromes, but two features must be emphasized. First, while psychoanalytic and psychodynamic interpretations were classically offered to explain these conditions, it now appears that they are often the result of cerebral damage (Joseph, 1986; Luautá & Bidault, 1994; Luautá, Sansone, Bidault, Schneider, & Tiberghien, 1999). Second, and consequently, these syndromes tend to be interpreted in a cognitive, information-processing approach (Ellis & Young, 1990; Luauté et al., 1999).

The face is not only the input to a person's identity. Indeed, before considering emotional facial expression, it must be mentioned that the face is also the substrate of other social, nonverbal communicative cues, such as lipreading and gaze direction. The detection of gaze direction is an important component of face-to-face social interaction. In particular, social interaction is highly affected by the sensitivity to frontal eye gaze (i.e., the ability of detecting whether we are looked at directly). Sensitivity to frontal eye gaze is high in humans as one is able to detect deviations of less than 1° of visual angle. Gaze direction is also a powerful cue for the orientation of selective attention.

Campbell, Heywood, Cowey, Regard, and Landis (1990) experimentally studied this ability in two prosopagnosic patients. The patients were asked to decide which of two faces was "looking straight at you." Both faces were shown simultaneously for the forced choice, with one face looking directly at the observer (angular deviation = 0) and the other looking at a particular angular deviation (5°, 10°, or 20°). K. D., a 66-year-old female, suffered a right posterior cerebral artery infarct and became prosopagnosic when she was 60 years old. Her performance on the gaze test was slightly disturbed, but no worse than that of a sample of right-brain injured, nonprosopagnosic patients, and it displayed a normal pattern of sensitivity to the angular deviation of gaze. Conversely, A. B., a 27-year-old female, suffered a developmental prosopagnosia, and her performance on the gaze test was clearly defective, including an absence of effect of the angular deviation. However, her deficit was not due to a disturbance of elementary sensory visual functions.

Lipreading is a nonverbal communicative cue that can assist and improve verbal communication. It is used by the deaf as well as by people with normal hearing when perceptual conditions are degraded. Campbell, Landis, and Regard (1986) assessed lipreading abilities of two contrasting brain-damaged patients. Mrs. D., a 61-year-old female, suffered a right posterior cerebral artery stroke and became prosopagnosic when she was 58 years old. Mrs. D. could lip-read speech efficiently. Conversely, Mrs. T., a 65-year-old female, suffered a left posterior brain injury and did not become prosopagnosic, but was alexic and impaired at lipreading.

Obviously, the major nonverbal communicative function of the face concerns emotional expression. Moreover, neuropsychological reports show that this function is dissociable of, and independent from, the other main function of the face, namely, as the medium of a person's identity. Indeed, prosopagnosic patients are often able to process facial emotional expressions normally, as illustrated by the above example of Mr. W. (Bruyer et al., 1983; see also Parry, Young, Saul, & Moss, 1991; Schweich & Bruyer, 1993). Conversely, several neurological conditions—focal cerebral damage and diffuse chronic organic brain syndromes or closed head injuries—can give rise to deficits in the recognition of emotional facial expressions, while the recognition of face identity is spared (Kurucz & Feldmar, 1979; Kurucz, Feldmar, & Werner, 1979; Kurucz, Soni, Feldmar, & Slade, 1980; Parry et al., 1991). Thus, double dissociation is observed between facial identity and facial expression.

In addition, even within the field of emotional facial expressions, four types of dissociations are revealed or suggested by brain lesions. First, there is a debate in the neuropsychological literature as to whether it would be useful to dissociate emotions according to their positive versus negative valence (the lateralization of lesions could differ according to this dimension); however, the debate is still not resolved (for early reviews, see Bruyer, 1980; Tucker, 1981).

Second, recognition of expressions should be dissociated from production of expressions. Indeed, while patients with deficits of recognition (see above) usually produce facial expressions normally, other subjects suffer a deficit in producing expressions while recognition is spared. For instance, Ross and Mesulam (1979) examined a 39-year-old female school teacher and a 62-year-old male surgeon who, after brain damage, were unable to express emotions through speech and action, while their ability to "feel" and to recognize emotions was intact.

Third, neuropsychological data suggest an additional dissociation inside the production of facial expressions. Indeed, it could be that brain mechanisms underlying the production of spontaneous expressions differ from those underlying the production of posed expressions, but this discussion remains open.

Fourth, some types of brain damage can lead to a deficit of recognition that is limited to specific facial emotional expressions. D. R., a 51-year-old woman, was examined by Young and colleagues (Young, Aggleton, Hellawell, Johnson, Broks, & Hanley, 1995; Young, Hellawell, Van de Wal, & Johnson, 1996). D. R. suffered bilateral partial lesions of the amygdala due to stereotaxic surgical electrocoagulations to control epileptic seizures. The investigation of her processing of facial stimuli evidenced a complex pattern: a poor memory for new faces, a deficit in the detection of gaze direction, and a deficit in recognizing and imagining emotional facial expressions. This picture is consistent with the hypothesis of a role for the amygdala in learning and social behavior.

However, lesions of the amygdala can lead to very specific deficits in the recognition of facial emotional expressions. D. R. was also examined by Calder, Young, Rowland, et al. (1996), together with S. E., a 64-year-old man who had an extensive lesion of the right hemisphere, including the amygdala, and a left lesion in the amygdalar region (these lesions were probably aftereffects of herpes simplex encephalitis at the age of 55 years). Both patients displayed deficits in recognizing emotional facial expressions, and the trouble was especially remarkable for the emotion of fear.

Adolphs, Tranel, Damasio, and Damasio (1994) studied S. M., a 30-year-old woman who suffered from a disease that caused bilateral destruction of the amygdala. Her processing of facial identity and recognition of emotional facial expressions were intact, with the exception that she was unable to recognize fear (and some blends of emotions displayed by a single expression); a complementary study showed that unilateral damage of the amygdala was not sufficient to lead to this specific deficit (Adolphs, Tranel, Damasio, & Damasio, 1995).

Implications

Obviously, many patients examined by neuropsychologists suffer nonverbal facial communicative disorders, some of them displaying genuine psychopathological patterns. Moreover, as discussed below, some psychopathological conditions can be understood in the framework of cognitive architectures. In addition, a remarkable feature of the literature reviewed in this section is the large diversity of clinical conditions, even within the very restricted domain considered in this chapter.

A corollary of this diversity is the high specificity of the deficits, which offers evidence of several kinds of (simple or double) dissociations. These dissociations are exploited in cognitive neuropsychology to assess cognitive models of normal functioning (see Bruyer, 1990). Moreover, neuropsychological observations have greatly contributed to the development of these models in conjunction with electrophysiological results and experimental (chronometric) data and analyses of everyday incidents in normal subjects. More recently, functional brain-imaging techniques applied to normal subjects joined this arsenal of tools to contribute to the understanding of human cognition.

Cognitive Architecture of Face Processing

During the 1980s, several authors attempted to model cognitive representations and operations involved in face processing, generally by means of information processing serial architectures. These proposals arose from cognitive models of word and object visual recognition (see Bruyer, 2000), and some of them tried to include cerebral functional asymmetries (for an overview of the filiation of these models, see Bruyer, 1987).

Given this cognitive root and the limitations of computers—processing facial images requires a considerable amount of memory resources—early models and research on face processing focused on the semantic and lexical stages of the identification of famous faces. However, recent developments in computer science have enabled researchers to take into consideration what is specific to faces, namely, the perceptual processing of facial images and the precise visual identification of particular exemplars. In addition, connectionist (not serial and not symbolic) models were published (e.g., Burton, Bruce, & Johnston, 1990; Kohonen, Oja, & Lehtio, 1981; O'Toole, Abdi, Deffenbacher, & Bartlett, 1991; Schreiber, Rousset, & Tiberghien, 1991), as well as some attempts to model phenomena that could be specific to faces: the disproportionate inversion effect (Valentine, 1991), the race effect (Valentine, 1991), the distinctivity effect (Valentine, 1991), the caricature effect (Rhodes, 1996), the categorical perception (Campanella, Hanoteau, Seron, Joassin, & Bruyer, in press), and so on.

The best summary of available data and the most-cited model is that of Bruce and Young (1986). Figure 8.1 was drawn from this model by taking into account the modifications suggested by Burton et al. (1990), the proposal of an initial "facial decision" process (Ellis, 1986), the addition of the detection of gaze direction (Campbell et al., 1990), and of processes involved in name retrieval and production (for a review, see Valentine, Brennen, & Brádart, 1996). Clearly, Fig. 8.1 shows the wealth and diversity of mental operations that can be made on a face and, consequently, the variety of possible impairments resulting from brain damage.

The principal features of the model are outlined briefly next (see Bruyer, 1994). The perceived stimulus must first be classified as a human face: This is made explicit by the first box in Fig. 8.1, which leads to facial decision according to the computational stages suggested by Marr (1982) for object recognition. Then, structural analyses allow the viewer to derive an invariant representation of the face seen, that is, a representation that is independent of the episodic and accidental characteristics (related to distance, source of lighting, pose, expression, etc.) of the picture currently seen. If the perceived face is that of a known person, matching occurs between the invariant representation and a representation stored in long-term memory during previous meetings, the face recognition unit. The activation of this unit corresponds to the process of recognition: "I know this face." Face recognition then gives access to the recognition of the person, and it is worth noting that the face is only one entry among others to person recognition (people can be recognized by other cues, such as voice, handwriting, etc.). Once the person has been recognized, the viewer retrieves semantic

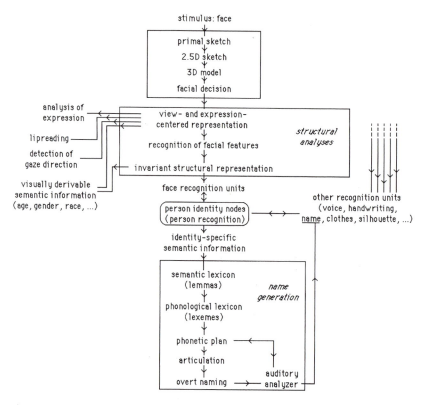

Fig. 8.1 Cognitive architecture of face identification. Adapted from "Face Recognition," by R. Bruyer. In V. S. Ramachandran, Ed., *Encyclopedia of Human Behavior* (Vol. 2, pp. 351–359), San Diego, CA: Academic Press, 1994.

pieces of information specific to the person seen—occupation, hobbies, address, and so on—and, finally, the name of the person is retrieved.

These various stages of person identification from the face can be selectively disturbed by brain injuries or experimental manipulations in the laboratory. In particular, prosopagnosia indicates a deficit concerning face recognition units. Prosopagnosia is different from person agnosia, which points to a deficit concerning the activation of person identity nodes (see the patient studied by Hanley, Young, & Pearson, 1989); from semantic person agnosia, which indicates a deficit in the activation of identity-specific semantic information (see the patient studied by De Haan, Young, & Newcombe, 1991); and from person anomia, which indicates a deficit related to a person's name retrieval (see the patients examined by Carney & Temple, 1993; Flude, Ellis, & Kay, 1989; Lucchelli & De Renzi, 1992; McKenna & Warrington, 1980; Shallice & Kartsounis, 1993).

Moreover, several forms of prosopagnosia can be distinguished on the basis of three—probably not independent—factors. First, as mentioned

above, signs of covert face recognition are found in some, but not all, prosopagnosic patients (for reviews, see Bruyer, 1991, 1993), which suggests that
the cognitive locus of the deficit is perceptual in some cases and postper-
ceptual in others (but see McNeil & Warrington, 1991). Second, all prosopagnosic patients do not recognize previously familiar faces, and many of
them cannot store representations of new faces met after the brain damage,
even if W. J. was able to store other nonverbal visual complex representations (McNeil & Warrington, 1993); however, some other prosopagnosic
subjects are able to memorize new faces. Third, De Haan and colleagues
studied three patients (P. H., M. S., and N. R.), evidencing three different
patterns when submitted to virtually the same tests.

The patient P. H. (De Haan, Young, & Newcombe, 1987a, 1987b; Young &
De Haan, 1988) was a prosopagnosic individual very similar to Mr. W.,
discussed above. Overtly, he was unable to recognize familiar faces, but
signs of covert recognition were evidenced when recognition was assessed
indirectly. For example, like Mr. W., P. H. performed better in the learning
of true rather than in the learning of false face/name associations (faces
unrecognized overtly were used). Also, like normal subjects, P. H. matched
better familiar—albeit unrecognized overtly—than unfamiliar faces in
same/different comparison tasks. Finally, like healthy subjects, P. H. displayed classical semantic interference and priming effects in several tasks
involving people names (faces unrecognized overtly were used as primes or
for interference; for example, he had to decide whether the name "Clinton"
corresponded to a politician or to a singer, and the name was accompanied
by the face of John F. Kennedy in one trial [priming] and by the face of
Frank Sinatra in another trial [interference]). Therefore, the authors concluded that, for P. H., face recognition units were spared, but their output
was damaged as covert recognition only could be evidenced by some effects
in later stages of processing.

Unlike P. H. and Mr. W., M. S. was unable not only to recognize overtly,
but also to recognize covertly the majority of familiar faces and objects
(Newcombe, Young, & De Haan, 1989). For instance, the subject's recognition of names benefited from a semantic priming by names, but not by faces
or pictures. Also, there was no difference between true and false associations in the learning of face/name associations. In addition, lexical decision
(to decide whether a string of letters corresponds to a real name) was
primed (facilitated) only by the few pictures overtly recognized by M. S.
Finally, the matching of pictures was facilitated by familiarity only when
pictures were overtly recognized. Consequently, the authors concluded that
a perceptual deficit was the basis of this clinical picture: Face recognition
units would be spared, but no longer activated, by the output of structural
processing. In other words, the input of the face recognition units would
be defective.

The patient N. R., like M. S., did not display signs of overt and covert
face recognition in usual tests (De Haan, Young, & Newcombe, 1992). How-

ever, he performed above chance when forced to decide which face was familiar in pairs in which one face was familiar and the other unfamiliar. This discrepancy between rudimentary overt recognition and the absence of covert recognition was explored in more depth. Several tests of priming were administered using faces that were and were not correctly classified in the forced-choice test. It appeared that priming was triggered only by faces recognized in the forced-choice test. Therefore, the authors concluded that N. R. suffered from a breakdown, or a degradation, of the face recognition units themselves.

The model summarized above shows that structural analyses can be performed on already known as well as on new, unfamiliar faces. Moreover, the perceptual representations can be the source of operations not related to, and independent of, face recognition and person identification. Indeed, according to pathological observations (see the first section of the chapter) and experimental data collected in normal subjects, a perceived face enables analysis of emotional expression, lipreading, detection of gaze direction, and access to visually derivable semantic pieces of information, such as approximate age, gender, and ethnic properties. As mentioned, some of these cues are directly related to nonverbal communication.

Actually, this architecture is more a descriptive summary of available data than a true valuable model with an explanatory power. In particular, one has to take into account the neurocognitive proposal of Bauer (1984, 1986), according to which there are two routes to face recognition. The main, ventral route is occipitotemporal and is responsible for conscious (overt, explicit) recognition; this pathway would be damaged in prosopagnosia. The dorsal route is occipito-parieto-limbic and is generally spared in prosopagnosia, allowing unconscious (covert, implicit) recognition when the ventral route is damaged. It should be noted in passing that this conceptual frame offered by Bauer is less parsimonious than that suggested by De Haan et al. (1987a, 1987b; Young & De Haan, 1988; case P. H., above) to explain the differences between overt and covert face recognition as two different routes were hypothesized by Bauer, while De Haan et al. suggested simply a deficiency of the output of face recognition units to explain covert recognition without overt recognition. However explained, according to Bauer, the dorsal route gives the face its emotional meaning.

Cognitive Architecture and Psychopathological Pictures

Ellis and Young (1990) used the framework offered by Bauer (1984, 1986) to understand the clinical picture of patients with *Capgras's syndrome*. These patients believe that the perceived person is the double of a known person. Ellis and Young (1990) suggested that patients with Capgras's syndrome seem to have an intact ventral route, while their dorsal pathways would be damaged, the mirror image of the impairments underlying

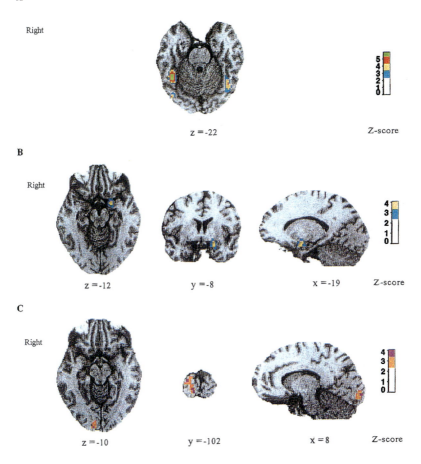

Fig. 8.2 Specific activations observed by Dubois and coworkers: A, fusiform gyri, activated in the three face tasks (the anterior activation in the right fusiform gyrus is the fusiform face area, FFA); B, left amygdala, activated by the gender categorization task on unfamiliar faces; C, right calcarine sulcus, deactivated by the gender categorization task on familiar faces. Values ± x, y, and z correspond to left/right, anterior/posterior, and top/bottom coordinates, respectively. Row A displays an axial (or transverse or horizontal) section of the brain. Rows B and C display, from left to right, axial (or transverse or horizontal), frontal (or vertical or coronal), and sagittal (or lateral) sections. For axial and frontal sections, the right hemisphere is on the left side of the figure. From "Effect of Familiarity on the Processing of Human Faces," by S. Dubois et al., 1999, *NeuroImage, 9,* 278–289. Copyright 1999 Academic Press, Inc. Reprinted with permission.

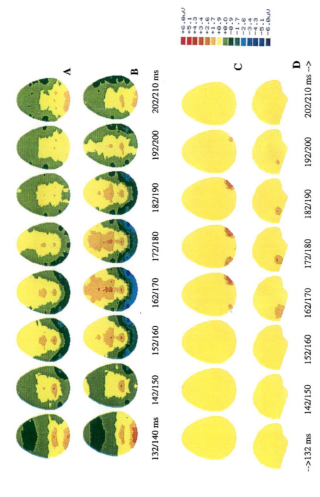

Fig. 8.3 The effect of inversion observed by Rossion and coworkers and its temporal evolution (from left to right): A, normal faces; B, inverted faces; C, subtraction (inverted-normal), horizontal view; D, subtraction, lateral (right side) view. From "Spatiotemporal Localization of the Face Inversion Effect: An Event-Related Potentials Study," by B. Rossion et al., 1999, *Biological Psychology, 50,* 173–189. Copyright 1999 Elsevier Science. Adapted with permission.

prosopagnosia with covert face recognition (see also Young & Ellis, 1989b).

Other delusional misidentification syndromes can be understood by means of the frame summarized in Fig. 8.1 (Ellis & Young, 1990). The patients with *Frégoli syndrome* are convinced that a person is disguised as another. This picture resembles some incidents occurring in the daily life of normal people (Schweich et al., 1992; Young, Hay, & Ellis, 1985). Indeed, when a specific person is expected, sometimes we misidentify a stranger as that person. While in normal people the mistake is transient and is corrected when perceptual evidence appears, in the Frégoli syndrome the perceptual inconsistency is attributed to disguise. Thus, the impairment of patients with Frégoli syndrome would be in the relationships between a person identity node and the cognitive system (not shown in the figure), which is the locus of decisional processes. Patients with *intermetamorphosis syndrome* believe that the physical appearance of some people may change radically to correspond to the appearance of someone else. Thus, this clinical picture could be conceived as an inappropriate firing of a face recognition unit for which, for instance, the threshold of excitation is lowered.

Obviously, additional empirical evidence is needed, but the few available data suggest that these psychopathological clinical pictures are conceptually very close to neuropsychological pictures. On the one hand, functional or structural cerebral anomalies are often detected in patients with a delusional misidentification syndrome (Joseph, 1986; Luauté et al., 1999; Luauté & Bidault, 1994). On the other hand, these syndromes can be interpreted in a cognitive, information-processing approach (Ellis & Young, 1990; Luauté et al., 1999), which implies that these patients should be systematically investigated by means of neuropsychological tests.

The remainder of this chapter returns to the two main functions of face processing—face identity and facial nonverbal communication (including expression)—and illustrates recent neuropsychological studies in the field. Current analyses of brain-damaged patients are not forgotten, but particular emphasis is given to modern neuroimaging experiments conducted with normal subjects (for an overview of studies with brain-injured patients, see Bruyer, 1993). Research is emphasized.

Contribution of Neuroimaging Studies

In a rather pessimistic recent overview of behavioral investigations of face processing, Uttal (2001) concluded that current studies are probably unable to solve theoretical debates in that field. However, as a behaviorist, Uttal did not consider neuropsychological and neuroimaging research, which is more promising.

Recent developments for computers and software allow researchers to "see" the cerebral activity of healthy subjects when they are performing several kinds of cognitive tasks; this can be done with noninvasive procedures. Therefore, neuroimagery is an ideal complementary alternative to the study of brain injuries and avoids the interpretative difficulties linked with the general effects of brain damage.

The three main techniques used today are event-related potentials (ERPs), positron emission tomography (PET), and functional magnetic resonance imaging (fMRI), although others, like magnetoencephalography (MEG) and transcranial magnetic stimulation (TMS), seem to be promising. ERPs are derived from the well-known electroencephalogram (EEG) technique and capture the local electrical brain activity induced by a stimulus, or the perceptual and cognitive processing of it, or response components; PET and fMRI detect correlates of metabolic modifications due to local increases of blood flow resulting from augmentations of local brain activity. Spatial resolution of PET and fMRI is high, and it is lower for ERP; temporal resolution is high for ERP, moderate for fMRI, and low for PET, indicating the complementarity of these methods. Books introducing the benefits of these techniques in cognitive neurosciences are those by Frackowiak, Friston, Frith, Dolan, and Mazziotta (1997), Papanicolaou (1998), and Posner and Raichle (1997); the relevance of these techniques in neuropsychology is well illustrated in the book edited by Kertesz (1994).

It is worth mentioning that, beyond very complex technical constraints, brain-imaging techniques are not without methodological difficulties with respect to the study of cognitive processes (see Bruyer, 1999; Sergent, 1994). Also, given the novelty of these methods, few studies related to the processing of faces have been published to now, and a theoretical conclusion is not offered (however, the ERP technique is somewhat older, and initial ERP studies of face processing have been critically reviewed by Bruyer, 1988).

Processing of Facial Identity

Several stages of the cognitive architecture displayed in Fig. 8.1 have been investigated by neuroimaging studies. Interestingly, some of them examined two or more stages in a single investigation, while some others compared equivalent stages with faces versus peoples' names as input.

With regard to the initial facial decision, the ERP study by Jeffreys (1996) evidenced face-specific neuronal populations, distinct from the neuronal populations sensitive to objects even if both populations were found in the same brain areas, located bilaterally in the inferior occipitotemporal region. Puce, Allison, Asgari, Gore, and McCarthy (1996) reported an fMRI study that showed that faces activated the occipitotemporal regions of the right hemisphere (whereas strings of letters activated the same regions of the left hemisphere) as well as the fusiform gyrus bilaterally. In addition, the fMRI studies of Kanwisher, McDermott, and Chun (1997) and of McCarthy, Puce, Gore, and Allison (1997) evidenced a region situated in the anterior part of the right fusiform gyrus that was specifically sensitive to faces (currently the so-called fusiform face area, FFA).

With respect to structural analyses, the ERP study of N. George, Evans, Fiori, Davidoff, and Renault (1996) reported temporal regions—mainly in the right hemisphere—in which positive potentials were recorded with a latency of about 200 ms, these potentials being specifically elicited by normal faces (as compared to faces with the eyes and mouth inverted). Bentin, Allison, Puce, Perez, and McCarthy (1996) recorded a negative ERP, mainly in the right hemisphere and with a latency of about 170 ms, that was specifically triggered by faces and eyes.

Jemel, George, Olivares, Fiori, and Renault (1999) reported an ERP study in which the subjects were first shown a famous face without eyes and then a complete face; this complete face was either the normal face of the famous person or that face with the eyes of another face. Incongruent faces triggered a positive wave, with a latency of about 140 ms, in the inferior temporal region of the right hemisphere; the source of this wave was located in the posterior part of the parietal lobe (the precuneus).

The fMRI study of Wojciulik, Kanwisher, and Driver (1998) showed that the activity of the FFA can be modulated by covert attention (i.e., by facial stimuli situated outside the attentional focus). Finally, in our research unit, a PET study by Rossion, Dricot, et al. (2000) showed that the right FFA was more activated by whole faces than by face parts, whereas this pattern was reversed in the left homologous area; in addition, this pattern was specific to faces.

The goal of structural analyses is to derive an invariant representation. This representation either can be matched to a preexisting face recognition unit (familiar faces) that is then activated and gives rise to recognition, or leads to the creation of a new, episodic face recognition unit (unfamiliar faces). With respect to the creation of new face recognition units, several studies deserve mention. On the one hand, the PET study conducted by Haxby et al. (1996) showed that the encoding of new faces gives rise to activations in the right hippocampus and the left prefrontal region, while the recognition of these faces activates the right prefrontal area. In the PET study reported by M. S. George et al. (1993), the subjects had to recognize an unfamiliar target face in a pair of unfamiliar faces; this led to an activation of the region of the amygdala on the left side.

A similar design was used by Haxby, Ungerleider, Horwitz, Rapoport, and Grady (1995), who in addition manipulated the delay between the presentation of the target and that of the pair of faces. There appeared (a) an activation in the right frontal region not affected by the delay and probably signifying the encoding and storage of the view-dependent representation of the face and (b) an activation of a large fronto-parieto-temporal network in the right hemisphere, which increased with the delay, probably reflecting operations devoted to the memory registration of a stable structural representation.

On the other hand, authors have displayed series of unfamiliar faces, some of them being shown two (or more) times, ·and have examined the effect of this repetition on brain activity. In some studies, the subject was explicitly asked to decide whether the face was seen for the first time or not. Thus, in the PET study of Kapur, Friston, Young, Frith, and Frackowiak (1995), this episodic recognition induced a selective activation of the left hippocampus. In the ERP study of Sommer, Komoss, and Schweinberger (1997), this repetition triggered a positive wave at the vertex, slightly more important on the right side, with a latency of about 400 to 800 ms; in addition, when the same task was repeated with unfamiliar first names, a positive frontal wave, slightly more important on the right side, appeared together with a negative posterior wave that was slightly more important on the left side.

In other studies, the subject sees the stimuli passively. Thus, Seeck et al. (1997) concluded, from their ERP study, that face recognition takes place as early as 50 ms after the repetition. However, this conclusion has been challenged. N. George, Jemel, Fiori, and Renault (1997) observed this same early phenomenon for faces as well as for nonfacial stimuli; thus, the wave recorded after 50 ms was probably due to a repetition effect and was not an effect of face recognition. Furthermore, Debruille, Guillem, and Renault (1998) showed, in a similar complementary ERP study using both unfamiliar and familiar faces, that face familiarity (i.e., face recognition) had an effect after about 100 ms—a much more plausible latency.

With this last study, the other goal of structural analyses began to be considered, namely, the activation of face recognition units leading to the recognition of familiar faces. Classically, the store of face recognition units is assessed by a familiarity decision task: The subject is asked to decide whether the perceived face is well known (i.e., famous or familiar) or new (unfamiliar). Such a decision task was administered to the subjects enrolled by Sergent, MacDonald, and Zuck (1994) for their PET study; the cerebral correlate of this task was an activation of occipitotemporal regions in the right hemisphere. Interestingly, the same task applied to persons' names led to a symmetric activation in the left hemisphere. In our research unit, a PET study was reported by Rossion, Schiltz, Robaye, Pirenne, and Crommelinck (2001), who displayed chimaerical stimuli designed by morphing unfamiliar and familiar faces—in various proportions—for a familiarity decision. It appeared that the familiarity decision is token in an all-or-none, rather than a proportional, fashion (a categorical process; see the final comments of this chapter) and is associated with abrupt changes of activation in the right ventral pathway of the brain.

Once the face and then the person have·been recognized, the viewer can normally retrieve identity-specific semantic information about the person seen. This processing stage was investigated by Sergent, Ohta, and MacDonald (1992), who asked their subjects to categorize famous faces as actors versus nonactors. Brain correlates of this cognitive operation (PET scan) were found in the right hippocampus and, bilaterally, in the fusiform gyrus and the anterior temporal cortex. The same task was used in the PET study of Sergent, Ohta, MacDonald, and Zuck (1994), who observed an activation in the right occipitotemporal region similar to that in the already mentioned PET study of Sergent, MacDonald, et al. (1994). Interestingly, in this last study, the same task with famous names as input led to symmetrical activation in the left hemisphere. The subjects of the above-mentioned PET study of Kapur et al. (1995) were also asked to categorize famous faces as politicians versus nonpoliticians: Activations were found in the right hippocampus and the right occipital visual areas.

The final stage of the cognitive architecture shown in Fig. 8.1 is that of the access to the name of the face seen. Curiously, while some neuroimaging studies used names as input (see above), it seems that no study has examined the access to names with faces as input. However, a recent PET study by our team (Campanella, Joassin, et al., 2001) evidenced the activation of a network of three brain areas, in the left hemisphere, when subjects had to retrieve from long-term memory specific face/name associations: the inferior frontal gyrus, medial frontal gyrus, and supramarginal gyrus of the inferior parietal lobe. An ERP study is in progress to track the temporal sequence of activations of these three regions.

Facial Nonverbal Communication

Until now, three channels of facial nonverbal communication have been investigated: gender categorization, detection of gaze direction, and emotional expression.

With respect to gender categorization, the subjects of Sergent et al. (1992, PET study) also had to classify unfamiliar faces as male versus female; this led to specific activation of the extrastriate right occipital cortex. The same task was submitted to the subjects of Sergent, MacDonald, et al. (1994a, PET study), with activation in the occipitotemporal region of the right hemisphere; in this study, the same task using Christian names led to a symmetrical occipitotemporal activation in the left hemisphere. Thus, in this study, three tasks were used: gender categorization, familiarity decision, and semantic decision. Occipitotemporal activations appeared to be situated more and more anteriorly from the first to the third task, and they were observed in the right hemisphere for faces, but in the left one for names.

The subjects enrolled by Kapur et al. (1995, PET study) also had to classify unfamiliar faces by gender, and this led to activations in the right hippocampus and visual cortex. Note that, in this study, episodic recognition, semantic categorization, and gender classification activated occipital areas as well as the right hippocampus. Morris, Friston, et al. (1998a, PET study) asked their subjects to categorize faces as male or female, which led to activation in occipital visual areas. However, in this study, emotional facial expression was manipulated, as discussed below.

According to the canonical model displayed by Fig. 8.1, the processing of face identity and the processing of gender of face are two distinct, parallel processes. However, it is worth noting that recent research in experimental psychology led to the conclusion that this independence has to be qualified, and that a single route should be considered (e.g., Ganel & Goshen-Gottstein, 2002; Goshen-Gottstein & Ganel, 2000; in our team, see Rossion, 2002).

Concerning the perception of gaze direction, it is known that gaze direction is a powerful trigger for the shifting of attention of the observer. In my group, Schuller and Rossion (2001) reported an ERP study that revealed that this shifting was associated with very early occipital activity.

Concerning the processing of emotional facial expressions, the subjects of M. S. George et al. (1993, PET study) also had to match unfamiliar faces with respect to their expression, which led to activations of the anterior part of the right cingular cortex and of frontal (mainly left-sided) regions. The subjects enrolled by Sergent, Ohta, et al. (1994, PET study) also had to evaluate the positive versus negative emotional valence of expressions displayed by unfamiliar faces; this induced an activation in the lateral part of the right occipital cortex. Furthermore, in this study, the limbic cortex was activated by this task and by the actor/nonactor semantic task. Emotional faces were displayed by M. S. George et al. (1995, PET study), and they invited their subjects to remember personal affective events corresponding to the emotion shown. Sadness induced an activation of limbic structures, while happiness led to a deactivation in the right prefrontal area and in the bilateral temporoparietal structures.

Morris et al. (1996, PET study) showed that fear induced an activation of the left amygdala, while happiness induced a deactivation of the same structure; in both cases, the activation or deactivation was proportional to the intensity of the displayed expression. Then, using a masking procedure, the same team (Morris, Öhman, & Dolan, 1998, PET study) showed that fear activates the left amygdala only if the subject consciously perceives the expression, whereas the right amygdala is activated by unconscious perception of fear. Finally, the subjects of Morris, Friston, et al. (1998, see above, PET study) did not have to process expression voluntarily, but fear produced a specific activation of the left amygdala, and expressions modulated the activations induced by the gender categorization task. Clearly, these last neuroimaging studies relate to the single-case reports mentioned in the second section of this chapter.

An Integrated Approach

In spite of its ultraanalytic look, the cognitive architecture of face processing is an integrated device, and many components are mandatory. Therefore, it would appear to be useful to consider it in an integrated manner, which leads to several methodological constraints: (a) Several components have to be investigated in a single study; (b) the same material has to be used in the different tasks; and (c) a single set of subjects must be enrolled for these various tasks. Such an approach was adopted, for instance, by Sergent et al. (1992; Sergent, MacDonald, et al., 1994). Moreover, when long-term face recognition units are involved, authors often use famous faces (i.e., faces of celebrities whose familiarity has been assessed by pretests). However, individual differences are important with respect to the process of familiarization (kind of encoding, duration, etc.) and as a function of personal self-interests. Therefore, it seems to be better to monitor the process of familiarization. Studies of our research group were planned to meet these methodological constraints (see also the final comments of this chapter).

Our group reported a PET study in which the subjects were first visually familiarized with new faces over 3 days by means of videotapes; after a first PET session, they were again familiarized with the same faces by means of videotapes, but additional pieces of information were given—semantic information (occupations) and lexical information (names)—and a second PET session followed. The results of the first PET session were published by Dubois et al. (1999); those of the second PET session are as yet unpublished, but see Dubois et al. (1997).

During the first PET session, the subjects performed four tasks: gender categorization of the faces learned, gender categorization of new faces, familiarity decision, and a control task (a visual pattern discrimination task). Two main results were observed (see Fig. 8.2). On the one hand, bilateral activation of the fusiform gyri (including the FFA in the right fusiform gyrus) was specifically triggered by faces regardless of task. On the other hand, face familiarity had an effect on gender categorization, a result not predicted by the model (however, see the single-route hypothesis, above). Thus, this task led to an activation of the left amygdala when unfamiliar faces were used and to a deactivation of early visual areas when familiar faces were shown.

During the second PET session—after the semantic and lexical learning—it appeared that representations of names should be kept distinct from representations of semantic information. Indeed, the retrieval of semantic information recruited a large cortical network, while the retrieval of names activated a subcortical network, including the putamen, the thalamus, and the cerebellum.

A very similar design was used in another ERP study by my group (Rossion, Campanella, et al., 1999). The main result was the recording of a ver-

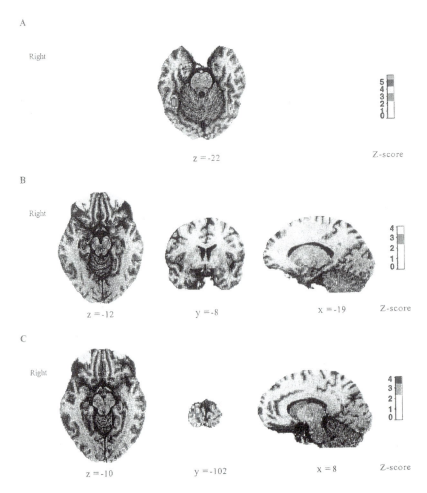

Fig. 8.2 Specific activations observed by Dubois and coworkers: A, fusiform gyri, activated in the three face tasks (the anterior activation in the right fusiform gyrus is the fusiform face area, FFA); B, left amygdala, activated by the gender categorization task on unfamiliar faces; C, right calcarine sulcus, deactivated by the gender categorization task on familiar faces. Values ± x, y, and z correspond to left/right, anterior/posterior, and top/bottom coordinates, respectively. Row A displays an axial (or transverse or horizontal) section of the brain. Rows B and C display, from left to right, axial (or transverse or horizontal), frontal (or vertical or coronal), and sagittal (or lateral) sections. For axial and frontal sections, the right hemisphere is on the left side of the figure. From "Effect of Familiarity on the Processing of Human Faces," by S. Dubois et al., 1999, *NeuroImage, 9,* 278–289. Copyright 1999 Academic Press, Inc. Reprinted with permission.

tex positive potential (VPP) around 160 ms after the onset of the stimulus that was specific to faces, but independent of the kind of task and of face familiarity. The source of this potential was in the region of the fusiform gyrus. In addition, this study gave rise to methodological developments with regard to analysis of brain potentials. Campanella, Gomez, et al. (1999) used the data of this study to compare grand average and individual analyses with respect to their sensitivity. It appeared that early peaks can be detected better by individual analyses, while the grand average method is more suitable to detect later components.

Final Comments

Obviously, current progress in our knowledge of the mechanisms underlying face processing depends closely on the convergence of neuropsychological analyses of deficits resulting from brain damage, neuroimaging experiments in healthy subjects, and electrophysiological studies in animals. These three modes of investigation are increasingly integrated (for instance, ERP studies are conducted on prosopagnosic patients: Bentin, Deouell, & Soroker, 1999; Eimer & McCarthy, 1999; Renault, Signoret, Debruille, Breton, & Bolgert, 1989) and constitute the *cognitive neurosciences*, an interdisciplinary scientific field that has to incorporate data provided by experiments in cognitive psychology, including developmental and comparative approaches (for an overview of high-level visual processes, see Bruyer, 2000). Four topics are briefly mentioned in this final section to recall current theoretical debates and progress: an evolutionary perspective, specificity, categorical perception of faces and facial expressions, and rehabilitation.

An Evolutionary Perspective

The visual identification of conspecifics by their faces and the recognition of emotional facial expressions are observed soon after birth, but these skills continue to develop over a long period during childhood (see Ellis, 1992; Johnson & Morton, 1991) and are not even the exclusivity ofe to the human species since they are present not only in nonhuman primates, but also in other mammals (like the ovines) and even in Gallinaceae (for a review, see the special issue of *Behavioural Processes* edited by Zayan, 1994). Moreover, in primates and other species, electrophysiologists did record cortical cells responding specifically to some facial identities, to some facial features, or to some facial expressions (see Gross, 1992; Heywood & Cowey, 1992; Perrett, Hietanen, Oram, & Benson, 1992; Rolls, 1992, 1994).

Naturally, one has to verify whether the specific brain areas identified in this way in animals correspond functionally and anatomically to areas damaged in humans suffering from deficits in face processing (e.g., prosopagnosia) and to areas identified by neuroimaging techniques in healthy humans. In addition, the identification of such selective cells contributes to the debate about the specificity of face-processing mechanisms.

Specificity

The question of specificity of face perception feeds an ancient and unresolved debate (see Davidoff, 1986; Ellis & Young, 1989; Hay & Young, 1982) and is closely related to Fodor's (1983) thesis of modularity. Fodor's assumption is that peripheral devices of the information-processing system are modular, with a module defined by a set of properties: It is domain specific (it is triggered by a specific kind of information, i.e., faces); its operations are mandatory (provided the specific stimulus is encountered); only the output of its processing is available to nonmodular devices, such as awareness, attention, memory, and the like (the results of intermediate, internal operations of the module are not available); it functions quickly; it is informationally encapsulated (it cannot be modulated in a top-down manner by beliefs, motivations, expectancies, memory, etc.); its output is superficial (it does not depend on background knowledge); it is neurally hardwired; its deficiency results in a specific behavioral deficit; and its development is specific, suggesting innate rules. Thus, the point is that a module would be dedicated to the processing of faces, another one to language, and so on.

Given this conceptual framework, the question of specificity is one version of the question of specialness: Are faces special (Teuber, 1978)? In a broad and superficial sense, faces are obviously special—see some of the arguments listed below, but for a more precise definition of specialness, it appeared useful to draw a distinction between uniqueness and specificity (Hay & Young, 1982). Uniqueness would be the stronger form of specialness: Faces are unique in that they are handled by a system that is separate from the systems used for processing other objects, and this system works differently from the other ones (modularity). Specificity would be the weaker form of specialness; a separate system exists for faces, but it may or may not work in a way similar to the other systems, sharing mechanisms with these systems. Let us note that specialness of a given class of stimuli would mean, formally, that all other classes are processed by the same mechanisms, a thesis defended by a few authors (e.g., Tovée, 1998).

Several arguments are used to defend specificity: (a) the crucial psychosocial importance of faces in daily life activities; (b) the impressive abilities—or expertise—of humans in discriminating facial identities and expressions, which needs the precise identification of exemplars within a very specific category formed by a great number of members; (c) the very precocious nature (innateness?) of these abilities; (d) the high specificity of deficits resulting from brain damage and affecting the processing of faces;

(e) electrophysiological recordings of face-sensitive cells in animals; (f) neuroimaging studies in healthy humans that indicate face-sensitive brain areas; and (g) experimental behavioral effects, particularly the effect of inversion on episodic recognition, which is disproportionate for faces compared to other complex and mono-oriented visual stimuli.

However, several of these arguments are still controversial today, so the hypothesis of specificity, albeit highly plausible, is not yet firmly verified, at least in its modular form (uniqueness) (see Rossion, 2000). For example, the disproportionate effect of inversion (Yin, 1969, 1970) has been used to suggest that normal (right-side-up) faces are processed by specific mechanisms that cannot operate when the faces are inverted; the disproportionate effect of inversion would result from the inability to process the "physiognomy" because the configural perceptual mechanisms are not recruited by upside-down faces (Sergent, 1984a, 1984b; Tanaka & Farah, 1993). Now, experimental studies have shown that such a disproportionate effect of inversion can be observed with other categories of visual complex stimuli, provided the viewer has acquired expertise for processing members of these categories (for dog breeders, Diamond & Carey, 1986; for experts in handwriting, Bruyer & Crispeels, 1992; for experts for "greebles," Gauthier & Tarr, 1997). Thus, the specificity of faces would be simply that virtually all human beings are expert in processing this material.

Given the theoretical importance of this effect, numerous behavioral studies have been devoted to it. However, the literature is virtually free of studies exploring the neural bases of the inversion effect with an appropriate temporal resolution; our group has attempted to fill in this gap. Rossion, Delvenne, et al. (1999) recorded ERP of subjects performing a delayed matching task on right-side-up and upside-down unfamiliar faces. The sole significant effect of inversion was observed at occipitotemporal sites about 160 ms after the onset of the stimulus, mainly in the right hemisphere (see Fig. 8.3): The inversion delayed and amplified the electrophysiological activity. Moreover, a complementary study showed that this specific effect of inversion on brain activity did not apply to other complex visual stimuli (Rossion, Gauthier, et al., 1999, 2000).

Finally, several studies question the truth of the informational encapsulation of the "module" devoted to faces. For instance, a recent ERP study of our team (Jemel, Pisani, Calabria, Crommelinck, & Bruyer, in press) shows priming effects even on very early components of brain activity generated by familiar and unfamiliar faces.

Categorical Perception of Faces and Facial Expressions

Current developments in computer science allow generation of pictures that constitute a continuous transition from one complex, multidimensional visual image to another. In particular, morphing software can be

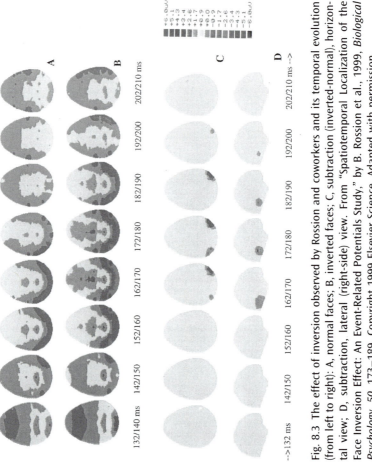

Fig. 8.3 The effect of inversion observed by Rossion and coworkers and its temporal evolution (from left to right): A, normal faces; B, inverted faces; C, subtraction (inverted-normal), horizontal view; D, subtraction, lateral (right-side) view. From "Spatiotemporal Localization of the Face Inversion Effect: An Event-Related Potentials Study," by B. Rossion et al., 1999, *Biological Psychology, 50*, 173–189. Copyright 1999 Elsevier Science. Adapted with permission.

used to create chimerical faces, that is, facial configurations formed with pixels issued from a given face and pixels issued from another one, in controlled proportions (e.g., 30% from Model A and 70% from Model B). Figure 8.4 illustrates this technique.

Thanks to this method, an ancient debate about the perception of emotions has been solved (Ekman, 1982). Indeed, some authors claimed that the range of emotions is formed with continuous, gentle dimensional transitions, while others claimed that emotions are discrete categories. Recent experiments with morphed faces support the second hypothesis. Indeed, even if continuous transitions between emotional facial expressions are shown, the subject perceives discrete categories with a sharp perceptual boundary between them (identification task, allowing definition of the boundary). Moreover, when pairs of morphed faces are displayed for same/different judgments (matching task), the subject is able to discriminate much better chimerical expressions issued from both sides of the boundary than chimerical expressions issued from the same side (Bruyer & Granato, 1999; Calder, Young, Perrett, Etcoff, & Rowland, 1996; De Gelder, Teunisse, & Benson, 1997; Etcoff & Magee, 1992; Granato & Bruyer, 2002; Granato, Bruyer, & Révillion, 1996; Young, Rowland, Calder, Etcoff, Seth, & Perrett et al., 1997).

In addition, the technique of morphing—using the identification task and then the matching task—provided the opportunity to reveal that the perception of facial identity (as well as of face gender; Campanella, Chrysochoos, & Bruyer, 2001) is also categorical. This has been shown for unfamiliar faces by Beale and Keil (1995) and for both unfamiliar and familiar faces by Campanella et al. (in press). Our research team is currently trying to detect cerebral correlates of this categorical perception of facial identities; the results of these studies are summarized next.

In the ERP study by Campanella, Hanoteau, Bruyer, Crommelinck, and Guérit (1999), the subjects were submitted to delayed same/different judgments on pairs of chimerical (morphed) faces. When faces differed, the physical difference between them was always the same (30%), but the two faces were issued either from the same side of the boundary (intracategorical condition) or from both sides (intercategorical condition). The amplitude of temporal negative waves associated with correct trials appeared to be higher in the intercategorical condition compared to the intracategorical condition and to same trials, and this brain correlate of categorical perception of identities was observed in the right hemisphere. More precisely (Campanella, Hanoteau, et al., 2000), the cerebral source of the categorical perception of facial identities was detected in the right occipitotemporal region about 170 ms after the onset of the second face of the pair (N_{170}).

In the PET study by Rossion, Schiltz, et al. (1999), the subjects were first familiarized over 3 days with initially unknown faces. Then, brain activity was recorded while the subjects performed a gender classification task on

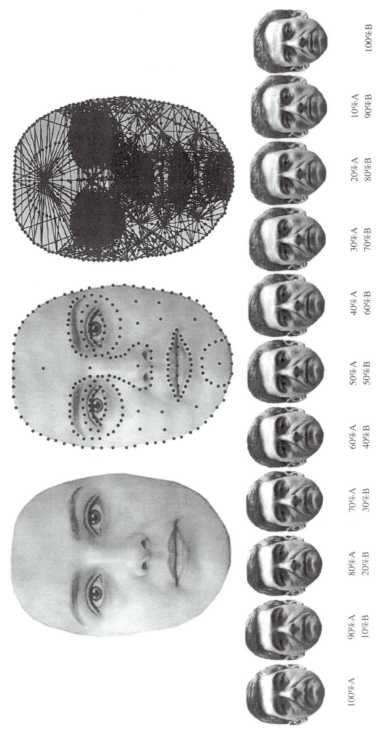

Fig. 8.4 Morphing from Face A to Face B in steps of 10%. Computations were performed for each of the corresponding anatomic landmarks indicated in the top picture; the resulting "faces" were then smoothed.

100%A 90%A 80%A 70%A 60%A 50%A 40%A 30%A 20%A 10%A 100%B
10%B 20%B 30%B 40%B 50%B 60%B 70%B 80%B 90%B

chimerical faces generated by a morphing procedure of each learned face with a new, unfamiliar face. Despite the continuous transition from unfamiliar to familiar faces, and while subjects did not have to perform an explicit recognition task, their brain activity was clearly and categorically (sharp boundary) related to face familiarity. The activity of the right middle occipital gyrus and of the right parahippocampal gyrus was negatively correlated with familiarity; in addition, their activity was sensitive to face novelty, but with no effect as to the level of novelty. These structures appeared to be components of a neural network sensitive to novelty, but not to familiarity, also including the right fusiform gyrus and the left cerebellum.

Finally, the ERP study reported by Campanella, Quinet, Bruyer, Crommelinck, and Guérit (2002) was designed to identify neural correlates of categorical perception of emotional facial expressions. It was shown that categorical perception was associated with an early activation of occipito-temporal regions.

Rehabilitation

One important dimension of neuropsychology is rehabilitation. Unfortunately, this chapter ends on a rather deceptive tonenote. Indeed, the literature is devoid of reports of neuropsychological therapy conducted on patients suffering from deficits of face processing resulting from brain damage. Moreover, Ellis and Young (1988) did report such an attempt in a case of childhood prosopagnosia, but the rehabilitation program failed.

By way of conclusion, I speculate on what rehabilitation or a clinical intervention might look like. First, given the diversity of potential disorders (identity, emotions, gender, etc.), a single kit of recommendations cannot be suggested. Second, even within a specific kind of information conveyed by faces, the locus of the deficit in the cognitive architecture will guide the rehabilitation strategy. Let us consider facial identity, for instance. If a perceptual deficit underlies the clinical defect by altering structural encoding, the therapist should probably reinforce configural visual strategies or recruit mental imagery. If, on the other hand, the deficiency concerns operations beyond the activation of face recognition units, then the strategy would be to reinforce some kinds of associations in long-term memory. Finally, the presence versus absence of signs of covert recognition will qualify the rehabilitation program; clearly, such signs—if any—should be used as a basis for reconstruction.

References

Adolphs, R., Tranel, D., Damasio, H., & Damasio, A. (1994). Impaired recognition of emotion in facial expressions following bilateral damage to the human amygdala. *Nature, 372*, 669–672.

Adolphs, R., Tranel, D., Damasio, H., & Damasio, A. R. (1995). Fear and the human amygdala. *Journal of Neuroscience, 15*, 5879–5891.

Alley, T. R. (Ed.). (1988). *Social and applied aspects of perceiving faces.* Hillsdale, NJ: Erlbaum.

Bauer, R. M. (1984). Autonomic recognition of names and faces: a neuropsychological application of the Guilty Knowledge Test. *Neuropsychologia, 22,* 457–469.

Bauer, R. M. (1986). The cognitive psychophysiology of prosopagnosia. In H. Ellis, M. Jeeves, F. Newcombe, & A. Young (Eds.), *Aspects of face processing* (pp. 253–267). Dordrecht, The Netherlands: Nijhoff.

Beale, J. M., & Keil, C. F. (1995). Categorical effects in the perception of faces. *Cognition, 57,* 217–239.

Bentin, S., Allison, T., Puce, A., Perez, E., & McCarthy, G. (1996). Electrophysiological studies of face perception in humans. *Journal of Cognitive Neuroscience, 8,* 551–565.

Bentin, S., Deouell, L. Y., & Soroker, N. (1999). Selective visual streaming in face recognition: Evidence from developmental prosopagnosia. *NeuroReport, 10,* 823–827.

Bruce, V. (1988). *Recognising faces.* Hove, England: Erlbaum.

Bruce, V., & Burton, M. (Eds.). (1992). *Processing images of faces.* Norwood, NJ: Ablex.

Bruce, V., Cowey, A., Ellis, A. W., & Perrett, D. I. (Eds.). (1992). Processing the facial image [Special issue]. *Philosophical Transactions of the Royal Society of London, series B.*

Bruce, V., & Humphreys, G. (Eds.). (1994). *Object and face recognition.* Hove, England: Erlbaum.

Bruce, V., & Young, A. (1986). Understanding face recognition. *British Journal of Psychology, 77,* 305–327.

Bruce, V., & Young, A. (1998). *In the eye of the beholder: The science of face perception.* Oxford, England: Oxford University Press.

Bruyer, R. (1980). Implication différentielle des hémisphères cérébraux dans les conduites émotionnelles [Differential implication of cerebral hemispheres in emotional behavior]. *Acta Psychiatrica Belgica, 80,* 266–280.

Bruyer, R. (Ed.). (1986). *The neuropsychology of face perception and facial expression.* Hillsdale, NJ: Erlbaum.

Bruyer, R. (1987). *Les Mécanismes de reconnaissance des visages* [Mechanisms of face recognition]. Grenoble, France: Presses Universitaires de Grenoble.

Bruyer, R. (1988). Brain asymmetries in face processing: A critical review of electrophysiological studies from a psychological point of view. *Journal of Physiology (Paris), 83,* 3–10.

Bruyer, R. (1990). Cognitive implications of studies on facial asymmetry. *International Journal of Psychology, 25,* 229–236.

Bruyer, R. (1991). Covert face recognition in prosopagnosia: A review. *Brain and Cognition, 15,* 223–235.

Bruyer, R. (1993). Failures of face processing in normal and brain-damaged subjects. In F. Boller & J. Grafman (Eds.), *Handbook of neuropsychology* (Vol. 8, pp. 411–435). Amsterdam, The Netherlands: Elsevier.

Bruyer, R. (1994). Face recognition. In V. S. Ramachandran (Ed.), *Encyclopedia of human behavior* (Vol. 2, pp. 351–359). San Diego, CA: Academic Press.

Bruyer, R. (1999). Regard d'un cognitiviste sur l'apport des techniques d'imagerie cérébrale fonctionnelle: quelques mises en garde [Contribution of functional brain imagery: Some comments from a cognitive viewpoint]. *Archives de Psychologie, 67,* 179–195.

Bruyer, R. (2000). *Le cerveau qui voit* [The seeing brain]. Paris: O. Jacob.

Bruyer, R., & Crispeels, G. (1992). Expertise in person recognition. *Bulletin of the Psychonomic Society, 30,* 501–504.

Bruyer, R., & Granato, P. (1999). Categorical effects in the perception of facial expressions: MARIE, a simple and discriminating clinical tool. *European Review of Applied Psychology, 49,* 3–10.

Bruyer, R., Laterre, C., Seron, X., Feyereisen, P., Strypstein, E., Pierrard, E., et al. (1983). A case of prosopagnosia with some preserved covert remembrance of familiar faces. *Brain and Cognition, 2,* 257–284.

Burton, A. M., Bruce, V., & Johnston, R. A. (1990). Understanding face recognition with an interactive activation model. *British Journal of Psychology, 81,* 361–380.

Calder, A. J., Young, A. W., Perrett, D. I., Etcoff, N. L., & Rowland, D. (1996). Categorical perception of morphed facial expressions. *Visual Cognition, 3,* 81–117.

Calder, A. J., Young, A. W., Rowland, D., Perrett, D. I., Hodges, J. R., & Etcoff, N. L. (1996). Facial emotion recognition after bilateral amygdala damage: Differentially severe impairment of fear. *Cognitive Neuropsychology, 13,* 699–745.

Campanella, S., Chrysochoos, A., & Bruyer, R. (2001). Categorical perception of facial gender information: Behavioural evidence and the face-space metaphor. *Visual Cognition, 8,* 237–262.

Campanella, S., Gomez, C., Rossion, B., Liard, L., Debatisse, D., Dubois, S., et al. (1999). Etude comparative en potentiels évoqués des données fournies par le biais d'analyses de groupes et individuelles [Comparison of group and individual analyses of ERPs]. *Neurophysiologie Clinique, 29,* 325–338.

Campanella, S., Hanoteau, C., Bruyer, R., Crommelinck, M., & Guérit, J. M. (1999). ERP correlates of face categorization [abstract]. *Society for Neuroscience, 25,* 353.

Campanella, S., Hanoteau, C., Dépy, D., Rossion, B., Bruyer, R., Crommelinck, M., et al. (2000). Right N_{170} modulation in a face discrimination task: An account for categorical perception of familiar faces. *Psychophysiology, 37,* 796–806.

Campanella, S., Hanoteau, C., Seron, X., Joassin, F., & Bruyer, R. (in press). Categorical perception of unfamiliar facial identities and the face-space metaphor. *Visual Cognition, 10.*

Campanella, S., Joassin, F., Rossion, B., De Volder, A., Bruyer, R., & Crommelinck, M. (2001). Association of the distinct visual representations of faces and names: A PET activation study. *Neuroimage, 14,* 873–882.

Campanella, S., Quinet, P., Bruyer, R., Crommelinck, M., & Guérit, J. M. (2002). Categorical perception of happiness and fear facial expressions: An ERP study. *Journal of Cognitive Neuroscience, 14,* 210–227.

Campbell, R., Heywood, C. A., Cowey, A., Regard, M., & Landis, T. (1990). Sensitivity to eye gaze in prosopagnosic patients and monkeys with superior temporal sulcus ablation. *Neuropsychologia, 28,* 1123–1142.

Campbell, R., Landis, T., & Regard, M. (1986). Face recognition and lipreading. *Brain, 109,* 509–521.

Capgras, J., & Reboul-Lachaux, J. (1923). L'illusion des "sosies" dans un délire systématique chronique [Illusion of double in a case of chronic and systematic delusion]. *Bulletin de la Société Clinique de Médecine Mentale, 2,* 6–16.

Caramazza, A. (1986). On drawing inferences about the structure of normal cognitive systems from the analysis of patterns of impaired performance: The case for single-patient studies. *Brain and Cognition, 5,* 41–66.

Caramazza, A., & Martin, R. C. (1983). Theoretical and methodological issues in the study of aphasia. In J. B. Hellige (Ed.), *Cerebral hemisphere asymmetry: Method, theory, and application* (pp. 18–45). New York: Prager.

Carney, R., & Temple, C. M. (1993). Prosopanomia? A possible category-specific anomia for faces. *Cognitive Neuropsychology, 10,* 185–195.

Courbon, P., & Fail, G. (1927). Syndrome "d'illusion de Frégoli" et schizophrénie [Frégoli syndrome and schizophrenia]. *Bulletin de la Société Clinique de Médecine Mentale, 15,* 121–124.

Courbon, P., & Tusques, J. (1932). Illusions d'intermétamorphose et de charme [Illusions of intermetamorphosis and of charm]. *Annales Médico-Psychologiques, 90,* 401–406.

Davidoff, J. B. (1986). The specificity of face perception: Evidence from psychological investigations. In R. Bruyer (Ed.), *The neuropsychology of face perception and facial expression* (pp. 147–166). Hillsdale, NJ: Erlbaum.

Davies, G., Ellis, H., & Shepherd, J. (Eds.). (1981). *Perceiving and remembering faces.* London: Academic Press.

Debruille, J. B., Guillem, F., & Renault, B. (1998). ERPs and chronometry of face recognition: Following-up Seeck et al. and George et al. *NeuroReport, 9,* 3349–3353..

De Gelder, B., Teunisse, J. P., & Benson, P. J. (1997). Categorical perception of facial expressions: Categories and their internal structure. *Cognition and Emotion, 11,* 1–23.

De Haan, E. H. F., Young, A. W., & Newcombe, F. (1987a). Face recognition without awareness. *Cognitive Neuropsychology, 4,* 385–415.

De Haan, E. H. F., Young, A. W., & Newcombe, F. (1987b). Faces interfere with name classification in a prosopagnosic patient. *Cortex, 23,* 309–316.

De Haan, E. H. F., Young, A. W., & Newcombe, F. (1991). A dissociation between the sense of familiarity and access to semantic information concerning familiar people. *European Journal of Cognitive Psychology, 3,* 51–67.

De Haan, E. H. F., Young, A. W., & Newcombe, F. (1992). Neuropsychological impairment of face recognition units. *Quarterly Journal of Experimental Psychology, 44A,* 141–175.

Diamond, R., & Carey, S. (1986). Why faces are and are not special: An effect of expertise. *Journal of Experimental Psychology: General, 115,* 107–117.

Dubois, S., Rossion, B., Schiltz, C., Bodart, J. M., Michel, C., Bruyer, R., et al. (1999). Effect of familiarity on the processing of human faces. *NeuroImage, 9,* 278–289.

Dubois, S., Rossion, B., Schiltz, C., Bodart, J. M., Michel, C., Bruyer, R., et al. (1997). Specific activation related to proper name retrieval associated with faces [abstract]. *Society for Neuroscience, 23,* 491.

Eimer, M., & McCarthy, R. A. (1999). Prosopagnosia and structural encoding of faces: evidence from event-related potentials. *NeuroReport, 10,* 255–259.

Ekman, P. (Ed.) (1982). *Emotion in the human face*. Cambridge, England: Cambridge University Press.

Ellis, H. D. (1986). Introduction: Processes underlying face recognition. In R. Bruyer (Ed.), *The neuropsychology of face perception and facial expression* (pp. 1–27). Hillsdale, NJ: Erlbaum.

Ellis, H. D. (1992). The development of face processing skills. In V. Bruce, A. Cowey, A. W. Ellis, & D. I. Perrett (Eds.), *Processing the facial image* (pp. 105–111). Oxford, England: Clarendon Press.

Ellis, H. D., Jeeves, M. A., Newcombe, F., & Young, A. (Eds.). (1986). *Aspects of face processing*. Dordrecht, The Netherlands: Nijhoff.

Ellis, H. D., & Young, A. W. (1988). Training in face-processing skills for a child with acquired prosopagnosia. *Developmental Neuropsychology, 4*, 283–294.

Ellis, H. D., & Young, A. W. (1989). Are faces special? In A. W. Young & H. D. Ellis (Eds.), *Handbook of research on face processing* (pp. 1–26). Amsterdam, The Netherlands: North-Holland.

Ellis, H. D., & Young, A. W. (1990). Accounting for delusional misidentifications. *British Journal of Psychiatry, 157*, 239–248.

Etcoff, N. L., & Magee, J. J. (1992). Categorical perception of facial expressions. *Cognition, 44*, 227–240.

Feyereisen, P. (1999). The neuropsychology of expressive movements. In L. Messing & R. Campbell (Eds.), *Gesture, speech, and sign* (pp. 3–25). New York: Oxford University Press.

Flude, B. M., Ellis, A. W., & Kay, J. (1989). Face processing and name retrieval in an anomic aphasic: names are stored separately from semantic information about people. *Brain and Cognition, 11*, 60–72.

Fodor, J. A. (1983). *The modularity of mind*. Cambridge, MA: MIT Press.

Frackowiak, R. S. J., Friston, K. J., Frith, C. D., Dolan, R. J., & Mazziotta, J. C. (Eds.) (1997). *Human brain function*. San Diego, CA: Academic Press.

Ganel, T., & Goshen-Gottstein, Y. (2002). The perceptual integrality of sex and identity of faces: Further evidence for the single-route hypothesis. *Journal of Experimental Psychology: Human Perception and Performance, 28*, 854–867.

Gauthier, I., & Tarr, M. J. (1997). Becoming a "greeble" expert: Exploring mechanisms for face recognition. *Vision Research, 37*, 1673–1682.

George, M. S., Ketter, T. A., Gill, D. S., Haxby, J. V., Ungerleider, L. G., Herscovitch, P., et al. (1993). Brain regions involved in recognizing facial emotion or identity: An oxygen-15 PET study. *Journal of Neuropsychiatry and Clinical Neurosciences, 5*, 384–394.

George, M. S., Ketter, T. A., Parekh, P. I., Horwitz, B., Herscovitch, P., & Post, R. M. (1995). Brain activity during transient sadness and happiness in healthy women. *American Journal of Psychiatry, 152*, 341–351.

George, N., Evans, J., Fiori, N., Davidoff, J., & Renault, B. (1996). Brain events related to normal and moderately scrambled faces. *Cognitive Brain Research, 4*, 65–76.

George, N., Jemel, B., Fiori, N., & Renault, B. (1997). Face and shape repetition effects in humans: A spatio-temporal ERP study. *NeuroReport, 8*, 1417–1423.

Goshen-Gottstein, Y., & Ganel, T. (2000). Repetition priming for familiar and unfamiliar faces in a sex-judgment task: Evidence for a common route for the processing of sex and identity. *Journal of Experimental Psychology: Learning, Memory, and Cognition, 26*, 1198–1214.

Granato, P., & Bruyer, R. (2002). Measurement of the perception of facially expressed emotions by a computerized device. *European Psychiatry, 17*, 339–348.

Granato, P., Bruyer, R., & Révillion, J. J. (1996). Etude objective de la perception du sourire et de la tristesse par la méthode d'analyse de recherche de l'intégration des émotions, "MARIE" [Study of the perception of happiness and sadness by the analysis of research and integration of emotions]. *Annales Médico-Psychologiques, 154*, 1–9.

Gross, C. G. (1992). Representation of visual stimuli in inferior temporal cortex. In V. Bruce, A. Cowey, A. W. Ellis, & D. I. Perrett (Eds.), *Processing the facial image* (pp. 3–10). Oxford, England: Clarendon Press.

Hanley, J. R., Young, A. W., & Pearson, N. A. (1989). Defective recognition of familiar people. *Cognitive Neuropsychology, 6*, 179–210.

Haxby, J. V., Ungerleider, L. G., Horwitz, B., Maisog, J. M., Rapoport, S. I., & Grady, C. L. (1996). Face encoding and recognition in the human brain. *Proceedings of the National Academy of Sciences of the USA, 93*, 922–927.

Haxby, J. V., Ungerleider, L. G., Horwitz, B., Rapoport, S. I., & Grady, C. L. (1995). Hemispheric differences in neural systems for face working memory: A PET-rCBF study. *Human Brain Mapping, 3*, 68–82.

Hay, D. C., & Young, A. W. (1982). The human face. In A. W. Ellis (Ed.), *Normality and pathology in cognitive functions* (pp. 173–202). New York: Academic Press.

Heywood, C. A., & Cowey, A. (1992). The role of the "face-cell" area in the discrimination and recognition of faces by monkeys. In V. Bruce, A. Cowey, A. W. Ellis, & D. I. Perrett (Eds.), *Processing the facial image* (pp. 31–38). Oxford, England: Clarendon Press.

Jeffreys, D. A. (1996). Evoked potential studies of face and object processing. *Visual Cognition, 3*, 1–38.

Jemel, B., George, N., Olivares, E., Fiori, N., & Renault, B. (1999). Event-related potentials to structural familiar face incongruities processing. *Psychophysiology, 36*, 437–452.

Jemel, B., Pisani, M., Calabria, M., Crommelinck, M., & Bruyer, R. (in press). Is the early face-sensitive ERP component cognitively penetrable? Evidence from repetition priming of Mooney faces of familiar and unfamiliar persons. *Cognitive Brain Research.*

Johnson, M. H., & Morton, J. (1991). *Biology and cognitive development: The case of face recognition.* Oxford, England: Blackwell.

Joseph, A. B. (1986). Focal central nervous system abnormalities in patients with misidentification syndromes. *Bibliotheca Psychiatrica, 164*, 68–79.

Kanwisher, N., McDermott, J., & Chun, M. M. (1997). The fusiform face area: A module in human extrastriate cortex specialized for face perception. *Journal of Neuroscience, 17*, 4302–4311.

Kanwisher, N., & Moscovitch, M. (Eds.) (2000). *The cognitive neuroscience of face processing* [special issue of *Visual Cognition*]. New York: Psychology Press.

Kapur, N., Friston, K. J., Young, A., Frith, C. D., & Frackowiak, R. S. J. (1995).

Activation of human hippocampal formation during memory for faces: A PET study. *Cortex, 31,* 99–108.

Kertesz, A. (Ed.) (1994). *Localization and neuroimaging in neuropsychology.* San Diego, CA: Academic Press.

Kohonen, T., Oja, E., & Lehtio, P. (1981). Storage and processing of information in distributed associative memory systems. In G. Hinton & J. A. Anderson (Eds.), *Parallel models of associative memory* (pp. 105–143). Hillsdale, NJ: Erlbaum.

Kurucz, J., & Feldmar, G. (1979). Prosopo-affective agnosia as a symptom of cerebral organic disease. *Journal of the American Geriatrics Society, 27,* 225–230.

Kurucz, J., Feldmar, G., & Werner, W. (1979). Prosopo-affective agnosia associated with chronic organic brain syndrome. *Journal of the American Geriatrics Society, 27,* 91–95.

Kurucz, J., Soni, A., Feldmar, G., & Slade, W. R. (1980). Prosopo-affective agnosia and computerized tomography findings in patients with cerebral disorders. *Journal of the American Geriatrics Society, 28,* 475–478.

Luauté, J. P., & Bidault, E. (1994). Capgras syndrome: Agnosia of identification and delusion of reduplication. *Psychopathology, 27,* 186–193.

Luauté, J. P., Sansone, S., Bidault, E., Schneider, P., & Tiberghien, G. (1999). Reconnaissance des visages et information émotionnelle dans les délires d'identification des personnes [Face recognition and emotional information in delusional persons' identification]. *European Review of Applied Psychology, 49,* 131–140.

Lucchelli, F., & De Renzi, E. (1992). Proper name anomia. *Cortex, 28,* 221–230.

Marr, D. (1982). *Vision: a computational investigation into the human representation and processing of visual information.* San Francisco, CA: Freeman.

McCarthy, G., Puce, A., Gore, J. C., & Allison, T. (1997). Face-specific processing in the human fusiform gyrus. *Journal of Cognitive Neuroscience, 9,* 605–610.

McKenna, P., & Warrington, E. K. (1980). Testing for nominal dysphasia. *Journal of Neurology, Neurosurgery and Psychiatry, 43,* 781–788.

McNeil, J. E., & Warrington, E. K. (1991). Prosopagnosia: A reclassification. *Quarterly Journal of Experimental Psychology, 43A,* 267–287.

McNeil, J. E., & Warrington, E. K. (1993). Prosopagnosia: A face-specific disorder. *Quarterly Journal of Experimental Psychology, 46A,* 1–10.

Morris, J. S., Friston, K. J., Büchel, C., Frith, C. D., Young, A. W., Calder, A. J., et al. (1998). A neuromodulatory role for the human amygdala in processing emotional facial expressions. *Brain, 121,* 47–57.

Morris, J. S., Frith, C. D., Perrett, D. I., Rowland, D., Young, A. W., Calder, A. J., et al. (1996). A differential neural response in the human amygdala to fearful and happy facial expressions. *Nature, 383,* 812–815.

Morris, J. S., Öhman, A., & Dolan, R. J. (1998). Conscious and unconscious emotional learning in the human amygdala. *Nature, 393,* 467–470.

Newcombe, F., Young, A. W., & De Haan, E. H. F. (1989). Prosopagnosia and object agnosia without covert recognition. *Neuropsychologia, 27,* 179–191.

O'Toole, A. J., Abdi, H., Deffenbacher, K. A., & Bartlett, J. C. (1991). Classifying faces by race and sex using an autoassociative memory trained for recognition. In K. J. Hammond & D. Gentner (Eds.), *Proceedings of the thirteenth annual conference of the Cognitive Science Society* (pp. 847–851). Hillsdale, NJ: Erlbaum.

Papanicolaou, A. C. (1998). *Fundamentals of functional brain imaging.* Lisse, The Netherlands: Swets and Zeitlinger.

Parry, F. M., Young, A. W., Saul, J. S. M., & Moss, A. (1991). Dissociable face processing impairments after brain injury. *Journal of Clinical and Experimental Neuropsychology, 13,* 545–558.

Perrett, D. I., Hietanen, J. K., Oram, M. W., & Benson, P. J. (1992). Organization and functions of cells responsive to faces in the temporal cortex. In V. Bruce, A. Cowey, A. W. Ellis, & D. I. Perrett (Eds.), *Processing the facial image* (pp. 23–30). Oxford, England: Clarendon Press.

Posner, M. I., & Raichle, M. E. (1997). *Images of mind* (2nd ed.). New York: Scientific American Library.

Puce, A., Allison, T., Asgari, M., Gore, J. C., & McCarthy, G. (1996). Differential sensitivity of human visual cortex to faces, letterstrings, and textures: A functional magnetic resonance imaging study. *Journal of Neuroscience, 16,* 5205–5215.

Renault, B., Signoret, J. L., Debruille, B., Breton, F., & Bolgert, F. (1989). Brain potentials reveal covert facial recognition in prosopagnosia. *Neuropsychologia, 27,* 905–912.

Rhodes, G. (1996). *Superportraits: Caricatures and recognition.* Hove, England: Psychology Press.

Rhodes, G., & Zebrowitz, L. A. (Eds.) (2002). *Facial attractiveness: Evolutionary, cognitive, and social perspectives.* London: Ablex.

Rolls, E. T. (1992). Neurophysiological mechanisms underlying face processing within and beyond the temporal cortical visual areas. In Bruce, V., Cowey, A., Ellis, A. W., & Perrett, D. I. (Eds.). *Processing the facial image* (pp. 11–21). Oxford, England: Clarendon Press.

Rolls, E. T. (1994). Brain mechanisms for invariant visual recognition and learning. *Behavioural Processes, 33,* 113–138.

Ross, E. D., & Mesulam, M. M. (1979). Dominant language functions of the right hemisphere? *Archives of Neurology, 36,* 144–148.

Rossion, B. (2000). *Mise à l'épreuve de la modularité de la reconnaissance des visages par l'imagerie cérébrale fonctionnelle* [Assessment of modularity of face recognition by means of functional brain imagery]. Unpublished doctoral dissertation, University of Louvain, Department of Experimental Psychology, Belgium.

Rossion, B. (2002). Is sex categorisation from faces really parallel to face recognition? *Visual Cognition, 9,* 1003–1020.

Rossion, B., Campanella, S., Gomez, C. M., Delinte, A., Debatisse, D., Liard, L., et al. (1999). Task modulation of brain activity related to familiar and unfamiliar face processing: An ERP study. *Clinical Neurophysiology, 110,* 449–462.

Rossion, B., Delvenne, J. F., Debatisse, D., Goffaux, V., Bruyer, R., Crommelinck, M., et al. (1999). Spatio-temporal localization of the face inversion effect: an event-related potentials study. *Biological Psychology, 50,* 173–189.

Rossion, B., Dricot, L., De Volder, A., Bodart, J. M., Crommelinck, M., de Gelder, B., et al. (2000). Hemispheric asymmetries for whole-based and part-based face processing in the human fusiform gyrus. *Journal of Cognitive Neuroscience, 12*, 793–802.

Rossion, B., Gauthier, I., Tarr, M. J., Despland, P., Bruyer, R., Linotte, S., et al. (2000). The N_{170} occipito-temporal component is delayed and enhanced to inverted faces but not to inverted objects: An electrophysiological account of face-specific processes in the human brain. *NeuroReport, 11*, 69–74.

Rossion, B., Gauthier, I., Tarr, M. J., Pirenne, D., Debatisse, D., & Despland, P. A. (1999). The N_{170} occipito-temporal component is delayed to inverted faces but not to inverted objects: electrophysiological evidence of face-specific processes in the human brain [abstract]. *NeuroImage, 9*, S864.

Rossion, B., Schiltz, C., Robaye, L., Pirenne, D., Bruyer, R., Devolder, A., et al. (1999). The neural basis of human face categorization: a parametric PET study [abstract]. *NeuroImage, 9*, S865.

Rossion, B., Schiltz, C., Robaye, L., Pirenne, D., & Crommelinck, M. (2001). How does the brain discriminate familiar and unfamiliar faces ? A PET study of face categorical perception. *Journal of Cognitive Neuroscience, 13*, 1019–1034.

Schreiber, A. C., Rousset, S., & Tiberghien, G. (1991). Facenet: A connectionist model of face identification in context. *European Journal of Cognitive Psychology, 3*, 177–198.

Schuller, A. M., & Rossion, B. (2001). Spatial attention triggered by eye-gaze increases and speeds up early visual activity. *Neuroreport, 12*, 2381–2387.

Schweich, M., & Bruyer, R. (1993). Heterogeneity in the cognitive manifestations of prosopagnosia: the study of a group of single cases. *Cognitive Neuropsychology, 10*, 529–547.

Schweich, M., Van der Linden, M., Brédart, S., Bruyer, R., Nelles, B., & Schils, J. P. (1992). Daily-life difficulties in person recognition reported by young and elderly subjects. *Applied Cognitive Psychology, 6*, 161–172.

Seeck, M., Michel, C. M., Mainwaring, N., Cosgrove, R., Blume, H., Ives, J., et al. (1997). Evidence for rapid face recognition from human scalp and intracranial electrodes. *NeuroReport, 8*, 2749–2754.

Sergent, J. (1984a). Configural processing of faces in the left and right cerebral hemispheres. *Journal of Experimental Psychology: Human Perception and Performance, 10*, 554–572.

Sergent, J. (1984b). An investigation into component and configural processes underlying face perception. *British Journal of Psychology, 75*, 221–242.

Sergent, J. (1994). Brain-imaging studies of cognitive functions. *Trends in Neurosciences, 17*, 221–227.

Sergent, J., MacDonald, B., & Zuck, E. (1994). Structural and functional organization of knowledge about faces and proper names: A positron emission tomography study. In C. Umiltà & M. Moscovitch (Eds.), *Attention and performance XV* (pp. 203–228). Cambridge, MA: MIT Press.

Sergent, J., Ohta, S., & MacDonald, B. (1992). Functional neuroanatomy of face and object processing: A positron emission tomography study. *Brain, 115*, 15–36.

Sergent, J., Ohta, S., MacDonald, B., & Zuck, E. (1994). Segregated processing of facial identity and emotion in the human brain: A PET study. *Visual Cognition, 1*, 349–369.

Shallice, T. (1979). Case study approach in neuropsychological research. *Journal of Clinical Neuropsychology, 1*, 183–211.

Shallice, T. (1988). *From neuropsychology to mental structure.* Cambridge, England: Cambridge University Press.

Shallice, T., & Kartsounis, I. D. (1993). Selective impairment of retrieving people's names: A category-specific disorder? *Cortex, 29,* 281–291.

Sommer, W., Komoss, E., & Schweinberger, S. R. (1997). Differential localization of brain systems subserving memory for names and faces in normal subjects with event-related potentials. *Electroencephalography and Clinical Neurophysiology, 102,* 192–199.

Tanaka, J., & Farah, M. J. (1993). Parts and wholes in face recognition. *Quarterly Journal of Experimental Psychology, 46A,* 225–245.

Teuber, H. L. (1978). The brain and human behavior. In R. Held, H. W. Leibowitz, & H. L. Teuber (Eds.), *Handbook of sensory physiology* (Vol. 8, pp. 879–920). Berlin: Springer-Verlag.

Tovée, M. J. (1998). Is face processing special? *Neuron, 21,* 1239–1242.

Tucker, D. M. (1981). Lateral brain function, emotion and conceptualization. *Psychological Bulletin, 89,* 19–46.

Uttal, W. R. (2001). Are reductive (explanatory) theories of face identification possible? Some speculations and some findings. In M. J. Wenger & J. T. Towsend (Eds.), *Computational, geometric, and process perspectives on facial cognition: Contexts and challenges* (pp. 467–501). London: Erlbaum.

Valentine, T. (1991). A unified account of the effects of distinctiveness, inversion and race in face recognition. *Quarterly Journal of Experimental Psychology, 43A,* 161–204.

Valentine, T. (Ed.). (1995). *Cognitive and computational aspects of face processing: Explorations in face space.* London: Routledge.

Valentine, T., Brennen, T., & Brédart, S. (1996). *The cognitive psychology of proper names: On the importance of being Ernest.* London: Routledge.

Wenger, M. J., & Townsend, J. T. (Ed.). (2001). *Computational, geometric, and process perspectives on facial cognition: Contexts and challenges.* London: Erlbaum.

Wojciulik, E., Kanwisher, N., & Driver, J. (1998). Covert visual attention modulates face-specific activity in the human fusiform gyrus: fMRI study. *Journal of Neurophysiology, 79,* 1574–1578.

Yin, R. K. (1969). Looking at upside-down faces. *Journal of Experimental Psychology, 81,* 141–145.

Yin, R. K. (1970). Face recognition by brain injured patients: A dissociable ability? *Neuropsychologia, 8,* 395–402.

Young, A. W. (1994). Covert recognition. In M. J. Farah & G. Ratcliff (Eds.), *The neuropsychology of high-level vision* (pp 331–358). Hillsdale, NJ: Erlbaum.

Young, A. W. (1998). *Face and mind.* Oxford, England: Oxford University Press.

Young, A. W., Aggleton, J. P., Hellawell, D. J., Johnson, M., Broks, P., & Hanley, J. R. (1995). Face processing impairments after amygdalotomy. *Brain, 118,* 15–24.

Young, A. W., & De Haan, E. H. F. (1988). Boundaries of covert recognition in prosopagnosia. *Cognitive Neuropsychology, 5,* 317–336.

Young, A. W., & Ellis, H. D. (Eds.). (1989a). *Handbook of research on face processing.* Amsterdam, The Netherlands: North-Holland.

Young, A. W., & Ellis, H. D. (1989b). Semantic processing. In A. W. Young &

H. D. Ellis (Eds.), *Handbook of research on face processing* (pp. 235–262). Amsterdam, The Netherlands: North-Holland.

Young, A. W., Hay, D. C., & Ellis, A. W. (1985). The faces that launched a thousand slips: Everyday difficulties and errors in recognizing people. *British Journal of Psychology, 76*, 495–523.

Young, A. W., Hellawell, D. J., Van de Wal, C., & Johnson, M. (1996). Facial expression processing after amygdalotomy. *Neuropsychologia, 34,* 31–39.

Young, A. W., Rowland, D., Calder, A. J., Etcoff, N. L., Seth, A., & Perrett, D. I. (1997). Facial expression megamix: Tests of dimensional and category accounts of emotion recognition. *Cognition, 63,* 271–313.

Zayan, R. (Ed.) (1994). Individual and social recognition [Special issue]. *Behavioural Processes, 33,* 1–246.

PART III

NONVERBAL BEHAVIOR
IN SPECIFIC CLINICAL DISORDERS

9

Nonverbal Deficits and Interpersonal Regulation in Alcoholics

PIERRE PHILIPPOT, CHARLES KORNREICH,
AND SYLVIE BLAIRY

It is widely recognized that alcohol dependency is one of the most prevalent and socially handicapping mental disorders affecting Western countries (National Institute of Alcohol Abuse and Alcoholism, 1990). While many theories of alcoholism have focused on biochemical models (e.g., Hunt, 1990; Pohorecky, 1991), a promising avenue has been opened with the development of social-psychological models of alcoholism. Most of these models credit emotion and emotion regulation with a focal role in the etiology of alcoholism. As noted by Lang, Patrick, and Stritzke (1998), emotion is at the center of the arena of alcoholics' behavior: The very definition of a psychoactive substance, which includes alcohol, directly addresses the notion of altered states of emotion or consciousness. Indeed, an important motive in alcohol use and abuse is its presumed capacity to alter anxiety, depression, or other dysphoric moods (Goldman, Brown, & Christiansen, 1987).

In this chapter, we defend the notion that emotion communication, and foremost nonverbal communication of emotion, plays a critical role in alcoholism. To support our assertion, we first examine the effects of alcohol in nonalcoholics and of alcoholism on social interactions and emotion regulation in interpersonal contexts. Based on this review of the literature, we propose a model that relates nonverbal competence, interpersonal conflict, and alcohol abuse. In the second part of the chapter, the literature relevant to the hypotheses derived from the model is examined. In particular, we focus on the research examining the impact of alcohol in nonalcoholics and alcoholism on facial expression decoding and encoding. In this context, we will research undertaken in our laboratory that addresses the biases shown by alcoholics in their perception of others' emotion from nonverbal cues.

Finally, we draw the clinical implications of the research findings and point to possible directions for future research.

The Effect of Alcoholism on Interpersonal Regulation and Emotion Communication

In this section, we first review evidence that shows alcoholics are confronted with frequent interpersonal conflicts and tension. We demonstrate that these conflicts take place during social interactions with emotional meaning, and then we show that emotion communication plays a critical role in the occurrence and maintenance of these conflicts. Finally, we discuss how expectations about alcohol effects on emotion regulation and communication are critical in the consumption of alcohol and in the social and emotional behaviors subsequently displayed.

Interpersonal Problems, Emotion, and Alcoholism

Several studies have documented that, in their daily functioning, alcoholics are confronted with severe interpersonal problems (Duberstein, Conwell, & Caine, 1993; Nixon, Tivis, & Parsons, 1992), especially the use of violence (Evans, 1980; Myers, 1984). These interpersonal problems are almost always related to emotional situations. In particular, alcoholics seem to have difficulties dealing with negative emotions, especially anger. Marlatt (1979) documented that the main reason for relapse in alcoholism is difficulties coping with anger and frustration. For instance, 29% of relapsing alcoholics report having started to drink alcohol again in a situation in which they were angry and/or frustrated. Similarly, Miller and Eisler (1977) reported a case study on assertiveness in alcoholics. They observed that alcoholics present particular difficulties in expressing negative emotions. These difficulties are particularly pronounced in heavy drinkers.

Using an experimental design, Marlatt, Kosturn, and Lang (1975) demonstrated that heavy drinkers drink more alcohol in difficult situations when they are prevented from expressing their emotions. They compared alcohol consumption in heavy drinkers assigned to one of three experimental conditions. In the first two conditions, participants were provoked into anger, while they were not in the third control condition. In the first condition, participants had no opportunity to express their emotions or to react, while in the second condition, they could react and express their emotions. The results showed that participants in the first condition subsequently drank more alcohol than participants in the two other conditions. Thus, experiencing anger was not sufficient to increase alcohol consumption; it was also necessary that participants were prevented from expressing their anger. In other words, these results suggest that the pivotal aspect of alcoholics' coping difficulties with negative emotion could be related to emotional expression in heavy drinkers.

The relationship between emotion and alcohol consumption has also been observed in normal drinkers. Klein and Pittman (1993) assessed the emotional states of more than a thousand individuals when they took their last alcoholic drink. It appears that, while women were more likely to be in a positive state than in a negative state, the reverse was true for men, especially married men. These authors proposed that men are more likely than women to use alcohol as a strategy to cope with stress and marital difficulties. Although this aspect was not specifically assessed in this study, it may be possible that these men were confronted with communication difficulties in their marital relationship, and that they used alcohol as an avoidant—and thus maladaptive—coping strategy. Indeed, Noller (1984) has shown that most difficult marital relationships are marked by communication problems, especially in the nonverbal domain.

In conclusion, these empirical observations point to the fact that alcohol consumption, as well as alcohol abuse, are related to interpersonal problems. These problems arise in emotional situations and are characterized by negative affectivity, especially anger and frustration, at least in men. Moreover, there are some indications that being prevented to express emotion induces greater alcohol consumption in heavy drinkers. Similarly, there seems to be more alcohol consumption in men with marital difficulties, a situation typically characterized by communication problems. The last two observations lead to the question of the role played by emotion communication during interpersonal problems in alcoholism.

Emotion Communication in Alcoholism

Very little work has directly addressed emotion communication style in alcoholism. However, two lines of research provide indirect information. One line of research investigates the impact of an alcoholic family's emotion communication style on the children of the family. The other line of research addresses the efficacy of communication training in alcoholics.

In terms of emotion communication in families of alcoholics, it has been shown that families with an alcoholic member are characterized by more conflicts, criticisms, and avoidance (Gabarino & Strange, 1993). Some have suggested that these characteristics deeply affect emotion communication in these families; in turn, this communication style has a negative effect on children from alcoholic families (Jones & Houts, 1992).

Using this perspective, several studies have investigated the type of communication in families with an alcoholic member. For instance, Segrin and Menees (1996) asked a group of students about their perceptions of their families, the level of criticism from their parents, the emotional support received from their parents, and how much parents denied their emotions. In comparing the answers of students with an alcoholic parent to those of students without an alcoholic parent, the results showed that children of alcoholics had a more negative view of their family, and that they had experienced more criticism and denial of their emotions from their parents.

Jones and Houts (1992) conducted a similar study with a sample of young adults. They investigated four communication characteristics within the family: criticism from the parents, child perception of the family, parental attention to children's needs and feelings, and reversal of emotional roles (children providing emotional support to a parent). They reported very similar results: Children from families with alcohol problems reported less positive perceptions of their family and more denial of their needs and feelings. These children also reported fewer abilities in decoding verbal and nonverbal communication of emotion. In sum, these two studies demonstrated that children from families of alcoholics reported more negative communication styles, marked by criticism and denial of emotion in their families.

In terms of research on training, several studies have investigated the effectiveness of a communication training program in the treatment of alcoholism. For instance, Monti et al. (1990) compared the effectiveness of three group treatment conditions for alcoholic men. In the communication skills training (CST) condition, participants were taught communication skills and interpersonal problem-solving skills, including the capacity to deal with criticisms regarding their alcohol consumption. The second condition was similar to the first one, with the addition that a family member of the alcoholic also participated in the group treatment (CST-F). In a third treatment condition, cognitive behavioral mood management training (CBMMT), participants were taught how to control their desire to consume alcohol in difficult situations.

The results of Monti et al. (1990) showed that all three treatment conditions had a positive impact on social skills and on reducing anxiety in participants. The CST and CST-F conditions were somewhat superior to the CBMMT condition in this respect, attesting to the importance of communication deficit in alcoholics' problems. Moreover, participants in the CST and CST-F conditions drank less alcohol up to 6 months after treatment than participants in the CBMMT condition. However, no differences between conditions were observed in terms of alcoholism relapse or days of total abstinence. Unfortunately, this study suffered from the absence of a control condition to provide an appropriate base of comparison to estimate the real effectiveness of the treatment conditions. Nevertheless, it suggests that emotion communication plays a very important role in the problems with which alcoholics are confronted. Other authors have stressed the role of social and communication skills training in the treatment of alcoholism (Kornreich, Dan, Fryns, Gozlan, & Verbanck, 1992; Oei & Jackson, 1984).

We directly addressed the question of communication problems in alcoholism in a study focusing on emotion communication within couples with an alcoholic member (Sferrazza et al., 2002). Both wife and husband independently completed a questionnaire addressing the type, intensity, rumination about, and control of emotion, first for themselves, then for their spouses, and finally for what they believed their spouses were perceiving about their own (respondent's) emotion. A second questionnaire comprised questions about emotional reactions and communication during a specific and recent emotional event that the couple had experienced together. Both partners from 25 alcoholic and 25 matched control couples participated in this study.

Overall, the results showed marked differences in emotional experiences and expression between couples with an alcoholic member and control couples. Very interestingly, there were very few differences between the alcoholic member of the couple and his or her spouse, but both were clearly different from the nonalcoholic control couples. Specifically, members of alcoholic couples reported experiencing more intense emotions in general and in particular for anger, guilt, sadness, anxiety, shame, and disgust. Interestingly, while alcoholics and their spouses reported they felt more guilt, they attributed more anger to their partner. Alcoholic couples also reported less emotional control. When they spoke about their emotion, they felt more discomfort, they did not know how to react and how to express themselves, did not feel understood, or did not feel they had opportunities to express their feelings. They also attributed more negative and fewer positive effects to their emotional expression. Thus, compared to matched controls, both members of couples with an alcoholic member reported that they experienced, in general, more intense and negative emotions, that they had difficulties in expressing and controlling their emotions, and that the consequences of their emotional expression were negative.

Turning to the analysis of the specific emotional events, alcoholic couples reported more guilt, shame, and anxiety than control couples. While all of the control couples had spoken about this event to someone, members of alcoholic couples were less likely to have shared the event, with only 86% speaking of it. Moreover, when they did speak about it, they waited longer to speak about it. Control couples were more likely to share the event with their spouse, while alcoholic couples spoke more with a physician or psychotherapist. They also ruminated more about the event, and experienced more negative emotions during these ruminations.

In sum, this study showed that couples with an alcoholic member experience more negative and more intense emotions, and they are confronted with communication difficulties regarding their emotions: They spoke less about their emotions, waited longer before doing so, and felt more discomfort about it. Finally, they reported that expressing their emotions had more negative consequences than positive ones. It is remarkable that both members of the alcoholic couple reported the same difficulties and negative experiences, suggesting that the impact of alcohol consumption on their functioning as a couple was mediated by a relationship and emotion communication dysfunction. Finally, as suggested by reciprocal determinism theory (Bandura, 1969, 1986), if alcoholism might produce poor marital adjustment, marital dysfunction might in turn be associated with excessive alcohol consumption.

In conclusion, the research reported in this part of the chapter showed that the immediate social environment, such as the family of alcoholics, is characterized by more negative affect than the environment of nonalcoholics. Specifically, children reported more criticism and denial of individual feelings and needs in alcoholic families; couples with an alcoholic member confessed more negative emotions, more difficulties in expressing them, and more negative consequences of emotion expression. This is suggestive of an important deficit in emotion communication in alcoholics' families. The importance of the communicative aspect in alcohol problems is further documented by the effectiveness of treatments focusing on communication training. Not only do such treatments improve social skills, but they also diminish stress and alcohol consumption.

Alcoholics' Expectations Regarding Alcohol's Effects on Emotion

The literature reviewed above showed that alcoholics are confronted with important interpersonal and emotion communication problems. They have specific difficulties in coping with frustration and anger. Their families are characterized by a higher level of criticism and more denial of emotion. Confronted with these problems, alcoholics tend to react by consuming alcohol. An interesting suggestion of social psychological theories of alcoholism (e.g., Cooper, Frone, Russell, & Mudar, 1995) is that this reaction is supported by alcoholics' belief that alcohol may help diminish negative affect, increase positive affect, and alleviate social and communicative difficulties.

Using this perspective, several studies have documented alcoholics' expectation about the effect of alcohol on emotion regulation. Goldman et al. (1987) concluded from several studies on expectation about alcohol effects that alteration of mood and affective reactions were probably the most pivotal and relevant of the beliefs leading to alcohol consumption. In more recent research, Rather and colleagues (Rather & Goldman, 1994; Rather, Goldman, Roehirch, & Brannick, 1992) used multidimensional scaling and other multivariate statistical techniques to map the organization of alcohol expectancies. Their results indicate that arousal (activation versus sedation) and affective/social valence (positive versus negative) are the primary dimensions along which alcohol expectancies are structured. It is noteworthy that the affective/social valence is mostly a dimension that reflects the expectation that alcohol will either reduce negative affect in social situations or increase positive affect in the same situations. Further, these dimensions can be used to distinguish heavy from light drinkers, the former holding stronger beliefs about positive effects of alcohol than the latter. In sum, research has shown that people hold specific expectations about the effect of alcohol on emotion and social emotion regulation. In addition, these expectations distinguish light from heavy drinkers. The question is now whether such expectations play a causal role in alcohol consumption.

Recent work by Cooper et al. (1995) suggests that these expectations are, in fact, the basis of motives for drinking. In their model, supported by extensive longitudinal data, they propose that desire to regulate positive and negative mood acts as the main motive to consume alcohol. Further, they distinguished between motivation to enhance positive emotions from motivation to reduce negative ones. They showed, for instance, that people drinking to enhance positive emotion tend to be sensation seekers who hold strong expectations that alcohol will facilitate positive experience. In contrast, people drinking to reduce negative emotion tend to be depressed and to rely on avoidant and other maladaptive coping strategies. In sum, there is evidence that shows that expectations about alcohol effects on emotion have an impact on motivation to drink and reported drinking. Our work suggests that alcoholics are characterized by a regulation deficit in emotional arousal, with either too high or too low levels. Alcohol consumption would therefore be used to achieve an optimal level of emotional arousal, either by increasing or by dampening it. Indeed, we have observed in our work that during emotion induction, alcoholics report either higher or lower levels of emotional arousal than controls (Kornreich et al., 1998).

From the work reviewed above, one could propose that expectations about effects of alcohol on social and emotional behavior determine the type of social and emotional behavior when intoxicated. This was explored by Marlatt et al. (1975) in an ingenious study in which social drinkers were made to believe that they had drunk either an alcoholic drink or a nonalcoholic drink (expected drink). Actually, they had received either alcohol or a placebo (actual drink) in both conditions. Participants were then exposed to an aggressive, insulting confederate. The authors observed only a main effect of the expected drink: Social drinkers who believed they had consumed alcohol behaved more aggressively than social drinkers who believed they had consumed a nonalcoholic drink, irrespective of what they had actually been drinking. These results clearly show that the emotional and social behaviors of the participants were not determined by the physiological effects of alcohol, but by their expectations and beliefs regarding alcohol. This observation, though, needs to be replicated with a population of alcoholics to demonstrate its generality.

In another study, Knight and Godfrey (1993) further examined the relationships among alcohol expectation, alcohol consumption, and emotional and social performance. Male students were exposed to a stressful situation in which they were videotaped during an interaction with a stranger who was an attractive female confederate. Participants were allocated to one of three conditions. In the first condition, they had to drink a fixed dose of alcohol (0.5 g/kg body weight), although they could drink more alcohol afterward if they wished. In the second condition, participants were free to consume as much alcohol as they wished. Finally, in the last control condition, no alcohol was offered. In all conditions, participants reported having strong expectations regarding the capacity of alcohol to reduce their social anxiety. Indeed, when provided with the opportunity (i.e., in the two first conditions), the more anxious the participants were, the more they consumed alcohol. However, their expectations were not upheld by their behavior: From the analysis of the videotapes, the authors reported that alcohol tended to decrease the adequacy of participants' social performance. In sum, this study showed that the decision to consume alcohol is related to beliefs about the emotional regulation effects of alcohol, even if this prediction does not correspond to objective effects of alcohol.

In conclusion, research shows that people in general hold strong beliefs that alcohol has an impact on emotion regulation. Alcohol is presumed to enhance positive affect and to alleviate negative affect. This impact on emotion regulation is often related to emotion occurring in social situations. Further, alcohol expectations distinguish between light and heavy drinkers and between sensation-seeking drinkers and depressed-avoidant ones. Finally, these expectations influence alcohol consumption and emotional and social behavior when intoxicated.

Conclusions

In this part of the chapter, we reviewed literature that showed that alcoholics are confronted with interpersonal and emotional problems in daily life. Alcoholics have special difficulty dealing with situations involving anger and frustration. Their close social environment, like their family, suffers from a negative emotional and communicative climate and is characterized by expression of criticism and denial of others' needs and feelings (as reported by their children). Ironically, alcoholics believe that drinking alcohol will help them cope with these situations. Consequently, alcohol consumption increases in situations involving stress, conflict, anger, or frustration. However, social behavior, communication, and functioning are degraded rather than enhanced by alcohol.

One can see how a vicious circle is easily initiated: In difficult interpersonal situations involving anger and frustration, alcoholics tend to rely on alcohol consumption as a coping strategy. However, their social perception and behavior deteriorate when intoxicated; they behave more aggressively, and they perceive less accurately their impact on others. This situation is very likely to maintain or to increase the occurrence of interpersonal problems, locking in the feedback loop.

Finally, to add a more positive note to this bleak conclusion, remediation programs that focus on communication in interpersonal and emotional situations seem to have a positive impact on alcoholics' well-being, social functioning, and alcohol consumption. However, more research on this topic is needed to confirm this hopeful statement.

Rationale for a Deficit in Nonverbal Communication of Emotion in Alcoholics

There are several empirical arguments that suggest a deficit in nonverbal communication of emotion in alcoholism. Some arguments pertain to the immediate effects of alcohol, while others are related to the effect of alcohol dependency.

Regarding the immediate effects of alcohol, it has been well demonstrated that alcohol impairs higher cognitive functioning, and that this impairment has an impact on several emotional processes (Lang et al., 1999). For instance, emotional appraisal appears to be impaired. This produces consequences both for the type of emotion that is experienced and expressed and for the way nonverbal cues of emotion are decoded. Quite obviously, less nonverbal decoding accuracy would be expected when under the influence of alcohol.

Second, as discussed above, alcohol changes expectations and self-perception. As males expect to be more prone to anger when intoxicated, they are likely to behave more aggressively (Keane & Lisman, 1980), to express more anger nonverbally, and to interpret others' nonverbal cues as indicating provocation or threat. Indeed, studies reviewed above documented that social performance and perception deteriorate while individuals are intoxicated.

Other reasons to suspect a nonverbal deficit are related to consequences of alcohol dependency. Alcoholics seem to experience many interpersonal conflicts. In particular, they have difficulties dealing with negative emotions, especially with anger and frustration. Finally, they report more problems expressing their emotions and more negative consequences of such expression. As a large part of emotion communication relies on nonverbal cues, and as social competence and harmonious functioning require the mastery of nonverbal communication, the problems of alcoholics in solving interpersonal conflicts and in communicating their emotions are suggestive of a deficit in nonverbal competence.

Based on the preceding rational and literature review, we propose that alcoholics are characterized by specific deficits in the expression and decoding of nonverbal cues of emotion. Specifically, they should express more intense emotions, especially negative emotions related to anger and frustration. They should also overperceive such negative displays in others.

This nonverbal deficit also would likely impair alcoholics' social competence. They would be more likely to find themselves in interpersonal conflicts, and more important, in such situations they would misperceive nonverbal cues from their partners, misattributing anger and hostile feelings to them. This misperception of the situation would diminish alcoholics' capacities to react efficiently and to find an appropriate and constructive solution to the conflict that would remain active and unresolved. Confronted with such difficult situations, alcoholics would then turn to alcohol as a coping strategy (although a faulty one).

The use of alcohol as an avoidant coping strategy is likely to maintain interpersonal problems and even to increase them. A first positive-feedback loop would then be created: Increased interpersonal tension would result in increased alcohol consumption, feeding back into the interpersonal tension. Further, as alcohol intoxication diminishes nonverbal decoding capacity, a second feedback loop would be created: Alcohol intoxication would lead to more nonverbal impairments, which nourish interpersonal tension, which then results in more alcohol consumption. This process is illustrated in Fig. 9.1.

In sum, we are proposing a mechanism by which a nonverbal deficit precipitates and maintains alcohol consumption and dependency. This effect is mediated by a deterioration in social competency: Because of their inability to read the emotional state of others correctly, alcoholics would generate interpersonal tensions and would be less well armed to solve them constructively than would nonalcoholics. Further, to avoid feelings of helplessness generated by their inability to solve these situations, alcoholics would turn to alcohol consumption as a coping strategy. In the next part of the chapter, we review the literature relevant to the hypotheses generated by the model we have outlined. We specifically focus on the empirical literature pertaining to nonverbal expression of emotion in alcoholism, and we attempt to relate it to social competence in alcoholics.

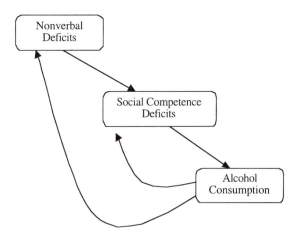

Fig. 9.1 The cycle of nonverbal deficits, social competence deficits, and alcohol consumption.

Facial Expression of Emotion and Alcohol

In this part of the chapter, we focus on the influence of alcohol on the expression and on the recognition of emotion from facial expression. First, the effect of alcohol on facial reactivity is examined in normal drinkers in emotional and nonemotional situations. To our knowledge, no experimental study has yet investigated the effects of alcohol dependency on facial expressivity. Consequently, we present work pertaining to the effect of alcohol on nonverbal decoding in normal drinkers. Then, we turn to the effect of chronic alcohol consumption on nonverbal decoding and present the results of our research program on this topic. A remarkable feature of this research domain is that it is still largely unexplored, and very little experimental work has yet been reported.

Effect of Alcohol on Nonverbal Encoding in Normal Drinkers

In an early study of the effect of alcohol on nonverbal encoding, Levenson (1987) videotaped the facial expression of participants who were exposed to stressful emotional situations after alcohol or placebo intake. He observed that alcohol reduces the overall intensity of facial expressivity as well as attempts to control facial expression. Sayette, Smith, Breiner, and Wilson (1992) reported a similar study, with comparable results. Using the Facial Action Coding System (FACS) (Ekman & Friesen, 1978), they observed that alcohol intoxication reduced negative emotional facial expressivity in response to manipulated stress.

However, a study using a more sensitive measure of facial activity partially failed to demonstrate this reduction in negative facial expression under intoxication. Stritske, Patrick, and Lang (1995) showed pleasant, neutral, and unpleasant slides to sober and intoxicated participants. They measured a number of physiological responses (startle reactivity, electrodermal response, and heart rate) as well as corrugator activity with electromyographic (EMG) recording. The measure of the activity of the corrugator (a small muscle of the forehead that brings together the two brows, i.e., frowning) is a reliable index of negative facial expressivity that can even index nonvisible changes (Cacioppo, Tassinary, & Fridlund, 1990). They observed that facial startle was reduced by alcohol intoxication, but that the normal affective modulation (i.e., when compared to the neutral condition, startle is stronger in the negative affect condition and weaker in the positive affect condition) remained intact in the alcohol condition. They also found that drinking resulted in a dramatic suppression of arousal across several physiological modalities, including heart rate and skin conductance. However, the activity of the corrugator was unaffected by alcohol and showed reliable differentiation in reaction to pleasant, neutral, and unpleasant stimuli.

This last result appears to be contradictory to the observations of Levenson (1987) and of Sayette and colleagues (1992) that negative facial expression is reduced during alcohol intoxication. Different explanations can be provided for this apparent contradiction. Stritske and colleagues (1995; Lang et al., 1999) argued that facial EMG is more sensitive than even fine-grain observational coding schemes such as FACS (Ekman & Friesen, 1978). Facial EMG would thus be more likely to provide evidence for subtle and transient facial reactions. We believe that the main explanation is that, as EMG is a relative measure, intensity differences between subjects' measurements are dubious (Cacioppo et al., 1990). The absence of intensity differences in corrugator EMG between intoxicated and sober participants should thus be interpreted with great caution. Furthermore, the experiments of Levenson (1987) and of Sayette and colleagues (1992) investigated only negative emotional states. No conclusion regarding the expression of positive emotion can thus be drawn from these results.

In sum, these studies suggest that alcohol dampens the intensity of affective reaction, including facial expression. It is still unclear whether this decrease is specific to or more pronounced for negative states. Indeed, the two studies reporting an effect of alcohol on facial expressions addressed specifically and only effects of alcohol on facial expression induced by stress. Unfortunately, very little experimental work has been conducted in this domain, which remains an unexplored but very promising field for future research. Even less investigated is the impact of alcohol dependency on facial expressivity: To our knowledge, no study has been published in this specific domain. We thus turn to the other side of the facial expression coin and examine how alcohol affects the recognition of emotion from facial expression.

Effect of Alcohol on Nonverbal Decoding in Normal Drinkers

In examining the effect of alcohol on nonverbal decoding in nonalcoholics, O'Sullivan, Micklewright, Ekman, Jones, and Friesen (1975) investigated the ability of male normal drinkers to identify emotion from facial expression before and after receiving alcohol (1 cc/kg body weight), marijuana, or a placebo. They presented their participants with photographs of faces showing joy, anger, fear, sadness, surprise, and disgust/contempt. They reported that alcohol significantly decreased the accuracy of judgment of faces expressing anger and sadness.

Borrill, Rosen, and Summerfield (1987) reconsidered the same question with different levels of alcohol (1 or 2.5 cc vodka/kg body weight) and male and female participants. They observed that male and female participants made more errors of judgment in the high alcohol condition, and that participants in the low alcohol condition made fewer errors than participants in the placebo condition. This effect was significant for anger in both genders and for disgust/contempt in males.

In sum, the results of these two studies are remarkably consistent. They also point to the impact that alcohol can have on violent behavior. Borrill et al. (1987) proposed that, if individuals consuming alcohol are disabled in their perception of anger in others, they may behave in ways that are annoying or provoking to others and thus become susceptible to interpersonal problems. Further, if they perceive (or misperceive) more contempt in others, they may themselves behave more aggressively.

Experimental Studies of Nonverbal Decoding in Alcoholics

Despite the importance of the question both from a clinical and from a theoretical perspective, no empirical study has investigated nonverbal decoding skills in alcoholics. To our knowledge, the first experimental investigation of facial expression in alcoholics was conducted by Oscar-Berman, Hancock, Mildwordf, Hutner, and Altman-Weber (1990). They compared alcoholic Korsakoff patients, non-Korsakoff alcoholics, and nonalcoholic controls regarding their ability to identify and recognize emotional material. Some tasks included photographs of facial expressions of emotion. They observed that alcoholic Korsakoff patients and non-Korsakoff alcoholics attributed more emotional intensity to facial expressions than controls. Further, the ability to match facial expressions with written labels was determined by the interaction between experimental group and age of the subject. Unfortunately, as the purpose of this study was to relate brain mechanisms to emotional perception and memory functions, Oscar-Berman and colleagues did not specify or interpret this interaction.

Although faces portraying different types of emotion were used in the study of Oscar-Berman et al., the authors did not report that alcoholics attributed more emotional intensity to certain emotions more than to others. Apparently, the authors did not explore this possibility or examine alcoholics' accuracy in the decoding of facial expression. Indeed, it is possible that alcoholics, while overattributing emotional intensity to facial stimuli, still decode the expressions accurately; that is, they do not misinterpret the emotion displayed. A possible explanation for the limitations of this pioneering study is that Oscar-Berman and colleagues used prototypical facial expressions, displaying full-blown emotions. Not only do these extreme stimuli have little ecological validity, but they also are easy to decode, and the use of such material is likely to produce ceiling effects (Hess, Blairy, & Keck, 1997).

To further document possible biases or impairments in the way alcoholics interpret emotional facial expression, we started a systematic research program in our laboratories. In the first study (Philippot et al., 1999), we addressed three questions. First, we wondered whether we could replicate the observation of Oscar-Berman et al. (1990) that alcoholics overattribute emotional intensity to facial stimuli. Second, we examined whether alcoholics are less accurate than nonalcoholics in recognizing the type of emotion portrayed by a facial expression. Third, we asked if alcoholics show systematic biases in interpreting facial expression. In other words, do they tend to misattribute some types of emotion more than others?

In the study, we presented a large set of photographs of facial expressions to 25 inpatients diagnosed with alcohol dependence according to *Diagnostic and Statistical Manual of Mental Disorders, Third Edition, Revised* (*DSM-III-R*; American Psychiatric Association [APA], 1987) criteria and to 25 controls who were matched for sex, age, and level of education. Each sample had 18 men and 7 women, the mean age was 43 years, and the sample individuals did not differ in terms of mental efficiency according to the Mini-Mental State Examination scale (Folstein, Folstein, & McHugh, 1975). Inpatients were in their third week of the detoxification process and were not receiving any psychotropic drugs at the time of assessment. To avoid ceiling effects and to use material reflecting real-life expressions, stimuli varied in the level of emotional intensity of the expression. Specifically, a series of emotional facial expressions constructed by Hess and Blairy (1995) was employed. We used a set of this series in which two actors portray five emotions (happiness, anger, sadness, disgust, and fear) at four intensity levels (0% [i.e., neutral], 30%, 70%, 100%). These stimuli were presented in a random order on a computer screen. Finally, to increase the sensitivity of our measures, participants rated each facial expression on 7-point scales for a large profile of eight emotions (happiness, sadness, fear, anger, disgust, surprise, shame, and contempt).

The results of this first study clearly demonstrated that alcoholics showed a deficit in the interpretation of emotional facial expressions. Several facets characterize this deficit. First, compared to controls, alcoholic participants overestimated the intensity of the emotion conveyed by facial expressions. Our data thereby replicated a similar observation reported by Oscar-Berman et al. (1990) for full-blown expressions. Further, our study extended this finding to emotional expressions of moderate and weak intensity and even to neutral faces. Thus, it documented that alcoholics tend to perceive more intense emotion than controls in the face of an interaction partner, even if no emotion is expressed.

Second, alcoholic participants misinterpreted facial expressions more than controls: They were more likely to believe that someone presenting a happy face was actually in a negative mood. They further tended to misattribute negative expressions (except for fear). For disgust, they presented a systematic bias, attributing emotions of anger and contempt, two emotions typical of interpersonal conflict, to an interaction partner. Finally, despite their poor performance, the alcoholics did not report more difficulties with the decoding task than controls. It is thus likely that they do not perceive their deficit in the decoding of emotional facial expression.

In sum, this first study portrayed alcoholics as living in a world in which they perceive more emotional signals from their interaction partners, emotional signals that they tend to misinterpret with a negative and hostile bias, without noticing their deficits in this domain.

However, the alcoholic participants in this first study were inpatients at the end of the detoxification process. We do not know whether they already presented a facial expression decoding deficit before they became dependent on alcohol, and we do not know whether the deficit is maintained in long-term abstinent alcoholics. In other words, we need to ask whether poor social skills, including poor emotion perception, represent a vulnerability that precipitates the process of alcoholism, or whether the poor social skills are a consequence of the alcoholic condition.

Indeed, two interpretations of the deficits in the decoding of emotional facial expressions observed by Philippot et al. (1999) can be made. On the one hand, the deficits might be the consequence of a general neurocognitive deterioration caused by alcohol that is known to impair multiple functions in chronic alcoholics. As most of these cognitive impairments remit with long-term abstinence, one would expect the deficits in the decoding of facial expression to be alleviated with long-term abstinence (Johnsson, Cronholm, & Izikovitz, 1962). On the other hand, emotional decoding deficits in alcoholics might be related to more fundamental impairments that might even precede the onset of alcohol dependency. Indeed, social skills deficits in alcoholics seem to be present before the onset of alcoholism (Rosenthal-Gaffney, Thorpe, Young, Colett, & Occhipinti, 1998). There could be a vulnerability factor in childhood and adolescence that predisposes individuals to high levels of alcohol consumption. Similarly, visuospatial deficits that might interfere with the decoding of facial expression have also been documented as present before the onset of alcoholism (Schandler, Clegg, Thomas, & Cohen, 1996).

Thus, the study of the evolution of the decoding abilities before, during, and after an episode of alcohol dependency would bring important information on the determinants and consequences of nonverbal decoding skills deficits in people at risk of, or suffering from, alcoholism. Using this perspective, we designed a second study (Kornreich, Blairy, Philippot, Hess, et al., 2001) in which we compared the performance of abstainers (former alcoholics abstinent for at least several months) with the performance of recently detoxified alcoholics in the facial expression decoding task. If it could be shown that there are no differences between these two populations, such an observation would rule out the possibility that the deficits are a consequence of a general cognitive deterioration that is alleviated with abstinence.

The same procedure as in Philippot et al. (1999) was carried out with 25 alcoholics abstinent for at least 2 months who were recruited either at a long-stay postcure center (16 patients with an abstinence time between 2 and 6 months, called intermediate-term abstainers) or through Alcoholics

Anonymous (9 patients with an abstinence time between 1 and 9 years, called long-term abstainers). These 25 participants were matched for age, sex, and educational level with the participants of Study 1.

The analysis of the data revealed an interesting pattern of results. Indeed, while some nonverbal impairments were no longer present in abstainers, other persisted. Specifically, the overattribution of emotional intensity to facial expression was not observed in abstainers. Similarly, the misinterpretation of happy and sad faces shown by recently detoxified alcoholics was not present in abstainers. However, their decoding accuracy deficit still persisted for facial expressions of anger and disgust; for these emotions, there were no differences between recently detoxified and abstinent alcoholics. Similarly, despite their poorer performance, abstainers did not report more difficulties than controls and were similar to recently detoxified alcoholics.

Overall, this pattern of results suggests that different facets of alcoholics' nonverbal impairments are determined by different processes. Some decline with time; others seem to persist long after alcohol detoxification, like the misinterpretation of some negative emotions. However, it remains to establish whether these deficits were present before the onset of alcohol dependency. Indeed, the fact that they remain, even years after the recession of alcohol abuse, does not imply that they are preexisting or independent from alcohol abuse. For instance, alcoholics may have a protracted withdrawal syndrome and brain dysfunction that need years of abstinence to remit: There is still a performance difference between alcoholics and controls on several neurocognitive tests 14 months after detoxification (Glenn, Parsons, & Sinha, 1994). After an interval of 4 years, considerable improvement may occur (Fabian & Parsons, 1983). There is a parallel decline in psychological distress (DeSota, O'Donnell, Allred, & Lopes, 1985). Psychiatric symptoms diminish to a near-normal level with the first 5 years of abstinence and continue to decline slowly during the following 5 years (DeSota, O'Donnell, & DeSota, 1989).

To explore further the hypothesis that a deficit in nonverbal decoding skills precedes the onset of alcoholism, one possibility would be to compare the nonverbal decoding performances of children and adolescents from families with several first- or second-degree relatives suffering from alcoholism with children and adolescents from families without a record of alcohol dependency. This strategy has been used regarding another impairment known to affect alcoholics: the visuospatial deficit (Beatty, Hames, Balnco, Nixon, & Tivis, 1996). Beatty and colleagues have shown that this deficit was already present in children from alcoholic families. Such evidence makes it more plausible that these deficits are present before the onset of alcoholism, and that they may play a role in the etiology of that condition.

Another question that needs to be addressed is whether the precise nonverbal deficits that we have observed in alcoholics are specific to the alcoholic population. Indeed, a major methodological consideration in alcoholism research involves the ability to show that an observed effect is specific to alcoholism. To demonstrate such a specificity, alcoholics must differ on the studied dimension from control groups with other behavior problems as well as from "normal" control groups (Sher, Trull, Bartholow, & Vieth, 1999).

To answer this question in part, we replicated our first study using two nonalcoholic control groups, one with psychopathology (i.e., obsessive-compulsive disorder [OCD]) and one without psychopathology (Kornreich, Blairy, Philippot, Dan, et al., 2001). We chose an OCD control group because alcoholism and OCD display symptomatic similarities, but do not share common etiologies. Indeed, several investigators have noted similarities between urges and desires to drink heavily and obsessive-compulsive disorders. Researchers in the field of alcohol have characterized alcohol abusers as having a "compulsion" to use alcohol (Caetano, 1985; Edwards & Gross, 1976; Modell, Glaser, Cyr, & Montz, 1992). It has also been suggested that the craving for alcohol seen in alcohol abusers resembles obsessive thought patterns (Anton, Moak, & Latham, 1995; Modell et al., 1992). Furthermore, the lifetime risk for obsessive-compulsive disorder among close relatives of alcoholics is 1.4%, which does not support the existence of a common genotype for the two disorders (Schuckit et al., 1995). It seemed therefore relevant to use a sample with obsessive-compulsive disorder as a control group with psychopathology.

We used the same procedure as in our former studies, but with a restricted set of stimuli given the (obsessively) long response time of participants with OCD. We recruited 22 outpatients suffering from obsessive-compulsive disorder according to the *DSM-IV* (APA, 1994) in a general hospital outpatient department. They were matched for age, sex, and educational level with 22 volunteers with no psychiatric record and 22 inpatients diagnosed with alcohol dependence according to *DSM-IV* criteria. The last group was at the end of the detoxification process in the same hospital and abstinent for between 2 and 3 weeks. They were not receiving any psychotropic medication at the time of assessment.

The analysis of the data showed that the results of Study 1 were replicated: Recently detoxified alcoholics attributed more emotional intensity to facial stimuli, were less accurate in identifying the emotion portrayed, and did not report more difficulties in the decoding task. The patients with OCD, however, did not differ from the normal controls. Thus, the facial expression decoding deficits observed in alcoholics could not be found in OCD patients, another psychopathological population presenting similarities to alcoholics.

At the least, these results demonstrated that the deficits we evidenced in alcoholics are not ubiquitous in psychopathological populations. Still, more investigations are needed to establish how specific these deficits are. Are they linked to a social skills deficit? If that is the case, they should also

be observed in a population of social phobics presenting social skills deficits. Are they linked to some specific processes in substance abuse? If this
possibility were true, such deficits should also be shown by abusers of sub-
stances other than alcohol. To answer these questions, we are currently
preparing studies that compare recently detoxified alcoholics with social
phobics with poor social competence and illegal substance abusers in the
detoxification process.

Above, we defended the notion that the impairments shown by alcoholics in the recognition of emotion from nonverbal cues might generate interpersonal difficulties. These conflictual social relations might increase the
probability of alcohol use and abuse as faulty coping strategies. Alcohol
intoxication might in turn impair the capacity of alcoholics to interpret
others' internal state accurately from their nonverbal behavior. They would
then begin a vicious circle, leading to more interpersonal conflict and to
more alcohol consumption.

If this hypothesis is correct, the deficit in nonverbal decoding observed
in alcoholics should be accounted for by their deficit in interpersonal relations. To examine this possibility, we conducted a fourth study in which
we replicated the procedure of Study 3 with 29 recently detoxified alcoholics and 29 controls matched for age, sex, and educational level. In addition,
we administrated to all participants the interpersonal problem inventory
of Horowitz, Rosenberg, Baer, Ureno, and Villasenor (1988). This scale
comprises 127 items assessing six domains of potential interpersonal difficulties: assertiveness, sociability, submissiveness, intimacy, excessive self-
control, and excessive self-responsibility.

Again, the results indicated that alcoholics were less accurate in decoding facial expression, and they attributed more emotional intensity to the
facial stimuli, but they did not report more difficulties with the task than
the control participants. As expected, alcoholics reported more interpersonal difficulties for all domains (except self-control), with an especially
large difference for intimacy, sociability, responsivity, and assertiveness
compared to controls. We then examined whether the nonverbal decoding
deficits of alcoholics were still statistically observable after partialling
out the variance accounted for by their interpersonal difficulties. The
ANCOVAs (analyses of covariance) revealed that alcoholics and controls
were no more different in terms of nonverbal decoding accuracy after partialling out the variance accounted for by interpersonal difficulties. This
last observation suggests that the relationship between nonverbal deficit
and alcoholism is mediated by interpersonal problems and tension.

Conclusions

From the literature reviewed in this section, it appears that alcohol dampens the intensity of facial expression in normal drinkers. This effect might
decrease the readability of nonverbal cues in intoxicated individuals. Un-

fortunately, although the nonverbal expression of emotion has not been studied yet in alcoholics, our self-report study suggested that emotion expression is increased in alcoholics.

Regarding the effect of alcohol on facial expression decoding, the performance of normal drinkers is deteriorated by alcohol, especially in the recognition of anger, disgust, and contempt. This points to the impact that alcohol can have on violent behavior. Intoxicated individuals may behave in ways that are annoying or provoking to others and thus become susceptible to interpersonal problems. Further, if they perceive more contempt in others, they may themselves behave more aggressively.

Finally, we examined chronic alcoholics' nonverbal competence. We systematically found that chronic alcoholics present three deficits in the interpretation of facial expression. First, they overestimate the intensity of the emotion felt by their interactant. Second, they present a systematic bias, overattributing emotions of anger and contempt. Third, alcoholics are not aware of their nonverbal deficits. This pattern of deficits seems specific to alcoholics, although more research is needed regarding this point. These deficits are enduring as abstinent alcoholics present the same pattern of deficits except that they no longer overestimate emotional intensity. Finally, these nonverbal deficits are related to interpersonal difficulties, which act as a mediator between nonverbal deficits and alcohol abuse. Thus, all predictions regarding nonverbal decoding derived from the model proposed at the end of the first section of this chapter are supported by the data.

Clinical Consequences of Nonverbal Decoding Deficits in Alcoholics

Throughout this chapter, we have demonstrated that alcoholics tend to generate tension and conflict when interacting with others, including their close relatives and family members. Furthermore, alcoholics present special difficulties in dealing with anger and frustration, two feelings that are often generated by interpersonal tension and conflicts. Difficulties in dealing with and expressing these feelings are the best predictors of relapse (Marlatt, 1979). In other words, relapse prevention programs should focus on teaching alcoholics appropriate coping strategies and expression modes in situations in which they feel angry or frustrated.

The different domains of research we reviewed suggest that communication deficits, especially those relating to emotion, might be central in the deficient coping strategies used by alcoholics confronted with interpersonal tension. The mechanism that we propose is that, because of their inability to read correctly others' emotional states, alcoholics generate interpersonal tensions and are less well armed to solve these tensions constructively. Further, to avoid feelings of helplessness generated by their inability to solve these situations, alcoholics turn to alcohol consumption as a coping strategy. They thus initiate two positive-feedback loops. Alcohol intoxication first aggravates interpersonal tensions and second depletes the already limited nonverbal skills.

In conclusion, we suggest that training programs aimed at developing nonverbal sensitivity in alcoholics should decrease interpersonal tension, increase appropriate coping skills, and consequently decrease alcohol consumption and relapse. Such training programs should especially focus on emotional intensity and expression of emotion related to interpersonal tension such as anger, contempt, and disgust. Our future research will address the design and effectiveness of such relapse prevention programs.

References

American Psychiatric Association. (1987). *Diagnostic and statistical manual of mental disorders* (3rd ed., rev.). Washington, DC: Author.

American Psychiatric Association. (1994). *Diagnostic and statistical manual of mental disorders* (4th ed.). Washington, DC: Author.

Anton, R. F., Moak, D. H., & Latham, P. (1995). The Obsessive Compulsive Drinking Scale: A self-rated instrument for the quantification of thoughts about alcohol and drinking behavior. *Alcoholism: Clinical and Experimental Research, 19,* 92–99.

Bandura, A. (1969). *Principles of behavior modification.* New York: Holt, Rinehart, & Winston.

Bandura, A. (1986). *Social foundation of thought and action: A social cognitive theory.* Englewood Cliffs, NJ: Prentice-Hall.

Beatty, W. W., Hames, K. A., Balnco, C. R., Nixon, S. J., and Tivis, L. J. (1996). Visuospatial perception, construction and memory in alcoholism. *Journal of Studies on Alcoholism, 57,* 136–143.

Borrill, J. A., Rosen, B. K., & Summerfield, A. B. (1987). The influence of alcohol on judgment of facial expressions of emotion. *British Journal of Medical Psychology, 60,* 71–77.

Cacioppo, J. T., Tassinary, L. G., & Fridlund, A. J. (1990). The skeletomotor system. In J. T. Cacioppo & L. G. Tassinary (Eds.), *Principles of psychophysiology: Physical, social, and inferential elements* (pp. 325–384). New York: Cambridge University Press.

Caetano, R. (1985). Alcohol dependence and the need to drink: A compulsion. *Psychosomatic Medicine, 15,* 463–469.

Cooper, M. L., Frone, M. R., Russell, M., & Mudar, P. (1995). Drinking to regulate positive and negative moods: A motivational model of alcohol use. *Journal of Personality and Social Psychology, 69,* 990–1005.

DeSota, C. B., O'Donnell, W. E., Allred, L. J., & Lopes, C. E. (1985). Symptomatology in alcoholics at various stages of abstinence. *Alcoholism: Clinical and Experimental Research, 9,* 505–512.

DeSota, C. B., O'Donnell, W. E., & DeSota, J. L. (1989). Long term recovery in alcoholics. *Alcoholism: Clinical and Experimental Research, 13,* 693–697.

Duberstein, P. R., Conwell, Y., & Caine, E. D. (1993). Interpersonal stressors, substance abuse, and suicide. *Journal of Nervous and Mental Disorders, 181,* 80–85.

Edwards, G., & Gross, M. M. (1976). Alcohol dependence: Provisional description of a clinical syndrome. *British Medical Journal, 1,* 1058–1061.

Ekman, P., & Friesen, W. V. (1978). *Facial action coding system: A technique for the measurement of facial movement.* Palo Alto, CA: Consulting Psychology Press.

Evans, V. (1980). Alcohol, violence, and aggression. *British Journal of Alcohol and Alcoholism, 15,* 104–117.

Fabian, M. S., & Parsons, O. A. (1983). Differential improvement of cognitive functions in recovering alcoholics. *Journal of Abnormal Psychology, 92,* 87–95.

Folstein, M. F., Folstein, S. E., & McHugh, P. R. (1975). "Mini-Mental State": A practical method for grading the cognitive state of patients for the clinician. *Journal of Psychiatric Research, 2,* 189.

Gabarino, C., & Strange, C. (1993). College adjustment and family environments of students reporting parental alcohol problems. *Journal of College Student Development, 34,* 261–266.

Glenn, S. W., Parsons, O. A., & Sinha, R. (1994). Assessment of recovery and neuropsychological functions in chronic alcoholics. *Biological Psychiatry, 36,* 443–452.

Goldman, M. S., Brown, S. A., & Christiansen, B. A. (1987). Expectancy theory: Thinking about drinking. In H. Blane & K. Leonard (Eds.), *Psychological theories of drinking and alcoholism* (1st ed., pp. 181–226). New York: Guilford Press.

Hess, U., & Blairy, S. (1995). *Set of emotional facial stimuli.* Montreal, Quebec, Canada: Department of Psychology, University of Quebec at Montreal.

Hess, U., Blairy, S., & Kleck, R. E. (1997). Intensity of emotional facial expression and decoding accuracy. *Journal of Nonverbal Behavior, 21,* 241–257.

Horowitz, L. M., Rosenberg, S. E., Baer, B. A., Ureno, G., & Villasenor, V. S. (1988). Inventory of interpersonal problems: Psychometric properties and clinical applications. *Journal of Consulting and Clinical Psychology, 56,* 885–892.

Hunt, W. A. (1990). Brain mechanisms that underlie the reinforcing effects of ethanol. In M. Cox (Ed.), *Why people drink: Parameters of alcohol as a reinforcer* (pp. 71–92). New York: Gardner.

Johnsson, C., Cronholm, B., & Izikovitz, S. (1962). Intellectual changes in alcoholics: Psychometric studies on mental sequela of prolonged intensive use of alcohol. *Quarterly Journal of Studies on Alcohol, 23,* 221–242.

Jones, D. C., & Houts, R. (1992). Parental drinking, parent-child communication and social skills in young adults. *Journal of Studies on Alcohol, 53,* 48–56.

Keane, T. M., & Lisman, S. A. (1980). Alcohol and social anxiety in males: Behavioural, cognitive and physiological effects. *Journal of Abnormal Psychology, 89,* 213–223.

Klein, H., & Pittman, D. J. (1993). The relationship between emotional state and alcohol consumption. *International Journal of Addictions, 28,* 47–61.

Knight, R. G., & Godfrey, H. P. (1993). The role of alcohol-related expectancies in the prediction of drinking behaviour in a simulated social interaction. *Addiction, 88,* 1111–1118.

Kornreich, C., Blairy, S., Philippot, P., Dan, B., Foisy, M.-L., Le Bon, O., Pelc, I., & Verbanck, P. (2001). Impaired emotional facial expression recognition in alcoholism compared to obsessive compulsive disorder and normal controls. *Psychiatry Research, 102*, 235–248.

Kornreich, C., Blairy, S., Philippot, P., Hess, U., Noël, X., Streel, E., Le Bon, O., Dan, B., Pelc, I., & Verbanck, P. (2001). Deficits in recognition of emotional facial expression are still present after mid-to long-term abstinence in alcoholics. *Journal of Studies on Alcohol, 62*, 533–542.

Kornreich, C., Dan, B., Fryns, A., Gozlan, S., & Verbanck, P. (1992). Approche cognitivo-comportementale de l'alcoolisme: Premiers enseignements de la réalisation d'un groupe thérapeutique. *Acta Psychiatrica Belgica, 13*, 279–293.

Kornreich, C., Philippot, P., Verpoorten, C., Baert, I., Dan, B., Le Bon, O., Verbanck, P., & Pelc, I. (1998). Alcoholism and emotional reactivity: More heterogeneous film-induced emotional responses in newly detoxified alcoholics compared to controls: A preliminary study. *Addictive Behaviors, 23*, 413–418.

Lang, A. R., Patrick, C. J., & Stritzke, W. G. K. (1999). Alcohol and emotional response: A multidimensional-multilevel analysis. In K. E. Leonard & H. T. Blane (Eds.), *Psychological theories of drinking and alcoholism* (2nd ed., pp. 328–371). New York: Guilford Press.

Levenson, R. W. (1987). Alcohol, affect, and physiology: Positive effects in the early stage of drinking. In E. Gottheil, K. Druley, S. Pasko, & S. Weinstein (Eds.), *Stress and addiction* (pp. 173–196). New York: Brunner Mazel.

Marlatt, C. A. (1979). *Alcohol use and problem dinking: A cognitive behavioral analysis.* New York: Academic Press.

Marlatt, C. A., Kosturn, C. F., & Lang, A. R. (1975). Provocation to anger and opportunity for retaliation as determinants of alcohol consumption in social drinkers. *Journal of Abnormal Psychology, 84*, 652–659.

Miller, P. M., & Eisler, R. M. (1977). Assertive behavior of alcoholics, a descriptive analysis. *Behaviour Therapy, 8*, 146–149.

Modell, J. G., Glaser, F. B., Cyr, L., & Montz, J. M. (1992). Obsessive and compulsive characteristics of craving for alcohol in alcohol abuse and dependence. *Alcoholism: Clinical and Experimental Research, 16*, 272–274.

Monti, P. M., Abrams, D. C., Binkoff, J. A., Zwick, W. R., Liepman, M. R., & Rohsenow, D. J. (1990). Communication skills training: Communication skills training with family, and cognitive behavioral mood management for alcoholics. *Journal of Studies on Alcohol, 51*, 263–270.

Myers, T. (1984). Alcohol and violence: Self-reported alcohol consumption among violent and nonviolent male prisoners. In N. Karsner, J. S. Madden, & R. J. Walker (Eds.), *Alcohol-related problems* (pp. 339–353). Chichester, England: Wiley.

National Institute of Alcohol Abuse and Alcoholism. (1990). *Seventh special report to the U.S. Congress on alcohol and health.* Rockville, MD: Author.

Nixon, S. J., Tivis, R., & Parsons, O. A. (1992). Interpersonal problem-solving in male and female alcoholics. *Alcoholism: Clinical and Experimental Research, 16*, 684–687.

Noller, P. (1984). *Nonverbal communication and marital interaction.* Exeter, England: Pergamon Press.

Oei, T. P. S., & Jackson, P. R. (1984). Some effective therapeutic factors in group cognitive behavioral therapy with problem drinkers. *Journal of Studies on Alcohol, 45*, 119–123.

Oscar-Berman, M., Hancock, M., Mildwordf, B., Hutner, N., & Altman-Weber, D. (1990). Emotional perception and memory in alcoholism and aging. *Alcoholism: Clinical and Experimental Research, 14*, 384–393.

O'Sullivan, M., Micklewright, J., Ekman, P., Jones, R., & Friesen, W. V. (1975, April). *The influence of alcohol and marijuana on the perception of facial expression of emotion.* Paper presented to the Western Psychological Association convention, Sacramento, CA.

Philippot, P., Kornreich, C., Blairy, S., Baert, Y., Den Dulk, A., Le Bon, O., Verbanck, P., Hess U., & Pelc, I. (1999). Alcoholics' deficits in the decoding of emotional facial expression. *Alcoholism: Clinical and Experimental Research, 23*, 1031–1038.

Pohorecky, L. A. (1991). Stress and alcohol interaction: An update of human research. *Alcoholism: Clinical and Experimental Research, 15*, 438–459.

Rather, B. C., & Goldman, M. S. (1994). Drinking related differences in the memory organization of alcohol expectancies. *Experimental and Clinical Pharmacology, 2*, 167–183.

Rather, B. C., Goldman, M. S., Roehirch, L., & Brannick, M. (1992). Empirical modeling of and alcohol expectancy memory network using multidimensional scaling. *Journal of Abnormal Psychology, 101*, 174–183.

Rosenthal-Gaffney L., Thorpe, K., Young, R., Colett, R., & Occhipinti, S. (1998). Social skills, expectancies, and drinking in adolescents. *Addictive Behaviors, 23*, 587–599.

Sayette, M. A., Smith, D. W., Breiner, M. J., & Wilson, J. T. (1992). The effect of alcohol on emotional response to a social stressor. *Journal of Studies on Alcohol, 53*, 541–545.

Schandler, S. L., Clegg, A. D., Thomas, C. S., & Cohen, M. J. (1996). Visuospatial information processing in intoxicated, recently detoxified, and long-term abstinent alcoholics. *Journal of Substance Abuse, 8*, 321–333.

Schuckit, M. A., Hesselbrock, V. M., Tipp, J., Nurnberger, J. I., Anthenelli, R. M., & Crowe, R. R. (1995). The prevalence of major anxiety disorders in relatives of alcohol dependent men and women. *Journal of Studies on Alcohol, 56*, 309–317.

Segrin, C., & Menees, M. M. (1996). The impact of coping style and family communication on the social skills of children of alcoholics. *Journal of Studies on Alcohol, 46*, 137–146.

Sferrazza, R., Philippot, P., Kornreich, C., Tany, C., Noel, X., Pelc, I., & Verbanck, P. (2002). Dysfonctionnement relationel au sein des couples alcooliques [Relational dysfunctioning in alcoholic couples]. *Alcoologie et Addictologie, 24*, 117–125.

Sher, K. J., Trull, T. J., Bartholow, B. D., & Vieth, A. (1999). Personality and alcoholism issues methods and etiological processes. In K. E. Leonard & H. T. Blane (Eds.), *Psychological theories of drinking and alcoholism* (2nd ed., pp. 54–105). New York: Guilford Press.

Stritske, W. G. K., Patrick, C. J., & Lang, A. R. (1995). Alcohol and human emotion: Adimensional analysis incorporating startle probe methodology. *Journal of Abnormal Psychology, 104*, 114–12.

10

Ethology and Depression

ANTOINETTE L. BOUHUYS

In the past decades, much effort has been devoted to understanding why people become depressed and what determines the duration of the depression or its recurrence. The resulting theories primarily focus on risk factors (i.e., factors that may have a causal relation with the onset, persistence, and recurrence of depression). Relatively little energy has been devoted to the possible contribution of ethology in this search for causal factors. This chapter focuses on the role of ethology in relation to the putative risk factors for onset, persistence, and recurrence of depression. As I show, human ethology—the study of the mechanisms and evolution of behavior—relies on careful observation of nonverbal human behavior.

Theoretical Framework

Depression is a serious and debilitating mood disorder. According to a generally accepted classification system (*DSM-IV*; American Psychiatric Association, 1994) the features of depressed mood and loss of interest or pleasure often coincide with sleep disturbances, cognitive impairments, feelings of worthlessness, concentration difficulties, and the slowing of motoric behavior. Depression (major depression) in the general population has a lifetime prevalence of 5%–10% and represents a large proportion of mental health outpatient contacts and psychiatric hospital admissions. Depression is associated with high medical use as well; depressed persons have medical costs twice those of nondepressed controls matched for medical illness. Therefore, the personal, economic, and health care costs of depression are high (von Korff, Ormel, Katon, & Lin, 1992).

Many mental health experts have become increasingly pessimistic about the outcome of depression. Despite the development of various types of pharmacotherapies and psychotherapies, about 30% of depressed patients do not respond to treatment. Particularly when patients are evaluated beyond immediate remission, relapse and recurrence of depression following successful treatments are common (Paykel, 1994). Relapse rates as high as 50%–70% after a first episode and 80%–90% after a subsequent episode have been reported (Angst, 1988). The recurrence rates 1.5–2.0 years after remission are 30%–50% (Ramana et al., 1995; Surtees & Barkley, 1994). Women are twice as likely to experience clinical depression as men (Paykel, 1991; Weissman & Klerman, 1977). These figures on the prevalence and outcome of depression underscore the need to understand mechanisms that underlie depression onset, persistence, and recurrence.

One of the prevailing etiological theories of depression is the diathesis-stress model. The theory includes individual differences in reactivity to the environment and two-way interplay between individual features and environmental influences. It states that depression can occur when a specific vulnerability (diathesis) interacts with negative stressful life events. It has been demonstrated that personality factors such as a neurotic or dependent personality (Bagby et al., 1994; Boyce, Parker, Barnett, Conney, & Smith, 1991; Franche & Dobson, 1992; Hirschfeld et al., 1989; Kendler, 1993; Ormel & Wohlfarth, 1991; Zuroff, 1994) as well as negative cognitions may serve as a diathesis (Crowell, O'Connor, Wollmers, & Sprafkin, 1991; Gotlib & Hammen, 1992; Segal, Williams, Teasdale, & Gemar, 1996).

According to Beck's model (Beck, Rush, Shaw, & Emery, 1979), vulnerability to depression comprises tendencies to negatively interpret the self, the environment, and the future. It has frequently been suggested that such enhanced negative processing plays a role in the onset and recurrence of depression (see Segal et al., 1996). This negative bias is assumed to operate most strongly regarding cognitions about interpersonal relationships (Hammen, 1992; Segal et al., 1996). It has been proposed that high levels of neuroticism are related to negative cognitions (Mathews & MacLeod, 1994), and that negative cognitions may generate stressful interpersonal events (Potthoff, Holahan, & Joiner, 1995), which enhance the risk for depression. Moreover, negative appraisal of stressful events and ineffective coping with these events is supposed to contribute to the development of depression (Hammen, 1992; Lazarus & Folkman, 1984). In some theories on depression, people in the environment of a depression-prone person are considered to play a role in the development, persistence, and recurrence of depression. It has been proposed that depressives' significant others finally react to dependent and support-seeking behavior with rejection, resulting in clinical depression (Coyne, 1976; Coyne, Burchill, & Stiles, 1990).

Depression has repeatedly been shown to be associated with disturbances in autonomic nervous system regulation (Zahn, Nurnberger, Berretti, & Robinson, 1991). In depression, disturbed cortisol secretion and parasympathetic tone are common. Consensus exists that impaired hypothalamic-pituitary-adrenocortical (HPA) axis function (e.g., high levels of cortisol) is associated with the depressed state (Holsboer, 1989). However, these high levels of cortisol tend to normalize at remission. In spite of this normalization, it has been reported that, at remission, high cortisol is related to risk of depression recurrence (Cosgriff, Abbott, Oakley Browne, & Joyce, 1990). Hyperreactivity of sympathetic-adrenomedullary and pituitary-adrenocortical axes may worsen cognitive biases in perception and stress appraisal and induce avoidance coping.

Several observations have led to the presumption that, with increasing experience of depressed episodes, subjects are more at risk to recurrence of depression. First, with successive recurrences of episodes, intervals between them become progressively shorter (Berti, Ceroni, & Pezzoli, 1984; Post, 1992; Sturt, Kumarkura, & Der, 1984). Second, with increasing episodes, psychosocial stressors contribute less to the recurrence of the next episode (see Post, 1992). Neurobiological sensitization has been postulated as an explanation. Each episode of depression lays a path for new episodes to emerge in response to increasingly minimal cues. On the one hand, the theory implies that psychosocial and cognitive factors have less causal impact for recurrence of the next depressive episode with increasing experience of depressive episodes. On the other hand, it has been argued that depressed persons who experienced many episodes show more cognitive and behavioral impairments than persons who experience their first depression. Hence, psychosocial and cognitive factors associated with depression are assumed to evolve over time as a function of depression recurrences (Akiskal, Hirschfeld, & Yerevanian, 1983; Lewinsohn, Steinmetz, Larson, & Franklin, 1981; Segal et al., 1996). The proposition that risk of recurrence of depression will increase due to vulnerability accumulation after progressive episodes is called the *vulnerability-accumulation hypothesis.*

Figure 10.1 summarizes the hypotheses of how basic cognitive, behavioral, and physiological mechanisms might link the personality risk factor neuroticism to depression and represent putative mechanisms through which neuroticism may influence risk for depression. High neurotic subjects, compared to low neurotic subjects, will show a negative bias in the processing of socially relevant stimuli (1 in Fig. 10.1) and have a negative

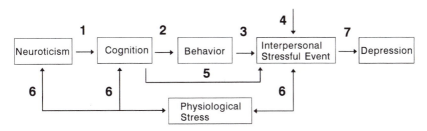

Fig. 10.1 Summary of hypotheses on how basic cognitive/behavioral and physiological mechanisms might link the personality risk factor neuroticism to depression.

perception of (significant) others that interferes negatively with interpersonal behavior (2). Consequently, this negative interpersonal behavior may generate more interpersonal stressful events (3), which may also arise independent of the subject's behavior (4). These individuals label interpersonal stressful events as more negative (due to a putative negative bias in the cognitive processing of socially relevant stimuli) and show more negative appraisal and ineffective coping with hypothetical stressful events (5) and show disturbances in autonomic nervous system responsivity to stressors (6). Given Items 1–6, they will be at higher risk for depression (7).

Based on the arguments and reasoning above, it may be concluded that the social environment, interpersonal processes, and the interpretation of environmental stimuli—in other words, social communication—play a role in depression onset, persistence, and recurrence. Moreover, this may be especially true as the number of depressive episodes experienced increases. Placed in this theoretical framework, ethology may contribute to the unraveling of mechanisms underlying risk for depression.

The Ethological Approach

In biology, the analysis of behavioral interactions between individuals and their (social) environment has been elaborated by ethology. Ethology has provided analytical and experimental tools to analyze communication structures and has contributed insight into the fundamental processes that underlie effective communication between individuals (Hauser, 1996). In contemporary ethology, behavior is studied from four perspectives by asking four fundamental questions (Tinbergen, 1951):

1. Which external stimuli cause the behavior under study? The stimuli that cause the behavior are proximate factors.
2. Which processes and factors are involved in the ontogeny, that is, the development (the organization), of the behavior?
3. Which biologically relevant function does the behavior serve; that is, what are the consequences of the signals with respect to expectancies for survival of the individuals and of their offspring? The biological relevance of behavior is related to fitness. The fitness measure includes all aspects related to the survival of the individuals and their offspring. The beneficial effects of behavior with respect to fitness are called ultimate factors.
4. How can the development of the behavior be understood from the perspective of evolutionary processes?

These questions can be asked regarding human behavior as well. Questions 3 and 4 above represent an evolutionary perspective. Several interesting evolutionary theories of depression have been postulated; these theories emphasize involuntary subordination (Gilbert, 1992; Price, Sloman, Gardner, Gilbert, & Rohde, 1994; Price & Gardner, 1995; Sloman, Price, Gilbert, & Gardner, 1994) or unbalanced altruism (McGuire, 1994; McGuire & Troisi, 1998) as cause of depression (for a review, see Gilbert, 1992; McGuire, Marks, Nesse, & Troisi, 1992; McGuire & Troisi, 1998). However, evolutionary theories of depression are beyond the scope of this chapter and are hard to validate empirically. The study of proximate factors has the advantage that it can be embedded better in an empirical tradition. In the next sections, examples of a proximate ethological approach of psychopathology are presented.

Dyadic interactions are very basic in diagnostic and psychotherapeutic processes. Consequently, in relation to psychopathology, the dyadic interaction can be considered an interesting starting point for the ethologist. Ethological studies have demonstrated that the (continuous) recording of the occurrence of behavioral elements has the potential to unravel an underlying organization of behavior. In our ethological approach, we first started with the search for an organizational structure of patient-interviewer behavior (see the section regarding the search for an organizational structure of nonverbal behavior during an interaction). This search resulted in a limited set of factors that described the behavior of the patient and the interviewer during an interaction. A clear example of a causal analysis of behavior is shown in the section, "Nonverbal Coordination and the Course of Depression." We experimentally manipulated the interviewer's behavior to establish causal connections between the interviewer's behavior and the patient's behavioral response.

The main theme of our studies concerns associations between behavior factors of patients and interviewers during a baseline interview (for instance, at admission) and future outcome. Although these studies are correlational, they are a first step in tracing factors that may account for persistence of depression. The same holds true for our studies on cognitions about nonverbal behavior and personality traits, which I report below.

Depression as Reflected in Observable Nonverbal Behavior

It has been convincingly demonstrated that depression is reflected on the level of nonverbal behavior (see Ellgring, 1989; Perez & Riggio, chapter 2, this volume; Siegman, 1985). Depressed patients speak less often, more monotonously, and with longer pauses than controls. They look less at an interviewer and show less interpersonal involvement (Jones & Pansa, 1979). Furthermore, it has been found that the level of interpersonal behavior increases when depression improves (Ellgring, 1989; Fossi, Faravelli, & Paoli, 1984; Rosen, Tureff, Lyons, & Davis, 1981). Some symptoms of depression (e.g., retardation—slowing of motoric behavior and cognitive processes—or agitation) can be reliably measured on the level of patients' nonverbal interpersonal behavior (Bouhuys, Jansen, & Van den Hoofdakker, 1991; Ulrich &

Harms, 1985; see also Schelde, 1994). No differences in interpersonal non-verbal behavior have been found between the various subcategories of depression, as described in the common diagnostic classification system (*DSM*) (Troisi, Pasini, Bersani, Grispini, & Ciani, 1990).

One may question whether the time-consuming method of measuring how depression is nonverbally expressed during the depressed state may have any value compared to global clinical observations. I believe that a proximate approach is, in fact, relevant in psychopathology, especially when it concerns the prediction of the course of depression. In the sections below, I focus on the predictive value of nonverbal behavior for both the persistence and the recurrence of depression. Because our research group has focused on these issues, I lean heavily on our investigations of depression.

The Search for an Organizational Structure for Nonverbal Behavior During an Interaction

What typifies an ethological approach in psychopathology?

First, although social psychologists also use observational techniques to answer their research questions, it can be argued that their methods differ from those of ethologists in this way: Commonly, in the domain of social psychology, isolated elements of behavior are studied that are presumed to serve a particular function (e.g., gesticulating, looking). In contrast, in the ethological approach of my group, we do not make a priori assumptions about behavioral functions, but study the structure of the behavioral elements. Such an approach may enable the tracing of possible biological and psychological functions of associated behaviors.

Second, in ethology, communication is a central issue. Senders and receivers of signals are of equal importance. My group applied this notion regarding a common psychiatric setting, the clinical interview. Therefore, we analyzed the behavior of the patients and also of the interviewer. In addition, in analyzing the behaviors of both persons, we paid particular attention to reciprocal behavioral influences because the behavior of the patient may influence that of the interviewer and vice versa.

My coworkers and I analyzed the behaviors displayed during a clinical interview between a caregiver and depressed patients just admitted to an inpatient clinic (Bouhuys et al., 1991; Bouhuys & Van den Hoofdakker, 1993). The interviews were videotaped and time coded. Various behaviors were recorded continuously by means of an event-recording system that enabled computer registration of the start and the end of particular behaviors. Each video recording was played more than once to record all behaviors of patients and interviewers. The time coding of the behaviors made the preservation of their time relationships possible.

The following behaviors were measured: speaking, listening, verbal back-channel behavior (hmm, hmm, yes, yes), looking, general head movements, nodding yes, shaking no, leg movements, and various hand movements. The hand movements were distinguished with respect to what was touched (own body or objects) and their intensity (low and high intensity move-ments). In addition, hand movements that supported speech (e.g., gesticu-lating) were recorded. My group analyzed the behaviors relative to speaking and listening of the interacting persons. This allowed us to adjust for varia-tion in the duration of speaking or listening that affects the duration or frequency of other behaviors. We studied the frequencies and the durations of each of the above behaviors during the persons' speaking turns, and the same variables were assessed during listening.

Based on statistical criteria (correlational analyses, i.e., factor analyses), the various elements were grouped into a limited set of behavioral factors. In a study of interactions between depressed patients and one psychiatrist, my group distinguished six factors for the patient and seven for the psychi-atrist. The patients and the psychiatrist shared four factors, which can be classified as follows: restlessness involving leg movement and light body touching; restlessness involving object touching; speech (duration and fre-quency of speaking); and active listening (intensive body touching during listening). Specific patient factors were eagerness (nodding yes and shaking no) and speaking effort (looking and gesticulating while speaking). Specific interviewer factors were turn taking (leg movements and gesticulating dur-ing patients' speaking), encouragement (verbal back-channel and nodding yes), and change looking (frequency of alternately looking at and away from a patient's face). These 13 behavioral factors best describe the behavioral structure during a diagnostic conversation. Our next step was to investigate whether these 13 behavioral factors may predict the subsequent course of depression.

Nonverbal Behavior of Patient and Interviewer and the Course of Depression

Theoretical Framework

As discussed, deficits in human communication are postulated to play an important role in many theories of depression (Coyne, 1976; Coyne et al., 1990; Gotlib & Hammen, 1992). Deficient social behavior of depression-prone persons is supposed to perpetuate depressogenic processes by elicit-ing negative reactions in others (Segrin & Abramson, 1994). It has been pro-posed that depressives' significant others finally react to dependent and support-seeking behavior with rejection. This may subsequently result in high interpersonal stress and lack of social support, which has been related to onset, persistence, and recurrence of depression (Brown, Harris, Hepworth, & Robinson, 1994; Coyne & Downey, 1991). The mechanisms involved in eliciting such rejecting attitudes have not yet been identified.

I propose that nonverbal behavioral involvement plays a role in the development of rejecting attitudes. Involvement of patients is probably represented by support-seeking behavior and involvement of the interviewer by support-giving behavior. Ideally, people in the patients' environment reciprocate the patients' support-seeking behavior with support-giving behavior. The reciprocity of involvement during an interaction seems of particular relevance for a positive experience of a dyadic interaction. Consequently, lack of involvement may cause negative feelings about the interaction, which may result in rejection of the depression-prone subjects, leading to depression.

Furthermore, personality may affect or be represented on the level of interactional behavior. For example, nonverbal overinvolvement in an interaction may be indicative of a dependent personality.

Ethological Observations

Nonverbal involvement of the depressed patients is presumably reflected by the speaking effort behavior factor and involvement of the other interactant by the encouragement factor (see Hale, Jansen, Bouhuys, 1997). Bouhuys and Albersnagel (1992) studied, at admission, these nonverbal involvement behaviors of depressed patients and a psychiatrist. It was found that the persistence of depression over a 10-week period could be predicted from patients' speaking effort and the psychiatrist's encouragement factors. More involvement of the patients and of the psychiatrist was associated with an unfavorable course of the depression.

My group replicated these results in another population of patients with winter depression (also known as seasonal affective disorder, SAD) who received light therapy (Geerts, Bouhuys, Meesters, & Jansen, 1995). The effects of light treatment were evaluated 19 days after the baseline interview. Note that, in both studies, we statistically corrected for differences in the severity of baseline depression. Therefore, it is not likely that variance in initial severity of depression can explain our results. However, in later studies, we could not confirm that patient's speaking effort and interviewer's encouragement factors had predictive quality (Geerts & Bouhuys, 1998; Geerts, Kouwert, Bouhuys, Meesters, & Jansen, 2000; Hale et al., 1997). In two of five studies, we found a relation between patient's speaking effort at admission and the persistence of depression. The predictive quality of the interviewer's encouragement was found in three of five studies. Hence, the findings for speaking effort and on encouragement in relation to the course of depression are equivocal.

Work by other authors, using different methods, did not clarify this issue. Troisi and coworkers (Troisi, Pasini, Bersani, Grispini, & Ciani, 1989) could predict the response to tricyclic treatment of depressed outpatients based on observed behaviors assessed during baseline interviews. They found that high levels of affiliative behavior (probably related to our speaking effort factor) predicted nonresponse to amitriptyline. This result is in agreement with the studies of my group that showed that depressed patients' high levels of involvement at admission were related to poor treatment outcomes.

Several authors assumed that high levels of body-focused hand movements are indicative of low involvement in an interaction (Coker & Burgoon, 1987; Segrin & Abramson, 1994). Bouhuys and Albersnagel (1992) found a tendency for low levels of body-focused hand movements (during listening) to be associated with poor outcome. Under the assumption that high levels of body-focused hand movements indicate low involvement, these results are in line with the studies above. However, in later studies my group could not replicate this finding.

Moreover, Ranelli and Miller (1981) found that depressed patients with high levels of body-focused hand movements during an interview at admission were less likely to improve. That study suggests that low involvement is associated with poor outcome, whereas the above results suggest the opposite. Consequently, conflicting evidence exists on the predictive quality of body-focused hand movement for the course of depression. Fossi and coworkers (1984) investigated depressed patients' ward behavior at admission in relation to later improvement. Examples of ward behavior are affiliation behaviors (touching one other, waiting, greeting, smiling), assertion behavior (leaving, refusal to obey command, pushing one other, intrusion in conversation), task-related behavior (reading, watching television), and pathological behavior (shaking, agitation, talking to oneself, withdrawal). They found no link between the various behaviors they distinguished at admission and later outcome.

It is important to try to account for these discrepancies. Perhaps the fact that different behaviors were observed is important in explaining the discrepancies. It is very likely that the samples from these different studies were assessed at different stages of depression (i.e., with respect to the start of the depressive episode and with respect to the number of episodes previously suffered). In light of the above-mentioned vulnerability-accumulation hypothesis, one may expect that patients who differ in depression history will also differ in behaviors that predict the course of the depression. In addition, these discrepant results may be explained by differences in the contextual aspects of the investigated interactions, such as different interviewers or differences in the type of interaction observed (clinical interviews versus interactions between patients and partners). For example, Fossi, Faravelli and Paoli (1984) observed behavior in a variety of rooms and during a variety of interactions, whereas other studies observed behavior during a dyadic interaction involving a clinical interview. Finally, the different intervals between the baseline measurements and the assessment of outcome may account for discrepant results.

All in all, results are inconsistent with respect to the predictive quality of patients' speaking effort and interviewers' encouragement factors for the course of the depression. About 50% of the studies showed that the behavior of the depressed patients had predictive value for the future course of depression; 60% of the studies showed that the interviewers' behavior had predictive quality. It should be noted that, as far as significant relationships exist between behavior at admission and later outcome, they were confined to interview situations. In interview situations, interactants are more or less "forced" to interact. This may contrast with the relatively less evocative psychiatric ward situations.

Consequently, some evidence exists that high levels of involvement of depressed patients are associated with poor outcome. As mentioned, Coyne's (1976; Coyne, Burchill, & Stiles, 1990; Coyne & Downer, 1991) interpersonal theory presumes that support-seeking behavior of depressive patients may serve as a depression-maintaining factor. In addition, dependent persons are more at risk to become depressed than other personality types. One may speculate that the patient's speaking effort factor reflects support-seeking behavior and that the encouragement factor reflects support-giving behavior. Thus, we may have traced a nonverbal mechanism by which dependency may be enacted during an interaction.

One may ask whether the high levels of patients' nonverbal involvement may underlie rejection attitudes of others. However, the levels of the interviewer's encouragement behavior seem to contradict this presumption: The interviewer showed increased levels of encouragement with respect to patients who did not improve later. Perhaps a more significant other would have emitted low levels of encouragement. My group found some support for this possibility. The interactions of depressed patients and their partners were compared to interactions of the same depressed patients interacting with a stranger (Hale et al., 1997). With application of the same methods described above, we found that partners of depressed patients showed less involvement (encouragement) in their interaction with the patient than controls (matched for the age and sex of the partners). In the same study, we found that less involvement (measured as speaking time) of the partners predicted an unfavorable course of depression over 6 months. These results may indicate that low levels of nonverbal involvement of a partner may depict lack of social support. We know from epidemiological studies that social support is an important protective factor for depression recurrence (Brown et al., 1994), and that lack of social support negatively affects the duration of depressive episodes (McLeod, Kessler, & Landis, 1992).

In sum, results seem to show that the type of relationship determines the nonverbal response of the environment to depressed persons. High levels of encouragement factor displayed to a depressed subject by an unfamiliar person are associated with persistence of depression. However, in the case for which a familiar person (e.g., the partner) is interacting with the depressed person, his or her low involvement predicts depression persistence. These results are consistent with interpersonal theories of depression: Initially, the environment reacts to the presentation of depressed symptoms with acceptance and encouragement (see interviewer behavior), but later the high levels of support-seeking behavior of the patients may result in rejection of significant others in the environment (see partners' behavior). Furthermore, under the assumption that speaking effort behavior reflects support seeking, our data confirmed that some dependent subjects show a less favorable course of depression.

Whereas the results reviewed above may seem disappointingly conflicting, the next section shows that ethological assessments of an interaction at admission can show more consistent relations with future course of depression. Specifically, measures that actually assess the lack of reciprocity in behavior of interactants are considered.

Nonverbal Coordination and the Course of Depression

Theoretical Framework

Coordination in social interaction refers to the ways that people adjust their actions to those of their partners. Coordination includes, among other things, the matching of behavior, the adoption of behavioral rhythms, and the manifestation of simultaneous movement of individual behaviors (Bernieri & Rosenthal, 1991). Some authors have investigated the temporal aspects of behavioral coordination during an interaction (Bernieri & Rosenthal, 1991; Burgoon, Le-Poire, & Rosenthal, 1995). The results from their studies show that coordination of behavior develops over time.

Figure 10.2 depicts a theoretical concept of coordination: Two persons (A and B) start an interaction. Initially, the amount of behavior (i.e., level) of persons A and B will differ. For instance, A shows higher frequencies of a certain behavior than B. However, due to reciprocal influences, their levels of behavior will converge. This results in smaller differences between

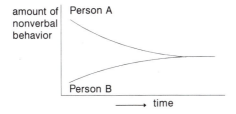

Fig. 10.2 Theoretical concept of nonverbal coordination between two persons (A and B). During the interaction, the amounts of behavior of Persons A and B converge to equal levels.

the levels of behavior displayed by A and B and finally similar levels of behavior.

Coordination has been found for various types of behavior (e.g., speech, nodding yes, and body movement [Bernieri, 1988; Gregory, Webster, & Huang, 1993]). In various studies, it was found that the degree of coordination in social interactions was related to satisfaction with the interaction or with other interpersonal outcomes such as attraction and attachment (Cappella, 1997; Cappella & Palmer, 1990; Hall, Harrigan, & Rosenthal, 1995). These associations support the coordination-rapport hypothesis, which presumes such relations (Tickle-Degnen & Rosenthal, 1990).

From a developmental perspective, adjustments of behaviors between caregivers and infants are presumed to be a prerequisite for normal developmental change (Fogel, 1993). Studies of interactions between mothers and newly born children suggest that high levels of nonverbal coordination are related to secure attachment. Pairs that were coordinated and that synchronized their behaviors were found to be attached more securely than pairs that were primarily noncoordinated (Isabella & Belsky, 1991; Isabella, Belsky, & Eye, 1989). Attachment is considered a basic and biologically necessary aspect of human nature, and many studies support the hypothesis that insecure attachment in early life may underlie later depression (Bowlby, 1969, 1981; Gotlib, 1992; Hammen et al., 1995; Main, 1996). It is assumed that attachment with parents and with intimate partners in adolescence and adulthood continue to reflect the imprint of the early attachment experiences with the primary caregiver (Diamond & Doane, 1994; Gotlib & Hammen, 1992; Parker, Hadzi Pavlovic, Greenwald, & Weissman, 1995). Thus, nonverbal coordination may form a stable factor: In early life, it allows secure attachment and healthy development. In later life, good coordination is associated with positive interpersonal functioning and satisfaction with the interaction.

Reciprocal behavior may be pertinent to the diathesis-stress model and interpersonal theories of depression: A lack of coordination may cause interpersonal problems, with the above-outlined consequences (see Fig. 10.1 and accompanying text).

Ethological Observations

Between depressed patients and interviewers, coordination occurs for nonverbal behaviors that express involvement in the interaction. My coworkers and I found a significant positive correlation between patients' and interviewers' nonverbal involvement behaviors (i.e., the factors speaking effort and encouragement) (Bouhuys & Van den Hoofdakker, 1991). This suggests that depressive patients and their interviewers attune nonverbal involvement behavior. That these factors are causally related was shown in another study (Geerts, Bouhuys, & Bloem, 1997). Depressed patients were interviewed for 20 min. During this interaction, the interviewer gave 10 min high nonverbal involvment and 10 min low nonverbal involvement (encouragement) in a crossover design. My group found that the patients' speaking effort was significantly higher in the high encouragement condition compared to the low encouragement condition. Hence, patients' level of involvement followed that of experimentally manipulated involvement of the interviewers, indicating that these involvement behaviors are causally related.

As mentioned, good coordination is related to interpersonal satisfaction. Accordingly, my group hypothesized that a lack of coordination between patients' speaking effort and interviewer's encouragement factors may underlie the unsatisfactory interactions observed in depression and therefore may be related to persistence of depression. To investigate this hypothesis, the coordination between speaking effort and encouragement was studied during interviews 15 to 20 min long. The interviews were subdivided in five periods of equal duration. Then, the two behavioral involvement factors were calculated for each period. Coordination was operationalized as the absolute difference between the patient's speaking effort and the interviewer's encouragement. A small absolute difference represented high levels of coordination. Accordingly, a decrease of absolute differences between speaking effort and encouragement over the interview showed that patients and interviewers were becoming better coordinated. Lack of coordination at admission was found to be related to depression persistence. We found that, with decreasing coordination between patients and interviewers over the interview, patients responded less favorably to subsequent treatment. This has been found in four of five studies. Two studies were of inpatients whose treatment was evaluated after 6–10 weeks. The patients received treatment according to their individual needs, such as antidepressive drugs or psychotherapy. Two other studies concerned patients with winter depression. In these studies, the effects of light therapy were evaluated 19 days after the baseline interview. In one study of an outpatient group ($n = 26$) that received "care as usual," coordination did not predict outcome (Geerts & Bouhuys, 1998; Geerts, Bouhuys, & Van den Hoofdakker, 1996; Geerts et al., 2000 Geerts et al., personal communication, 2003). Apparently, the predictive value of lack of coordination for an unfavorable course of depression does not depend on type of treatment.

In conclusion, lack of coordination is related to the persistence of depression. This association has now been confirmed by four of five studies, which differed with respect to type of patients (winter depression, inpatient and outpatient population) and to type of interviewers (clinician, researcher, or research assistant; male or female).

What accounts for the lack of coordination? The presumption that the depressed person is not able to coordinate with another person because of depression and that this may explain the results is not very likely. In our analyses, we controlled for patients' differences in severity of the depression. Hence, the severity of depression cannot account for the predictive quality of lack of coordination for the unfavorable course of depression. However, we cannot exclude the possibility that lack of coordination only can be observed during the depressed state. Longitudinal studies that include both depressed and remitted states are necessary for insight on these issues.

As indicated in the theoretical background above, our measure for coordination may be related to (early) attachment. In children, insecure attachment was found to be associated with lack of coordination. Lack of coordination may then be a traitlike quality that later in life constitutes risk for depression persistence. Moreover, one may speculate that unsatisfactory and problematic relationships may be mediated by lack of coordination. The lack of coordination may play a causal role in the maintenance of depression. In sections below, I integrate our findings with current theories on depression.

Cognitions and the Course of Depression

Theoretical Framework

According to Beck's cognitive theory, depression is characterized by mood-congruent biases that operate at all aspects of processing, such as attention, reasoning, and memory (Beck, Rush, Shaw, & Emery, 1979). It has frequently been suggested that a bias toward the processing of negative cues plays a role in the recurrence of depression (see Mathews & MacLeod, 1994). This bias is assumed to operate most strongly regarding cognitions about interpersonal relationships (Hammen, 1992; Segal et al., 1996). My group has been focusing on interpersonal relationships by studying cognitions about the facial expressions of others.

The face signals emotional states and regulates the behavior of others (Darwin, 1872/1965; Ekman, 1992). Although evidence is still conflicting, it has been reported that depressed patients show an impaired ability to decode facial expressions (Gur et al., 1992; Mikhailova, Vladimirova, Iznak, Tsusulkovskaya, & Sushko, 1996; Rubinow & Post, 1992) and show decreased sensitivity to emotion-related stimuli compared to controls (Wexler, Levenson, Warrenburg, & Price, 1994). Hence, depressed patients seem less able to decide which emotion is involved in others. Apart from this impaired sensitivity to social signals that may hamper normal interactions, some depressed subgroups show a negative bias in the judgment of facial expressions as well (George et al., 1998; Gur et al., 1992; Mandal & Palchoudhury, 1985; Rubinow & Post, 1992).

However, other authors could not support this evidence (Archer, Hay, & Young, 1992; Gaebel & Woelwer, 1992; Mandal, 1987; Walker, McGuire, & Bettes, 1984; Zuroff & Colussy, 1986). Thus, some studies suggest that depressed patients are inclined to interpret the emotions of others wrongly or more negatively. Such deficits in interpretation of facial expressions may generate stressful interpersonal events, which are presumed to contribute to an increased risk for depression (Potthoff et al., 1995). In addition, once stressful interpersonal events have emerged, subjects' negative cognitive style may hamper their ability to cope with these events.

Furthermore, it has been proposed that children who have experienced insecure attachment in early life—a concept related to deficits in coordination, as discussed above—develop "working models" (Bowlby, 1969, 1981) or cognitive "schemas" (Beck et al., 1979) with negative cognitions. These negative cognitions may form a risk (possibly via interpersonal behaviors) for later depression (Crowell et al., 1991; Gotlib & Hammen, 1992; Segal et al., 1996).

Ethological Observations

Recently, my group found supportive evidence that a bias toward the processing of negative social stimuli may mediate persistence of depression and relapse into depression. Decoding abilities of schematic facial expressions were assessed with a questionnaire. Subjects judged a series of 12 schematic faces (line drawings) consisting of four eyebrow types, three mouth types, and one eye-and-nose type (see Fig. 10.3). The use of ambigu-

Fig. 10.3 Schematic faces judged on five negative emotions (fear, anger, disgust, sadness, and rejection) and two positive emotions (elation and invitation). Faces 3, 4, and 5 represent so-called ambiguous faces.

ous or blended faces, conveying equal amounts of positive and negative emotions, is of particular interest in depression research. First, in cognitive theories on the development of depression, ambiguous situations are supposed to be causal (Beck et al., 1979). Second, it has been found in healthy subjects that the judgment of ambiguous pictures (i.e., equal with respect to positive and negative cues) is more strongly influenced by feeling states than clearer pictures (Isen & Shalker, 1982). The same tendency was found for ambiguous faces (Terwogt, Kremer, & Stegge, 1991). Faces 3, 4, and 5 of Fig. 10.3 represent the ambiguous faces in the current study (see Bouhuys, Bloem, & Groothuis, 1995, for statistical arguments).

Under each facial expression, a list of adjectives that expressed different emotions was presented. The patients were instructed to judge how strongly each facial expression displayed each emotion and to rely on their first impression. The subjects judged the 12 faces with respect to the five primary emotions: fear, happiness, anger, sadness, and disgust. Two other adjectives (rejection and invitation) were included due to findings that depressed patients judge social interactions more negatively than controls only if they imagined that these interactions were directed at themselves (Hoehn-Hyde & Rush, 1982). Five of the seven adjectives (fear, sadness, anger, disgust, and rejection) were grouped in a general category called negative emotions, and the remaining two adjectives (happiness and invitation) were grouped as positive emotions. The reason behind this grouping is the suggestion that self-reported affect can best be categorized in positive and negative emotions (Watson & Tellegen, 1985). Factor analysis of my group's data on the judgment of facial expressions confirmed this positive-negative distinction (Bouhuys, Geerts, & Mersch, 1997).

My group found that perception of high levels of negative facial emotions from ambiguous faces at admission was associated with poor outcome of depression after 6 weeks (Geerts & Bouhuys, 1998). This association was confined to women (Bouhuys, Geerts, & Gordijn, 1999b). Our previously reported results that suggested relations in the opposite direction in an outpatient setting (Bouhuys, Geerts, Mersch, & Jenner, 1996) could possibly be explained by these gender differences. Furthermore, we investigated the perception of emotions in the depressed state and in the remitted state in relation to a possible subsequent relapse within 6 months after remission. We found that perception of high levels of negative emotions from ambiguous faces, either assessed at admission or at discharge (in remitted state), was associated with relapse into depression (Bouhuys, Geerts, & Gordijn, 1999a). So, the patients who were inclined to interpret ambiguous faces more negatively were more likely to relapse within 6 months. We found no relations between judgment of positive emotions and relapse.

Different theories try to explain the relations between emotion processing and mood. According to the differential activation hypothesis, vulnerability to depression depends (among other things) on the patterns of information processing that become activated in states of mild depression

(Teasdale, 1988). According to this view, the processing of a vulnerable individual may be affected in a depressed mood state, but may be quite normal when remitted and in an asymptomatic state (state dependent). So, the hypothesis presumed that cognitive processing is state dependent. This perspective contrasts with the view that constantly present and enduring negative biases in basic cognitions are the primary vulnerability factors. According to this view, negative cognitions are considered a trait (Beck et al., 1979; Gilboa & Gotlib, 1997; Hedlund & Rude, 1995).

My group's study of the judgment of facial expression in depressed and remitted states may provide more insight into these state-trait possibilities. In the depressed state and the remitted state, we investigated the association between the perception of emotions and subsequent relapse. It was found that the perception of negative emotions is state dependent: Patients saw more negative emotions when in a depressed state than when the depression had been cleared. We already reported on the possible traitlike quality of negative cognitions that may be concluded from the observations that the negative bias was predictive in the depressed and remitted states. Therefore, our results seem to support both presumptions, that is, that the negative bias of the depressed patients has traitlike and statelike qualities. Tentatively formulated, our data provide support for a bias toward the perception of others' negative (ambiguous) facial emotional expressions as an enduring vulnerability factor to depression relapse (traitlike quality), whereas depressed mood amplifies this negative bias in perception (statelike quality).

Furthermore, my group found evidence that negative cognitions of the depressed persons may affect the cognitions of their partners (or vice versa) (Hale, Jansen, & Bouhuys, 1998). Depressed patients, their partners, and control persons (matched on sex and age of the partner) were asked to judge the faces of Fig. 10.3 with respect to the various emotions they display. Both the patients and the partners judged the facial expressions less positively and tended to judge the expressions more negatively than controls. Patients and partners did not perceive the expressions differently. Thus, depressed persons and their partners shared a tendency for negative thinking. One may ask whether this negative bias of the partners may be related to the patients' later outcome. Given the above-outlined theories, such association may be achieved via a reduction of the partners' social support. However, this presumption was not corroborated: The relative negative judgment of the partners was not associated with later outcome. However, more extensive studies with larger populations should confirm this unexpected result.

In conclusion, evidence is accumulating that cognitions about nonverbal behavior in terms of the perception of facial expressions are relevant for the course of depression. Patients who see relatively high levels of negative emotions in ambiguous faces are more likely to have longer depressive episodes and are more likely to relapse into depression after remission. Furthermore, partners seem to be affected by the negative interpretations of the depressives.

Personality and (Cognitions About) Nonverbal Behavior: Support for the Etiological Model?

The previous sections presented evidence that showed that behavioral co-ordination and negative cognitions are related to depression persistence and that negative cognitions are related to relapse into depression. Before I address the consequences of these findings for the model presented in Fig. 10.1, some possible interrelationships in this model are considered.

The available evidence for the interrelationships between the various variables presented in Fig. 10.1 and depression is considerable, but not beyond dispute. However, studies of relationships between behavioral and cognitive variables are scarce. The causal relationships among these variables, if any, have not been demonstrated yet.

My group hypothesized that (a) lack of behavioral coordination mediated the link between putative personality risk factors (neuroticism and extraversion) and later persistence of or relapse into depression, and (b) negative cognitions about facial expression may mediate the link between neuroticism and later persistence and relapse. These presumptions were tested in a study of 60 patients with winter depression. Coordination of patients' support seeking (the speaking effort factor) and interviewers' support giving (the encouragement factor) were assessed together with neuroticism and extraversion. We found that the less the patient and the interviewer became coordinated over the baseline interview and the lower the extraversion was, the more unfavorable the outcome of light therapy was 19 days later (Geerts et al., 1999). Neuroticism was not associated with outcome. We found that extraversion has a predictive quality for outcome in the expected direction. However, our prediction that the relation between extraversion and outcome would be mediated by behavioral coordination was not confirmed.

In a subsequent study of 26 depressed inpatients, my group found that low extraversion and high neuroticism predicted poorer outcomes after 6 weeks, as did high negative cognitions and a relative lack of coordination (Geerts & Bouhuys, 1998). In this study, we also found no support for lack of coordination as a mediating link between neuroticism or extraversion and persistence of depression. Thus, again, coordination of nonverbal behavior does not serve a mediating function between personality and outcome. In this study, we did find support for the notion that negative cognitions mediate the relation between neuroticism and outcome.

We found further support for the mediating function of negative cognitions in the relationship between neuroticism and relapse into depression. Relapse into depression was predicted by high levels of neuroticism and perception of negative emotions assessed in patients just remitted from an episode of depression (Bouhuys, 2002). The link between neuroticism at remission and relapse disappeared after negative cognitions were partialled out. In other words, neuroticism may predispose individuals to process others' emotions negatively, which then influences the course of depression negatively (persistence or relapse).

Thus, my group did not find support for the notion that nonverbal coordination serves a mediating role between notorious risk factors and outcome. On the contrary, we tested the variables nonverbal coordination, extraversion, and negative cognitions in a regression model. The question was asked whether these variables contributed independently to the prediction of outcome. We found that each of the variables had its own unique predictive quality, independent of the other variables (Geerts & Bouhuys, 1998). These results do not support a mediating role for nonverbal coordination, but suggest that these variables represent different aspects of interpersonal processes that are related to depression. What are the relevant differences between the variables and what typifies the differences between the variables? An important difference seems to be the level of assessment: directly observed behavior versus self-report questionnaires about subjects' attitude in interpersonal situations. Thus, coordination represents the actual behavior during interpersonal interactions, whereas extraversion and negative cognitions represent depressed subjects' knowledge and notions about (their) emotions and behavior in interpersonal situations.

The model of my group also predicted that negative cognitions would be associated with cortisol. We tested this in a group of 34 depressed inpatients; we assessed the perception of facial expressions and 24-hr urinary cortisol during their depressed state. We found that the tendency to perceive ambiguous faces as negative was associated with relatively high levels of cortisol excretion (Bouhuys, 2002). This finding supports the connection between cortisol and negative cognitions proposed in Fig. 10.1.

Vulnerability-Accumulation and Nonverbal Coordination

The vulnerability-accumulation hypothesis holds that, with increasing experience of depressed episodes, subjects are more at risk for recurrence of depression. Having found that deficits in coordination of nonverbal involvement may form a risk for depression persistence, my group hypothesized that coordination would be impaired with the increasing experience of depressive episodes (Bouhuys & Sam, 2000).

My group assessed coordination in remitted patients who had either suffered a first lifetime episode or experienced a recurrent depression during an interview of 15 min. Three aspects of coordination were considered: (a) the above-mentioned time course of coordination during an interaction,

(b) the mean coordination over the interview, and (c) the variability of coordination. This last measure needs explanation. Suppose that a pair is trying to equalize their involvement behavior (see Fig. 10.2). One may postulate that subjects control their coordination via a simple feedback mechanism (see McFarland, 1971). We showed that involvement of depressed patients and interviewers is causally related (Geerts et al., 1997). Consequently, the involvement behavior of a sender may serve as a feedback signal for a receiver to regulate the receiver's level of involvement behavior. This feedback mechanism may be represented in time by a curve that depicts diminishing fluctuations around a mean until a steady state has been achieved. If no steady state in coordination has been reached or fluctuations in coordination stay large over time, this may indicate lack of control.

The interview was divided into five equal periods of 3 min. For each period, the degree of coordination was assessed. Variability of coordination was defined as the standard deviation of the five period scores.

My group found, in a subgroup of remitted patients with a recurrent depression, larger variability of coordination compared to patients remitted from a lifetime episode. The other aspects of coordination did not differ between these two groups. The significant differences were restricted to a subgroup that consisted of remitted subjects who had just suffered a severe episode of depression. If remission was preceded by a less severe depressive episode, no differences in variability of coordination were found. In other words, the hypothesis that patients who had suffered more depressed episodes are more likely to be impaired in coordination when interacting with an interviewer, compared to patients who just remitted from a first lifetime depression, found some support.

These results can be placed in a developmental perspective. The deficits in coordination my group found between interviewers and patients with recurrent depression may be grounded in the early experience of the patients in coordination with their caregivers. Deficits in coordination in early life may have resulted in insecure attachment, which is considered a vulnerability for later depression. Deficits in coordination in later life may be related to depression risk as acquired in early mother-child interactions. In addition, suffering additional depressive episodes may then affect this already acquired vulnerability, resulting in an increase in this vulnerability factor and in elevated risk for depression recurrence (probably via unsatisfactory interactions). Further longitudinal research is needed to determine the interrelationship between early and late coordination and attachment and to elucidate how these factors place subjects at elevated risk for depression.

In conclusion, some support was found for the notion that nonverbal vulnerability accumulates in depression and that the severity of prior depression modifies this process. The deficits in coordination—perhaps acquired in early life—are supposed to become clearer with increasing expe-

rience of depressive episodes, causing unsatisfactory interactions, leading
to elevated risk for depression recurrence.

Final Remarks and Future Research

The main theme of this chapter was to consider interactional aspects in
depression from a ethological perspective and to see how these interactional aspects may fit into current etiologic models of depression (see Fig.
10.1). Etiologic models that propose causal explanations should preferably
be based on longitudinal designs. Therefore, the chapter referred mainly to
longitudinal studies of depressed patients. Instead of the commonly assessed cognitions concerning patients' reflections about thoughts and attitudes assessed by questionnaires, cognitions about nonverbal social signals
were added to the model. Furthermore, instead of questionnaires that assess
quality of relationships between people, directly observed nonverbal behavioral interactions, presumably reflecting interactional quality, were
measured.

The associations between cognitions about others' emotions seem to fit
into the prevailing theories of depression. Neuroticism is related to negative
cognitions, and these cognitions mediate the link between neuroticism and
outcome. Moreover, high levels of negative cognitions coincide with high
levels of the stress hormone cortisol. Here, data derived from an ethological
viewpoint confirm the proposed model. In addition, the data of my group
suggest that cognitions about others' emotions may form a relevant addition
to the model. However, the claim that negative cognitions may affect the
course of depression via their negative effect on interpersonal relationships
is an issue for future research. No causal relationships with the onset or
course of depression have been demonstrated.

Strong evidence has been presented to show that lack of coordination
between involvement behaviors of depressed patients and a conversation
partner has predictive quality with respect to the course of depression.
However, coordination predicted poor outcome independent of personality
factors and negative cognitions. In this respect, coordination does not fit
into the model, for which interpersonal aspects of behavior were thought
to be affected by negative cognitions. Apparently, the interpersonal observations my group applied seem to represent a novel aspect in depression
research. Therefore, the model may be extended by conceiving of coordination as a vulnerability factor. More research should be done on this issue
to gain insight into the meaning of lack of coordination for the depression
course. The relation between lack of coordination and interpersonal satisfaction deserves further attention. Moreover, it has been argued that coordination may stem from very early experience relevant to attachment and
security. In future research, my group will address this issue.

Hence, concerning the model presented in Fig. 10.1, it was possible (a) to prove the unique contribution of interpersonal processes to risk for depression, compared to putative risk factors such as neuroticism and extraversion (see Geerts et al., 1999; Geerts & Bouhuys, 1998), and (b) to show that cognitions about socially relevant stimuli fit into the model. Apparently, the embedding of ethological research in psychosocial theoretical frameworks has value.

After these optimistic statements, some drawbacks should be mentioned. Ethology in psychiatry is a recent research domain, and results should be replicated by different research groups. Moreover, research on etiology of depression would benefit from premorbid behavioral assessment instead of assessing patients and former patients. However, ethological assessments are time, and therefore money, consuming. Because of the consistency of results with respect to lack of coordination that predicts persistence of depression, less time consuming methods that assess the same aspects of interpersonal behavior are needed.

I am hopeful that in the near future ethological assessments can be applied to guide treatment strategies. The assessment of both coordination and nonverbal cognitions may contribute to develop new or additional treatments for potential nonresponders or subjects prone to relapse. Possible other implications for therapeutic interventions should get attention: Interpersonal and cognitive therapy are successful interventions in the prevention of relapse (see Frank & Spanier, 1995; Scott, 1996). For instance, in the cognitive behavior therapy model, patients are encouraged to prepare for future stressful events by rehearsing and augmenting their repertoire of coping behaviors. It is tempting to speculate that, if these approaches target in particular the depressive's negative bias in the perception of others' emotions and the potential consequences for interpersonal stress, they would even be more successful in the prevention of relapse.

My group found that, especially in women, negative cognitions were related to future persistence of depression. Depression shows a $2:1$ female predominance (Paykel, 1991; Weissman & Klerman, 1977). Surprisingly little attention has been devoted to possible gender differences in cognitive mechanisms that may underlie development and maintenance of depression. Some authors have postulated that women and men follow different pathways to depression development and maintenance, with cognitive factors implicated more in depression for women than for men (Butler & Nolen-Hoeksema, 1994; Nolen-Hoeksema, 1990; Teasdale, 1988).

Furthermore, evidence exists that women and men differ in cognitive processing of nonverbal signals. Overall, women are more accurate and sensitive decoders than men (Hall, 1978; Mufson & Nowicki, 1991). Apart from these possible gender differences in information processing, some authors reported that women and men may differ in coping strategies and interpersonal functioning. Gender differences in styles of responding to or coping with depressed mood have been demonstrated: Women are more likely than men to self-focus ruminatively when depressed, a response style that maintains and exacerbates the depressed mood (Bruder-Mattson & Hovanitz, 1990; Nolen-Hoeksema, 1990). In addition, women seem more likely than men to attribute their depression to interpersonal problems (Robbins & Tanck, 1991; Spangler, Simons, Thase, & Monroe, 1996). Future research should certainly take possible gender differences into account.

I hope that ethological studies of depression may enlarge our understanding of mechanisms and risk factors responsible for onset, persistence, and relapse of depression. Human ethology and psychiatry may both gain by further integration of their research.

Acknowledgment

I am very grateful to Erwin Geerts for his critical comments on an earlier draft of this chapter.

References

Akiskal, H. S., Hirschfeld, R. M. A., & Yerevanian, B. I. (1983). The relationship of personality to affective disorders. *Archives of General Psychiatry, 40*, 801–810.

American Psychiatric Association. (1994). *Diagnostic and statistical manual of mental disorders* (4th ed.). Washington, DC: Author.

Angst, J. (1988). Clinical course of affective disorders. In T. Helgason & R. J. Daly (Eds.), *Depressive illness: Prediction of course and outcome* (pp. 1–44). Berlin: Springer-Verlag.

Archer, J., Hay, D. C., & Young, A. W. (1992). Face processing in psychiatric conditions. *British Journal of Clinical Psychology, 31*, 45–61.

Bagby, R. M., Schuller, D. R., Parker, J. D. A., Levitt, A., Joffe, R. T., & Sharon, S. M. (1994). Major depression and the self-criticism and dependency personality dimension. *American Journal of Psychiatry, 151*, 597–599.

Beck, A. T., Rush, A. J., Shaw, B. F., & Emery, G. (1979). *Cognitive therapy of depression*. New York: Guilford Press.

Bernieri, F. J. (1988). Coordinated movement and rapport in teacher-student interactions. *Journal of Nonverbal Behavior, 12*, 120–138.

Bernieri, F. J., & Rosenthal, R. (1991). Interpersonal coordination: Behavior matching and interactional synchrony. In R. S. Feldman & B. Rimé (Eds.), *Fundamentals of behavior* (pp. 401–432). Cambridge, England: Cambridge University Press.

Berti, G., Ceroni, G., & Pezzoli, A. (1984). Chronicity in major depression: A naturalistic prospective study. *Journal of Affective Disorders, 10*, 121–144.

Bouhuys, A. L. (2002). *Cortisol and depression*. Unpublished data.

Bouhuys, A. L., & Albersnagel, F. A. (1992). Do interactional capacities based on observed behaviour interfere with improvement in severely depressed patients? *Journal of Affective Disorders, 25*, 107–116.

Bouhuys, A. L., Bloem, G. M., & Groothuis, T. G. G. (1995). Induction of depressed and elated mood by music influences the perception of facial emotional expressions in healthy subjects. *Journal of Affective Disorders, 33*, 215–226.

Bouhuys, A. L., Geerts, E., & Gordijn, M. C. M. (1999a). Depressed patients' perception of facial emotions in depressed and remitted state is associated with relapse: A longitudinal study. *Journal of Nervous and Mental Disease, 187,* 595–602.

Bouhuys, A. L., Geerts, E., & Gordijn, M. C. M. (1999b). Gender specific mechanisms associated with outcome of depression: Perception of emotions, coping and interpersonal functioning. *Psychiatry Research, 85,* 247–261.

Bouhuys, A. L., Geerts, E., Mersch, P. P., & Jenner, J. A. (1996). Nonverbal interpersonal sensitivity and persistence of depression: The perception of emotions in schematic faces. *Psychiatry Research, 64,* 193–203.

Bouhuys, A. L., Geerts, E., & Mersch, P. P. A. (1997). Relationship between perception of facial emotions and anxiety in clinical depression: Does anxiety-related perception predict persistence of depression? *Journal of Affective Disorders, 43,* 213–223.

Bouhuys, A. L., Jansen, C. J., & Van den Hoofdakker, R. H. (1991). Analysis of observed behavior displayed by depressed patients during a clinical interview: Relationships between behavioral factors and clinical concepts of activation. *Journal of Affective Disorders, 21,* 79–88.

Bouhuys, A. L., & Sam, M. M. (2000). Coordination of nonverbal behaviour between patients and interviewers as a potential risk factor to depression recurrence: Vulnerability accumulation in depression. *Journal of Affective Disorders, 57,* 189–200.

Bouhuys, A. L., & Van den Hoofdakker, R. H. (1991). The interrelatedness of observed behavior of depressed patients and of a psychiatrist: An ethological study on mutual influence. *Journal of Affective Disorders, 23,* 63–74.

Bouhuys, A. L., & Van den Hoofdakker, R. H. (1993). A longitudinal study of interaction patterns of a psychiatrist and severely depressed patients based on observed behavior: An ethological approach of interpersonal theories of depression. *Journal of Affective Disorders, 27,* 87–99.

Bowlby, J. (1969). *Attachment and loss.* London: Hogarth.

Bowlby, J. (1981). *Attachment and loss, Vol. 3: Loss: Sadness and depression.* Middlesex, England: Harmondsworth.

Boyce, P., Parker, G., Barnett, B., Conney, M., & Smith, F. (1991). Personality as a vulnerability factor to depression. *British Journal of Psychiatry, 159,* 106–114.

Brown, G. W., Harris, T. O., Hepworth, C., & Robinson, R. (1994). Clinical and psychosocial origins of chronic depressive episodes II: A patient inquiry. *British Journal of Psychiatry, 165,* 457–465.

Bruder-Mattson, S. F., & Hovanitz, C. A. (1990). Coping and attributional styles as predictors of depression. *Journal of Clinical Psychology, 46,* 557–565.

Burgoon, J. K., Le-Poire, B. A., & Rosenthal, R. (1995). Effects of preinteraction expectancies and target communication on perceiver reciprocity and compensation in dyadic interaction. *Journal of Experimental Social Psychology, 31,* 287–321.

Butler, L. D., & Nolen-Hoeksema, S. (1994). Gender differences in responses to depressed mood in a college sample. *Sex Roles, 30,* 331–346.

Cappella, J. N. (1997). Behavioral and judged coordination in adult informal social interactions: Vocal and kinesic indicators. *Journal of Personality and Social Psychology, 72,* 119–131.

Cappella, J. N., & Palmer, M. T. (1990). Attitude similarity, relational history, and attraction: The mediating effects of kinesic and vocal behaviors. *Communication Monographs, 57*, 161–183.

Coker, D. A., & Burgoon, J. K. (1987). The nature of conversational involvement and nonverbal encoding patterns. *Human Communication Research, 13*, 463–494.

Cosgriff, J. P., Abbott, R. M., Oakley Browne, M. A., & Joyce, P. R. (1990). Cortisol hypersecretion predicts early depressive relapse after recovery with electroconvulsive therapy. *Biological Psychiatry, 28*, 1007–1010.

Coyne, J. C. (1976). Depression and the response to others. *Journal of Abnormal Psychology, 85*, 186–193.

Coyne, J. C., Burchill, S. A. L., & Stiles, W. B. (1990). An interactional perspective on depression. In C. R. Snyder & D. O. Forsyth (Eds.), *Handbook of social and clinical psychology* (pp. 325–349). New York: Pergamon.

Coyne, J. C., & Downey, G. (1991). Social factors and psychopathology: Stress, social support, and coping processes. *Annual Review of Psychology, 42*, 401–425.

Crowell, J. A., O'Connor, E., Wollmers, G., & Sprafkin, J. (1991). Mothers' conceptualizations of parent-child relationships: Relation to mother-child interaction and child behavior problems. Special issue: Attachment and developmental psychopathology. *Development and Psychopathology, 3*, 431–444.

Darwin, C. (1965). *The expression of the emotions in man and animals.* Chicago: University of Chicago Press. (Original work published 1872)

Diamond, D., & Doane, J. A. (1994). Disturbed attachment and negative affective style: An integrational spiral. *British Journal of Psychiatry, 164*, 770–781.

Ekman, P. (1992). Are there basic emotions? *Psychological Review, 99*, 550–553.

Ellgring, H. (1989). *Nonverbal communication in depression.* Cambridge, England: Cambridge University Press.

Fogel, A. (1993). *Developing through relationships: Origins of communication, self, and culture.* New York: Harvester, Wheatsheaf.

Fossi, L., Faravelli, C., & Paoli, M. (1984). The ethological approach to the assessment of depressive disorders. *Journal of Nervous and Mental Disease, 182*, 332–341.

Franche, R. L., & Dobson, K. (1992). Self-criticism and interpersonal dependency as vulnerability factors to depression. *Cognitive Therapy and Research, 16*, 419–435.

Frank, E., & Spanier, C. (1995). Interpersonal psychotherapy for depression: Overview, clinical efficacy, and future directions. *Clinical Psychology Science and Practice, 2*, 349–369.

Gaebel, W., & Woelwer, W. (1992). Facial expression and emotional face recognition in schizophrenia and depression. *European Archives of Psychiatry and Clinical Neuroscience, 242*, 46–52.

Geerts, E., & Bouhuys, A. L. (1998). Multi-level prediction of short-term outcome of depression: The role of nonverbal interpersonal and cognitive processes and of personality traits. *Psychiatry Research, 79*, 59–72.

Geerts, E., Bouhuys, A. L., & Bloem, G. M. (1997). Nonverbal support giving induces nonverbal support seeking in depressed patients. *Journal of Clinical Psychology, 53*, 41–49.

Geerts, E., Bouhuys, A. L., Meesters, Y., & Jansen, J. H. C. (1995). Observed behavior of patients with seasonal affective disorder and an interviewer predicts response to light treatment. *Psychiatry Research, 57*, 223–230.

Geerts, E., Bouhuys, A. L., & Van den Hoofdakker, R. H. (1996). Nonverbal attunement between depressed patients and an interviewer predicts subsequent improvement. *Journal of Affective Disorders, 40*, 15–21.

Geerts, E., Kouwert, E., Bouhuys, A. L., Meesters, Y., & Jansen, J. H. C. (2000). Nonverbal interpersonal attunement and extravert personality predict outcome of light treatment in seasonal affective disorder. *Journal of Affective Disorders, 59*, 193–204.

George, M. S., Huggins, T., McDermut, W., Parekh, P. I., Rubinow, D., & Post, R. M. (1998). Abnormal facial emotion recognition in depression: Serial testing in an ultra-rapid-cycling patient. *Behavior Modification, 22*, 192–204.

Gilbert, P. (1992). *Depression: The evolution of powerlessness*. London: Guilford Press.

Gilboa, E., & Gotlib, I. H. (1997). Cognitive biases and affect persistence in previously dysphoric and never-dysphoric individuals. *Cognition and Emotion, 11*, 517–538.

Gotlib, I. H. (1992). Interpersonal and cognitive aspects of depression. *Current Directions in Psychological Science, 1*, 149–154.

Gotlib, I. H., & Hammen, C. L. (1992). *Psychological aspects of depression; Towards a cognitive-interpersonal integration*. Chichester, England: Wiley.

Gregory, S. W., Webster, S., & Huang, G. (1993). Voice pitch and amplitude convergence as a metric of quality in dyadic interviews. *Language and Communication, 13*, 195–217.

Gur, R. C., Erwin, R. J., Gur, R. E., Zwil, A. S., Heimberg, C., & Kraemer, H. C. (1992). Facial emotion discrimination: II. Behavioral findings in depression. *Psychiatry Research, 41*, 241–251.

Hale, W. H., Jansen, J. H. C., & Bouhuys, A. L. (1997). Depression relapse and ethological measures. *Psychiatry Research, 70*, 57–64.

Hale, W. H., Jansen, J. H. C., & Bouhuys, A. L. (1998). The judgement of facial expressions by depressed patients, their partners and controls. *Journal of Affective Disorders, 47*, 63–70.

Hale, W. W., Jansen, J. H. C., Bouhuys, A. L., Jenner, J. A., & Van den Hoofdakker, R. H. (1997). Non-verbal behavioral interactions of depressed patients with partners and strangers: The role of behavioral social support and involvement in depression persistence. *Journal of Affective Disorders, 44*, 111–122.

Hall, J. A. (1978). Gender effects in decoding nonverbal cues. *Psychological Bulletin, 85*, 845–857.

Hall, J. A., Harrigan, J. A., & Rosenthal, R. (1995). Nonverbal behavior in clinician-patient interaction. *Applied and Preventive Psychology, 4*, 21–37.

Hammen, C. (1992). Cognitive, life stress, and interpersonal approaches to a developmental psychopathology model of depression. *Development and Psychopathology, 4*, 189–206.

Hammen, C. L., Burge, D., Daley, S. E., Davila, J., Paley, B., & Rudolph, K. D. (1995). Interpersonal attachment cognitions and prediction of symptomatic responses to interpersonal stress. *Journal of Abnormal Psychology, 104*, 436–443.

Hauser, M. D. (1996). *The evolution of communication.* Cambridge, MA: MIT Press.

Hedlund, S., & Rude, S. (1995). Evidence of latent depressive schemas in formerly depressed individuals. *Journal of Abnormal Psychology, 104,* 517–525.

Hirschfeld, R. M. A., Klerman, G. L., Lavori, P., Keller, M. B., Griffith, P., & Coryell, W. (1989). Premorbid personality assessments of first onset of major depression. *Archives of General Psychiatry, 46,* 345–349.

Hoehn-Hyde, D., & Rush, A. J. (1982). Perception of social interactions in depressed psychiatric patients. *Journal of Consulting and Clinical Psychology, 50,* 209–212.

Holsboer, F. (1989). Psychiatric implications of altered limbic-hypothalamic-pituitary-adrenocortical activity. *European Archives of Psychiatry and Neurological Sciences, 238,* 302–322.

Isabella, R. A., & Belsky, J. (1991). Interactional synchrony and infant-mother attachment: A replication study. *Child Development, 62,* 373–384.

Isabella, R. A., Belsky, J., & Eye, A. (1989). Origins of mother-infant attachment: An examination of interactional synchrony during infant's first year. *Developmental Psychology, 25,* 12–21.

Isen, A. M., & Shalker, T. E. (1982). The effect of feeling state on evaluation of positive, neutral, and negative stimuli: When you "accentuate the positive," do you "eliminate the negative"? *Social Psychology Quarterly, 45,* 58–63.

Jones, I. H., & Pansa, M. (1979). Some nonverbal aspects of depression and schizophrenia occurring during an interview. *Journal of Nervous and Mental Disease, 167,* 402–409.

Kendler, K. S. (1993). The prediction of major depression in women: Toward an integrated etiologic model. *American Journal of Psychiatry, 150,* 1139–1148.

Lazarus, R. S., & Folkman, S. (1984). *Stress, appraisal and coping.* New York: Springer.

Lewinsohn, P. M., Steinmetz, J. L., Larson, D. W., & Franklin, J. (1981). Depression-related cognitions: antecedent or consequence? *Journal of Abnormal Psychology, 90,* 213–219.

Main, M. (1996). Introduction to the special section on attachment and psychopathology: 2. Overview of the field of attachment. *Journal of Consulting and Clinical Psychology, 64,* 237–243.

Mandal, M. K. (1987). Decoding of facial emotions, in terms of expressiveness, by schizophrenics and depressives. *Psychiatry, 50,* 371–376.

Mandal, M. K., & Palchoudhury, S. (1985). Responses to facial expression of emotion in depression. *Psychological Reports, 56,* 653–654.

Mathews, A., & MacLeod, C. (1994). Cognitive approaches to emotion and emotional disorders. *Annual Review of Psychology, 45,* 25–50.

McFarland, D. J. (1971). *Feedback mechanisms in animal behaviour.* London: Academic Press.

McGuire, M., & Troisi, A. (1998). *Darwinian psychiatry.* New York: Oxford University Press.

McGuire, M. T. (1994). Altruism and mental disorders. *Ethology and Sociobiology, 15,* 299–321.

McGuire, M. T., Marks, I., Nesse, R. M., & Troisi, A. (1992). Evolutionary biology: A basic science for psychiatry? *Acta Psychiatrica Scandinavia, 86,* 89–96.

McLeod, J. D., Kessler, R. C., & Landis, K. R. (1992). Speed of recovery from major depressive episodes in a community sample of married men and women. *Journal of Abnormal Psychology, 101,* 277–286.

Mikhailova, E. S., Vladimirova, T. V., Iznak, A. F., Tsusulkovskaya, E. J., & Sushko, N. V. (1996). Abnormal recognition of facial expression of emotions in depressed patients with major depression disorder and schizotypal personality disorder. *Biological Psychiatry, 40,* 697–705.

Mufson, L., & Nowicki, S. (1991). Factors affecting the accuracy of facial affect recognition. *Journal of Social Psychology, 131,* 815–822.

Nolen-Hoeksema, S. (1990). *Sex differences in depression.* Stanford, CA: Stanford University Press.

Ormel, J., & Wohlfarth, T. (1991). How neuroticism, long-term difficulties, and life situation change influence psychological distress: A longitudinal model. *Journal of Personality and Social Psychology, 60,* 744–755.

Parker, G., Hadzi Pavlovic, D., Greenwald, S., & Weissman, M. (1995). Low parental care as a risk factor to lifetime depression in a community sample. *Journal of Affective Disorders, 33,* 173–180.

Paykel, E. S. (1991). Depression in women. *British Journal of Psychiatry, 158,* 22–29.

Paykel, E. S. (1994, December). Historical overview of outcome of depression. *British Journal of Psychiatry, Suppl.,* 6–8.

Post, R. M. (1992). Transduction of psychosocial stress into the neurobiology of recurrent affective disorder. *American Journal of Psychiatry, 149,* 999–1010.

Potthoff, J. G., Holahan, C. J., & Joiner, T. E. (1995). Reassurance seeking, stress generation, and depressive symptoms: An integrative model. *Journal of Personality and Social Psychology, 68,* 664–670.

Price, J., & Gardner, R. (1995). The paradoxical power of the depressed patient: A problem for the ranking theory of depression. *British Journal of Medical Psychology, 68,* 193–206.

Price, J., Sloman, L., Gardner, R., Gilbert, P., & Rohde, P. (1994). The social competition hypothesis of depression. Special issue: Depression. *British Journal of Psychiatry, 164,* 309–315.

Ramana, R., Paykel, E. S., Cooper, Z., Hayhurst, H., Saxty, M., & Surtees, P. G. (1995). Remission and relapse in major depression: A two-year prospective follow-up study. *Psychological Medicine, 25,* 1161–1170.

Ranelli, C. J., & Miller, R. (1981). Behavioral predictors of amitriptyline response in depression. *American Journal of Psychiatry, 138,* 30–34.

Robbins, P. R., & Tanck, R. H. (1991). Gender differences in the attribution of causes for depressed feelings. *Psychological Reports, 68,* 209–1210.

Rosen, A. J., Tureff, S. E., Lyons, J. S., & Davis, J. M. (1981). Pharmacotherapy of schizophrenia and affective disorders: Behavioral assessment of psychiatric medications. *Journal of Behavioral Assessment, 3,* 133–148.

Rubinow, D. R., & Post, R. M. (1992). Impaired recognition of affect in facial expression in depressed patients. *Biological Psychiatry, 31,* 947–953.

Schelde, T. (1994). Ethological research in psychiatry. *Ethology and Sociobiology, 15,* 349–368.

Scott, J. (1996). Cognitive therapy of affective disorders: A review. *Journal of Affective Disorders, 37*, 1–11.

Segal, Z. V., Williams, J. M., Teasdale, J. D., & Gemar, M. (1996). A cognitive science perspective on kindling and episode sensitization in recurrent affective disorder. *Psychological Medicine, 26*, 371–380.

Segrin, C., & Abramson, L. Y. (1994). Negative reactions to depressive behaviors: A communication theories analysis. *Journal of Abnormal Psychology, 103*, 655–668.

Siegman, A. (1985). Expressive correlates of affective states and traits. In A. Siegman (Ed.), *Multichannel integrations of nonverbal behavior* (pp. 37–68). Hillsdale, NJ: Erlbaum.

Sloman, L., Price, J., Gilbert, P., & Gardner, R. (1994). Adaptive function of depression: Psychotherapeutic implications. *American Journal of Psychotherapy, 48*, 401–416.

Spangler, D. L., Simons, A. D., Thase, M. E., & Monroe, S. M. (1996). Gender differences in cognitive diathesis-stress domain match: implications for differential pathways to depression. *Journal of Abnormal Psychology, 105*, 653–657.

Sturt, E., Kumarkura, N., & Der, G. (1984). How depressing life is: Lifelong morbidity risk for depression in the general population. *Journal of Affective Disorders, 6*, 104–122.

Surtees, P. G., & Barkley, C. (1994). Future imperfect: The long-term outcome of depression. *British Journal of Psychiatry, 164*, 327–341.

Teasdale, J. D. (1988). Cognitive vulnerability to persistent depression. *Cognition and Emotion, 2*, 247–274.

Terwogt, M. M., Kremer, H. H., & Stegge, H. (1991). Effects of children's emotional state on their reactions to emotional expressions: a search for congruency effects. *Cognition and Emotion, 5*, 109–121.

Tickle-Degnen, L., & Rosenthal, R. (1990). The nature of rapport and its nonverbal correlates. *Psychological Inquiry, 1*, 285–293.

Tinbergen, N. (1951). *The study of instinct.* Oxford, England: Oxford University Press.

Troisi, A., Pasini, A., Bersani, G., Grispini, A., & Ciani, N. (1990). Ethological assessment of the *DSM-III* subtyping of unipolar depression. *Acta Psychiatrica Scandinavia, 81*, 560–564.

Troisi, A. T., Pasini, A., Bersani, G., Grispini, A., & Ciani, N. (1989). Ethological predictors of amitryptiline response in depressed outpatients. *Journal of Affective Disorders, 17*, 129–136.

Ulrich, G., & Harms, K. (1985). A video analysis of the non-verbal behaviour of depressed patients before and after treatment. *Journal of Affective Disorders, 9*, 63–67.

von Korff, M., Ormel, J., Katon, W., & Lin, E. H. (1992). Disability and depression among high utilizers of health care: A longitudinal analysis. *Archives of General Psychiatry, 49*, 91–100.

Walker, E., McGuire, M., & Bettes, B. (1984). Recognition and identification of facial stimuli by schizophrenics and patients with affective disorders. *British Journal of Clinical Psychology, 23*, 37–44.

Watson, D., & Tellegen, A. (1985). Toward a consensual structure of mood. *Psychological Bulletin, 98*, 219–235.

Weissman, M. M., & Klerman, G. L. (1977). Sex differences and the epidemiology of depression. *Archives of General Psychiatry, 34*, 98–111.

Wexler, B. E., Levenson, L., Warrenburg, S., & Price, L. H. (1994). Decreased perceptual sensitivity to emotion-evoking stimuli in depression. *Psychiatry Research, 51*, 127–138.

Zahn, T. P., Nurnberger, J. I., Berretti, W. H., & Robinson, T. N. (1991). Concordance between anxiety and autonomous nervous system activity in subjects at genetic risk for affective disorder. *Psychiatry Research, 36*, 99–110.

Zuroff, D. C. (1994). Depressive personality styles and the five-factor model of personality. *Journal of Personality Assessment, 63*, 453–472.

Zuroff, D. C., & Colussy, S. A. (1986). Emotion recognition in schizophrenic and depressed patients. *Journal of Clinical Psychology, 42*, 411–416.

11

Nonverbal Behavior in Schizophrenia

ANN M. KRING AND KELLY S. EARNST

In the outspoken forms of schizophrenia, the
emotional deterioration stands in the forefront
of the clinical picture. . . . Many schizophrenics
. . . sit about the institutions to which they are
confined with expressionless faces, hunched-
up, the image of indifference.

Bleuler (1911/1950)

Historically, emotional disturbances in schizophrenia were considered prominent features of the disorder, as evidenced in the above quote by Bleuler (1911/1950). It is noteworthy that the nonverbal behavior component of emotion (facial expression, postures) was the focus of these early clinical descriptions. Indeed, theorists wrote often about an apparent mismatch between schizophrenia patients' nonverbal emotion displays and their subjective experience of emotion. The writings of Bleuler, Kraepelin (1919/1971), and others provided descriptions of schizophrenia patients who reported experiencing strong emotions, but who did not readily display those feelings outwardly. Despite the theoretical and clinical importance of these observations, systematic research into the nature of emotional disturbances was not conducted until fairly recently.

In this chapter, we examine the nature of nonverbal emotion disturbances in schizophrenia, beginning with a consideration of theoretical approaches to the study of emotion and schizophrenia and the research paradigms that have arisen from these approaches. It is our contention that greater progress toward understanding the nature of emotional disturbances in schizophrenia has been made from studies based in the theoretical and methodological traditions of basic emotion research. We review a number of schizophrenia studies that have employed paradigms from the basic emotion literature and then present some new data that demonstrate that schizophrenia patients exhibit very subtle nonverbal facial expressions not outwardly observable. We conclude by summarizing what we do and do not know about emotion disturbances in schizophrenia, note treatment and assessment implications, and suggest a number of directions for additional research.

Theoretical and Methodological Approaches to Studying Emotion in Schizophrenia

Many early theories of emotion disturbance in schizophrenia were based on clinical observations with schizophrenia patients, and they were derived to account for the diverse symptom picture comprising the illness, not just the emotional features of schizophrenia. Recognizing the varied number of schizophrenia symptoms, Bleuler (1911/1950) posited that schizophrenia symptoms could be categorized as either fundamental (i.e., pathognomonic) or accessory. In Bleuler's theory, there were four fundamental symptoms, one of which was affective disturbance. Bleuler, who coined the term *schizophrenia* to reflect the "splitting of associative threads" that occurs in schizophrenia, suggested that this associative disturbance was a direct reflection of the disease process, whereas other symptoms, including affective symptoms, reflected the disease process interacting with an individual patient's environment. Moreover, Bleuler's ideas about schizophrenia were heavily influenced by psychoanalytic theory. For example, he suggested that this line of theorizing could account for the content of delusions and hallucinations.

Also grounded in psychoanalytic theory, Rado (1956) conjectured that the primary emotion disturbance in schizophrenia was a failure to experience positive emotions, which he referred to as the "welfare emotions." As a consequence of this pleasure deficit, Rado argued that schizophrenia patients would experience negative emotions (the "emergency emotions") more strongly.

More recent theories in psychiatry have attempted to integrate psychological and biological factors to account for the overt signs and symptoms of the disorder. For example, Carpenter and colleagues (e.g., Carpenter, Buchanan, Kirkpatrick, Tamminga, & Wood, 1993; Carpenter, Heinrichs, & Wagman, 1988) argued that schizophrenia patients who have negative symptoms that are both enduring and primary represent a distinct etiologic subtype referred to as the deficit syndrome. Furthermore, these investigators hypothesized that dysfunction involving frontal cortex and limbic structures might account for deficit symptomatology (e.g., Buchanan et al., 1994; Tamminga et al., 1992). Interestingly, the essence of deficit symptoms is based on Kraepelin's (1919/1971) notion of an avolitional process, described as "emotional dullness, failure of mental activities, loss of mastery over volition, of endeavor, and of ability for independent action" (p. 74);

thus, not surprisingly, a number of the deficit symptoms involve emotional features (e.g., diminished emotional range, curbing of interests, and restricted affect).

The development of more recent theories of schizophrenia has been complemented with the development of more reliable methods for symptom assessment, such as the Scale for the Assessment of Negative Symptoms (SANS; Andreasen, 1983) and the Schedule for the Deficit Syndrome (SDS; Kirkpatrick, Buchanan, McKinney, Alphs, & Carpenter, 1989; for a review, see Earnst & Kring, 1997). These scales were developed so that a trained observer could interview a patient and then rate the degree to which the patient manifested a number of different symptoms, including emotional symptoms. For example, the SANS includes an Affective Flattening subscale. Patients who are rated as having flat affect may speak in a monotonic voice, use few expressive gestures, have poor eye contact, and show few changes in facial expression.

The development of these rating scales contributed to a resurgence of interest in emotional features of schizophrenia because they provided investigators with much-needed, reliable measures of emotion-related symptoms. Using these scales, evidence indicates that flat affect is a fairly common symptom of schizophrenia, although there is considerable cross-cultural variability (Jenkins, 1994). Among Euro-American schizophrenia patients, flat affect is relatively stable across time (Kring & Earnst, 1999; Pfhol & Winokur, 1982; but see Keefe et al., 1991), related to a poor prognosis (Carpenter, Bartko, Strauss, & Hawk, 1978; Fenton & McGlashan, 1991; Knight & Roff, 1985), and more common in schizophrenia than in depression (Andreasen, 1979).

Although the use of these rating scales has contributed to the understanding of the symptom flat affect (among others), the scales are not without limitations. First, the clinical interview on which symptom ratings are made may not actually elicit emotion from the participants. Questions are typically centered on the patient's illness experience, and while this may be emotion eliciting for some patients, it may be quite benign for others. Thus, ratings of expressive behavior may be constrained by the interview (Kring, Alpert, Neale, & Harvey, 1994). In addition, these scales typically assess only one component of emotion: The Affective Flattening subscale assesses the expressive component of emotion. However, emotion is best construed as having multiple components. An approach that assesses multiple emotion components, therefore, will provide a more complete evaluation of emotional responding among schizophrenia patients.

Because many psychiatric theories are developed to account for the diversity of schizophrenia symptoms, emotion does not often claim center stage in these accounts. Yet, a long and fruitful theoretical tradition on basic emotion function can inform studies of emotion dysfunction in schizophrenia. From the emotion literature, many theorists consider emotions to be responses that have developed over the course of human evolution to enable individuals to deal with problems, situations, and events in the environment (e.g., Buck, 1994; Ekman, 1992; Izard, 1993a, 1993b; Keltner & Kring, 1998; Kring & Bachorowski, 1999; Lang, Bradley, & Cuthbert, 1990). Emerging from these functional accounts, an emotion response is defined by a constellation of components, including a cognitive or appraisal component, a behavioral or expressive component, an experiential component, and a physiological component.

Methods for studying emotion that have originated from the basic emotion tradition typically involve the presentation of emotion-eliciting stimuli, such as emotional film clips, emotional slides, imagery, or social interaction. Facial expressions are often videotaped and later coded, and self-reports of emotional experience following the presentation of the emotionally evocative stimuli are gathered. Some investigators include psychophysiological measures, such as heart rate or skin conductance (SC), to assess the physiological component of emotion. These studies are usually done in laboratory settings; however, other, more naturalistic, approaches include daily assessments of emotional expression and experience over longer periods of time (e.g., Feldman-Barrett, 1997, 1998).

Findings from Empirical Studies of Emotion Disturbances in Schizophrenia

Using paradigms from basic emotion research, studies have found that, compared to nonpatient controls, schizophrenia patients are less facially expressive of both positive and negative emotions, yet they report experiencing as much positive and negative emotion while viewing emotion-eliciting films or pictures (Berenbaum & Oltmanns, 1992; Dworkin et al., 1993; Dworkin, Clark, Amador, & Gorman, 1996; Kring & Earnst, 1999; Kring, Kerr, Smith, & Neale, 1993; Kring & Neale, 1996). In paradigms involving a social interaction, schizophrenia patients are also less expressive than nonpatient controls (e.g., Krause, Steimer, Sanger-Alt, & Wagner, 1989; Mattes, Schneider, Heimann, & Birbaumer, 1995) and other patient groups (e.g., those with Parkinson's disease, depression, alcohol abuse) that have features similar to negative symptoms (Davison, Frith, Harrison-Read, & Johnstone, 1996; Gaebel & Wolwer, 1992; Pitman, Kolb, Orr, & Singh, 1987). Yet, despite their diminished expressive behavior, schizophrenia patients reported experiencing more negative emotion in these social interactions (Krause, Steimer-Krause, & Hufnagel, 1992). In addition, schizophrenia patients may show greater skin conductance reactivity to emotional film clips than nonpatients (Kring and Neale, 1996; but see also Kring, Germans, Triesch, & Putnam, 2003). Thus, studies that have incorporated methods from basic emotion have been able, for the first time, to confirm empirically the early clinical descriptions of Bleuler, Kraepelin, and others and indicate that schizophrenia patients manifest a disjunction among emotion response components.

These findings raise additional questions, however, with respect to non-verbal behavior in schizophrenia. First, it remains unclear whether schizophrenia patients are actually expressing (i.e., contracting the facial musculature), but at an intensity level that is undetectable by observers. Recent evidence indicates that schizophrenia patients do indeed manifest unobservable (covert) facial activity in a manner consistent with the valence of emotional stimuli, which suggests that the expressive component of emotion is not completely deficient among schizophrenia patients (Earnst et al., 1996; Kring, Kerr, & Earnst, 1999; Mattes et al., 1995). Second, the extent to which this subtle, unobservable facial activity among schizophrenia patients is related to other components of emotion is not known. However, understanding the relationships among emotion response components will help elucidate the nature of a possible disjunction among these components in schizophrenia.

Facial Expressions: Observable and Unobservable

Facial expressions are observable to the extent that facial muscle contraction leads to movement of various skin and connective tissue (e.g., lines, folds, wrinkles on the skin; movement of mouth, eyebrows, etc.). However, if facial muscle movement is sufficiently weak or if the muscle contractions discontinue before the corresponding connective tissues move, the muscle activity will not translate into an observable expression. Yet, this type of unobservable facial muscle activity can and does occur without these corresponding movements of skin and connective tissue.

Surface electromyographic (EMG) recording of facial muscle activity is a noninvasive method for measuring such unobservable facial muscle activity, and there are several important advantages to using EMG recording as a measure of facial behavior (Fridlund, 1988; Fridlund & Izard, 1983). For example, EMG recording allows for the detection of changes in the facial musculature that are too small to be observed. In addition, EMG is a more precise measure of facial muscle movement. Third, muscle movement is immediately detectable. EMG assessments of facial activity are not without disadvantages, however. The placement of electrodes on the face may interfere with spontaneous expressive behavior and may make an individual more aware of his or her facial behavior. To avoid this last problem, researchers typically give instructions to participants to divert attention from the face (e.g., "We are measuring unconscious brain waves"). In studies in which continuous emotional stimuli are presented, as in the case of film studies, EMG activity is most typically averaged over the entire film period and thus is not directly tied to particular moments of time in the film. In other words, an average of EMG activity across the film period is typically the dependent variable in analyses rather than the discrete events that are accumulated when assessing observable facial expressions.

Converging evidence from several studies using EMG in nonpatient populations indicates that EMG activity over the brow region (corrugator supercilii) increases and EMG activity over the cheek region (zygomaticus major) decreases during the presentation of unpleasant stimuli. In contrast, EMG activity over the cheek region increases and activity over the brow region decreases during the presentation of pleasant stimuli (e.g., Brown & Schwartz, 1980; Cacioppo, Bush, & Tassinary, 1992; Cacioppo, Petty, Losch, & Kim, 1986; Dimberg, 1982; Fridlund, 1991; Kring et al., 1999). This same pattern of findings has also been demonstrated with depressed patients (e.g., Schwartz, Fair, Salt, Mandel, & Klerman, 1976; Teasdale & Bancroft, 1977). In addition, corrugator activity is associated with reports of unpleasant emotion, and zygomatic activity is associated with reports of pleasant emotion (e.g., Fridlund & Izard, 1983; Greenwald, Cook, & Lang, 1989; Lang, Greenwald, Bradley, & Hamm, 1993; McCanne & Anderson, 1987).

Only recently have researchers included EMG assessments in studies of schizophrenia. For example, Kring et al. (1999) found that schizophrenia patients demonstrated greater zygomatic activity in response to pictures of positive facial expressions than to pictures of negative facial expressions and greater corrugator activity in response to pictures of negative facial expressions than to pictures of positive facial expressions. Interestingly, schizophrenia patients' EMG activity was greater than that of nonpatient controls. Mattes et al. (1995) found that schizophrenia patients exhibited more zygomatic activity during a happy film and a discussion of pleasant events than during a sad film and discussion of sad events, and they exhibited more corrugator activity during a sad film and discussion of sad events than during the happy film and discussion of pleasant events. Although patients exhibited slightly more corrugator activity than controls during the sad discussion, this difference was not significant. In addition, patients did not differ from controls in their corrugator activity during the sad film, and they exhibited less zygomatic activity than controls during the happy film and pleasant discussion.

Taken together, these findings suggest that, although schizophrenia patients' observable expressive behavior distinguishes them from nonpatient controls, more subtle and unobservable facial activity may be similar to or even greater than controls. This is particularly interesting in light of the findings that schizophrenia patients do not differ from controls in their self-reports of emotional experience. That is, their diminished observable expressivity cannot be readily accounted for by comparable diminished reports of experienced emotion. Rather, schizophrenia patients may have a different threshold for displaying observable expressions (Ekman, 1992).

Investigating Unobservable Facial Activity in Schizophrenia: New Findings

We recently completed a longitudinal investigation of emotional respond-ing in schizophrenia (Kring & Earnst, 1999). Our primary aim in that study was to investigate which effects, if any, neuroleptic medication might have on emotional responding in schizophrenia and to assess the extent to which emotional responding in schizophrenia is stable across time. To address those questions, we implemented a counterbalanced crossover design (Spohn & Strauss, 1989) by which all participants were tested on two occasions, ap-proximately 5 months apart. For the schizophrenia patients, the different testing occasions also represented a change in their medication status. About half of the patients were off medication at the first testing and then were retested while on medication, and the other half of the patients were on medication at the first testing and then retested while off medication. Nonpatient controls were tested at two times, with the amount of time be-tween testing occasions equivalent to the time between testing occasions for patients (for more detail on the study design, see Kring & Earnst, 1999).

A secondary aim of that study was to determine if schizophrenia pa-tients manifested subtle, unobservable facial movement in response to emo-tionally evocative stimuli to illuminate the boundaries of expressive behav-ior among schizophrenia patients. In particular, we were interested to see if schizophrenia patients exhibited EMG activity that was consistent with the valence of emotional films. Based on the few previous studies that as-sessed EMG activity in response to emotional stimuli among schizophrenia patients, we expected that their responses would vary in a reliable fashion depending on the valence of the film that they were watching. That is, we expected that schizophrenia patients would exhibit greater zygomatic activ-ity in response to positive film clips and greater corrugator activity in re-sponse to negative film clips. We were also interested in ascertaining whether schizophrenia patients would differ from nonpatients in their EMG activity. Based on the studies reviewed above, we expected that schizophrenia patients would show very similar levels of EMG activity across the films. Finally, we were interested to see if EMG activity among schizophrenia patients would be associated with the observable expressive, experiential, and physiological components of emotion.

Overview of Sample, Methods, and Prior Results

Our participants were 15 male patients with diagnoses of either schizophre-nia ($n = 13$) or schizoaffective disorder ($n = 2$) and 15 nonpatient controls with no personal or family history of psychopathology who were recruited from the community. The patient and nonpatient groups did not signifi-cantly differ in age, years of education, or racial composition.

For each testing occasion, we unobtrusively videotaped participants as they first viewed a neutral film clip, followed by two positive then two negative film clips or the reverse order (negative before positive). After each film, participants answered three brief questions about the film clip to assess attention and understanding. They then completed a self-report emotional experience measure that included adjectives to assess the valence (pleasant, unpleasant) and activation (high, low) dimensions of emotion (Larsen & Diener, 1992; Russell, 1980). EMG activity (zygomatic and corrugator) and skin conductance activity were recorded during a 10-min resting baseline period as well as continuously throughout the film clips.

Although the findings relevant to our primary questions about medication effects and stability of emotional responding have been published elsewhere (Kring & Earnst, 1999), we briefly reiterate the results here to provide a context for interpreting the EMG findings. Replicating prior studies of emotional responding in schizophrenia, we found that schizophrenia patients showed fewer positive and negative facial expressions than nonpatients in response to emotional film clips, yet did not differ substantially in their reports of experienced emotions. More specifically, patients and controls did not differ in their reports of pleasant, high, and low activation emotions; however, patients reported experiencing more unpleasant emotion across all film clips. With respect to medication effects, our findings indicated that schizophrenia patients' observable expressive behavior and reports of experienced emotion were stable across changes in both medication status and time. In other words, medication did not strongly affect observable facial expression or experienced emotion. The findings (both new and already published) regarding group differences are summarized in Table 11.1. That medication was not associated with a dampening of expressive behavior suggested to us that schizophrenia patients' diminished expressive behavior could not be understood solely as a side effect of their medication.

Table 11.1 Summary of Group Differences in Emotional Responding

No Differences	Controls > Patients	Patients > Controls
Zygomatic activity	Positive and negative facial expressions	Corrugator activity
Self-report: Pleasant, high activation, and low activation emotion		Self-report: Unpleasant emotion

New Findings

In this chapter, we present new findings from the longitudinal study relevant to our secondary aim of examining subtle manifestations of facial activity. Consistent with our expectations, the zygomatic activity of both schizophrenia patients and controls varied according to the valence of the film clip. That is, the zygomatic activity of both schizophrenia patients and nonpatient controls was greater in response to the positive films than to the negative and neutral films. Similarly, both schizophrenia patients and nonpatient controls exhibited greater corrugator activity in response to the negative films than to the positive or neutral films (see Figs. 11.1 and 11.2). Also consistent with our predictions, schizophrenia patients did not differ from nonpatients in the amount of zygomatic activity exhibited in response to the emotional films. Contrary to our expectations, however, schizophrenia patients exhibited greater corrugator activity than controls across all films.

Descriptive statistics for skin conductance reactivity scores are shown in Table 11.2. Reactivity scores were computed by subtracting the number of skin conductance responses during baseline from the number of skin conductance responses during each film. Importantly, schizophrenia patients did not significantly differ from controls in the number of skin conductance responses during the baseline period. The reactivity of schizophrenia patients and controls did differ, however, according to film type. Specifically, patients tended to have greater reactivity than controls to the neutral film, but not to the positive and negative films. In addition, controls had less

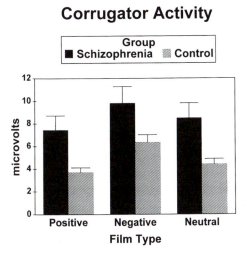

Fig. 11.1 Corrugator activity in schizophrenia patients and controls in response to emotional films.

Zygomatic Activity

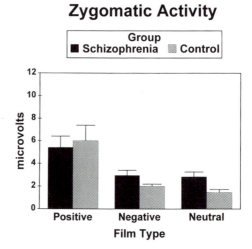

Fig. 11.2 Zygomatic activity of schizophrenia patients and controls in response to emotional films.

skin conductance reactivity to the neutral film than to the positive and negative films, but these differences were not significant for schizophrenia patients. It should be noted, however, that this relationship may reflect nothing more than the fact that the neutral film was always the first film clip presented. The film clip situation may have been more novel for patients than controls, thereby contributing to their increased skin conductance reactivity.

As shown in Table 11.3, there is much correspondence among observable facial expression, EMG, self-report, and skin conductance reactivity among nonpatient controls. That is, both observable expressive behavior and EMG activity were significantly positively correlated with self-report of emotional experience and skin conductance reactivity. In contrast, there

Table 11.2 Skin Conductance Reactivity Scores

| | Group | | | |
| | Schizophrenia | | Control | |
Film	M	SD	M	SD
Positive	0.30	0.94	0.65	0.99
Negative	0.23	1.02	0.32	1.00
Neutral	0.18	1.05	−0.26	0.63

Table 11.3 Correlations Among Emotion Components

	1	2	3	4	5	6	7	8	9	10
1. Obsv-Pos	—	.79**	.78**		.48*		.11		.47*	
2. Obsv-Neg	.15	—		.80**		.41*		.38		.44*
3. Zyg-Pos	.81**		—		.73**			.70**		
4. Corr-Neg		.33		—		.49*		.65*		.74**
5. Pleasant-Pos	.39		.44*		—	.59*	.87**		.91**	
6. Unpleasant-Neg		.36		.07		—		.59*		.70**
7. HiAct-Pos	.20		.49*		.79**		—		.60*	
8. HiAct-Neg		.19		−.08		.25		—		.66
9. SCR-Pos	.08		.41*		.44*				—	
10. SCR-Neg		−.37		−.52*		.23	.31	.24		—

Note: Schizophrenia patients' correlations are below the diagonal; nonpatient controls' correlations are above the diagonal. Pos = positive films; Neg = negative films; Obsv = observer ratings; Zyg = zygomatic; Corr = corrugator; SCR = skin conductance reactivity; HiAct = high activation; LoAct = low activation.

** $p < .01$, * $p < .05$, one-tailed tests.

is relatively little correspondence among these components for schizophrenia patients, substantiating findings of a disjunction between emotion response components. Neither observable expressive behavior nor corrugator activity was significantly related to self-reported emotional experience and skin conductance reactivity. Of note, zygomatic activity was related to observable expressive behavior, self-report, and skin conductance reactivity, a finding that is consistent with the findings for controls.

Discussion and Implications

These findings provide preliminary answers to the questions pertinent to the secondary aim of our study. Schizophrenia patients do manifest expressive behavior, albeit at an unobservable level, in response to emotionally evocative material. Although contraction of the facial muscles is part of both observable and unobservable facial activity, the magnitude of the corrugator and zygomatic responses obtained in this study suggests that, on average, the facial behavior assessed via EMG was subtle and likely not observable. In addition, we conducted analyses using observable facial expressions as a covariate in an attempt to statistically isolate EMG activity that was not related to observable facial activity; results from these analyses were virtually identical to those reported above.

Cacioppo and colleagues posited the "motor recruitment hypothesis" to conceptualize the relationship between unobservable and observable facial behavior (Cacioppo, Petty, & Marshall-Goodell, 1984; Cacioppo, Petty, & Tassinary, 1989; Tassinary & Cacioppo, 1992). More specifically, they argued that, at low levels of emotional intensity, facial behavior varies by valence (positive and negative) and as such is ideally measured using EMG. At higher levels of emotional intensity, however, facial behavior becomes observable and is further differentiated into specific emotions (e.g., disgust display, smile). Although both patients and controls exhibited valence-specific EMG activity, controls also displayed more observable expressions (although discrete emotional expressions were not measured in this study, it is likely that the observable behavior could be distinguished into more specific emotion displays). This raises the interesting possibility that schizophrenia patients have a different intensity threshold for producing observable displays. In other words, schizophrenia patients may require stimuli of even greater intensity before their expressive behavior becomes observable. On the other hand, schizophrenia patients' expressive behavior may be unrelated to the intensity of the stimulus and may instead reflect a component of a concomitant neuromotor dysfunction (e.g., Dworkin et al., 1996).

Although schizophrenia patients displayed less observable expressive behavior than controls, they exhibited comparable zygomatic activity and even greater amounts of corrugator activity. These findings were somewhat surprising, although they have been replicated in other studies (Kring et al., 1999; Mattes et al., 1995). Separate consideration of the findings regarding zygomatic and corrugator activity is warranted since the findings differed, at least with respect to group differences.

Why might patients differ from controls in their observable positive facial behavior, but not in their zygomatic activity? Indeed, for both patients and controls, observable positive facial expressions were correlated with zygomatic activity, suggesting that greater muscle activity is associated with greater observable facial displays. Thus, it seems somewhat paradoxical that patients and controls differed in their observable displays but not in their unobservable displays given the observed positive correlation between these two measures of expressive behavior.

Measurement considerations are certainly plausible to account for the apparent discrepancy between observable positive facial behavior and zygomatic activity. Recall that our measure of zygomatic activity was an average of activity across the entire film clip. By contrast, our measure of observable displays was based on discrete events during the film period. That is, coders rated observable changes in the face from a neutral to nonneutral display and recorded the valence, intensity, and duration of those changes (Kring & Sloan, 1991). It may be the case that zygomatic activity is differentially distributed across the film periods for patients and controls. Although it is probable that most of the positive observable displays involved contraction of the zygomatic muscle, the schizophrenia patients likely had additional contractions either that were not of sufficient intensity to be observable or that dissipated before the attendant skin and connective tissues were moved.

With respect to corrugator activity, schizophrenia patients exhibited greater activity than controls in response to the films. This finding is consistent with other recent studies that assessed EMG or frowning among schizophrenia patients (Davison et al., 1996; Kring et al., 1999; Mattes et al., 1995). Why do patients exhibit greater corrugator activity (i.e., frown) than controls? It might be tempting to conclude that this activity has little to do with emotional expression; however, patients' corrugator activity varied according to the film type in the expected manner. In other words, they displayed greater corrugator activity in response to the negative films than to either the positive or neutral films. Nonetheless, a number of previous studies demonstrated that corrugator activity often reflects processes not directly linked to emotion expressive behavior. For example, Smith and colleagues (Pope & Smith, 1994; Smith, 1989) demonstrated that corrugator activity reflects not only unpleasant emotion, but also "anticipated effort." Cacioppo, Petty, and Morris (1985) suggested that the frown also indicates concentration or puzzlement. According to these views, watching the films may have required more actual (or perceived) effort for patients than for controls. If this is the case, it remains unclear what part of this experimental situation (viewing films) was more effortful for the patients.

In prior studies, we (Kring et al., 1993; Kring & Neale, 1996) speculated that schizophrenic patients might be actively inhibiting or suppressing their facial expressions. Active inhibition likely requires effortful process-ing and would thus be consistent with elevated corrugator activity. How-ever, that the schizophrenic patients' skin conductance reactivity was simi-lar in response to both emotional and nonemotional (neutral) films does not favor an inhibition hypothesis. Indeed, although there is some disagree-ment in the literature as to whether suppressing expressive behavior corre-sponds to an increase (e.g., Gross & Levenson, 1993, 1997) or decrease (e.g., Zuckerman, Klorman, Larrance, & Spiegel, 1981) in skin conductance re-sponse, what seems clear is that the psychophysiological effects of emo-tional suppression are specific to emotional stimuli.

Alternatively, the patients may have been rather puzzled by the experi-mental situation. If this is the case, this puzzlement only manifested itself during the films as the patients and controls did not significantly differ in their baseline corrugator activity. Nonetheless, that the schizophrenia patients' corrugator activity reflects more than emotional responding is sup-ported by the weak and nonsignificant correlations between corrugator ac-tivity and self-reports of emotional experience and skin conductance reac-tivity. In contrast, zygomatic activity was related to emotion self-reports and skin conductance reactivity for both patients and controls. Thus, these findings provide further support for a disjunction among emotion response components among schizophrenia patients, particularly for negative emo-tion expressive behavior.

Conclusions and Future Directions

Empirical investigations into the nature of emotional disturbances in schizophrenia have confirmed what early theorists observed. Adopting methods from basic emotion research has allowed investigators to study multiple components of emotional response in emotionally evocative situa-tions. These studies revealed that schizophrenia patients display fewer ob-servable facial expressions than nonpatients, yet they report experiencing similar, and in some instances greater, amounts of experienced emotion. Using a more sensitive measure of expressive behavior has led to a number of interesting discoveries. First, schizophrenia patients manifested subtle, unobservable displays in response to emotional stimuli. Second, schizo-phrenia patients' EMG activity was similar to or greater than the displays of nonpatients. Third, the zygomatic activity of schizophrenia patients was associated with observer ratings of positive facial expression, self-reports of pleasant emotions, and skin conductance reactivity. In contrast, patients' corrugator activity was not significantly related to other components of emotional response.

Despite this progress in our understanding of emotional features in schizophrenia, a number of unanswered questions remain. First, it remains unclear whether the observed emotion deficits in schizophrenia are ante-

cedent to, concomitant with, or a consequence of the disorder. If these disturbances pre-date the onset of schizophrenia or persist beyond symptomatic remission, claims about their causal importance can be more clearly
made. Moreover, positioning these disturbances in the temporal sequence
of the disorder has important treatment and assessment implications. Unfortunately, very few studies have addressed this important issue (Kring,
1999, 2001).

However, indirect evidence suggests that at least some of the observed
emotion disturbances may pre-date the onset of schizophrenia. For example, Walker and colleagues (Walker, Grimes, Davis, & Smith, 1993) coded
facial expressions from home movies and found that preschizophrenic girls
displayed fewer joy expressions, and that both preschizophrenic boys and
girls displayed more negative facial expressions compared to their healthy
siblings (Walker et al., 1993). Studying childhood records of adults who
developed schizophrenia, Knight and Roff (1983, 1985) found evidence that
affective disturbances appeared in childhood and persisted into adulthood.
Although the findings from these studies are interesting, it remains unclear
whether this pattern of emotional behavior was related to the onset of
schizophrenia and if the pattern was specific to schizophrenia since these
studies were retrospective and had fairly limited samples (e.g., patients
seen in clinics as children or who had home movies are not necessarily
representative of all schizophrenia patients).

However, findings from high-risk studies also suggest that emotional disturbances may pre-date the onset of the illness. High-risk studies identify a
group of children at risk for developing schizophrenia (typically, high risk
is defined as having a biological parent with schizophrenia) and then follow them from childhood through the period of risk (Neale & Oltmanns,
1980). Teacher ratings from the Copenhagen high-risk study indicated that
boys and girls who were later diagnosed with schizophrenia were more
emotionally labile, socially withdrawn, socially anxious, and relatively un-
expressive than children who did not develop schizophrenia (Olin, John, &
Mednick, 1995; Olin & Mednick, 1996). Findings from the New York High-
Risk Project indicated that flat affect was greater among adolescents at risk
for developing schizophrenia than among adolescents at risk for developing
affective disorders (Dworkin et al., 1991).

Although there is indirect evidence that at least some type of emotion
disturbance in schizophrenia may pre-date the onset of the disorder, many
of the observed emotion disturbances in schizophrenia are perhaps most
accurately construed as concomitants of the disorder. Indeed, most of the
research on emotion in schizophrenia has been cross sectional and has included patients with at least some degree of residual symptoms.

With respect to whether emotion disturbances in schizophrenia can be
construed as consequences of the disorder, there is some evidence that
emotional disturbances in schizophrenia are fairly stable. For example, results from our longitudinal study (Kring & Earnst, 1999) indicated that di-

minished emotional expression was stable across 5 months. However, our study did not specifically include assessments during and following a symptomatic episode. In sum, additional research is needed to elucidate whether emotional disturbances in schizophrenia are an antecedent to or a consequence of the illness or both.

An additional unanswered question is whether these findings of emotion disturbances will be observed among women with schizophrenia. Almost none of the studies above included women patients in their sample. Studies that did include women did not look for gender differences. Yet, research from basic emotion suggests that there are substantial gender differences in expressive behavior (e.g., Brody & Hall, 1993; Kring & Gordon, 1998). In a study of adult schizophrenia patients' childhood movies, Walker et al. (1993) found that preschizophrenic girls displayed fewer expressions of joy from infancy to adolescence compared to their healthy siblings, but displayed more negative expressions in adolescence. Although the basic emotion literature suggests fewer differences between men and women in other components of emotion response, it is nonetheless important to examine gender in studies of emotion and schizophrenia, particularly given that there are a number of gender differences in schizophrenia (for a review, see Salem & Kring, 1998).

A third important question is whether these findings will replicate across cultures. There is evidence to suggest that negative symptoms, including flat affect, may not be as prevalent in other cultures. For example, Ramirez, Johnson, and Opler (1992) found that Puerto Rican schizophrenia patients manifested fewer negative symptoms, including flat affect and anhedonia, than Anglo American patients. Dassori, Miller, and Saldana (1995) found that Mexican American schizophrenia patients exhibited more withdrawal than Anglo American patients, but these groups did not differ on other measures of negative symptoms. Perhaps more important, however, the meaning of these symptoms across cultures may vary dramatically. Jenkins (1988) found that various manifestations of mental illness (including schizophrenia, but also including depression and anxiety) were characterized as *nervios* rather than (or in addition to) mental illness by Mexican American families. When these family members were given the opportunity to describe what *nervios* was like, their descriptions were categorized in emotional terms: easily angered, anxious, and sad or depressed. This finding suggests that emotional features of schizophrenia may be among the more salient characteristics of the disorder among Mexican Americans (yet these features are not necessarily considered part of a mental illness).

Implications for Assessment and Treatment

The adoption of paradigms and methods from the emotion research literature has allowed us to study more precisely schizophrenia patients' pattern of emotional responding, and the findings generated from these studies have important treatment and assessment implications. Schizophrenia patients' emotional responding is stable across time and does not appear to be strongly affected by more typical neuroleptic medications (Kring & Earnst, 1999). What remains to be seen, however, is whether some of the newer, "atypical" medications might have an impact on emotional responding, particularly flat affect. Recent research on the atypical neuroleptics, such as clozapine, suggests that these agents may be more effective in treating negative symptoms, including flat affect (e.g., Kane, Honigfeld, Singer, & Meltzer, 1988; Meltzer, 1991; Miller, Perry, Cadoret, & Andreasen, 1994; Umbricht & Kane, 1995).

One of the more effective forms of psychosocial interventions for schizophrenia involves social skills training (Benton & Schroeder, 1990; Corrigan, 1991; Dilk & Bond, 1996). Certainly, expressive behavior is an important part of socially skilled behavior. However, recent evidence suggests that the emotional deficits in schizophrenia are distinct from social skills deficits (Salem & Kring, 1999), and thus interventions aimed at improving social skills may not necessarily change expressive behavior. These interventions could be strengthened by including components that specifically target emotional disturbances (e.g., expressing emotion at the right time in the appropriate contexts; interpreting emotions in others) as well as the performance of socially skilled behavior. Moreover, researchers and clinicians could augment their outcome assessment procedures to include measures of both emotional and social functioning.

The findings reviewed above also have important implications for the assessment of emotional features in schizophrenia. In particular, laboratory-based measures of emotional responding can provide important information that is not easily accessed with clinical rating scales. For example, ratings of flat affect might be misinterpreted to mean that a schizophrenia patient is without feeling. Indeed, studies that rely solely on clinical rating scales that typically assess only one component of emotion may fail to capture the essence of the emotional disturbance adequately in schizophrenia, which appears to be the lack of coordinated engagement of emotion response components. For those who work with schizophrenia patients clinically, it will be important to ascertain how schizophrenia patients feel in different situations even if they do not show many outward signs of emotion.

Although the experimental control offered by a laboratory manipulation of emotion answers important questions, its generalizability is limited. However, results from these laboratory studies can suggest a number of hypotheses that can then be tested in a more ecologically valid (but less well controlled) setting. For example, examining emotional response tendencies in contexts such as social interaction with family members is a direction that deserves further empirical attention. In addition, psychologists would do well to adapt methods, such as ethnographies and narrative analyses, used by other disciplines (including anthropology, linguistics, and sociology) to capture more adequately the subjective experience of emotion in daily life among schizophrenia patients (Corin, 1990; Jenkins, 1994; Kleinman, 1995). A combination of laboratory and field methods would be an ideal marriage, for example, to study the social consequences of diminished emotional expression and inability to describe one's feelings to others (Keltner & Kring, 1998). In addition, narrative analyses would provide useful information on the contexts in which patients are likely to experience diminished pleasure and positive emotion. Such a methodological approach can also provide important information about the meaning of emotional symptoms both within and across cultures (Jenkins, 1997).

Acknowledgment

During the preparation of this chapter, Ann Kring was supported in part by a grant from NARSAD.

References

Andreasen, N. (1979). Affective flattening and the criteria for schizophrenia. *American Journal of Psychiatry, 34*, 208–212.

Andreasen, N. C. (1983). *The Scale for the Assessment of Negative Symptoms (SANS)*. Iowa City: University of Iowa.

Benton, M. K., & Schroeder, H. E. (1990). Social skills training with schizophrenics: A meta-analytic evaluation. *Journal of Consulting and Clinical Psychology, 58*, 741–747.

Berenbaum, H., & Oltmanns, T. F. (1992). Emotional experience and expression in schizophrenia and depression. *Journal of Abnormal Psychology, 101*, 37–44.

Bleuler, E. (1950). *Dementia praecox or the group of schizophrenias* (J. Zinkin, Trans.). New York: International Universities Press. (Original work published 1911)

Brody, L. R., & Hall, J. A. (1993). Gender and emotion. In M. Lewis & J. M. Haviland (Eds.), *Handbook of emotions* (pp. 447–460). New York: Guilford Press.

Brown, S., & Schwartz, G. E. (1980). Relationships between facial electromyography and subjective experience during affective imagery. *Biological Psychology, 11*, 49–62.

Buchanan, R. W., Strauss, M. E., Kirkpatrick, B., Holstein, C., Breier, A., & Carpenter, W. T. (1994). Neuropsychological impairments in deficit versus nondeficit forms of schizophrenia. *Archives of General Psychiatry, 51*, 804–811.

Buck, R. (1994). Social and emotional functions in facial expression and communication: The readout hypothesis. *Biological Psychology, 38*, 95–115.

Cacioppo, J. T., Bush, L. K., & Tassinary, L. G. (1992). Microexpressive facial actions as a function of affective stimuli: Replication and extension. *Personality and Social Psychology Bulletin, 18*, 515–526.

Cacioppo, J. T., Petty, R. E., Losch, M., & Kim, H. S. (1986). Electromyographic activity over facial muscle regions can differentiate the valence and intensity of emotional reactions. *Journal of Personality and Social Psychology, 50*, 260–268.

Cacioppo, J. T., Petty, R. E., & Marshall-Goodell, B. S. (1984). Electromyographic specificity during simple physical and attitudinal tasks: Location and topographical features of integrated EMG responses. *Biological Psychology, 18*, 85–121.

Cacioppo, J. T., Petty, R. E., & Morris, K. J. (1985). Semantic, evaluative, and self-referent processing: Memory, cognitive effort, and somatovisceral activity. *Psychophysiology, 22*, 371–384.

Cacioppo, J. T., Petty, R. E., & Tassinary, L. G. (1989). Social psychophysiology: A new look. *Advances in Experimental Social Psychology, 22*, 39–91.

Carpenter, W. T., Bartko, J. J., Strauss, J. S., & Hawk, A. B. (1978). Signs and symptoms as predictors of outcome: A report from the International Pilot Study of Schizophrenia. *American Journal of Psychiatry, 135*, 940–945.

Carpenter, W. T., Buchanan, R. W., Kirkpatrick, B., Tamminga, C., & Wood, F. (1993). Strong inference, theory testing, and the neuroanatomy of schizophrenia. *Archives of General Psychiatry, 50*, 825–831.

Carpenter, W. T., Heinrichs, D. W., & Wagman, A. M. I. (1988). Deficit and non-deficit forms of schizophrenia: The concept. *American Journal of Psychiatry, 145*, 578–583.

Corin, E. E. (1990). Facts and meaning in psychiatry. An anthropological approach to the lifeworld of schizophrenics. *Culture, Medicine, and Psychiatry, 14*, 153–188.

Corrigan, P. W. (1991). Social skills training in adult psychiatric populations: A meta-analysis. *Journal of Behavior Therapy and Experimental Psychiatry, 22*, 203–210.

Dassori, A. M., Miller, A. L., & Saldana, D. (1995). Schizophrenia among Hispanics: Epidemiology, phenomenology, course, and outcome. *Schizophrenia Bulletin, 21*, 303–312.

Davison, P. S., Frith, C. D., Harrison-Read, P. E., & Johnstone, E. C. (1996). Facial and other non-verbal communicative behaviour in chronic schizophrenia. *Psychological Medicine, 26*, 707–713.

Dilk, M. N., & Bond, G. R. (1996). Meta-analytic evaluation of skills training research for individuals with severe mental illness. *Journal of Consulting and Clinical Psychology, 64*, 1337–1346.

Dimberg, U. (1982). Facial reactions to facial expressions. *Psychophysiology, 19*, 643–647.

Dworkin, R., Clark, S. C., Amador, X. F., & Gorman, J. M. (1996). Does affective blunting in schizophrenia reflect affective deficit or neuromotor dysfunction? *Schizophrenia Research, 20*, 301–306.

Dworkin, R., Clark, S. C., Lipsitz, J. D., Amador, X. F., Kaufmann, C. A., Opler, L. A., White, S. R., & Gorman, J. M. (1993). Affective deficits and pain insensitivity in schizophrenia. *Motivation and Emotion, 17*, 245–276.

Dworkin, R. H., Bernstein, G., Kaplansky, L. M., Lipsitz, J. D., Rinaldi, A., Slater, S. L., Cornblatt, B. A., & Erlenmeyer-Kimling, L. (1991). Social competence and positive and negative symptoms: A longitudinal study of children and adolescents at risk for schizophrenia and affective disorder. *American Journal of Psychiatry, 148*, 1182–1188.

Earnst, K. S., & Kring, A. M. (1997). Construct validity of negative symptoms: An empirical and conceptual review. *Clinical Psychology Review, 17*, 167–189.

Earnst, K. S., Kring, A. M., Kadar, M. A., Salem, J. E., Shepard, D. A., & Loosen, P. T. (1996). Facial expression in schizophrenia. *Biological Psychiatry, 40*, 556–558.

Ekman, P. (1992). Facial expression and emotion. *American Psychologist, 48*, 384–392.

Feldman-Barrett, L. (1997). The relationships among momentary emotional experiences, personality descriptions, and retrospective ratings of emotion. *Personality and Social Psychology Bulletin, 23*, 1100–1110.

Feldman-Barrett, L. (1998). Discrete emotions or dimensions? The role of valence focus and arousal focus. *Cognition and Emotion, 12*, 579–599.

Fenton, W. S., & McGlashan, T. H. (1991). Natural history of schizophrenia subtypes II: Positive and negative symptoms and long-term course. *Archives of General Psychiatry, 48*, 978–986.

Fridlund, A. J. (1988). What can asymmetry and laterality in EMG tell us about the face and brain? *International Journal of Neuroscience, 39*, 53–69.

Fridlund, A. J. (1991). Sociality of solitary smiling: Potentiation by an implicit audience. *Journal of Personality and Social Psychology, 60*, 229–240.

Fridlund, A. J., & Izard, C. E. (1983). Electromyographic studies of facial expressions of emotions and patterns of emotions. In J. T. Cacioppo & R. E. Petty (Eds.), *Social psychology: A sourcebook* (pp. 243–286). New York: Guilford Press.

Gaebel, W., & Wolwer, W. (1992). Facial expression and emotional face recognition in schizophrenia and depression. *European Archives of Psychiatry and Clinical Neuroscience, 242*, 46–52.

Greenwald, M. K., Cook, E. W., & Lang, P. J. (1989). Affective judgment and psychophysiological response: Dimensional covariation in the evaluation of pictorial stimuli. *Journal of Psychophysiology, 3*, 51–64.

Gross, J. J., & Levenson, R. W. (1993). Emotional suppression: Physiology, self-report, and expressive behavior. *Journal of Personality and Social Psychology, 64*, 970–986.

Gross, J. J., & Levenson, R. W. (1997). Hiding feelings: The acute effects of inhibiting negative and positive emotion. *Journal of Abnormal Psychology, 106*, 95–103.

Izard, C. E. (1993a). Four systems for emotion activation: Cognitive and noncognitive processes. *Psychological Review, 100*, 68–90.

Izard, C. E. (1993b). Organizational and motivational functions of discrete emotions. In M. Lewis & J. M. Haviland (Eds.), *Handbook of emotions* (pp. 631–641). New York: Guilford Press.

Jenkins, J. H. (1988). Ethnopsychiatric conceptions of schizophrenic illness: The problem of nervios within Mexican-American families. *Culture, Medicine, and Psychiatry, 12,* 303–331.

Jenkins, J. H. (1994). Culture, emotion, and psychopathology. In S. Katayama & H. Markus (Eds.), *Emotion and culture: Empirical studies of mutual influence* (pp. 307–335). Washington, DC: American Psychological Association Press.

Jenkins, J. H. (1997). Subjective experience of persistent schizophrenia and depression among US Latinos and Euro-Americans. *British Journal of Psychiatry, 171*, 20–25.

Kane, J., Honigfeld, G., Singer, J., & Meltzer, H. (1988). Clozapine for the treat-ment-resistant schizophrenic: A double-blind comparison with chlorproma-zine. *Archives of General Psychiatry, 45*, 789–796.

Keefe, R. S. E., Lobel, D. S., Mohs, R. C., Silverman, J. M., Harvey, P. D., David-son, M., Losonczy, M. F., & Davis, K. L. (1991). Diagnostic issues in chronic schizophrenia: Kraeplinian schizophrenia, undifferentiated schizophrenia, and state-independent negative symptoms. *Schizophrenia Research, 4*, 71–79.

Keltner, D., & Kring, A. M. (1998). Emotion, social function, and psychopathol-ogy. *Review of General Psychology, 2*, 320–342.

Kirkpatrick, B., Buchanan, R. W., McKinney, P. D., Alphs, L. D., & Carpenter, W. T. (1989). The Schedule for the Deficit Syndrome: An instrument for re-search in schizophrenia. *Psychiatry Research, 30*, 119–123.

Kleinman, A. (1995). Suffering and its professional transformation. In A. Klein-man, *Writing at the margin: Discourse between anthropology and medicine* (pp. 995–119). Berkeley: University of California Press.

Knight, R. A., & Roff, J. D. (1983). Childhood and young adult predictors of schizophrenic outcome. In D. F. Ricks & B. S. Dohrenwend (Eds.), *Origins of psychopathology: Problems in research and public policy* (pp. 129–153). Cambridge, England: Cambridge University Press.

Knight, R. A., & Roff, J. D. (1985). Affectivity in schizophrenia. In M. Alpert (Ed.), *Controversies in schizophrenia: Change and constancies* (pp. 280–313). New York: Guilford Press.

Kraepelin, E. (1971). *Dementia praecox and paraphrenia* (R. M. Bradley, Trans.). Huntington, NY: Krieger. (Original work published 1919)

Krause, R., Steimer, E., Sanger-Alt, C., & Wagner, G. (1989). Facial expressions of schizophrenic patients and their interaction partners. *Psychiatry, 52*, 1–12.

Krause, R., Steimer-Krause, E., & Hufnagel, H. (1992). Expression and experi-ence of affects in paranoid schizophrenia. *Revue européenne de Psychologie Appliquée, 42*, 131–138.

Kring, A. M. (1999). Emotion in schizophrenia: Old mystery, new understand-ing. *Current Directions in Psychological Science, 8*, 160–163.

Kring, A. M. (2001). Emotion and psychopathology. In T. J. Mayne and G. Bo-nanno (Eds.), *Emotion: Current issues and future directions* (pp 337–360). New York: Guilford Press.

Kring, A. M., Alpert, M., Neale, J. M., & Harvey, P. D. (1994). A multichannel, multimethod assessment of affective flattening in schizophrenia. *Psychiatry Research, 54*, 211–222.

Kring, A. M., & Bachorowski, J.-A. (1999). Emotion and psychopathology. *Cogni-tion and Emotion, 13*, 575–599.

Kring, A. M., & Earnst, K. S. (1999). Stability of emotional responding in schizo-phrenia. *Behavior Therapy, 30*, 373–388.

Kring, A. M., Germans, M. K., Triesch, S., & Putnam, K. M. (2003). *Heightened electrodermal reactivity to emotional stimuli in schizophrenia: Specificity and boundaries.* Manuscript in preparation.

Kring, A. M., & Gordon, A. H. (1998). Sex differences in emotion: Expression, experience, and physiology. *Journal of Personality and Social Psychology, 74*, 686–703.

Kring, A. M., Kerr, S. L., & Earnst, K. S. (1999). Schizophrenic patients show facial reactions to emotional facial expressions. *Psychophysiology, 36*, 186–192.

Kring, A. M., Kerr, S. L, Smith, D. A., & Neale, J. M. (1993). Flat affect in schizophrenia does not reflect diminished subjective experience of emotion. *Journal of Abnormal Psychology, 102*, 507–517.

Kring, A. M., & Neale, J. M. (1996). Do schizophrenic patients show a disjunctive relationship among expressive, experiential, and psychophysiological components of emotion? *Journal of Abnormal Psychology, 105*, 249–257.

Kring, A. M., & Sloan, D. (1991). *The facial expression coding system (FACES): A users guide.* Unpublished manuscript.

Lang, P. J., Bradley, M. M., & Cuthbert, B. N. (1990). Emotion, attention, and the startle reflex. *Psychological Review, 97*, 377–395.

Lang, P. J., Greenwald, M. K., Bradley, M. M., & Hamm, A. O. (1993). Looking at pictures: Affective, facial, visceral, and behavioral reactions. *Psychophysiology, 30*, 261–273.

Larsen, R. J., & Diener, E. (1992). Promises and problems with the circumplex model of emotion. *Review of Personality and Social Psychology, 13*, 25–59.

Mattes, R. M., Schneider, F., Heimann, H., & Birbaumer, N. (1995). Reduced emotional response of schizophrenic patients in remission during social interaction. *Schizophrenia Research, 17*, 249–255.

McCanne, T. R., & Anderson, J. A. (1987). Emotional responding following experimental manipulation of facial electromyographic activity. *Journal of Personality and Social Psychology, 52*, 759–768.

Meltzer, H. Y. (1991). Pharmacologic treatment of negative symptoms. In J. F. Greden & R. Tandon (Eds.), *Negative schizophrenic symptoms: Pathophysiology and clinical implications* (pp. 217–231). Washington, DC: American Psychiatric Press.

Miller, D. D., Perry, P. J., Cadoret, R. J., & Andreasen, N. C. (1994). Clozapine's effect on negative symptoms in treatment-refractory schizophrenics. *Comprehensive Psychiatry, 35,* 8–15.

Neale, J. M., & Oltmanns, T. F. (1980). *Schizophrenia.* New York: Wiley.

Olin, S. S., John, R. S., & Mednick, S. A. (1995). Assessing the predictive value of teacher reports in a high risk sample for schizophrenia: An ROC analysis. *Schizophrenia Research, 16*, 53–66.

Olin, S. S., & Mednick, S. A. (1996). Risk factors of psychosis: Identifying vulnerable populations premorbidly. *Schizophrenia Bulletin, 22*, 223–240.

Pfhol, B., & Winokur, G. (1982). The evolution of symptoms in institutionalized hebephrenic/catatonic schizophrenics. *British Journal of Psychiatry, 141*, 567–572.

Pitman, R. K., Kolb, B., Orr, S. P., & Singh, M. M. (1987). Ethological study of facial behavior in nonparanoid and paranoid schizophrenic patients. *American Journal of Psychiatry, 144*, 99–102.

Pope, L. K, & Smith, C. A. (1994). On the distinct meaning of smiles and frowns. *Cognition and Emotion, 8*, 65–72.

Rado, S. (1956). *Psychoanalysis of behavior: Collected papers.* New York: Grune & Stratton.

Ramirez, P. M., Johnson, P. B., & Opler, L. A. (1992, May). *Ethnicity as a modifier of negative symptoms.* Paper presented at the annual meeting of the American Psychiatric Association, Washington, DC.

Russell, J. A. (1980). A circumplex model of affect. *Journal of Personality and Social Psychology, 39*, 1161–1178.

Salem, J. E., & Kring, A. M. (1998). The role of gender differences in the reduction of etiologic heterogeneity in schizophrenia. *Clinical Psychology Review, 18*, 795–819.

Salem, J. E., & Kring, A. M. (1999). Flat affect and social skills in schizophrenia: Evidence for their independence. *Psychiatry Research, 87*, 159–167.

Schwartz, G. E., Fair, P. L., Salt, P., Mandel, M. R., & Klerman, G. L. (1976). Facial muscle patterning to affective imagery in depressed and nondepressed subjects. *Science, 192*, 489–491.

Smith, C. A. (1989). Dimensions of appraisal and physiological response in emotion. *Journal of Personality and Social Psychology, 56*, 339–353.

Spohn, H. E., & Strauss, M. E. (1989). Relation of neuroleptic and anticholinergic medication to cognitive functions in schizophrenia. *Journal of Abnormal Psychology, 98*, 367–380.

Tamminga, C. A., Thaker, G. K., Buchanan, R., Kirkpatrick, B., Alphs, L. D., Chase, T. N., & Carpenter, W. T. (1992). Limbic system abnormalities identified in schizophrenia using positron emission tomography with fluorodeoxyglucose and neocortical alterations with deficit symptoms. *Archives of General Psychiatry, 49*, 522–530.

Tassinary, L. G., & Cacioppo, J. T. (1992). Unobservable facial actions and emotions. *Psychological Science, 3*, 28–33.

Teasdale, J. D., & Bancroft, J. (1977). Manipulation of thought content as a determinant of mood and corrugator activity in depressed patients. *Journal of Abnormal Psychology, 86*, 235–241.

Umbricht, D., & Kane, J. M. (1995). Risperidone: Efficacy and safety. *Schizophrenia Bulletin, 21*, 593–606.

Walker, E. F., Grimes, K. E., Davis, D. M., & Smith, A. J. (1993). Childhood precursors of schizophrenia: Facial expressions of emotion. *American Journal of Psychiatry, 150*, 1654–1660.

Zuckerman, M., Klorman, R., Larrance, D. T., & Spiegel, N. H. (1981). Facial, autonomic, and subjective components of emotion: The facial feedback hypothesis versus the externalizer-internalizer distinction. *Journal of Personality and Social Psychology, 41*, 929–944.

12

Clinical Implications of Research in Nonverbal Behavior of Children With Autism

GAIL McGEE AND MICHAEL MORRIER

Autism is manifested by irregularities in both verbal and nonverbal social behaviors. Beginning with Kanner's (1943) first description of infantile autism, autistic disorder has been characterized as a condition in which there is a severe lack of responsiveness to the environment. The first case studies of children with autism described a lack of interest in people and avoidance of eye contact.

Although autism is a neurodevelopmental disorder, the diagnosis is based on a certain pattern of social, communication, and behavioral symptoms. Behavioral interventions have been shown to be effective in improving the language and behavioral challenges associated with autism. However, social dysfunction often continues to debilitate individuals with autism throughout their life span. Because many children with autism do not have meaningful language, nonverbal social behaviors are of special importance in identifying and treating autism. Even after the development of language, the majority of people with autism continue to present with fundamental difficulties in both expression and understanding of nonverbal social cues.

Consideration of the criteria for a diagnosis of autism illustrates the centrality of nonverbal behaviors in this developmental disability. To summarize, autism is characterized by (American Psychiatric Association, 1994)

1. Qualitative impairments in social interaction
2. Qualitative impairments in communication
3. Restricted, repetitive, and stereotyped patterns of behavior, interests, and activities

Technically, autism is just one of a spectrum of pervasive developmental disorders, including autistic disorder, Asperger syndrome, Rett syndrome, childhood disintegrative disorder, and pervasive developmental disorders—not otherwise specified (PDD-NOS). Children in all of these subtypes present with the fundamental social irregularities displayed by children with autism, even though the number and severity of symptoms varies.

Nonverbal behaviors that are commonly associated with autism include impairment in behaviors that regulate social interaction, such as inconsistent eye contact, a lack of communicative gestures, or the absence of socially directed smiles. Another symptom, failure to develop age-appropriate peer interactions, may be manifested when a child with autism "walks through" other children as if they were not present. A third social symptom is a lack of effort to share enjoyment, interests, or achievements with others. In other words, children with autism do not initiate interactions by showing, bringing, or pointing out objects of interest to other people. The most common and pervasive social symptom involves a lack of social or emotional reciprocity. Thus, people with autism often fail to notice the nonverbal social behaviors displayed by others, and they lack the interest and skills needed to respond effectively to social approaches made by others.

There are also symptoms categorized in the communication and behavioral domains that relate directly to nonverbal behaviors. Thus, idiosyncratic language attributes include speaking in a monotone or a high-pitched voice or using very soft speech, which makes it difficult for others to interpret the speaker's emotional state accurately. Similarly, stereotyped motor mannerisms include unusual posturing or body movements, which are commonly unrelated to communicative intent.

The following sections highlight, in turn, research on the nonverbal behavioral symptoms that are specific to autism and practical research applications in the area of diagnosis and treatment of autism. Recent attempts to merge the study of nonverbal behavior with investigations of the neurobiology of autism are also outlined, along with suggestions for future research that may lead to a clinically significant impact.

Irregularities in Nonverbal Behavior Specific to Autism

A large and growing body of research in developmental psychology has been aimed at identification of the deficits that are independent of impairments in cognitive and linguistic functioning and therefore are unique to autism. A methodological convention has evolved that consists of comparing children with autism to groups of children with more generic developmental delay or younger typical children, and groups are matched according to verbal or nonverbal scores on intelligence tests. Nonverbal mental age is thought to provide the most accurate estimate of intellectual functioning of children with autism because their verbal mental ages are often confounded by characteristic language delays. The selection of a control group has an impact on research results in important ways, as may be evident in differing outcomes across the studies outlined here. Inconsistency of findings across studies may also result from task variability, as well as from the participation of subjects of differing ages and levels of functioning. The review that follows is organized according to studies in face recognition, perception of emotions, display of affective expressions, and the use of gestures for communication.

Skills in Face Recognition

There is a substantial body of research on the abilities of people with autism to recognize faces and discriminate facial characteristics. Although deficits in face recognition abilities are not a symptom of autism per se, it is likely that difficulties in this area may reflect an overall lack of focus on the social environment.

At least one study found no face recognition deficits in children and adolescents with autism. The subjects, aged 9 to 18 years, presented with wide-ranging levels of intellectual ability (Volkmar, Sparrow, Rende, & Cohen, 1989). When their performance was compared on tasks requiring the assembly of puzzles made of human faces, the subjects with autism were found to perform similarly to a control group matched for both nonverbal mental age and chronological age. However, it was unclear whether the puzzle task required social judgment or could simply be completed as a visual motor task.

Face-processing abilities of children and adults with autism were also studied by comparing their performances on a comprehensive clinical test battery to those of same-aged typical children (Teunisse & De Gelder, 1994). The subjects with autism performed nearly as well as normal controls on a variety of face-processing tasks. However, their response patterns on more complex discrimination tasks were similar to those of younger typical children. As a group, the subjects with autism made the most errors on tasks that required matching a facial feature in the context of a complete face. In contrast, they gave near-perfect performances on tasks that required matching a particular facial feature from an array of similar stimuli.

Other studies have found that individuals with autism use atypical strategies to complete face recognition tasks, even when they show no overall face recognition deficits. For example, the ability of groups of younger (mean age 9 years, 8 months) and older (mean age 14 years, 1 month) children with autism to identify photographs of their peers was compared to younger and older groups of typical children (Langdell, 1978). Both groups of children with autism were able to identify pictures of their peers, but the younger children did so by focusing on the mouth area of the photographs. These findings stand in contrast to those of studies on the face recognition strategies used by nondisabled subjects, who tend to rely on the eyes when making face discriminations (Goldstein & Mackenberg, 1966). The older children with autism were able to identify the photographs equally well when provided with upper or lower facial features. Unlike same-aged subjects matched for nonverbal mental ages, and unlike the results of earlier face-processing research with nondisabled subjects (Valentine, 1988), the older subjects with autism showed no performance decrement when they were asked to identify faces that were turned upside down.

The relationship of cognitive ability to face recognition skill has also been examined in adolescents with autism (Boucher & Lewis, 1992). Regardless of whether the same-aged control groups were matched on nonverbal or verbal mental ages, the subjects with autism were found to be impaired on tasks requiring the recognition of unfamiliar faces. This impairment was specific to social stimuli because the youth with autism performed as well as normal subjects and subjects with learning disabilities on tasks that required recognition of buildings. Deficits in attention were ruled out as an explanatory factor, despite an overall correlation between the amount of time looking and the accuracy of responses. Specifically, the children with autism showed similar attention impairments on both the face and building discrimination tasks, yet their accuracy differed between the social and nonsocial tasks.

A recent study used the face recognition tasks from a standardized intelligence test (i.e., Kaufman ABC; Kaufman & Kaufman, 1983). It was found that children with autism did less well than a matched group of children with PDD-NOS and a group of children with nonspecified learning difficulties (Klin et al., 1999). The investigators speculated that face recognition deficits could be more apparent in younger children because adults may have learned compensatory strategies.

In sum, although there is variability of results, the predominant finding is that persons with autism display irregularities in face recognition ability that are not solely accounted for by developmental delay. It should be noted that virtually all of these studies assessed face recognition skills using static stimuli (i.e., photographs). Therefore, it remains unclear whether similar or even greater differences would be found in assessments of face processing in more dynamic situations, which better represent the discriminations called for in everyday life.

Abilities in Emotion Perception

An early study required adolescents with autism to match intact and incomplete stimulus faces against a standard of happy, unhappy, angry, or frightened faces (Hobson, Ouston, & Lee, 1988). The youths with autism were as capable as typical adolescents in matching the full faces to the standard faces. However, children with autism were less able to identify emotions as the faces became increasingly incomplete.

Using a set of standardized photographs (Ekman & Friesen, 1976), 12-year-old children with autism had difficulty selecting the picture of an emotional expression that differed from the other expressions presented (Tantam, Monaghan, Nicholson, & Stirling, 1989). Similarly, the children with autism were more impaired than a control group (matched for age, sex, and nonverbal intelligence) in labeling the emotional expressions of unfamiliar adults. However, the performance of children with autism was similar to that of controls on tasks that required them to label the expressions in inverted faces. The recognition and labeling deficits shown by the children with autism were also found to be specific to social content because the participants were able to label different types of buildings accurately.

Similarly, difficulties in comprehension of facial, vocal, or bodily expressions of affect have been shown to be disordered uniquely in children with more broadly defined pervasive developmental disorders (Braverman, Fein, Lucci, & Waterhouse, 1989). Thus, a group of children with pervasive developmental disorders performed less accurately than typical children on tasks that required matching emotional expressions. The subgroup of children with autism also did poorer on tasks that required comprehension of affective terms. Again, the decoding deficits were shown to be specific to social comprehension, and there were no group performance differences on object-matching tasks. There was, however, variability in the social comprehension skills within the group of children with autism spectrum disorders. The children with severe social impairments showed comprehension difficulty that was unrelated to their cognitive abilities. However, children with milder social impairments performed similar to typical children matched for gender and nonverbal intelligence.

Cognitive ability was also found to be related to performance on a task that required matching of emotions to context (Fein, Lucci, Braverman, & Waterhouse, 1992). Specifically, children were shown a series of photographs of emotion-evoking situations (e.g., two children fighting over cookies), and the face of one of the children was obscured. Participants were asked to select from an assortment of facial displays the one that best fit the missing face in the photograph. An object-matching control task that required no social judgment was also presented. No group differences were found in accuracy of performance on the social task. However, the children with pervasive developmental disorders did perform significantly better on the object-matching task than they did on the social task. The seeming inconsistency was accounted for by variability in cognitive functioning that existed within the group of children with pervasive developmental disorder.

The ability to describe and label complex emotions was examined in 12.5-year-old children with autism who did not have mental retardation (Capps, Yirmiya, & Sigman, 1992). Overall, the children with autism were surprisingly accurate in describing emotions of happiness and sadness. However, the children with autism had more difficulty than normal children (matched for verbal ability) in describing emotions of pride and embarrassment. Thus, it took them longer to answer questions about these emotional states, they required more prompts from the examiner, and they tended to give very general responses. Qualitative analysis of the response patterns suggested that the children with autism had a limited appreciation of the role that an audience plays in relation to the concept of embarrassment. Further, it appeared that they had learned rules that enabled them to give "scripted" answers to questions about emotions. Unlike the normal children, the children with autism were less likely to give examples based on their own experiences. These results suggest that children with autism may be able to learn to identify simple emotions even when they continue to have a limited personal understanding of complex emotions.

Children with autism have also been found to have difficulties in perspective taking, which in turn may contribute to a lack of empathy toward others (Dawson & Fernald, 1985). The strategies used to understand social situations have been directly examined in elementary school-aged children with autism (Pierce, Glad, & Schreibman, 1997). In this study, the performance of children with autism was compared to children with mental retardation who had been matched for verbal mental age. The experimental paradigm varied the number and type of cues on a social perception task. A series of videotaped vignettes presented between one and four social cues, and the child's task was to describe how the character in the vignette was feeling and why the character was feeling as he did. Cues varied according to tone, content, and verbal and nonverbal behaviors. For example, in one of the vignettes in which only nonverbal cues were presented, two girls were seated at a picnic table, and they smiled as a third girl approached them. In a vignette with multiple cues, two boys seated at a picnic table watched as a third boy said in an angry tone, "You're doing it wrong," and proceeded to grab a bag from one of the boys who was seated. The children with autism answered factual questions as accurately as the control subjects (i.e., they correctly identified how many people were present in the scene and the gender of the participants). However, they did worse on all social perception questions. Interestingly, the accuracy of the children with autism was best on vignettes that presented single rather than multiple cues.

These findings were interpreted as evidence that general attention deficits contributed to impairment in social perception. However, the mixture of both verbal and nonverbal cues that were used in this study presented the potential for confound that may limit interpretations of core deficits. Specifically, vignettes presenting multiple cues always included verbal stimuli, whereas scenes with only single cues included only nonverbal stimuli.

Another study found that, when children with autism were asked to sort stimuli according to their preferences, they did not make typical choices regarding the valence of facial expressions (Celani, Battacchi, & Arcidiacono, 1999). For example, children with autism did not judge happy faces to be related to pleasantness. In addition, although the participants with autism did have some ability to recognize emotions, they were less accurate than groups of typical children and children with Down syndrome who were matched on verbal intelligence.

One of the few studies of emotional identification skills in young children with autism involved a comparison of 12 preschool-aged children with autism and 12 age-matched typical children (Feldman, McGee, Mann, & Strain, 1993). The task was to view videotaped vignettes of child actors engaged in naturalistic social situations. When the vignette was freeze-framed between segments, the experimenter queried, "Show me the boy who is feeling angry." As predicted, the children with autism were less accurate than were typical subjects on identification of happy, sad, and angry expressions. However, children with autism did identify happy expressions at better-than-chance levels. Because happy expressions are also the first discrimination learned by younger typical children, these findings suggest that the decoding skills of children with autism may simply be delayed rather than deviant. As reported in prior research, intellectual ability was not correlated with accuracy of decoding responses (Braverman et al., 1989).

In short, as with face recognition abilities, children with autism demonstrate some ability to discriminate the emotional expressions of other people. However, most studies have reported either deficits or irregularities in the social perception of children with autism, with some variance across ages. Finally, although there may be some influence of cognitive ability in emotion detection skills, the peculiarities associated with autism are not fully accounted for by level of intelligence.

Display of Emotional Expressions

Although the expression of emotion by persons with autism has been studied less often than the ability to decode the emotional expressions of others, some data are available. Preschool-aged children with autism were found to differ from children with more generic developmental delays; the children with autism displayed positive emotions in positive contexts less often than did comparison subjects (Snow, Hertzig, & Shapiro, 1987).

Affective differences appear to persist as children with autism get older. Thus, when school-aged children with autism were instructed to make happy and sad faces, judges rated their attempts as poor (Langdell, 1981). Similarly, high-functioning adults with autism have been found to have persistent difficulties in the expression, as well as labeling, of emotions (Macdonald et al., 1989).

The pattern of emotional encoding by young children with autism was detailed in a structured laboratory task that required interaction with an unfamiliar adult (Yirmiya, Kasari, Mundy, & Sigman, 1989). Children with autism were found to show approximately the same overall levels of affect as did children with mental retardation and typical children. However, the children with autism were unique in that they showed more negative emotional responding and incongruent emotional blends than did children in the comparison groups.

Another study examined the emotional expressions of children with autism and typical children during naturally occurring preschool activities (McGee, Feldman, & Chernin, 1991). Again, children with autism were found to display levels of emoting similar to those of the typical children, and both groups had neutral expressions approximately 76% of the time. Unlike previous findings (Snow et al., 1987; Yirmiya et al., 1989), most of the children in both groups displayed predominantly happy facial expressions when their faces were not neutral. These differences may have been related to the fact that the children in this sample were observed during play in an everyday environment rather than during participation in a testing situation. These preschool subjects had also been receiving intensive early intervention.

However, there were major differences between the groups in terms of the situations in which the children's happy faces occurred. When typical children looked happy, they were either interacting with a teacher (76% of intervals scored happy) or a peer (19%), and they were virtually never playing alone (5%). In contrast, when the children with autism looked happy, they were less likely to be in situations with teachers (50%) or peers (9%), and they were much more likely to be found playing alone (42%).

The contextual congruence of children's emotional expressions was further examined to determine whether happy (or sad or angry) facial expressions occurred in situations that would normally be expected to evoke a happy (or sad or angry) emotion in typical children. As predicted, the typical children showed nearly perfect contextual congruence, so that they looked happy when they were in a positive situation (e.g., the teacher was smiling and asking questions about the child's activity). When typical children looked sad, they were nearly always in a negative situation with adults or in solitary play (e.g., getting hurt on the playground); when they looked angry, they were usually in negative situations with other children (e.g., another child was taking away their toy). However, the children with autism were much less likely to display the expected match between context and emotional display. Thus, in addition to looking happy during solitary play, when the children with autism looked sad, they were more likely to be receiving a positive interaction from a teacher. There were not many angry scores for either population, but when the children with autism did look angry, they tended to be close to an adult or receiving a positive teacher interaction.

Affective encoding is important to social functioning because facial displays cue others when to approach for interaction. In addition, facial displays probably function as conditioned reinforcement for social approaches. For example, a peer may be more likely to approach a child who provides social reinforcement by looking up and smiling at him. In summary, the level of current and future opportunity for social interaction is likely to be limited when children do not display their emotions in an appropriate manner.

Use of Gestures for Communication

Observational studies of the peer interactions of children with and without autism have documented a general lack of gestural expression by children with autism (Attwood, 1986). Further, it has been shown that, although children with autism may use gestures for the purpose of making requests, they are far less likely to engage in gestural acts for the purpose of sharing an interest in an object (Curcio, 1978; Wetherby & Prutting, 1984).

The specificity of these deficits in "indicating" behaviors was clearly demonstrated in a comparison of groups of children with autism, children with mental retardation, and typical children (Mundy, Sigman, Ungerer, & Sherman, 1986). Subjects and comparison groups were matched for mental age (approximately 25 months) and maternal education level. The children with autism were found to differ significantly on behaviors such as pointing, showing, or making eye contact with others while holding an object or watching an item in motion. Moreover, these differences were evident regardless of a child's individual developmental level. Conclusions were that children with autism have unique deficits in the use of nonverbal behaviors to share an awareness or interest in objects or events with others.

To summarize, there is now a substantial literature describing a number of irregularities in social behavior that are unique to persons with autism. This research has more recently been extended downward in the age range. The result has been a transformation from a notably unreliable art of clinical diagnosis of autism to an empirically based diagnostic process.

Earliest Presentations of Autism

Guidelines were recently established by the American Academy of Neurology to encourage physicians to be alert for signs of autism in very young children (Filipek et al., 1999). Nonverbal behaviors that may be cause for concern include failure to smile in social situations, preference for playing alone, showing little interest in other children, or trying to get things independently rather than asking for help (Filipek et al., 1999). Operational descriptions of the nonverbal social behavior of young children with autism have critically important clinical implications because there is widespread agreement that intervention is most effective if it is started as early as possible (Fenske, Zalenski, Krantz, & McClannahan, 1985; Lovaas, 1987).

As in developmental studies of social behavior in normally developing children, this review examines a broader range of skills under the rubric of nonverbal social behavior (Riggio, 1992). Thus, imitation skills lay the foundation for developing reciprocal interactions with parents and other children, as do abilities and interest in establishing joint attention with others. The reports that follow show a trend toward obtaining an understanding of autism in children at increasingly early ages.

One study of the nonverbal communication skills of 26 children with autism, who were under the age of 4 years, compared parental reports to direct observations of the children's behavior (Stone, Hoffman, Lewis, & Ousley, 1994). The majority of the children observed were found to have multiple abnormalities in this domain. There was high agreement between parents and observers (>80%) that the children engaged in abnormal social play and good agreement (>65%) on the presence of impaired imitation skills.

Further specification of the early irregularities in nonverbal behavior shown in children with autism was accomplished by comparing children with autism and children with general learning impairments, all of whom were under the age of 3.5 years (Stone, Ousley, Yoder, Hogan, & Hepburn, 1997). In addition to overall deficits in spontaneous communication acts, the children with autism displayed significantly lower levels of pointing, showing objects, and eye gaze. They were also more likely to manipulate the examiner's hand in a manner that appeared to be using the hand as a tool. The children with autism exhibited overall deficits in the use of communicative gestures, and they were less likely to combine two or more nonverbal communicative acts (such as looking while pointing). In sum, the children with autism appeared to find it less rewarding to use nonverbal behaviors to share the attention of adults than did the children with other learning impairments. Conclusions were that the nonverbal communication impairments of young children with autism contribute to overall difficulties in monitoring the attention of communication partners.

Over the past decade, a great deal of research has focused on theory of mind (TOM) conceptualizations of autism. In a nutshell, TOM posits that the behavioral symptoms of children with autism evolve from a fundamental lack of ability to share the perspective of other people. Although cognitive irregularities are the primary focus of this theoretical construct, TOM experiments have frequently used paradigms that assessed nonverbal social behaviors. As an example, an autism screening questionnaire (i.e., the Checklist for Autism in Toddlers, or CHAT) was designed for reporting by mothers of young children (Baron-Cohen, Allen, & Gillberg, 1992). When the CHAT was completed for 80 toddlers (18 months old), 4 children who were later diagnosed with autism were found to have deficits in two or more of the following five items: social interest, social play, pretend play, pointing to show, and bringing an object to an adult. In contrast, 80% of the normal toddlers passed all of the items, and none failed more than one item.

The public health screening system in Sweden made possible an even larger prospective study of the CHAT (Baron-Cohen et al., 1996). Predictions were that young children would be at high risk for autism if they failed items related to protodeclarative pointing (pointing at an object to direct another person to look at the object as an end in itself), gaze monitoring (looking in the same direction in which an adult is looking), and pretend play. In fact, only 12 of 16,000 children failed all three of these items, and 10 of the 12 children were found to have autism when they were 3.5 years of age. Thus, the false-positive rate was only 16.6%, and there were no false negatives. Interestingly, of 22 children who failed only the items related to protodeclarative pointing and pretend play, none had autism, but 68% had language delays.

Retrospective Analyses of Home Videotapes

The increasing availability of home videotapes has made possible some important examinations of behavioral presentations of infants who were later found to have autism. One such study compared the videotapes of first birthday parties of typical children and children who had been subsequently diagnosed with autism (Osterling & Dawson, 1994). The children with autism differed from their same-aged peers in that they did not bring things to show to their parents, point to items of interest, look at other people, or appear to notice when their name was called. As with children at older ages, the exact social problems varied from child to child, and the absence of one social symptom did not rule out autism. However, all of the children who were later found to have autism presented identifiable problems in nonverbal social behavior when they were as young as 1 year of age.

Using a similar methodology, a broader range of variables was examined in a retrospective videotape comparison of infants (9–12 months old) who were subsequently diagnosed with autism (Baranek, 1999). The infants with autism were compared to a group of same-aged infants with various developmental disabilities as well as to a group of same-aged typical children. Findings were that the children with autism needed more prompting to orient toward a person calling their name. Children with autism also tended to show strong aversions to social touch, and they frequently mouthed objects. On the other hand, certain unusual nonverbal behaviors (i.e., stereotyped quality to object play, unusual posturing of body parts, diminished looking at camera, visual staring/fixation on objects, and less animated affective expressions) were found to occur more often in the children with more general developmental disabilities. The frequency of these atypical behaviors by children with autism fell between those of the other two groups.

Prospective Analysis of Nonverbal Social Behaviors

The reliability of autism diagnoses has also been examined in very young children with autism (Lord, 1995). Significant findings were that 2-year-olds who seldom lifted up their arms to be held or carried were often later diagnosed with autism. However, this same behavior was not a discriminator when children were 3 years of age. Other behavioral indices that discriminated autism in the 2-year-olds included seeking to share own enjoyment, use of other's body as a tool, directing attention, interest in other children, attention to voices, pointing and understanding gestures, hand and finger mannerisms, and unusual sensory behaviors. Behaviors that were not significantly different for children at age 2 years but were different at age 3 years were restricted range of facial expressions, coming to adults for comfort, and direct gaze. The best predictors of autism at age 2 years were deficits in direct attention and attention to voices, and by age 3 years, the single best predictor was a lack of seeking to share own enjoyment. Overall, the diagnosis of autism was fairly stable for children identified at age 2 years of age. However, accuracy was further improved when children were diagnosed at age 3 years or older because the normal children were easier to separate out at older ages.

Evolution of Gold Standard Diagnostic Instruments

Obviously, the assessment of nonverbal social behaviors predominates in the detection of autism in children of very young ages. The growing body of research on early presentation of autism has now been applied to the development of assessment instruments that are being used to standardize the diagnosis of autism. Specifically, the Autism Diagnostic Observation Schedules (ADOS) and the Autism Diagnostic Interview (ADI) are now recognized as so-called gold standard instruments—instruments that are widely accepted as the most valid and reliable—for obtaining a differential diagnosis of autism. These instruments provide tremendous promise for research in autism because now there is consensus on where diagnostic lines should be drawn. As a result, research findings can now be more readily translated across subpopulations of people with autism. By reducing confounds that arise in comparisons of poorly defined subject populations, the consistency of findings across studies should improve.

Both the ADOS and the ADI instruments were designed to assess criteria for autism as outlined in the *International Statistical Classification of Diseases, 10th Revision* (*ICD-10*; World Health Organization, 1992) and the *Diagnostic and Statistical Manual of Mental Disorders, 4th Edition* (*DSM-IV*; American Psychiatric Association, 1994). One of the primary purposes for empirical development of these instruments was to improve the accuracy of diagnosis for children with comorbid mental retardation, as well as for those at the higher end of the intellectual spectrum.

Autism Diagnostic Observational Schedule

The original version of the ADOS was an attempt to create a system of behavioral observations of children with autism who were between the chronological ages of 6 and 18 years and who had a mental age of at least 3 years (Lord et al., 1989). The assessment consisted of in vivo presentation of a series of tasks designed to elicit behaviors that indicate either the presence or absence of various characteristics of autism. To illustrate, a piece of candy is presented in a tightly closed jar. A typical child would be likely to initiate an interaction with an available adult to get help in opening the jar. In contrast, a child with autism would be more likely to persist in trying to open the jar independently, give up and walk away, or throw a tantrum. The tasks provided for direct assessment of a range of nonverbal behaviors, including gestures/mime, facial expressions, eye contact, smiling, maintenance of appropriate social distance, and demonstrations of shared enjoyment. The assessment proved to have good validity in discriminating between two groups of subjects with autism (one group with mild mental retardation and another group with no retardation), a group with other mental handicaps, and a group of normally developing children and adolescents. Acceptable test-retest reliability was also demonstrated.

The assessment was next extended down in the age range by development of the Pre-Linguistic Autism Diagnostic Observation Schedule (PL-ADOS), which was tied to the behavioral deficits presented by children with autism with developmental ages younger than 3 years (DiLavore, Lord, & Rutter, 1995). The emphasis was on assessment of the quality, and not just the presence or absence, of various social/communication behaviors associated with autism in young children. Among the nonverbal behaviors addressed were eye gaze, direction of facial expressions to others, social smile, gestural imitation, and other behaviors that indicate sharing of attention with others. It was found that items related to range of facial expressions, pointing, and showing gestures did not add discrimination power. In addition, reliance on scores of restrictive interests led to more incorrect identifications than a focus on social communication behaviors.

The two earlier observational schedules (i.e., the original ADOS and the PL-ADOS) have now been upgraded according to results of validity and reliability tests. In addition, the assessment has been sorted into four modules representing differing developmental levels. Interrater reliability of the new ADOS (the ADOS–Generic or ADOS-G) was found to be good (Lord, Risi, Lambrecht, Cook, Leventhal, DiLavore, et al., 2000). There was also evidence that the instrument can be used to discriminate autism from the PDD-NOS subtypes within the autism spectrum as well as between the autism spectrum and other disabilities.

Autism Diagnostic Interview

The ADI, which is a semistructured interview with a child's principal caregiver, provides information that is complementary to that yielded by the ADOS-G. The parent provides historical and current information on the social, communication, and behavioral characteristics required for a diagnosis of autism. The original ADI focused on children aged 5 years through early adulthood (Le Couteur et al., 1989). Items selected were sensitive to deviance and not just developmental delay. Of 16 social items, 4 sampled nonverbal behaviors, including anticipatory gestures at or before age 5 years, range of facial expressions, appropriate facial expressions, and greetings. Of 12 communication items, 3 also sampled behaviors that have nonverbal components, including abnormality in pointing, gesture, and imitation.

Acceptable test-retest item reliability was demonstrated in an administration of the ADI to parents of children with autism and to parents of comparable groups of children with mental retardation (Le Couteur et al., 1989). The ADI's overall validity as a tool for discriminating the presence or absence of autism was established in tests with a second sample of subjects, with no false positive or false negatives in the validity sample. However, no single symptom accurately predicted autism in the absence of supporting information.

The ADI was subsequently revised (ADI-R) to permit expansion to preschool-aged children (Lord, Rutter, & Le Couteur, 1994). Like the ADOS-G, the ADI-R was aimed at better detection of children with autism and profound mental retardation, as well as at improved diagnosis for higher functioning adults with autism. Items were added that elicited reports of behaviors that occur only in children with autism. New items were also added to sample reports of behaviors that would be present in children with normal or deficient intellectual ability, but without autism. A series of reliability (test/retest, interobserver) and validity (internal consistency) studies compared children with autism and children with other mental handicaps or language impairments. Findings were that the revised social and communication algorithms yielded correct diagnosis in 24 of 25 children who had a clinical diagnosis of autism. Only 2 of 25 children without autism received false-positive diagnoses. Nonverbal social items included direct gaze, smiles reciprocally to others, limited range of facial expression during communication, use of another person's body as a tool to communicate, and inappropriate facial expression. In addition, it was found that the children with autism used fewer social gestures, and they had more difficulty understanding the gestures of others. Although the overall algorithms yielded the best diagnostic accuracy, individual nonverbal items were better at discriminating autism than had been expected.

To summarize, the ADI-R represents an important advance in objective consolidation of clinical interview data in a manner that is sensitive to detecting autism in children of varying chronological and mental ages. An individual who meets or exceeds the ADOS and ADI-R algorithm cutoffs for autism will show significant abnormalities in social responsivity, the use of gestures, and the use of verbal language in social interaction. The ADOS is now available commercially (Lord, Rutter, DiLavore, & Risi, 1999), although training and certification at the University of Chicago or other approved sites is required for use of these assessments in research.

Translation of Descriptive Research to Use in Clinical Interventions

Research from a developmental perspective has cumulatively resulted in better understanding of the nonverbal deficits of children with autism, as well as in significantly improved diagnostic capability. On the other hand, the field of behavioral psychology has contributed most actively to the development and evaluation of clinical interventions for autism. There has been an unfortunate dearth of crossover between autism research in developmental and behavioral psychology. For example, there is abundant empirical information on the emotional decoding irregularities associated with autism, and challenges in appreciating the emotions of others may obviously interfere with adaptive social functioning. Yet there are virtually no published reports of clinical interventions aimed at correcting these deficits.

There are, however, a few areas in which developmental theory and descriptive research have been used to develop some promising interventions. Thus, descriptive research in areas such as eye contact, social distance, affection, and peer interactions provide excellent models for future autism investigations.

Eye Contact

Impairment in eye-to-eye gaze is one of the most frequently identified social symptoms associated with autism. Individuals with autism were found to establish less eye-to-eye contact than subjects with Down syndrome or typical children, although group differences were not found in comparison to persons with mental retardation of unknown etiology (Yirmiya, Pilowsky, Solomonica-Levi, & Shulman, 1999). Further, it was shown that, although chronological and mental ages can mediate deficits in eye gaze, intellectual ability does not fully account for the irregularities shown by children with autism. Thus, older and more verbal children with autism may learn to look at others given certain cues. However, they often continue to refrain from initiating eye contact, and they rarely check the eye contact of others to determine if their message has been conveyed.

The earliest laboratory interventions for nonverbal behavior of children with autism compared three strategies for increasing eye contact during interactions (Tiegerman & Primavera, 1981, 1984). Findings were that the strategy most effective in promoting eye contact was one of imitating the object play in which the children were engaged.

It has also been shown that a child's imitation ability is related to re-sponsiveness to interventions aimed at promoting eye gaze (Dawson & Gal-pert, 1986). A developmental intervention approach, similar to the imita-tion strategy described above, was based on research on the nonverbal so-cial interactions between normally developing infants and their mothers. Fifteen children with autism, aged 4 to 6 years, participated in this compar-ison of three imitation conditions. The children who had the lowest level of imitation ability, as measured on the Uzgiris-Hunt Scale (Uzgiris & Hunt, 1975), were found to increase their eye contact, social touching, and vocal-izations in a condition that corresponded to the lowest level of imitation development. Therefore, intervention consisted of the simultaneous imita-tion of children's toy play. The children with low imitation ability did not do as well when presented with a delayed model of their behavior or when novel behaviors were modeled. In contrast, the children who entered inter-vention with higher level imitation skills tended to respond to all three imitation conditions by increasing their eye contact and decreasing their levels of perseverative play.

These findings were then extended from the laboratory to an applied intervention, which was implemented by the mothers of children with au-tism between the ages of 2 and 6 years (Dawson & Galpert, 1990). During an initial assessment session in which the mothers were asked to imitate their child's play behaviors, the children showed immediate increases in the duration of eye gaze directed toward their mothers. Across the next 2 weeks, the mothers were asked to provide daily 20-min imitation sessions to their child at home. A postintervention assessment showed that the daily practice had produced cumulative increases in eye gaze, along with corre-sponding improvements in the quality of the children's play. Participating children responded positively to the intervention independent of their level of functioning, as measured in terms of preintervention imitation abil-ity, intellectual ability, play skills, Vineland social age, and the severity of their autistic symptoms.

Physical Proximity to Others

A preference for spending time alone, even when social opportunity is available, is another defining characteristic of autism. Social isolation has a cascading effect on social development because opportunities for social learning are further limited when children with autism remain aloof from other people.

Time spent in proximity to other people may be considered as the con-verse of social avoidance. In early clinical descriptions of autism, Lorna Wing and colleagues (Wing & Atwood, 1987; Wing & Gould, 1979) de-scribed three types of social interaction patterns of children with autism by categorizing them as oblivious, avoidant, or active but odd. Observational data on the naturally occurring peer-related social behavior of preschool-aged children with autism have provided operational definitions for similar categories of social interest (McGee, Morrier, Hynes, Parsons, & Lin, 1997). Three of nine children with autism displayed levels of proximity to other children that were below the mean and bottom ranges displayed by other children with autism (avoidant). Three additional children who had been in intervention for several years were found to demonstrate near-normal levels of responsiveness to peers, but they could not successfully elicit social bids from their peers (i.e., were active but odd). A third group of children was classified as having an interest in peers that appeared to be related to their interest in high-preference toys. This toy-related social interest involved a high probability that, when a child was focused on another child, the child was simultaneously focused on a toy. It was also noted that some children who were initially oblivious of their peers actually became more avoidant as they became more aware of social events in their environment.

The relevance of physical proximity to intervention outcomes was illustrated in a study that examined the relationship of peer proximity to "autistic behaviors" (McGee, Paradis, & Feldman, 1993). The behavior of 28 preschool-aged children with autism was sampled during regular activities in an inclusive preschool. When the children were in proximity (within 3 feet) to typical peers, the levels of their self-stimulatory behaviors were significantly lower than when they were in proximity to other children with autism. Intermediate levels of self-stimulatory and other odd motor behaviors occurred when the children were alone. This effect was not a treatment outcome because data were collected when the children were new to the preschool. It is possible that autistic behavior decreased as the result of a state of hyperarousal that occurs during situations in which social approaches are likely. However, as yet there are no direct data to verify a relationship between arousal and self-stimulatory behavior.

Simple exposure to typical peers has also been found to yield some positive influence on other nonverbal social behaviors of 6- to 8-year-old children with autism (Lord & Hopkins, 1986). A relatively minimal intervention consisted of placing children with autism together with typical peers, who were given a general instruction: "Show your partner how to play. Do your best to get him to play with you." The dependent measures were initiations, number of squares apart, orientation (facing playmates), self-stimulatory behavior, solitary play, responsiveness, and number and duration of interactions. Comparison conditions were studied with same-aged typical peers versus younger typical peers. After intervention, all of the subjects showed gains in proximity, orientation, and responsiveness. However, same-aged typical peers initiated more often than did the younger peers, and older children were better able to effectively adjust their initiations in a manner that successfully obtained responses from the children with autism.

In setting social goals, it helps to know exactly how much of the time typical children engage in various social behaviors. To establish some benchmarks, we compared the social behaviors of typical 3- and 4-year-old children were compared to the social behaviors of same-aged children with autism (McGee, Feldman, & Morrier, 1997). Results quantified the expected behavioral differences in peer proximity. Typical children were near other children an average of 80% of the time observed, while children with autism were near other children only 62% of the time. In addition, typical children were shown to spend more time directly focused on both adults and other peers. Finally, the relatively small gap between 3-year-olds with and without autism expanded substantially by the time children were 4 years of age. It does not appear that children with autism get worse with increasing age, but the gap between them and typical children expands because typical children experience such rapid social growth during the preschool years.

When peer proximity was targeted in an intervention for toddlers with autism, the results were relatively swift and impressive (McGee, Morrier, & Daly, 1999). Thus, following at least 9 months of intervention in a center-based program that included typical peers, a majority (71%) of the children with autism showed increases in peer proximity. An additional group (25%) maintained peer proximity levels within the ranges of typical children. When children are small, the intervention for peer proximity is logistically simple. A child with autism can be placed near other children during play activities, and seating arrangements for snack or study can be alternated between children with and without disabilities. Constant redirection is indicated to prevent some children from migrating away from groups of other children. If a child with autism is especially avoidant, then that child may be attracted to the location of other children by placing highly preferred toys in his or her vicinity. Alternatively, typical peers may be drawn close to the child with autism by placing preferred play materials near the child. Over time, it appears that the children with autism become "desensitized" to the presence of other children. In other words, this rather low-intensity intervention appears to build a tolerance for the presence of other people, thereby increasing the opportunity for further learning of appropriate nonverbal social behaviors.

Affection

Difficulties in understanding the emotional displays of other people may account for the common failure of people with autism to show empathy for the distress of others, as well as a failure to seek reassurance from others during potentially threatening situations (Bacon, Fein, Morris, Waterhouse, & Allen, 1998). For example, when exposed to situations in which an unfamiliar adult pretended to be hurt or distressed, children with autism engaged in virtually no displays of affection or offers of assistance. Rather, they either ignored or gave simple recognition responses. The lowest-functioning children showed no evidence of even noticing when another person had been hurt.

Effective behavioral interventions have been developed to teach and promote the giving and receiving of affectionate behavior by children with autism. One study compared two strategies for teaching affection responses to four children with autism, who were identified by their parents as failing to display affection to them and not responding to verbal displays of affection from them (Charlop & Walsh, 1986). The children were randomly assigned to receive instruction using one of two intervention procedures, including a "time delay" procedure and a "peer modeling" intervention. The time delay procedure began with a therapist directly prompting affection responses. On social opportunities that followed a child's correct responses, the therapist waited for increasing amounts of time before prompting the next affection responses. Thus, time delay procedures aim to produce independent responding by fading prompts along a dimension of increasing time intervals. The second procedure consisted of opportunity to model typical peers engaging in affection behaviors.

Although the peer modeling intervention was not effective in teaching affection responses, the children with autism did show increased eye contact in this condition. In contrast, all of the children with autism learned the affection responses trained through the time delay procedure, and their new affection repertoire generalized to recess on the playground. One child immediately transferred use of spontaneous hugs and kisses (as well as statements of affection) from the clinic to the home. Parents of the other participants were able to obtain affectionate responses from their children at home after learning the time delay procedures that had been used for teaching at the clinic. Parents and siblings described their child with autism as more social and lovable following intervention. Other therapeutic benefits of the time delay procedure included lower levels of inappropriate behaviors. Importantly, the affection behaviors did not transfer to unfamiliar adults, which is relevant because safety issues could arise if there was indiscriminate generalization of affection to strangers.

Another approach to promoting affection in children with autism was to blend encouragement to engage in specific affectionate behaviors into common preschool games (McEvoy et al., 1988; McEvoy, Twardosz, & Bishop, 1990). Examples of nonverbal target responses included "hug your friend" or "pat your friend on the back." These affection activities were shown to be effective not only for children with autism, but also for other children who displayed social withdrawal. An advantage of this approach is that it can be used with children who have little or no expressive language. In addition, the affection activities do not require sophisticated skills on the part of regular preschool teachers.

Although the ability to display affection in conventional ways may fall short of having an interest or skill in displaying empathy toward others, it is a foundation on which to build. In most cases, it appears that children with autism do indeed have attachments and preferences among people, and affection training gives them the tools to express themselves appropriately. At the least, if children with autism learn to demonstrate affection toward parents and significant others when they are quite young, family members will be better able to access some much-needed social reward from their children.

Peer Interactions

One of the diagnostic criteria for autism is the lack of peer-related social behaviors appropriate to developmental level. A number of strategies have been demonstrated as effective in teaching children with autism the "how to" of reciprocal peer interactions (McConnell, Sission, Court, & Strain, 1991). However, it has proven more difficult to have an impact on the generalization and maintenance of their newly learned social skills.

Peer interaction research has by and large targeted a combination of verbal and nonverbal social behaviors, which is logical given that the very nature of social interaction implies a complex interface between nonverbal social cues and verbal communications (Riggio, 1992). Although both verbal and nonverbal behaviors were measured in the research discussed next, the peer interaction responses learned by children with autism have been primarily nonverbal. Thus, even the children with autism who have functional verbal language tend to use a lower level of verbal communication with their peers than with adults. Adults commonly provide an array of subtle and direct language supports, while typical peers are unlikely to facilitate language unless specifically taught to do so. It is possible for verbally fluent children with autism to learn how to converse with their peers if given extended practice. However, the bulk of social interaction research to date has been aimed at relatively basic interaction skills.

The complexity of social behavior dictates the need for social goals to be clearly specified. Thus, for each target social behavior, there is a need to describe the desired topography (i.e., what the behavior should look like), context (i.e., which situation usually calls for the behavior), and frequency (i.e., how often the behavior should occur). This task requires knowledge of the naturally occurring social behavior of typical preschool-aged children. Unfortunately, the developmental literature offers surprisingly little normative information about the peer interactions of young children. Although applied behavior analysis interventions have traditionally been developed with a conspicuous lack of regard for developmental information, the need for logistical data has given impetus to a few descriptive studies of the social behavior of typically developing children.

In one of the first observational studies aimed at gathering information for use in the development of autism interventions, 61 normally developing preschool children were observed in the course of naturally occurring play activities (Tremblay, Strain, Hendrickson, & Shores, 1981). The children's peer interactions were then analyzed for the probability that a given behavior would be successful in soliciting a positive response from other children. Results indicated that the nonverbal behaviors most effective in obtaining positive peer responses were rough-and-tumble play, sharing, assisting, and providing affection. Vocal imitation and overt attempts to seek attention were less successful peer interaction strategies.

This information was subsequently used to select the target social behaviors for two series of behavioral interventions. In teacher-mediated approaches, the teacher directly prompted the interactions of the children with autism as they were playing with other children (cf. Odom & Strain, 1986). In peer-mediated approaches, the typical peers were trained and rewarded for prompting the interactions of children with autism (cf. Odom, Hoyson, Jamieson, & Strain, 1985).

Data from observations of the ongoing social behavior of typical children were used to target desired levels of social interactions for children participating in a peer incidental teaching intervention (McGee, Almeida, Sulzer-Azaroff, & Feldman, 1992). Findings were that typical children engaged in reciprocal interactions an average of 31% of the time during a preschool's unstructured free play, and their interactions decreased to an average of 13% of the time during a lunch period in which a teacher was constantly available and talking to the children. The intervention was then aimed at obtaining similar levels of reciprocal interactions between pairs of typical children serving as peer tutors to children with autism. The first step in preparing a peer tutor was to teach the tutor to use high-interest toys to elicit an initiation from a child with autism, who in turn learned to initiate interactions by reaching for or otherwise gesturing for a desired toy. Next, the peer tutor learned to respond to those initiations in a manner that yielded at least a two-turn interaction. Specifically, the peer tutor learned to ask, "What do you want?" and then to wait expectantly for a verbal request for the toy. When the child with autism responded, the peer tutor rewarded the child with praise, social contact (such as a tickle), and the toy.

Reciprocal peer interactions between the children with autism and their typical peer tutors increased as a function of the intervention. Importantly, the increased interactions were also maintained across conditions of gradually reduced teacher presence and encouragement of the peer tutors.

Implications are that when interventions produce artificially high levels of interactions, they are unlikely to be maintained by conditions normally available in everyday environments. Thus, it is unrealistic and potentially counterproductive for interventions to be aimed at getting reciprocal interactions to occur between 80% and 100% of the time, as has been common research and clinical practice.

The Role of Nonverbal Behavior in Understanding the Neurobiology of Autism

Research in the area of neurobiology is a relatively recent and potentially important approach to studying the nonverbal behavior of persons with autism (Rumsey, 1996). There is growing availability of technologies (e.g., functional magnetic resonance imaging [fMRI] and positron emission tomography [PET]) that permit direct study of brain structure and function, and the tasks used to study nonverbal behaviors unique to autism can be feasibly implemented concurrent with neuroimaging procedures. The significance is that, despite a professional consensus that autism is a neurological disorder, there is still relatively little known about the specific pathogenesis of autism (Gillberg & Coleman, 1992). It would be a major advance in understanding autism if a foundation of knowledge could be established on the relationship of brain function to irregularities in the nonverbal behaviors of persons with autism.

There are several theories that speculate how certain nonverbal social irregularities may be related to specific areas of neurological dysfunction. One theory, based on studies of socioemotional behavior in normal adults and primates, holds that lesions in the amygdala or anterior cingulate may play a central role in the social difficulties of people with autism. Although there is little direct evidence, impairment in these regions could explain the difficulty that people with autism have in interpreting the emotional content of social stimuli, as well as provide an explanation for their lack of social motivation (Fein, Pennington, & Waterhouse, 1987; Waterhouse, Fein, & Modahl, 1996). It has also been proposed that lesions in temporal and right hemisphere functioning may lead to deficits in the perception and expression of social cues, and that an inability to regulate attention can reduce social learning from environmental events and lead to confusion and social withdrawal (Dawson & Lewy, 1989).

An animal model for differences in social attachment suggests the possibility that neuropeptide dysfunction may play a role in autism (Insel, O'Brien, & Leckman, 1999). Specifically, two breeds of prairie voles have been shown to exhibit vastly different behavioral patterns for mating and rearing of their young. One breed of voles mates and remains together for life, and both parents nourish their offspring over an extended period of time. In contrast, another very similar breed of voles shows no mating affiliation, and the breed abandons its young at very early ages. There is only a minor genetic variance between the two kinds of voles, and this difference controls the functioning of receptor sites for two hormones, oxytocin and vasopressin. Interestingly, the hormone oxytocin is present in high levels in human mothers at the time they give birth. A known function of oxytocin is to produce lactation, but it is at least plausible that oxytocin plays a role in early mother-infant bonding. At this point, it is pure speculation whether the genes that control oxytocin and vasopressin in voles will be found to differ between normal humans and persons with autism. Yet the model illustrates the potential for crossover between studies of the neurobiology of autism and studies of the nonverbal behavioral manifestations of autism.

A considerable amount of research investigating the biological origins of autism has been focused on irregularities in the cerebellum, which are thought to interact with limbic system abnormalities in causing attentional deficits in selective attention (Courchesne, Yeune-Courchesne, Press, Hesselink, & Jernigan, 1988; Reiss, 1988). Based on examination of fMRI scans of the cerebellum in subjects with autism, the investigators hypothesized that the social disabilities associated with autism may result from impairment in selective attention. In turn, this impairment in selective attention may interfere with the ability of people with autism to use and understand social language and gestures (Courchesne, Akshoomoff, & Townsend, 1990).

An important "crossover" study examined the brain functioning of adults with autism during their participation in a face discrimination task (Schultz et al., 2000). Participants were 14 precisely diagnosed individuals with high-functioning autism or Asperger syndrome, and their performance was compared to that of young adults who had no history of brain trauma, psychiatric illness, or neurological problems. The groups were matched for age and intelligence test scores. A series of tasks required discrimination between faces, patterns, and pairs of objects (e.g., between two chairs, cars, etc.). The stimuli used in the face recognition task were photographs of persons of the same gender and age, and potential distractors such as hair, ears, and clothing were edited out of the pictures. On each experimental trial, the subjects pressed a button to indicate whether the stimuli in the pair were the same or different. The tasks were administered simultaneously with fMRI scanning.

Findings were that the young adults with autism showed brain activation patterns similar to the normal controls during the object discrimination tasks. However, during face discrimination tasks, the subjects with autism showed activation patterns that differed from those of control subjects. The brain activation patterns of subjects with autism were similar on both face and object discrimination tasks, while activation patterns differed across tasks for normal subjects. Specifically, relative to controls, the autism group had significantly greater activation in the inferior temporal gyri during face-processing tasks, along with reduced activation of the fusiform gyrus. Conclusions were that, when individuals with autism are making discriminations between faces, they demonstrate a pattern of brain activity that suggests a focus on facial features rather than on the whole of a facial stimulus. It may be recalled that there were similar behavioral findings in earlier research (Teunisse & De Gelder, 1994), and these serve to validate the findings on brain-processing differences of people with autism spectrum disorders.

It is possible that imaging studies may ultimately shed some light on various theoretical debates regarding the nature of nonverbal irregularities in autism. It remains unclear whether individuals with autism show decreased appreciation of emotions due to an innate inability to recognize emotions, an inability to process components of facial expression, hyperarousal, fundamental difficulty in understanding the concept of emotion in specific contexts, general cognitive impairment, or other factors. Imaging studies may also help to clarify whether fundamental neurological differences persist even among persons who have learned compensatory strategies for processing emotional stimuli.

Finally, there are virtually no studies of the relationship of nonverbal behaviors and neurological variables in children with autism at young ages. The reports of dramatic positive outcomes in young children with autism who have received intensive early intervention raise a number of lucrative questions. If it turns out that neurological plasticity (Huttenlocher, 1984, 1994) accounts for the apparent increase in responsiveness to treatment, then the issue of critical periods for intervention in specific nonverbal social behaviors becomes of considerable importance. Currently, there are numerous ethical, technical, and logistical challenges that limit the feasibility of imaging research with young children (Rumsey et. al., 1997). But the time will come that knowledge and technology can address issues of central importance to understanding the developmental course of nonverbal behavior, the biological basis of social development, and the interaction between nonverbal social behavior and brain development (Fein et al., 1992).

Additional Directions for Clinical Research and Practice

Although the body of information on the nonverbal social deficits of children with autism has expanded rapidly in recent years, there remain a number of empirical gaps that impede clinical applications of these findings. There is a need to understand better the development of typical and atypical nonverbal behaviors across time, as well as a need to design clinical interventions that address irregularities in higher level nonverbal behaviors.

Expanded information on typical/atypical developmental progressions in nonverbal social behaviors would help to isolate the variables related to social understanding and permit analysis of the components of nonverbal social communication. There is quite a bit of information on behaviors such as joint attention and establishing eye-to-eye gaze, yet gaps remain at various points in development (e.g., how teenagers establish joint attention with their peers).

For some symptoms of autism, clinical lore has not yet been supported with the empirical detail that might expedite intervention research. Thus, children with autism often mechanically use the bodies of other people to meet their needs, such as leading a parent by the arm to a cupboard where cookies are stored. Other children speak in a monotone regardless of the emotional content of their message. A gifted child with Asperger syndrome may lack an understanding of how to adapt social rules to various situations. Yet, there is a paucity of data to inform clinicians on how to treat or measure progress in these commonly reported problems.

We currently have little specific information on how many children with autism are affected by a given symptom, nor do we know much about which environmental events influence the display of various nonverbal social behaviors. Also of interest is information on the salience of specific social irregularities in relation to other social abilities and knowledge of how these relationships change across developmental periods. In a nutshell, it is hoped future research in nonverbal behavior will be focused on the clinically relevant details of what is typical and atypical nonverbal behavior.

A related issue pertains to the methodology used to study nonverbal behavior of children with autism. For the most part, the data available on the nonverbal skills of people with autism have been obtained during experimental tasks that required arbitrary judgments about still (or static) photographs. Relatively few studies have made use of dynamic stimuli that approximate the social situations commonly encountered in real life. In both behavioral (cf. McGee et al., 1991, versus Yirmiya et al., 1989) and neurobiological studies (Kilts, 2000), it has been shown that results may differ when behavior is examined in natural contexts rather than in experimental settings. Further, it is well known that persons with autism have substantial difficulty dealing with abstract information, and they are often unable to generalize their knowledge and skills across settings. In the general field of research in nonverbal behavior, there has been a trend toward use of increasingly naturalistic stimuli. However, in autism research, there has been continuing reliance on presentation of static stimuli in contrived laboratory tasks. There is clearly a need to expand studies of ongoing social behavior of children and adults with autism in their everyday environments.

Finally, the time is at hand for extension of clinical applications to higher level nonverbal skills, as well as for the development of enhanced strategies to improve transfer of nonverbal social skills across time, settings, and people. In certain areas, such extensions may simply require a shift in dependent variables. For example, procedures for teaching school-aged children with autism to self-monitor various adaptive or challenging behaviors (Koegel, Harrower, & Koegel, 1998) might be applied productively to nonverbal behaviors such as appropriate voice tone, body postures, or even the contextual congruence of facial expressions.

Perhaps most intriguing and most absent are empirically derived procedures for meeting the social challenges presented by high-functioning children and adults with autism or Asperger syndrome. Progress in early intervention, along with improvements in diagnosis, appear to be rapidly expanding the pool of people with autism who have little or no cognitive impairment. In the recent past, most intervention programs did not have the time available to intervene in more than the most obvious deficits (e.g., verbal communication, behavior challenges, and perhaps eye contact). Yet when children with autism begin intervention at increasingly early ages, and when they progress at more rapid rates, then the time and opportunity become available to address far more subtle social needs.

It may ultimately be possible to teach people with autism the age-appropriate skills needed for emotional expressiveness and sensitivity, as well as to regulate or control the flow of nonverbal messages in such a way as to manage conversations effectively (Riggio, 1992). In fact, such an ambitious paradigm is needed if a long-term goal is to increase the potential of persons with autism to increase their level of social contacts and support. Fulfillment of these gaps in knowledge of the nature and most efficacious intervention for various nonverbal behaviors could have crucially important implications for the lifelong success of people with autism.

References

American Psychiatric Association. (1994). *Diagnostic and statistical manual of mental disorders* (4th ed.). Washington, DC: Author.

Attwood, A. J. (1986). Do autistic children have unique learning problems? *Communication, 20,* 9–11.

Bacon, A. L., Fein, D., Morris, R., Waterhouse, L., & Allen, D. (1998). The responses of autistic children to the distress of others. *Journal of Autism and Developmental Disorders, 28,* 129–142.

Baranek, G. T. (1999). Autism during infancy: A retrospective video analysis of sensory-motor and social behaviors at 9–12 months of age. *Journal of Autism and Developmental Disorders, 29,* 213–224.

Baron-Cohen, S., Allen, J., & Gillberg, C. (1992). Can autism be detected at 18 months? The needle, the haystack, and the CHAT. *British Journal of Psychiatry, 161,* 839–843.

Baron-Cohen, S., Cox, A., Baird, G., Swettenhan, J., Nightingale, N., Morgan, K., Drew, A., & Charman, T. (1996). Psychological markers in the detection of autism. *British Journal of Psychiatry, 168,* 1–6.

Boucher, J., & Lewis, V. (1992). Unfamiliar face recognition in relatively able autistic children. *Journal of Child Psychology and Psychiatry, 33,* 843–859.

Braverman, M., Fein, D., Lucci, D., & Waterhouse, L. (1989). Affect comprehension in children with pervasive developmental disorders. *Journal of Autism and Developmental Disorders, 19,* 301–316.

Capps, L., Yirmiya, N., & Sigman, M. (1992). Understanding of simple and complex emotions of nonretarded children with autism. *Journal of Child Psychology and Psychiatry, 7,* 1169–1182.

Celani, G., Battacchi, M. W., & Arcidiacono, L. (1999). The understanding of the emotional meaning of facial expressions in people with autism. *Journal of Autism and Developmental Disorders, 29,* 57–66.

Charlop, M. H., & Walsh, M. E. (1986). Increasing autistic children's spontaneous verbalizations of affection: An assessment of time delay and peer modeling procedures. *Journal of Applied Behavior Analysis, 19*, 307–314.

Courchesne, E., Akshoomoff, N. A., & Townsend, J. (1990). Recent advances in autism. *Current Opinion in Pediatrics, 2*, 685–693.

Courchense, E., Yeune-Courchense, R., Press, G. A., Hesselink, J. R., & Jernigan, T. L. (1988). Hypoplasia of cerebellar vermal VI and VII in autism. *New England Journal of Medicine, 318*, 1349–1354.

Curcio, F. (1978). Sensorimotor functioning and communication in mute autistic children. *Journal of Autism and Childhood Schizophrenia, 2*, 264–287.

Dawson, G., & Fernald, M. (1985). Perspective-taking ability and its relationship to the social behavior of autistic children. *Journal of Autism and Developmental Disorders, 17*, 487–498.

Dawson, G., & Galpert, L. (1986). A developmental model for facilitating the social behavior of autistic children. In E. Schopler & G. Mesibov (Eds.), *Social behavior in autism* (pp. 237–261). New York: Plenum.

Dawson, G., & Galpert, L. (1990). Mother's use of imitative play for facilitating social responsiveness and toy play in young children. *Development and Psychopathology, 2*, 151–162.

Dawson, G., & Lewy, A. (1989). Arousal, attention, and socioemotional impairments of individuals with autism. In G. Dawson (Ed.), *Autism: Nature, diagnoses, and treatment* (pp. 49–74). New York: Guilford Press.

DiLavore, P. C., Lord, C., & Rutter, M. (1995). The Pre-Linguistic Autism Diagnostic Observation Schedule. *Journal of Autism and Developmental Disorders, 25*, 355–379.

Ekman, P., & Friesen, W. (1976). *Pictures of facial affect.* Palo Alto, CA: Consulting Psychologists Press.

Fein, D., Lucci, D., Braverman, M., & Waterhouse, L. (1992). Comprehension of affect in context in children with pervasive developmental disorders. *Journal of Child Psychology and Psychiatry, 33*, 1157–1167.

Fein, D., Pennington, B., & Waterhouse, L. (1987). Implications of social deficits in autism for neurological dysfunction. In E. Schopler & G. G. Mesibov (Eds.), *Neurobiological issues in autism* (pp. 127–144). New York: Plenum Press.

Feldman, R. S., McGee, G. G., Mann, L., & Strain, P. (1993). Nonverbal affective decoding ability in children with autism and in typical preschoolers. *Journal of Early Intervention, 17*, 341–350.

Fenske, E. C., Zalenski, S., Krantz, P. J., & McClannahan, L. E. (1985). Age at intervention and treatment outcome for autistic children in comprehensive intervention program. *Analysis and Intervention in Developmental Disabilities, 5*, 49–58.

Filipeck, P. A., Accardo, P. J., Baranek, G. T., Cook, E. H., Dawson, G., Gordon, B., Gravel, J. S., Johnson, C. P., Kallen, R. J., Levy, S. E., Minshew, N. J., Prizant, B. M., Rapin, I., Rogers, S. J., Stone, W. L., Teplin, S., Tuchman, R. F., & Volkmar, F. R. (1999). The screening and diagnosis of autistic spectrum disorders. *Journal of Autism and Developmental Disorders, 29*, 439–484.

Gillberg, C., & Coleman, M. (1992). *The biology of the autistic syndromes* (2nd ed.). New York: Cambridge University Press.

Goldstein, A. G., & Mackenberg, E. (1966). Recognition of human faces from isolated facial features. *Psychonomic Science, 6*, 149–150.

Hobson, R. P., Ouston, J., & Lee, A. (1988). What's in a face? The case of autism. *British Journal of Psychology, 79*, 441–453.

Huttenlocher, P. R. (1984). Synapse elimination and plasticity in developing human cerebral context. *American Journal of Mental Deficiency, 88*, 488–496.

Huttenlocher, P. R. (1994). Synaptogenesis in human cerebral cortex. In G. Dawson & K. W. Fischer (Eds.), *Human behavior and the developing brain* (pp. 137–152). New York: Guilford Press.

Insel, T. R., O'Brien, D. J., & Leckman, J. F. (1999). Oxytocin, vasopressin, and autism: Is there a connection? *Biological Psychiatry, 45*, 145–157.

Kanner, L. (1943). Autistic disturbances of affective contact. *Nervous Child, 3*, 217–250.

Kaufman, A. S., & Kaufman, N. L. (1983). *K-ABC: Kaufman Assessment Battery for Children, interpretative manual.* Circle Pines, MN: American Guidance Service.

Kilts, C. (2000). In vivo imaging of the pharmacodynamics and pharmacokinetics of lithium. *Journal of Clinical Psychiatry, 61*(Suppl. 9), 41–46.

Klin, A., Sparrow, S. S., de Bildt, A., Cicchetti, D. V., Cohen, D. J., & Volkmar, F. R. (1999). A normed study of face recognition in autism and related disorders. *Journal of Autism and Developmental Disorders, 29*, 499–508.

Koegel, L. K., Harrower, J. K., & Koegel, R. L. (1998). Support for children with developmental disabilities in full inclusion classrooms through self-management. *Journal of Positive Behavior Interventions, 1*, 26–33.

Langdell, T. (1978). Recognition of faces: An approach to the study of autism. *Journal of Child Psychology and Psychiatry, 19*, 255–268.

Langdell, T. (1981). *Face perception: An approach to the study of autism.* Unpublished doctoral dissertation, University of London.

Le Couteur, A., Rutter, M., Lord, C., Rios, P., Robertson, S., Holdgrafer, M., & McLennan, J. (1989). Autism Diagnostic Interview: A standardized investigator-based instrument. *Journal of Autism and Developmental Disorders, 19*, 363–387.

Lord, C. (1995). Follow-up of two-year-olds referred for possible autism. *Journal of Child Psychology and Psychiatry, 36*, 1365–1382.

Lord, C., & Hopkins, M. (1986). The social behavior of autistic children with younger and same-age nonhandicapped peers. *Journal of Autism and Developmental Disorders, 16*, 249–262.

Lord, C., Risi, S., Lambrecht, L., Cook, E. H., Leventhal, B. L., DiLavore, P. C., et al. (2000). The Autism Diagnostic Observation Schedule–Generic: A standard measure of social and communication deficits associated with the spectrum of autism. *Journal of Autism and Developmental Disorders, 30*, 205–223.

Lord, C., Rutter, M., DiLavore, P. C., & Risi, S. (1999). *Autism Diagnostic Observation Schedule (ADOS).* Los Angeles: Western Psychological Services.

Lord, C., Rutter, M., Goode, S., Heemsbergen, J., Jordan, H., Mawhood, L., & Schopler, E. (1989). Autism Diagnostic Observation Schedule: A standardized observation of communicative and social behavior. *Journal of Autism and Developmental Disorders, 19*, 185–212.

Lord, C., Rutter, M., & Le Couteur, A. (1994). Autism Diagnostic Interview–Revised: A revised version of a diagnostic interview for caregivers of individuals with possible pervasive developmental disorders. *Journal of Autism and Developmental Disorders, 24,* 659–685.

Lovaas, O. I. (1987). Behavioral treatment and normal educational and intellectual functioning in young autistic children. *Journal of Consulting and Clinical Psychology, 55,* 3–9.

Macdonald, H. Rutter, M., Howlin, P., Rios, P., Le Couteur, A., Evered, C., & Folstein, S. (1989). Recognition and expression of emotional cues by autistic and normal adults. *Journal of Child Psychology and Psychiatry, 30,* 865–877.

McConnell, S. R., Sission, L. A., Court, C. A., & Strain, P. S. (1991). Effects of social skills training and contingency management on reciprocal interaction of preschool children with behavioral handicaps. *Journal of Special Education, 24,* 473–495.

McEvoy, M. A., Nordquist, V. M., Twardosz, S., Heckaman, K. A., Wehby, J. H., & Denny, R. K. (1988). Promoting autistic children's interaction in an integrated early childhood setting using affectionactivities. *Journal of Applied Behavior Analysis, 21,* 193–200.

McEvoy, M. A., Twardosz, S., & Bishop, N. (1990). Affection activities: Procedures for encouraging young children with handicaps to interact with their peers. *Education and Treatment of Children, 13,* 159–167.

McGee, G. G., Almeida, M. C., Sulzer-Azaroff, B., & Feldman, R. S. (1992). Promoting reciprocal social interactions via peer incidental teaching. *Journal of Applied Behavior Analysis, 25,* 117–126.

McGee, G. G., Feldman, R. S., & Chernin, L. (1991). A comparison of affective display by children with autism and typical preschoolers. *Journal of Early Intervention, 15,* 237–245.

McGee, G. G., Feldman, R. S., & Morrier, M. J. (1997). Benchmarks of social treatment for children with autism. *Journal of Autism and Developmental Disorders, 27,* 353–364.

McGee, G. G., Morrier, M. J., & Daly, T. (1999). An incidental teaching approach to early intervention for toddlers with autism. *Journal of the Association for Persons with Severe Handicaps, 24,* 133–146.

McGee, G. G., Morrier, M. J., Hynes, S., Parsons, C., & Lin, C. (1997, May). *Assessment and treatment of social interest in children with autism.* Paper presented at the annual meeting of the Association of Behavior Analysis, Chicago.

McGee, G. G., Paradis, T., & Feldman, R. S. (1993). Free effects of integration on levels of autistic behavior. *Topics in Early Childhood Special Education, 13,* 57–67.

Mundy, P., Sigman, M., Ungerer, J., & Sherman, T. (1986). Nonverbal communication and play correlates of language development in autistic children. *Journal of Autism and Developmental Disorders, 20,* 115–128.

Odom, S. L., Hoyson, M., Jamieson, B., & Strain, P. S. (1985). Increasing handicapped preschoolers' peer social interactions: Cross-setting and component analysis. *Journal of Applied Behavior Analysis, 18,* 3–16.

Odom, S. L., & Strain, P. S. (1986). A comparison of peer-initiated and teacher-antecedent interventions for promoting social interaction of autistic preschoolers. *Journal of Applied Behavior Analysis, 19,* 59–71.

Osterling, J., & Dawson, G. (1994). Early recognition of children with autism: A study of first birthday home videotapes. *Journal of Autism and Developmental Disorders, 24,* 247–257.

Pierce, K., Glad, K. S., & Schreibman, L. (1997). Social perception in children with autism: An attentional deficit? *Journal of Autism and Developmental Disorders, 27,* 265–282.

Reiss, A. L. (1988). Cerebellar hypoplasia and autism. *New England Journal of Medicine, 319,* 1152–1153.

Riggio, R. E. (1992). Social interaction skills and nonverbal behavior. In R. S. Feldman (Ed.), *Applications of nonverbal behavioral theories and research* (pp. 3–30). Hillsdale, NJ: Erlbaum.

Rumsey, J., Filipek, P., Kennedy, D., Lange, N., Reiss, A., Evans, A., Giedd, J., Bookheimer, S., Cohen, M., Horiwitz, B., & Simpson, G. (1997). *Tools for pediatric neuroimaging workshop: Report of the working groups.* Rockville, MD: National Institutes of Health.

Rumsey, J. M. (1996). Neuroimaging studies in autism. In R. Lyon & J. Rumsey (Eds.), *Neuroimaging: A window to the neurological foundations of learning and behavior in children* (pp. 119–146). Baltimore, MD: Brookes.

Schultz, R. T., Gauthier, I., Klin, A., Fulbright, R. K., Anderson, A. W., Volkmar, F., Skudlarski, P., Lacadie, C., Cohen, D. J., & Gore, J. C. (2000). Abnormal ventral temporal cortical activity during face discrimination among individuals with autism and Asperger syndrome. *Archives of General Psychiatry, 57,* 331–340.

Snow, M. E., Hertzig, M. E., & Shapiro, T. (1987). Expression of emotion in young autistic children. *Journal of the American Academy of Child and Adolescent Psychiatry, 26,* 836–838.

Stone, W., Hoffman, E. L., Lewis, S. E., & Ousley, O. Y. (1994). Early recognition of autism: Parental reports versus clinical observation. *Archives of Pediatric and Adolescent Medicine, 148,* 174–179.

Stone, W. L., Ousley, O. Y., Yoder, P. J., Hogan, K. L., & Hepburn, S. L. (1997). Nonverbal communication in two- and three-year-old children with autism. *Journal of Autism and Developmental Disorders, 27,* 677–696.

Tantam, D., Monaghan, L., Nicholson, H., & Stirling, J. (1989). Autistic children's ability to interpret faces: A research note. *Journal of Child Psychology and Psychiatry, 30,* 623–630.

Teunisse, J., & De Gelder, B. (1994). Do autistics have a generalized face processing deficit? *International Journal of Neuroscience, 77,* 1–10.

Tiegerman, E., & Primavera, L. (1981). Object manipulation: An interactional strategy with autistic children. *Journal of Autism and Developmental Disorders, 11,* 427–438.

Tiegerman, E., & Primavera, L. H. (1984). Imitating the autistic child: Facilitating communicative gaze behavior. *Journal of Autism and Developmental Disorders, 14,* 27–38.

Tremblay, A., Strain, P. S., Henderickson, J. M., & Shores, R. E. (1981). Social interactions of normal preschool children: Using normative data for subject and target behavior selection. *Behavioral Modification, 5,* 237–253.

Uzgiris, I., & Hunt, J. M. (1975). *Assessment in infancy: Ordinal scales of psychological development.* Urbana: University of Illinois Press.

Valentine, T. (1988). Upside-down faces: A review of the effect of inversion upon face recognition. *British Journal of Psychology, 79*, 471–491.

Volkmar, F. R., Sparrow, S. S., Rende, R. C., & Cohen, D. (1989). Facial perception in autism. *Journal of Child Psychology and Psychiatry, 30*, 591–598.

Waterhouse, L., Fein, D., & Modahl, C. (1996). Neurofunctional mechanisms in autism. *Psychological Review, 103*, 457–489.

Wetherby, A. M., & Prutting, C. A. (1984). Profiles of communicative and cognitive-social abilities in autistic children. *Journal of Speech and Hearing Research, 27*, 364–377.

Wing, L., & Atwood, A. (1987). Syndromes of autism and atypical development. In D. J. Cohen & A. Donnelan (Eds.), *Handbook of autism* (pp. 3–19). New York: Wiley.

Wing, L., & Gould, J. (1979). Severe impairments of social interaction and associated abnormalities in children: Epidemiology and classification. *Journal of Autism and Developmental Disorders, 9*, 11–29.

World Health Organization. (1992). *The international statistical classification of diseases and related health problems, 10th revision (ICD-10)*. Geneva, Switzerland: Author.

Yirmiya, N., Kasari, C., Mundy, P., & Sigman, M. (1989). Facial expressions of affect in autistic, mentally retarded and normal children. *Journal of Child Psychology and Psychiatry and Allied Disciplines, 30*, 725–735.

Yirmiya, N., Pilowsky, T., Solomonica-Levi, D., & Schulman, C. (1999). Brief report: Gaze behavior and theory of mind abilities in individuals with autism, Down Syndrome, and mental retardation of unknown etiology. *Journal of Autism and Developmental Disorders, 29*, 333–341.

Index

Action tendency theory, 55
Affective-autonomic response dissociation, 150–52, 159–60
Affective information processing, 4
    distributed, 53–54
Affective/social valence, 214
Affect regulation. *See also* Emotion regulation
    psychodynamic perspective of, in communicative framework, 59–63
Alcohol
    as avoidant coping strategy, 218
    facial expression of emotion and, 219–27
    and nonverbal decoding in normal drinkers, 220–21
    and nonverbal encoding in normal drinkers, 219–20
Alcohol consumption. *See also* Alcoholism
    nonverbal deficits, social competence deficits, and, 218
Alcoholics, 209
    clinical consequences of nonverbal decoding deficits, 227–28
    deficit in nonverbal communication of emotion, 217–18
    expectations regarding alcohol effects on emotion, 214–16
    nonverbal decoding in, 221–26
Alcoholism, 209, 216–17
    emotion communication in, 210–14
    interpersonal problems, emotion, and, 210–11
Amygdala, 175–76, 186, 187
Anger, 149, 162, 210, 217. *See also* Negativity behavior

Angry faces, 29–30, 35, 132–34
Antidepressants, 22
Anxiety, 134. *See also* Social anxiety disorder
    cognitive biases in, 127–31, 136–39
    cognitive models of, 128, 136–37
    secondary, 7
    trait, 129, 130, 132, 133, 137, 138
Appraisal patterns, 156
Appraisal view of emotional states, 49
Arousal, 214
Associative network model of emotion, 128
Attachment, 244
Attention, crucial function for, 127
Attentional biases, 246. *See also* Selective attention
    for phobia-related stimuli, 135–36
    for threat/anxiety, 128–31, 139
Attentiveness (behavior)
    client, 94, 97, 98
    therapist-client, 76–78, 80, 93–94
        changes in match of, 95–97, 100
        gathering information about one another, 81–82
        learning the tasks of therapy, 85
        regulating change via exchange of information, 88–89
    vigilant, 82, 136–39
Autism, 287–88
    directions for clinical research and practice, 310–12
    earliest presentations of, 295–97
        prospective analysis of nonverbal social behaviors, 297–98
        retrospective analyses of home videos, 297

Autism (*continued*)
  evolution of gold standard diagnos-
    tic instruments, 298–301
  irregularities in nonverbal behav-
    ior, 288–89
  abilities in emotion perception,
    290–93
  display of emotional expressions,
    293–95
  skills in face recognition, 289–90
  use of gestures for communica-
    tion, 295
  nonverbal behavior and neurobiol-
    ogy of, 308–10
  (sub)types of, 287–88
  translation of descriptive research
    to use in clinical interventions,
    301
  affection, 304–6
  eye contact, 301–2
  peer interactions, 306–7
  physical proximity to others,
    302–4
Autism Diagnostic Interview (ADI),
  298–301
Autism Diagnostic Observational
  Schedule (ADOS), 298–300
Avoidant personality disorder, 22–23

Basic emotions view, 49
Beck, Aaron T., 128, 234, 246
Behavior therapy, 36, 212
Bereavement. *See also* Grief
  empirical studies of nonverbal emo-
    tional expression during, 150
  affective-autonomic response dis-
    sociation, 150–52, 159–60
  facial expressions of emotion,
    153–57
  limitations and directions for fu-
    ture research, 161–62
  theoretical and clinical implica-
    tions, 159–61
  social and functional perspective
    on emotion during, 145, 148–
    49, 163
  negative emotions, 149–50
  positive emotions and laughter,
    150
Between-systems coherence, 156
Bleuler, Eugen, 264
Borderline personality disorder,
  61–62

Brain damage, deficiencies of facial
  nonverbal communication
  after. *See also under specific
  disorders*
  contributions of neuroimaging stud-
    ies, 181–86
  integrated approach, 187–89
  implications, 176
  methodological considerations,
    172–73
  panel of clinical neuropsychologi-
    cal patterns, 173–76
  rehabilitation, 195
Butterfly effect, 62

Capgras's syndrome, 180
Change, regulation of
  via emotions, 89–90
  via exchange of information, 88–89
  via interpersonal influence and ad-
    aptation processes, 90–91
Checklist for Autism in Toddlers
  (CHAT), 296
Cognitive-affective modeling, 114
Cognitive behavioral mood management training (CBMMT), 212
Cognitive-behavioral treatments, 36
"Cognitive-motivational" view of at-
  tentional biases, 136–37
Communication, 63–64. *See also spe-
  cific topics*
  dynamic net of concurrent interac-
    tive processes, 52–56
  myth of ping-pong, 52–56
  superlens model of, 45, 56–58
  in therapy, 45–47
Communication skills training (CST),
  212
Communicative contact, 115
Cooperative intent, displaying, 82–83
Coordination (behavior), 76–78, 80,
  83–84, 86–87. *See also under*
  Depression
  dimensions of, 91
Coordination-rapport hypothesis, 244
Corrugator supercilii muscle activation, 49
Countertransference, 60–61

"Danger schemata," 128
Decoding, nonverbal. *See under* Alco-
  holics
Defense mechanisms, 60

Delusional misidentification syndromes, 174, 180–81
Denial during bereavement, 148
Depression, 233
  attentional biases for emotional faces in, 134, 246
  cognitions and course of
    ethological observations, 247–50
    theoretical framework, 246–47
  cognitive theories of, 248. *See also* Beck
  emotional control and, 32–35
  emotional expressiveness and, 21, 22, 24
  emotional sensitivity and, 26–27
  ethological approach, 236–37, 253–55
  future research, 253–55
  neurological functioning and, 234–35
  neuroticism and, 235–36, 250–51
  and nonverbal behavior in children, 21
  nonverbal behavior of patient and interviewer and course of
    ethological observations, 240–43
    theoretical framework, 239–40
  nonverbal coordination and course of
    ethological observations, 244–46
    theoretical framework, 243–44
  personality and cognitions about nonverbal behavior, 250–51
  as reflected in observable nonverbal behavior, 237–38
  social skill deficits and, 33
  theoretical framework, 233–36
  treatment, 21, 22
  vulnerability-accumulation and nonverbal coordination, 235, 251–53
Diagnostic tool, nonverbal behavior as, 7, 64
Diasthesis-stress model, 234, 244
Differential activation hypothesis, 248–49
Dimensional school of emotional states, 49
Dissociation(s), 175, 176
  double, 173, 175, 176
Duchenne expressions, 115, 118, 119, 155, 162

Electromyographic (EMG) activity, 267–70, 274
Emotional control (EC), 19, 31–35
Emotional expression(s), 45, 51
  in support of response to task mastery, 86
Emotional expressiveness, 19–24
Emotional expressivity (EE), 19
Emotional processes, interventions based on, 4
Emotional sensitivity (ES), 19, 24–31
  defined, 24
Emotional states, 51
  nonverbal behavior as determinant of, xiii, 5–6
  schools of thought regarding, 49
Emotion regulation, 31, 33–34, 65. *See also* Affect regulation
  depression as disorder of, 32–34
  emotion researchers' growing interest in, 4–5
  nonverbal behavior in, 6, 8
Emotion(s)
  cognitive models of, 128
  interpersonal consequences of dysphoric, 157–59
  regulating change via, 89–90
  secondary, 7–8
Empathy, 8
  multiple levels of, 58–59
  psychodynamic perspective of, in communicative framework, 59–63
Engagement-disengagement patterns/cycles, 87–90
Error-repair processes in relationships, 87, 90, 92
Ethological approach, 236. *See also under* Depression
  organizational structure for nonverbal behavior during interaction, 238–39
  to psychopathology, 238–39, 254
Event-related potentials (ERPs), 182, 184
Event-response coherence, 156
Extraversion and depression, 250
Eye movement studies, 134

Face, as medium of nonverbal communication, 171–72
Face identification, cognitive architecture of, 177, 178, 182, 185–87

Face processing, 189. *See also* Emotional sensitivity; *specific topics*
  cognitive architecture of, 176–80
  and psychopathological pictures, 180–81
  evolutionary perspective, 189–90
  specificity, 190–92
Face recognition, 57–58
  covert, 173
Facial Action Coding System (FACS), 77, 219
Facial affective behavior, 113–14
  and therapeutic outcome, 114–21
"Facial decision" process, 177
Facial expression, 186. *See also* Emotional sensitivity; *specific topics*
  categorical perception of faces and, 191, 193–95
  context analysis of, 113
  does not only express emotion, 48–50
  of emotion, coherence of, 156–57
  myth of emotional, 48–50
  myth of the meaningless, 50–52
  as rich source of information about sender, 50–52
Facial feedback, 55–56
Facial identity, processing of, 182–85
Facial nonverbal communication, 185–86
Fodor, J. A., 190
Fractionation of cognitive processes, 172–73
Frégoli syndrome, 181
Friendliness, displaying, 82–83
Functional magnetic resonance imaging (fMRI), 182–83
Fusiform face area (FFA), 183

Gaze direction, perception of, 186
Gender categorization of faces, 187, 193, 195
Gender differences
  in depression, 32, 254–55
  in emotional sensitivity and control, 32
Generalized anxiety disorder, 134
Global social skill/competence (SSI Total), 19
Grief. *See also* bereavement
  differentiating emotion and, 146–47

Grief work perspective on emotion and bereavement, 147–48

Imitation skills, 295–96, 301–2. *See also* Mimicry
Interaction regulation, nonverbal behavior in, 8
Intermetamorphosis syndrome, 181

Korsakoff patients, 221

Language disorders, 96
Laughter, 153–57, 161, 162
Laughter-as-dissociation, 157
Leitaffekt, 116–17, 120, 121
Lipreading, 174–75

Magnetic resonance imaging, functional (MRI), 182–83
Mental disorders, what makes them so persistent, 111–13, 119–20
Mentalization, 112, 113
Mimicry, motor, 54, 55, 61, 62, 65. *See also* Imitation skills
Mirror neurons, 54
Modularity, Fodor's theory of, 190
Morphing, 193, 195
Motor mimicry. *See* Mimicry, motor
Motor recruitment hypothesis, 274
Mutual affect, 115

Negativity behavior, 76, 77, 80, 82–83, 86, 92. *See also* Alcoholism; Depression
Nervios, 278
Neuroleptic medications, 21–22, 279
Neurological impairment, 28, 308–10. *See also* Brain damage
Neuroscience(s)
  cognitive, 189
  social, 64
Nonverbal behavior, 6. *See also specific topics*
  changes in morphology and function of over time, 91–92
  dimensions of, in clinical settings, 6
  as index of pathological processes, 7–8
  as neglected field in clinical psychology and psychotherapy, xiii, 3–5
  relevance for clinical research and practice, 5–6

Nonverbal researchers, increasing interest in clinical issues, 4

Obsessive-compulsive disorder (OCD), 225
Öhman's model of fear and anxiety, 131
Operationalized psychodynamic diagnostics (OPD), 112

Peer modeling intervention, 305
Perceptual deficit hypothesis, 27
Phobias
  preparedness theory of, 30
  social. *See* Social anxiety disorder
  spider, 135–36, 138
Pop-out task, 133–34
Positivity (behavior), 76–78, 80, 82–83, 86, 92–95
  changes in client positivity, 97, 99
  changes in match of therapist-client, 95–97, 101
Positron emission tomography (PET), 182–87
Pre-Linguistic Autism Diagnostic Observational Schedule (PL-ADOS), 299
Projective identification, 59–60, 62, 113, 114
Prosopagnosia, 173–75, 178–79
Psychoanalytic theory, 59–60, 264
Psychopathology
  nonverbal processes active in, 4
  nonverbal social skills and, 17–19, 35–37
Psychotherapy. *See* Therapy

Rado, Sandor, 264
Rapport. *See* Working alliance and rapport
Reciprocal affirmation, 115
Reflective functioning, 112. *See also* Mentalization
Relational culture. *See* Working relational culture
Repetition-compulsion, 111, 114
Riggio, Ronald E., 18–19

Schema model of anxiety, 128
Schemas, cognitive, 247
Schizophrenic patients, 20–21, 24, 28, 263
  approaches to studying emotion in, 20, 264–66

correlations among emotion components, 272–74
corrugator activity, 270, 271, 273–76
emotional control, 31–32
emotional sensitivity, 25–27, 31, 35
emotion disturbances in, 20–21, 24, 276–78
  empirical studies of, 266–67
  future directions, 276–78
  implications for assessment and treatment, 21–22, 278–80
observable and unobservable facial expressions, 267–76
perceptual deficit hypothesis, 27
skin conductance reactivity, 271, 272
zygomatic activity, 270–76
Seasonal affective disorder (SAD), 240
"Selection-for-action," 127
Selective attention. *See also* Attentional biases
  to aversive pictorial scenes, biases in, 136–39
  to emotional faces, biases in, 131–35
  role in anxiety, 127–31
Self-representation, 112, 234
Sex differences. *See* Gender differences
Shakespeare, William, 3
Smiling, 115, 118, 119, 153–56, 294
Social anxiety disorder/social phobia, 22–24, 28–29, 31, 34
Social control (SC), 19
Social expressivity (SE), 19
Social functional perspective on emotion, 152–54
Social Performance Rating Scale (SPRS), 22
Social referencing, 53
Social sensitivity (SS), 19
Social skills, 7
  defined, 18
  model for basic, 18–19
Social skills training, 36, 279
Speech disorders, 96
Spider-fearful individuals, 135–36, 138
Synchronization, 61, 62, 83, 84. *See also* Coordination (behavior)

Theory of mind (TOM) conceptualization of autism, 296
Therapeutic alliance(s), 81, 103 *n*.1.
See also Working alliance
association between nonverbal behavior and, 9, 93–94, 97,
102–3
at various times, 93–95
description of dyads according to
strength of, 95, 96
secure *vs.* insecure, changes in nonverbal behavior across periods
in dyads with, 95–101
Therapeutic outcome
emotional quality of therapeutic relationship and, 114–16
facial affective behavior and,
114–21
therapist-client nonverbal behavior
and, 75–76, 93, 94
Therapeutic relationship. *See also*
Working alliance
asymmetry, 86–87
curative factors of, 116–21
emotional quality of, and therapeutic outcome, 114–16
functions of nonverbal behavior
across three periods of, 79–88
gathering information about one another, 81–82
implementation of maladaptive relationship pattern in intersubjective field, 114
nonverbal behavior in, 8–9
regulating and influencing interpersonal involvement, 83–84
a study of nonverbal behavior and
development of, 92–102

Therapist, client's evaluation of,
8–9
Therapy. *See also specific topics*
learning the tasks of, 85
"Time delay" procedure, 305
Transcranial magnetic stimulation
(TMS), 182
Transference, 60, 61

"Vigilant-avoidant" pattern of bias in
anxiety, 136–39
Visual probe task, 129, 134–38
Vulnerability-accumulation hypothesis, 235, 251

Williams, J. M. G., 136–37
Working alliance and rapport, 75,
103 *n*.1. *See also* Therapeutic
alliance(s)
alliance rupture and repair, 87, 90,
92
changes in nonverbal behavior during development of, 79–81
development of rapport, 81–84
development of working alliance,
84–87
ongoing working relationship,
87–88
coordination and, 91. *See also* Coordination (behavior)
nonverbal behavior signs of, 9, 76–
77, 79, 97, 102–3
morphology and signal meaning,
77, 78
therapist-client nonverbal behavior
and rapport, 93, 94
Working relational culture, developing a, 86–87